LITTLE WHITE SQUAW

LITTLE WHITE SQUAW

a white woman's story of abuse, addiction, and reconciliation

Eve Mills Nash
and Kenneth J. Harvey

an imprint of Beach Holme Publishing

PROSPECT BOOKS

VANCOUVER, BC

This book is published by Beach Holme Publishing, 226–2040 West 12th Avenue, Vancouver, B.C. V6J 2G2. *www.beachholme.bc.ca* This is a Prospect Book.

The publisher gratefully acknowledges the financial support of the Canada Council for the Arts and of the British Columbia Arts Council. The publisher also acknowledges the financial assistance received from the Government of Canada through the Book Publishing Industry Development Program (BPIDP) for its publishing activities.

The Canada Council | Le Conseil des Arts
for the Arts | du Canada

BRITISH
COLUMBIA
ARTS COUNCIL
Supported by the Province of British Columbia

Editor: Michael Carroll
Design and Production: Jen Hamilton
Cover Art: *The Other Side* by Jerry Whitehead
Eve Mills Nash Photograph: Sasha Thompson
Kenneth J. Harvey Photograph: Janet Power
Interior Art: Jody L. M. Claus

Printed and bound in Canada by AGMV Marquis

National Library of Canada Cataloguing in Publication Data

Nash, Eve Deloris, 1950-
  Little white squaw

"A Prospect book."
ISBN 0-88878-427-9

  1. Nash, Eve Deloris, 1950- 2. Adult child sexual abuse victims—Canada—Biography. 3. Alcoholics—Canada—Biography.
I. Harvey, Kenneth J. (Kenneth Joseph), 1962- II. Title.
HV6570.4.C3N37 2002   362.76'4'092   C2002-910165-4

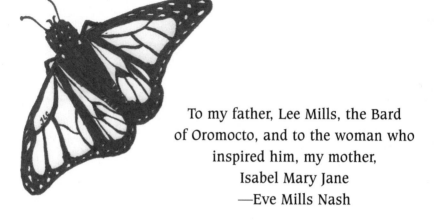

To my father, Lee Mills, the Bard
of Oromocto, and to the woman who
inspired him, my mother,
Isabel Mary Jane
—Eve Mills Nash

To the family
—Kenneth J. Harvey

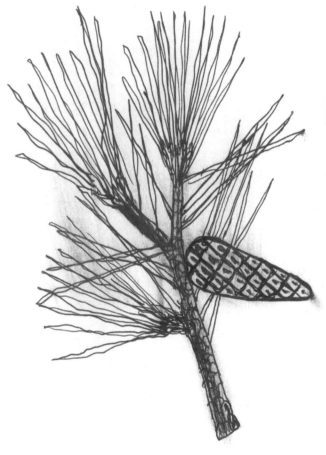

PART ONE

1955-1974

PINE

PROLOGUE: THE WOODS

I am on my back in the snow gazing up at the small brown hand with fingernails chewed too short from worry. It is my son Jody's hand, reaching out for me on a bitter cold March morning in 1986. Jody is only sixteen. He had taken care of me from a safe distance all night as I drank steadily and sank deeper into depression. He pretended to be engrossed in one of his video games, but every time I moved to collect another beer or make a trip to the bathroom I glimpsed the concern in his eyes.

"Why don't you go to bed, Mom?" he suggested. "You must be tired."

I shrugged and said, "Later." No matter how much I drank, the alcohol ceased to affect me. It might as well have been water.

When I set off into the woods behind my house, it was still dark. Dressed only in a T-shirt and jeans in the near-zero temperature, I had no idea where I was going. I only knew Jody was following me, afraid for what I might do. When he saw me lie in the snow, he ran up and put his hand out to help, as if I'd simply fallen, but then noticed I was motionless, as if I desired to rest on the soft snow.

I am crying, filled with horrific shame to have him see me this way after all the promises I've made. But I am living in a land of immeasurable blackness and defeat, a place of suffocating emotionless weight where the body is the curse that must be extinguished.

I know my kids have had enough, so I decided I'd walk away and die. Eliminate the parent and the kids would be fine. It made perfect sense.

"C'mon, Mom," Jody now insists, his breath misting greyish-white in the air. "You have to get up."

The snow feels comforting beneath my back as I stare up at trees that should be beautiful but only provoke my grief. Try as I might, I can't see their beauty.

"Come home," Jody urges, his voice quavering. "You need to go to bed."

"Go back," I whisper, shutting my eyes. *How many times has he covered up for me so I can pretend my life is normal? Calling my boss to tell him I'm sick with the flu when I'm actually hung over. Hiding bottles when a relative drops by...*

"Mom, please."

When I open my eyes to regard him, tears are ready to spill from his big brown doe eyes. Gentle. Trusting. What sort of ugliness have those accepting, docile eyes witnessed because of me and my men?

"Your mother's no good. I just want to go to sleep."

"Mom, you have to get up. I love you." His trembling has increased. I watch him shiver, yet can't feel a thing.

"Jody, please go home."

"You're the only mom I got."

I raise my fingers numbly toward him. Perhaps to touch his face, to smear a black streak across one so dear to me. Jody takes the opportunity to grab my hand with both of his. In a moment I'm sitting up, looking at him. My son. He's holding my coat open for me to slip my arms into despite the fact he's only in a T-shirt. I am on my feet. I've risen. Jody wraps the coat around my shoulders, and I pull him in under with me. We are like one person, huddled beneath the warmth.

I let him lead me back to the house.

BORN THE WRONG COLOUR

I was only six when I suspected my skin might be the wrong colour. We were living in Haneytown, a small country village about twenty miles from Fredericton, New Brunswick. I was in grade one and in love with Dickie Lee, a shy seven-year-old from somewhere in China. I loved the golden glow of his skin and his blue-black hair, which shone in the morning sunlight as he boarded the bus to the rural school we attended in Geary.

Just before my seventh birthday I decided Dickie was going to be my boyfriend and told him so. He never argued the point but, looking back, I'm not sure he even understood it, either; he spoke very little English. He did enjoy the homemade cakes and cookies I shared with him from my tin lunch pail.

"Do you like me, Dickie?" I asked him one day at school during recess.

"Yes, thank you very much," he replied with a smile as he swallowed a large bite from one of my mother's cinnamon rolls.

That was enough for me.

I was stimulated by thoughts of a culture so different from mine, a culture where dragons were magical creatures and children like Dickie were greeted with proud smiles by their fathers. As far as I could tell, Dickie's parents were never angry with him. I used to watch their faces glow every time they picked him up at school. It was as if he were someone special, and when Dickie paid attention to me I felt special, too.

I tried to imagine what it would be like to live on a foreign Asian shore where all the boys had black hair and brown skin. When Dickie moved away, only three months after we met, I was already hooked. My attraction to Dickie Lee was the beginning of an unusual addiction.

THE CURSE OF A POOR FAMILY

My mother, Isabel, a petite woman with shoulder-length light brown hair and plain good looks, was the best cook I've ever known. Even back when I was just a kid she was able to create a culinary master-piece out of something as simple as a can of sockeye salmon, onions, and a few potatoes. My mouth still waters when I imagine her plump brown loaves of bread or deep dishes of apple crumble cooling on the windowsill of our small brown-shingled home.

Mom didn't like to hug. When I tried to get close, she'd pat me on the head or back off awkwardly. I'd keep trying, but she would usually brush me away, saying, "Go on now. I've got to get this cooking done." Or sewing or ironing…

When she did hug me, her arms felt stiff, as though they were working against their will. A vacant look would overtake her small brown eyes when I tried to strike up a conversation, as if she were creating a wall between us so she wouldn't have to get to know me. She never seemed to act that way toward my brothers. Regardless, she always took extra care in baking special treats for us. And I came to understand *I love you* in the language of apple pies.

For many years I possessed the empty feeling that my mother didn't love me. I often felt as if I were nothing more than a bother to her.

Being born female had been the root of many of my mother's problems. From an early age she discovered it was a male's world as she waited on her drunken father and helped her mother care for six brothers. She spent her teen years in Barker's Point on the north side of Fredericton, and often she'd walk the two miles across the train bridge to deliver lunch or some necessity to her father while he dried out in the Brunswick Street jail. Her mother was too busy caring for her large brood single-handedly to spend any time playing with them, and my mom—being the eldest—was expected to assume a great deal of the responsibility.

In those days discipline meant beatings with a large leather strap or an alder switch. Often there was little to eat. There wasn't much to prompt the words *I love you* from a mother who matter-of-factly proclaimed, "Daughters are the curse of a poor family." I think those words lay dormant in my mother's mind, only to find new light when I crossed into adolescence.

My mom became pregnant before she and my father met. She was only seventeen when she gave birth to a girl with curly blond hair. She named the infant Eunice and tried to care for her while still helping at home, but it was impossible. The workload was too much to handle and a choice had to be made—the obvious one at the time. When Eunice was fifteen months old, my mother was forced to give her up for private adoption. No doubt that baby girl gouged a big chunk out of my mother's heart when she was handed over to strangers.

I couldn't understand my mother's growing coldness when I began developing into a young woman. Perhaps she was troubled by reminders of *her* past mistakes and was determined to make certain I wouldn't follow in her footsteps.

Our house was extremely small—a mere three rooms. No bathroom. No running water. Just two bedrooms and a combined kitchen and sitting room that contained another pullout bed for two of my brothers—Nelson and Carman. I occupied the top bunk in one of the bedrooms. Another brother, Allison, claimed the bottom bunk. Mom and Dad—who worked as a janitor for an apartment complex in Oromocto—had the remaining bedroom to themselves, except when there was a new baby or if someone was especially sick. Otherwise there was no way of getting close to my parents, of enjoying their comforting heat. Being especially sick was almost something worth looking forward to. I cherished the cold nights when my father would come and check to make certain we were all tucked in. Sometimes I'd throw my blankets off so he'd cover me up again and give my forehead a reassuring little pat.

The old house wasn't much to look at, just a brown-shingled shack. But it had plenty of character standing proudly in the middle of a large field about fifty feet from the woods. Our yard was as spotless as the inside of the house. My mother despised clutter, so even the garbage was hidden before it was taken to the dump five miles away to be burned. The grass was always clipped and manicured.

Everything on our property was neatly arranged and had been given its own space an exact measure of feet away from the nearest object. The outhouse was at least a hundred feet from the house and was surrounded by pine trees. About fifty feet in front of it, between the outhouse and the house, stood a small shack used for Dad's meagre collection of tools, shovels, picks, and the scythe I greatly feared.

On the north side of the house there was another outbuilding used for storage, and twenty feet behind that, off to the right, stood a woodshed. On the south side there was a picnic table next to a single swing that hung by rope from the thick branch of an ancient oak. Once in a while a multicoloured beach ball or a small red wagon might get left behind beside the picnic table, but usually any sign that play had taken place in the afternoon was quickly erased by suppertime.

In the front of the house, spaced exactly two feet apart, were three tires, each filled with flowers. Pansies grew in a circle on the outside, ringing the marigolds inside. Everything was so perfect;

even the flowers had their own little yards. It must have been my parents' way of compensating for the lack of space inside the house. They created a vast, ordered kingdom outdoors to help escape the claustrophobia of their inner lives.

A young cedar grew outside my bedroom window. Sometimes, on summer nights, the pungent perfume stole its way inside on a warm carpet of west wind. The lacy fingers of the tree would scratch on my window to signal the visit and I'd pretend the cedar was a special friend come to call. I'd think of Catherine in *Wuthering Heights*, one of my favourite novels. I'd picture Catherine visiting Heathcliff, tapping on the glass. I'd fantasize about the darkness that was Heathcliff, so much like my father, a handsome man with thick dark hair, brooding eyes, and high cheekbones that hinted at remote Native ancestry. I used to imagine my dad as a movie star. With his sober good looks and unpredictable mood changes, he exuded an air of mystery like some of the men I read about in my books.

I read incessantly anything I could get my hands on. Mom told me I had inherited my love of reading from my father. Growing up as a child in a poor family, he found that dictionaries were often the only books available to him, so he read them cover to cover many times. As for me, stories that portrayed gloomy, untamed men heightened my affinity with tragedy.

When I was twelve, Mom added wild rosebushes to the front yard, then a lilac tree and wild day lilies to her flower collection. Soon the front of our house was completely fenced in by aromatic flowers. Mixed with the scents of Mom's blueberry pies and lemon breads, the resulting blend rivalled the intoxicating fragrance from any perfume company.

I can't recall ever being cold or hungry. But I do remember the exhaustion in my father's eyes when he walked the more than three miles home after work before we had a car, frequently carrying a large burlap sack of potatoes or some other groceries on his back. Stepping in the door, he'd be faced with the news that there was another leak in the roof or the shed door needed a hinge. And always wood or water had to be carried.

There was no end to my mother's slaving. She was in constant motion—cooking, scrubbing, washing clothes by hand (and later in an old wringer washing machine), hanging them on the clothes-line, preparing lunches, planting flowers. Our house and our clothes always smelled of flowers, cinnamon, and cloves. I don't know if that scent of flowers lingered on my mother's hands or if she carried the pollen in the pores of her skin, but I can't think of my mother without picturing perfect rows of peach-coloured gladioli and deep red dahlias surrounded by the sky-blue of morning glories.

Neither my mother nor my father had time for imperfection or frivolity, and I was given to both. So I tried to stay out of their way. I hid in the woods for hours and talked to the trees, the flowers, the brook, and later, to my little stray cocker spaniel, Pal.

I'd tell my surroundings about my dreams, about how I was going to be a famous writer and have tons of money when I grew older. About how I would wear bright satin dresses and pearls braided in my long hair as I entertained my friends in a grand house and my babies slept in their separate beds upstairs.

I would have four healthy, happy children and I would be a good mother.

Sometimes I'd cry as I held Pal and asked him to love me and never go away. I talked about everything, except the visitors who came to touch me during the late hours. I was a child and had no way of properly facing those feelings or aligning them into words.

Sometimes I collected ants and spiders and made farms for them. My mother wasn't too thrilled with this pastime, but she allowed it as long as I stayed outside or in the shed, out of her way. It wasn't until I smuggled a garter snake into the house in a shoe box that she put an end to it all.

Cut off from my bug and snake interests, I took up reading and writing in earnest. I read comics, dictionaries, encyclopedias, *True Stories,* anything, as long as it offered a world to which I could escape. *Jane Eyre,* with another seething male protagonist, and *Wuthering Heights* became my literary Bibles, but I loved my Wonder Woman comic books just as much.

I never really minded being poor. Economically challenged— what an expression! It sounded like some sort of competition. Back then all we worried about was surviving. I know today what hardships my parents fought. They did the best they could. But, as a kid, I assumed I was the problem. My world was so small and introspective that I was sure I had to be the reason for their ill tempers, especially when my father raged about how unfair life was, or how he wished he'd never been born. Like most children, I took it personally.

GRANDMOTHERS

When I was quite young, my father's mother, Grammie Mills, visited us often. My paternal grandfather had died long before I'd been born, so Grammie Mills had been widowed quite a while. Emma was her name—a sweet little woman from Birmingham, England, who stood only five feet tall. She smelled like lilacs. I don't remember her hair being any other colour than grey. It was long, but she never wore it down. She kept it pinned up in a circle around her head that made her look to me like an angel with a silver halo. I'd stare up at her from her lap while she rocked me in her rocking chair and sang hymns that I embraced for their soothing melodies: "Rock of Ages cleft for me. Let me hide myself in thee."

I wasn't sure what kind of rock she was singing about, but I thought I understood. I'd once found a cave carved into the rock in the woods and figured it might be a good place to hide. I would go there and sit on the moss and pretend I was safe from my enemies. I used to think Grammie would have liked it, too.

Most often the songs she sang were about the home and mother she'd left behind when she immigrated to Canada at the age of seven. I believe she made up the words to most of the songs, because they didn't rhyme and they rambled aimlessly without reaching any destination, but I couldn't have cared less. She was singing them for *me*. Not only that, she would also read me stories and recite precious poetry.

"Two little girls in blue, two little girls in blue," she'd mumble over and over as she stroked my cheek. Gazing toward the sky outside our kitchen window, she always seemed to be off in another world.

"What are you thinking about, Grammie?" I'd often ask.

"You, little one, you," she'd say. And she would laugh throatily and gaze into my eyes with such love that I would feel my chest swell with pride. Sometime I thought I could detect a trace of fear in those soft eyes when she looked at me, but she spoke so few words that I could never be certain.

"Be a good girl, Eva, be a good girl" was all she'd say before once again retreating into her far-off world of daydream.

When Grammie Mills moved to Saint John to live with my Aunt Edna, I felt as if I'd lost a big piece of my newly special self. After a few months, the memory of her tranquillizing songs wore too thin to buffer my loneliness. We didn't visit Grammie Mills often because the one-hour drive was a costly venture for a family struggling to clothe and feed five people. I wrote to Grammie frequently and she would always reply. She kept all of my letters and read them repeatedly, my aunt later told me. I did the same with hers, even sniffing the letters. Her lingering scent and the delicate curl of her handwriting gave me solace.

I saw my maternal grandmother, Grammie Brewer, more regularly. She'd left my grandfather, George, the father my mother had brought lunches to in jail, before I was born and remarried a man with eight children after raising eight of her own. In later years she also raised her granddaughter, Nancy.

According to her birth certificate, Grammie Brewer had been born Effi Scoupi on December 24, 1903, in Germany. My mother said she'd come into the world with a veil of flesh over her eyes that had to be removed. This caul gave her "second sight" and established her reputation as a fortuneteller who often saw forerunners of people's imminent deaths. Her father, Franz, was also a noted fortuneteller. He hailed from Bohemia, and her mother, Franchiska, was from Austria. Other relatives lived in Romania.

As a child, Effi travelled with her family from village to village, searching for work, learning the art of tea-leaf fortunetelling and palm reading from her father, who repaired timepieces along the journey. They did this until they immigrated to Canada to escape persecution from an Austrian leader.

Once in Canada, her name was changed to Eva Skopie. At fourteen she met and married my grandfather. My mother was the eldest of the two girls in a predominantly male family. It wasn't until Grammie was in her mid-forties that she became Grammie Brewer after she married a farmer who lived in a small country village about forty minutes north of Oromocto.

Grammie Brewer, like Grammie Mills, was small in stature, measuring only four foot ten, but she was a force to be reckoned with when she was riled. One day I watched her chase a stray dog across the yard with a wooden spoon in her hand. The dog was almost as big as she, yet Grammie showed no sign of fear as she drove the mangy cur away from one of her prized white angora kittens.

Like my mother, Grammie Brewer wasn't openly affectionate,

but I always knew she had a soft spot for me. Every Valentine's Day I received a carefully wrapped gift from her in the mail—a small tin of heart-shaped sugar cookies with pink frosting.

When I was about eight, I coaxed her to tell my fortune, even though she seldom engaged in the practice around any of us kids. I'd gulped down my cup of tea, with only a little sugar, no milk, and spit bits of tea leaves into a dish towel as I paused for breath. I couldn't wait to hear what adventures lay in store for me.

"You needn't have drunk the tea," Grammie said a little too late.

I watched in fascination as she squinted into my cup, studying the patterns made by the leaves. When Grammie instructed me to make a wish, I was torn between choosing a new car for my father or happiness for myself. In the end I selected the car because I enjoyed our Sunday drives.

"What do you see, Grammie? What do you see?"

"Settle down and be quiet. This takes time."

It seemed like hours before she spoke again. She gazed intently into the cup, and I could hear her careful breath as her eyes focused on my future.

"You will travel many different paths in your life," she finally said, "and you will touch many people."

I was puzzled by her words and a little disappointed. I'd hoped to hear something about a new bike or maybe a note from Norman Gardner, one of the cute boys at school I had a crush on. When I started to open my mouth to ask, she gave me a silencing look.

"I see a man with very dark hair and dark skin in your future. You will be too young when you marry. Be careful, Eva, he is not a good man for you."

Grammie started to talk about paths again, but my mind was already engaged by the dark man who would be my future husband. *Maybe it will be Norman*, I giggled to myself. *Maybe we'll run away together and be happy forever.*

From that day forward I talked to Grammie Brewer about fortunetelling and dreams every chance I got. Whenever she could find time, she'd help me decipher the clumps of tea leaves in the cups of those who'd eaten at her table. If the leaves shaped a ship, it would mean an adventure or good fortune. When Grammie Brewer saw a cat, it forecast misfortune or betrayal. Letters or numbers might indicate significant dates or initials of people who would affect the seeker. Other times if a path was shaped by the leaves and something was obstructing it, a blocked course was suggested. Just when I started to demonstrate a talent for unravelling the signs of the people who had left their futures in their cups, Grammie insisted I stop.

"Nothing good comes to those who keep reading the cups," she told me. "That's why I don't like to do it anymore."

But it was too late. I was already starting to "see" things I didn't care to divine.

UNWANTED ATTENTION

When I was in elementary school, my mother's father, George, was a regular visitor to our home, especially on weekends. He was still a drunk, and on those occasions my mother was, too. Dad never drank much. He said he didn't care for the taste of it, but I suspect he just wanted to keep an eye on Mom. It was those disturbing visits that slowly began to erode my faith in the goodness of nature.

Some weekends I thought it might be different as I watched my grandfather, my mother, my father, and a few friends take up guitars, harmonicas, and fiddles on a Friday night. I appreciated the music, but it was the clinking of the bottles that terrified me. The poisoning liquor always seemed to twist the uplifting beat of the singing and dancing into angry brawls.

It was during this time, when I was about five, that I first found out men would be nice to me just for a touch of soft skin. I was already used to hiding my body from the lecherous gaze and searching fingers of an old family friend who dropped by a couple of times each month, but during these drunken parties there was nowhere to hide. So I pretended to be asleep when I couldn't stand the exploring fingers of one of the guests who might come into my room where the bottles were waiting. Mine was the biggest of the two rooms, with an open space behind the door, a logical choice for storage.

I knew it had to be something to do with what was inside the bottles that made my mother change from a quiet housekeeper to a screaming, angry wild woman. Usually it was my dad who was given to furious outbursts. Mom seldom raised her voice. If she was upset, she'd go off to the bedroom and cry in silence.

On one such Saturday night the house was full of people, several with guitars, fiddles, and harmonicas. As all the instruments came into play, even our spoons were used to take up the beat. I loved to hear the music because I knew my mother would soon begin to sing in a voice that reminded me of June Carter's from the country-and-western Carter Family.

Beautiful, beautiful brown eyes
Beautiful, beautiful brown eyes
Beautiful, beautiful brown eyes
I'll never love blue eyes again.

Tucked under the bedcovers, I'd pretend Mom was singing that song just to me. She was a fine stepdancer, too. Her feet never seemed to tire when she danced to the reels and jigs our visitors energetically played. She'd throw back her head and laugh as she moved in rhythm to "St. Anne's Reel" or old favourites like "Camptown Races."

Dad would never dance. Instead he'd sit and play a mournful harmonica, or sometimes the Jew's harp. Once in a while he'd attempt to sing along, but he had little confidence in his vocal abilities. I was the greatest admirer of his voice, especially when he sang about intriguing people like the sad Indian princess Red Wing.

On this particular Saturday night one of my father's friends seemed to be paying a lot of attention to my mother. The two of them even tried a dance step together, but the man was too wobbly to pull it off. Watching my mom, I grew increasingly disturbed to see her laugh and joke with this man. When she wasn't drinking, Mom never talked to anyone of the opposite sex who wasn't related to us.

I turned my attention to my father and noticed a change come over his face. His usual stern look had stiffened to a sinister expression. When the music paused so everyone could refill their glasses, my father glanced over at my mother and called out in a loud, commanding voice, "What do you think you're doing? Do you think I'm blind?"

"What're you talking about?" my mother asked. But I suspected she already knew. She'd behaved that way before and my father had made the same accusations.

Dad ordered everyone to leave, and as they started to rise from around the kitchen table, he said, "I can't trust you when you're like this."

My grandfather, not wanting to see the party break up so quickly, took my mother's side. The argument heated up until the three of them shifted outside into the clear night air with the departing guests. A shouting match soon commenced. My father and grandfather stood with fists raised, hurling insults that seemed to have nothing to do with what was going on. My mother cried and yelled for them to stop while a few of the guests waited for things to settle so they could resume their drinking. That was when I went to bed. My little brothers were already sleeping soundly and hadn't woken during the racket.

Eventually everything was quiet. The guests had reluctantly left the party. Later my grandfather slipped into my room. I felt his shadow in the doorway and sensed his breathing. I blamed the bottles for what was happening. The bottles changed people, gave them two different personalities. Sometimes I thought I might be the one who split into two people—one for the normal days and another for the grotesque nights.

The music in my head grew so loud that I couldn't hear my sobs. I imagined I was inside a cloud that was going to carry me to a land where there were no men at all except maybe my father. And my father would protect me. He would be there to look after me. He would hold me in his strong arms, and the night and its shadows would shrink away from where they had lodged deep in my frightened child's heart. I would marvel at his handsome face and his smiling eyes would save me.

The nighttime visitations continued—either my grandfather or friends of the family would find their way into my room. It wasn't until I sampled the remnants of liquid in the bottles that I found a way to black out the fear and sleep peacefully. I was six years old.

After only a few sips, I felt safe and happy as I floated inside my cloud to another fantasy land, a big green thicket occupied only by my grandmothers and their cats, a place where small cocker spaniel puppies lingered with all the other forest animals. They would watch me with innocent, depthless eyes and speak to me in our own private language. When they were near, there was only the feeling of ample goodness. There stood the animals, unmoving and plain, the gentle, welcoming forest behind them.

BORN-AGAIN CHRISTIAN CHILD

When I was nine, I attended the Billy Graham Crusade in Fredericton with my friend Sharon and her parents, who belonged to the local Baptist church. I was nervous about facing the new experience, but my hesitation fled the minute I walked into the coliseum. A young, pleasant man and woman stood at the entrance, greeting people as they arrived. The woman had brown waist-length hair. She gave me a warm handshake as she welcomed me to the meeting, then handed me a small piece of paper with the words "Jesus Loves You" written in red at the top.

We found seats in the fourth row from the front. There weren't many children present, mostly adults. We sat amid the assembly of close to five hundred people watching the man onstage trumpeting the high points of salvation. The buzz from the crowd, the sense of their intense devotion to the man booming out his words, mesmerized me. Suddenly I had the impression I was the only person in the room. Leaning forward in my chair, I clung to every word and savoured every musical note as I felt beckoned to the power of deliverance and angelic epiphany.

I studied the face of the man who was preaching. Something about him reminded me of Grammie Mills. There seemed to be a glow around his head. Maybe it was just the large overhead fluorescent lights giving an afterglow to images. I'd seldom been in a building with lights that bright.

When the preacher searched in my direction, his eyes returned my gaze.

He sees me, I thought. *He really sees me.*

"Jesus will give you happiness," he called out to me. "Jesus will be your friend. You just have to give Him your heart. Give Jesus your heart. Can you give Jesus your heart and let Him be your friend?" I rose from my chair and stumbled to the front, climbing the stairs to the stage with joyous tears streaming down my face, not even aware that Sharon and her parents had followed me up.

"Please, Jesus," I said, "take my heart." I wanted him to make it a better thing. I wanted to be saved. And, yes, I felt I was being saved.

The same woman with the long brown hair who had greeted me at the door joined me onstage and grasped my hand to pray. "Will you repeat the sinner's prayer with me?" she asked.

I nodded and swiped the tears from my eyes, oblivious to the crowd before me.

"If you say the prayer and mean it, God will forgive you for every bad thing you've ever done."

I nodded again.

"God will change your life for you. Do you want your life to change?"

"Yes."

"Close your eyes and pray with me." She shut her eyes and I shut mine. In a whisper I repeated the words the woman spoke: *God, be merciful to me a sinner...* And as I did so, I felt my heart swell to discharge its burden. My head grew light and I was gripped by an intense happiness I had never experienced. I was filled with holy light.

Opening my eyes, I looked out over the crowd. They were watching me and they were smiling and shouting out praise, happy that I had been saved.

Unfortunately the desperate situations at home didn't change in the face of my new salvation. I started to become discouraged, yet I didn't lose my faith. I continued attending church. I prayed and prayed for a better life. *God, please make my mom stop drinking. Make her love me. Give Daddy a better job so he won't be so angry all the time. And please make my grandfather go away.*

I devoted myself to praying. I wouldn't give up on God. When I was almost twelve, God answered my prayers. For years I had been imploring my parents to join me at church each Sunday. They would see me praying every day I thought, and might want to change, too. Then, to my astonishment and glee, they did begin attending church, and their drinking stopped. *Everything will be all right now,* I told myself. *Everything will be so absolutely perfect.*

My parents soon became pillars of the church. They renounced all worldly goods, a feat not that difficult to master considering their economic situation. The minister at the church became their direct pipeline to God, pronouncing new revelations that required greater sacrifice and more devout obedience. Women were commanded to stop wearing shoes with heels. They were to wear dresses that disguised their womanhood and hats that demonstrated their subservience to men. Even the baby girls were instructed to wear dresses that flowed to their ankles. Radios could only be switched on for the news, and televisions were positively evil, the sole creation of the devil.

On a warm spring day our family and a few of the church people gathered on the front lawn of our home. Before us sat our television, propped on a table. My father said a prayer of exorcism before raising the pickaxe and driving it through the tube. When the tube blew out a large puff of grey smoke, the small gathering cried, "Praise the Lord!" For them it was an offering. For me it meant no more Walt Disney, no more candy-coated escape into benign lands.

I was informed I had to stop wearing jeans, nail polish, and jewellery. I was warned never to cut my hair. I was to be excused from gym class. I wasn't even permitted to play baseball at noon hour.

I still had a crush on Norman, but he wasn't interested in church, so I decided I'd have to sacrifice my girlish feelings for my more serious devotion to Christ. I had never been allowed to spend time alone with boys, but now it was even worse. If I was caught alone with a boy, I'd be accused of all sorts of vile actions I didn't even know about yet. I was used to being groped and prodded by adults, but I couldn't so much as talk to a boy my own age.

Girls who thought about boys all the time were bad, sinister, wretched wenches. Since I did wonder about boys quite a bit, I suspected my parents were right. I must be bad. I must have the sinister worm of evil in me. Oddly I took a shine to that thought. It was a romantic notion: the seeds of insurrection neatly planted, the way it was in one of the characters in the books I'd read. If I was bad, then I'd need accomplices. That was when I started befriending the bad boys at school.

I was fascinated with a classmate named Raymond, a short, well-tanned French boy who could barely speak French. In fact, he couldn't speak English all that well, either. He would often stutter when he was forced to read in class. He always wore light-coloured T-shirts, black jeans, and boots—never shoes or sneakers—and usually his clothes were too small for his stocky frame. I figured he bought them at the Salvation Army discount store because I knew firsthand how hard it was to find just the right size there. Immediately I empathized with his dilemma.

Raymond lived with religious foster parents. He never did well in school and was picked on by most of the teachers and the other kids, probably because he was so emotionally numb. He wouldn't cry even when the principal strapped him for not answering a question. He told me he never even cried when his stepmother whipped him across the back with a belt and locked him in his room without supper.

I believed him and began to revere his suffering. He needed to be saved. He was in pain. I thought he was just about the bravest boy I'd ever met. I tried to help him learn how to spell so the teacher would stop calling him a dummy in class, but he never seemed to get the hang of it. He had a hard time pronouncing certain words and found it difficult to concentrate. Today he would be diagnosed with attention-deficit disorder or a learning disability. Back then he was just rebellious and incorrigible. His teachers told him he didn't want to learn, but they never saw how hard he tried when he was with me, or how honest tears would float in his eyes when he couldn't distinguish a *b* from a *d*. And he was so eager to please me.

I promised never to tell.

Raymond grew up with the tough-guy image clenched in every

muscle of his body but also in his heart. He hated the world. When we were in school, we were constantly warned about him. Everyone said he'd come to no good. And I guess, in their own narrow-minded way, they were right.

Raymond was twenty-five when his body was discovered at the bottom of Lake Ontario. Rumour was he'd been dumped after being killed by a rebel biker gang. I never found out for sure how he died. When I heard the news, all I remembered was the curly-haired guy who loved red cars, tabby cats, and the colour black. He was the one who gave me my first bouquet of flowers when I was only thirteen—daisies, bluebells, and buttercups—with a note that read: "To my best freind. Love, Raymond."

One of the most difficult consequences of my family's born-again values was the effect they had on my ambition. My dreams to become a professional writer or veterinarian or both were dashed. My father was a talented poet who had been dubbed the Bard of Oromocto by local media. His poetry and children's stories had been published in local newspapers and, as a tourism project, the Women's Institute had put together a collection of his poems in a book called *The Wake of Silence*.

"Crusoe Complex" was one of my favourites. The words helped explain the pained expression I so often witnessed in my father's eyes:

Heart is a lonely island ringed by reefs
And washed by endless tide
Love is a bridge to other islands
A brotherhood to lesser loneliness.
My island has no bridges,
The bitter tides are flotsam-filled
And reefs around my island are a cage.

Jim Coulter often read my father's poems on CFNB Radio, but Dad knew he'd never make any real money writing poetry no matter how much he dreamed about it, so I guess he was determined to save me from the same unrequited dreams. He was quick to say, "Put that foolishness out of your head." I was a female. Females were supposed to learn all the devotions required to be a good wife. "Never mind that career nonsense," he insisted with a fierceness that seemed much too severe to suit the situation.

He discouraged me from viewing writing as a career, but his objections came too late. I had already fallen in love with the recognition I'd received at school for my writing abilities. It was the only area of my life where I felt some measure of confidence. When I won a provincial essay contest at the age of twelve, my mind was made up. I *would* be a writer and I *would* make money at it.

My father discouraged me from learning about things usually considered the sole preoccupation of men—like cars. I asked him one day to show me, as he had my brothers, how to fix the fan belt in our car. He had no time for it. I cursed him twenty years later when I sat on the side of a deserted highway on my way home from St. Stephen trying to picture what little information I had been able to glean of the fan-belt installation before I was instructed to go help my mother and leave the fan belts to the men.

I was always at the top of my class in school. My marks hovered in the nineties. Sometimes I would even bring home papers with a proud 100 circled in red marker. But no one was particularly impressed except Grammie Mills. Whenever I wrote and told her about my marks, she'd always write back to let me know how proud she was of me.

Only if my grades slipped a point or two did I receive any feedback. Then it would be something like: *What happened there? Didn't you study? Had your mind on those boys again, didn't you?*

I had a hard time pretending my life was normal. Sexual abuse had forced me to be a fragmented woman long before I was even an adolescent, and the secret was making me sicker every day. My strict parents would never have believed I was innocent. If I confessed, it would be my fault. If I opened my mouth, it would all be my fault, my creation, my doing. My father was always suspicious of my dealings with the opposite sex. He'd often accuse me of sneaking away to meet a boy when I'd only been sitting in the woods by myself, wondering about my solitude and admiring the stillness.

Eventually the accusations got to me. The craziness in my head got to me. The life of misunderstanding and loneliness got to me. The part of me that was labouring to come to life just gave up. I didn't want to be there anymore. I thought maybe I could drown myself, but we didn't live handy to any suitably deep river or lake and I was terrified of water, anyway. I had heard that my great-grandfather had shot himself, but I didn't know how to use a gun. So I just started praying for an end when I went to bed at night.

"Please, God, don't let me wake up in the morning. I don't want to wake up anymore." I begged for God to take me so that my eyes would never witness daylight again. I would eventually drift off into the semblance of my hoped-for disappearance, but in the morning my eyes would open to the reality of yet another day.

Having grown up in a predominately morbid household, it was an easy transition to become preoccupied with fantasizing about death. How wonderful and peaceful it would be. How empty and weightless. How innocent and graceful.

But I continued living. After a while, I just stopped praying altogether.

If it wasn't for school, I might have found a definite way to do away with myself. I loved school. I loved books. I grew stronger under the steady regimen of classrooms and corridors. I delighted in cleaning dusty chalk boards and helping the teachers any way I could. I found the consistent presence of the teachers reassuring. I hated weekends. I hated the turbulent days when we were forced to stay at home because of storms.

And I hated summer vacations.

I had few friends at school, only a skinny girl a year younger than I named Beryl. She had light brown hair and sang country songs like my mother. Beryl was easygoing except for being troubled by constant nosebleeds. She lived about four miles away on Waterville Road. Some of my teachers were the kindest people I had ever come upon. Miss Murray, a slim young woman with curly brown hair and a generous smile, was my favourite of all the teachers. Whenever she spoke to me, she always put her hand affectionately on my shoulder. She seemed to care about me genuinely, even going as far as to tell me she was worried I was spending too much time with the boys at school.

"You have to be careful," she said, "especially around the older boys—like Norman."

A part of me wanted to ask why, but another part didn't want to hear anything more. My need for Norman far outweighed any advice from an adult who knew nothing of my brash and pure-hearted desires.

One of my principals, Mr. Davidson, loaned me extra books to read and always encouraged me to follow my dreams. He never seemed too busy to talk and he was quite excited when I showed him those 100s circled in red. It was as if he had journeyed from my imaginary country, that green fertile land with winding brooks, furry puppies, and gentle-handed grandmothers who served apple pie and cookies as they smiled and patted your cheek, a country where the sole male inhabitants lived on the other side of the brook and could visit only in the daytime under the plainness of sunlight. It was a world I still conjured up, even in high school.

Mr. Davidson wasn't concerned about training anybody to be a proper wife, and he certainly wasn't interested in my body. His generosity and kindness accented my parents' rigid fanaticism. It was through this comparison that I began to suspect my mother and father truly hated me.

In school I adored listening to lectures about far-off countries or distant planets. This information held my attention a lot longer than the seemingly frivolous games played during recess breaks. I was particularly fond of history, language arts, and social studies, but totally frustrated by mathematics after grade six. For the most part, I loved all my teachers, and I often fantasized what it would be like to stand in front of a classroom and lecture about Charles Dickens laboriously penning his stories of life in old England.

School became my entire world. I couldn't fail. That was who I was—a top student, willing and able to take on any project to please an adult. I wrote for the school newspaper and worked as the editor gathering articles from the reps in each of the classes. I often won writing competitions. These interests were particularly important because I needed my poet father to be proud of me. Outside school I possessed zero identity. To fail would have meant I ceased to exist as a human being.

In spite of my efforts, not all of my teachers admired my devotion. In particular, one of my math teachers, Mr. C., made it obvious he thought I wasn't worth any extra effort when it came to getting supplementary help to master difficult concepts in subjects like algebra. I approached him one day to seek assistance.

"Why would a top student like you need extra help?" he replied sarcastically, walking away. I knew better than to ask again.

Grade seven was a tough year for me. My lack of popularity among my peers became excruciatingly obvious. I wasn't allowed to attend school activities like dances or baseball games, functions that might have given me a chance to nurture friendships. So I tried deliberate rebellion, like failing to produce homework in order to appear *cool*, even though I usually completed assignments within an hour after school was dismissed.

One day I tried to act cool in class by making fun of the teacher, Miss Mazie Myles, behind her back so the other kids would laugh at me. And I did get their attention as I pretended to scratch my chin and mouth her favourite phrase: *I wasn't born in a swamp yesterday, you know*. Unfortunately my antics also caught Miss Myles's attention when she turned unexpectedly. Everyone laughed, but when I saw the look of disappointment in my teacher's eyes, a teacher who had treated me fairly, I felt stupid and ashamed. Miss Myles sent me out in the hallway to think about my behaviour, and I stood there in humiliation, realizing that a few laughs from the kids weren't worth hurting a teacher I actually liked.

That year I befriended Donna Carpenter. New to our class, she had moved with her family to Geary because her father was enlisted in the army at Base Gagetown. Donna was everything I ever wanted to be: popular and pretty with long, straight auburn hair and a flippant attitude about everything. We were practically the same size, both short, with long hair, and had been born in the same month and year, so I fantasized that she was my twin sister. I jigged school a couple of times with her, but fear of my parents' wrath ruined any fun I might have had on those excursions. Donna's parents were much more lenient. Most of the time she didn't even have a curfew. One of the days we jigged school, her mother actually drove us to Killarney Lake in Fredericton so we could swim.

I visited Donna's home a few times. She'd let me borrow her clothes, but I'd have to change before I went home. My parents would have died if they had seen me dressed in bell bottoms and a halter top.

Donna and I managed to stay friends in spite of our differences. I still went to church and she had no religious beliefs. She often attended school dances or skating parties at the school. Most of the time I listened to the highlights of these events as she retold them. I figured I was banished to the sidelines to watch others have fun. I had to face the facts: I was destined to be a nerd. The only hope I held on to was my love of writing. I would be a famous writer and then I would be so cool.

"You'll never amount to anything," Mr. C. told me one day, regarding me as if I were a loathsome creature he'd like to cast from his sight. "Those high marks don't mean a thing."

I was standing in front of my entire class. I had tried to pass a note to Donna while Mr. C. was teaching. His cutting words tore away what bit of self-confidence I had managed to cling to over my thirteen years. Something vital shrivelled into a cold heavy ball inside me. I had been humiliated again. The eyes of all my class-mates were upon me, and everyone now knew how worthless I truly was.

By the age of fourteen, I started to change, but not physically; that had happened a long time ago in grade two. I started to embrace my anger and turn it on other people. My thoughts of missionary work on some distant shore, or helping the pagans live better God-inspired lives, transformed into daydreams of lying naked beside some woodland stream with Ray Stewart, the brother of my next-door neighbour. Ray was the first boy I ever loved. I dreamed about marrying him and running away to Prince Edward Island where his family had lived before moving to New Brunswick. I wanted him to love me back. His cool, detached manner only heightened my desire for him. I didn't want to be a *nice* girl anymore. I wanted to be nasty. I wanted to control him with my body. The body that held the power, the body that people wanted.

Being a faithful churchgoer hadn't changed my life for the better. More than ever, I could never quite measure up. After being accused so many times of things I'd never yet experienced, I decided it was finally time to discover what I was missing, to fit the role, to bridge the gap between accusation and reality.

That was the year I willingly let Ray explore my body. We were into heavy necking and petting, but I wanted to give myself to him completely. Only the terror of a possible pregnancy kept me from going all the way. My mother's fervent warnings reared up in my head. My mother's sad life. My mother's dark regret. It had found its mark in me. I couldn't give myself over to my longings even though my parents were certain I already had.

A few months later Ray moved to the United States and joined the American army. I was heartbroken. He kept in touch for a while, writing short letters on lined paper, talking mostly about his training. They weren't romantic by any stretch. He even came back to see me once, showing up on my doorstep unexpectedly. He talked to my father about marrying me, which sent my heart soaring. When he was leaving, he kissed me goodbye, then said, "I'll write and we'll make plans." But I never heard from him again.

A CAREER IN WRITING

Winning the essay contest when I was twelve encouraged me to write with more regularity. Geary Consolidated School produced a student newspaper and I was a frequent contributor before I eventually took over as editor. I entered every essay contest I heard of and often won a prize. I developed a deep passion for writing exposition and non-fiction. Determined to be a reporter, I asked my principal, Mr. Davidson, where I should start. He suggested I contact the two local papers, *The Daily Gleaner* in Fredericton and the weekly *Camp Gagetown Gazette* in Oromocto.

At the tender age of fourteen I was writing a weekly column in both newspapers. I covered school news for *The Gleaner* and the *Social Scene* for the *Gazette*. The editor of the Oromocto paper at the time, Don Sisson, was satisfied with my writing and didn't hesitate to pass on his approval. Finding worth in his encouragement, I worked even harder to please him. When I became district representative for the Kindness Clubs, an organization dedicated to the prevention of animal abuse, I also began writing about the clubs' activities.

The material I wrote for *The Daily Gleaner* was on a gratis basis, but the *Camp Gagetown Gazette* paid me a weekly salary of about $10.

A year later my yearning to pursue a writing career was bolstered when I won yet another essay contest. Out of several hundred young people who entered from all across Canada and the United States, I was selected as one of thirty-nine winners. My essay, "Submission to His Commission," was based on Christ's message to carry His word of love to all people regardless of their state or location. It was published in *Young Ambassador* magazine out of Lincoln, Nebraska, in 1966. I nearly went out of my mind checking the mailbox every day for four or five months, anxious to see my story in print. When the magazine finally arrived, my mom was the first to see it. She opened the envelope, then showed it to me when I returned from school. She also proudly flaunted it to all her friends.

Within a few months of my newfound success south of the border, I was picking up a few dollars by covering events in the Oromocto area as a correspondent for *The Daily Gleaner*. At night, before sleeping, I'd imagine what it would be like to have a full-time job as a writer. I'd picture myself travelling to exotic locales, covering stories for *National Geographic* and *Life*.

Again I considered a career in the Christian ministry. I saw myself as a helpful saint, rushing to the aid of children in Third World countries, or ministering to the sick and dying in some dingy big-city hostel.

The summer before I turned sixteen, I went to live with Hector McGregor, a French evangelist on the Gaspé shore of Quebec. He had been a visitor to our Geary church and had spoken about the need for people to help with his new Protestant church. Brother McGregor was calling for musicians and singers, anyone willing to join him for the summer. He also required a person to assist with his four young children. On the night I heard him speak I approached him and said I would be interested in offering a hand. I was expected to help with the children and the church services, and the family would speak French exclusively so I might learn the language in this do-or-die situation.

I rode the train from Fredericton by myself. My parents saw me off. The church had taken up a collection, so I had money in my pocket. They presented it to me the Sunday before I left, and Mom and Dad managed to scrape up a few dollars to go with it. After the return train ticket was purchased, I had almost $60 and felt like an heiress setting out on her own for the first time. Along the way I spoke to a few people who were curious about my venture. When an old man asked if I was interested in accompanying him to the bar car for a drink, I stopped talking and took out my Bible to read. No one came near me after that.

When the train arrived in Gaspé City, Hector McGregor and his family were there to meet me. They drove me to a small village named Pointe-Navarre where they lived. As it turned out, I spent most of my time doing housework and baby-sitting while Hector and his wife visited people, attempting to build a congregation. I did manage to sing in French during a few services. After I was there about a month, Brother McGregor caught me talking one evening to a French boy who didn't attend church. The brother mercilessly scolded me, saying I'd go straight to Hell if I didn't change my ways, and I watched the French boy shrink away, taking his leave. A kind young minister named Jean Joyale tried to take my part while Brother McGregor delivered his wrath, but the damage had been done. The brother said, "I'll have no boy-crazy teenager making out in the churchyard and interfering with my ministry."

"You're a dirty-minded hypocrite!" I yelled back. "Your biggest ministry is having kids."

"Let's just talk about this," Brother Joyale interrupted in French.

"This isn't your concern," Brother McGregor said sternly.

That was that. I packed my things in silence and was delivered to the train station a few days later. Only the warm hugs from Brother McGregor's wife and children let me know I'd be missed.

When I returned home from my learning experience, I once more abandoned my dream of becoming a missionary. I knew I could never possibly live the uncompromising life my parents and the church expected of me.

ADDICTED TO BAD BOYS

My next big crush was on a young Maliseet boy named Alfred who used to visit his sister next door to where we lived. He was lean and brown with dark, menacing eyes—eyes so black I sometimes felt mesmerized when I looked into them. I was intrigued by the alluring primitiveness of his behaviour, the raw, passionate sex that seemed a foreboding certainty. He had a long, angular face with a hooked nose that reminded me of a hawk. He smelled like the cedar and pine he spent hours carving into animal figures. He was an artist, vaguely magical and mythical, and there for me.

I was hungry for the touch of those rough, callused fingers, but again I was too afraid to give in. Our summer romance was limited to probing tongues and awkward caresses that tried to coax shy nipples through the confines of cotton. I never knew he had another girlfriend—a tough, husky white girl—until one day she made her presence known. I was sitting outside on my doorstep when she stormed right up to me, a hostile figure suddenly too close for comfort.

"Who do you think you are?" she screamed. I stood and edged away from the house, not wanting my mother to hear what was going on. I didn't have a clue who the girl was.

"W-what are you talking about?" I stammered, noticing she had her fists clenched by her sides. I continued backing away as she advanced.

"What are you doing with my boyfriend?"

"What boyfriend? Who are you talking about?"

"Alfred." She raised her hands and lunged at me.

I stumbled, shocked into silence for a moment. "Alfred? I didn't know he had a girlfriend."

"Well, he does," she said, pointing at me, gritting her teeth. "And if I catch you messing around with him again, I'll drive that little white nose of yours down your throat."

My cheeks were flushed and I felt tears spring to my eyes. I had never been threatened before and I wasn't about to attempt fighting a girl with arms like a wrestler's.

"There's nothing going on between Alfred and me," I lied. "Besides, I already have a boyfriend."

"That better be true!" she screamed in my face. "If I find out different, I'll wrap that long hair around your throat!" She glared at me, deciding what to do next. Then she backed away, still watching me, before heading onto the road that would take her the three miles from Haneytown to Oromocto. *She sure does talk strange for a white girl*, I thought.

Fearing for my life, I told Alfred I couldn't see him anymore when he came to visit his sister a few days later. He didn't offer any objection. No decrees of love for me, no long pleas of devotion. I had a sneaky suspicion his girlfriend must have already warned him off. After all, she was twice as tough as he was.

GRAMMIE MILLS'S DEATH

I didn't see Grammie Mills as frequently as I would have liked in my early teen years, but I thought of her often. I wondered what she would say if I had been able to talk to her about boys. I didn't think she would get as mad as my mother when I tried broaching the subject. Grammie Mills never got mad at me.

It was a freezing cold morning, February 13, 1967, when my

father received the call informing him Grammie Mills was gone. Ordinarily I would have been at school, but on this particular morning I was home with a cold. My father was told there had been a fire caused by overheated ductwork in Aunt Edna's Lakewood home on the outskirts of Saint John. Aunt Edna had already left for work. A neighbour had noticed smoke billowing from the house and alerted the fire department. When the firemen arrived, it was too late. They had discovered my grandmother's body on the kitchen floor, three feet from the door. Aunt Edna's German shepherd, which had lain faithfully next to Grammie Mills, had also perished.

The policeman notified my father that Grammie had been overcome by the smoke. She never suffered. Not a bit.

"The police want me to go to Saint John," my father quietly told us, his hand still on the receiver. "To identify the body."

I couldn't believe my ears. I stood there, watching the pain etch deeper into my father's face. It was too much for me to bear. Without a word I headed to my bedroom. I stayed there, unwilling even to say goodbye to him as he left.

The following day, when my father returned from Saint John, he didn't talk about Grammie in front of me. He wouldn't mention her name. I noticed that some of his dark brown hair had turned white. It had happened in less than twenty-four hours. I'd read in one of my books about a man whose black hair turned completely white after coming face-to-face with a demonic spirit. I was afraid for my father, but I didn't want to know what had happened, what had made his hair change colour in what seemed like nothing more than an instant.

Grammie Mills's funeral was held in Fredericton. All during the service I stared at the casket, determined to rip it open and have one last look at her to make certain she was really inside. I couldn't believe they required such a big box for such a tiny woman. I wanted it all to be just a bad dream. I wanted to wake up and see her visiting us again for a big Sunday dinner. I wanted to hear her gruff little chuckle as she greeted me with a warm, perfume-scented hug and kiss.

Sitting with my mom and dad in the funeral chapel, I recalled how purely delighted my grandmother used to be when I brought her flowers. She didn't like winter and so it seemed unfair to me that we would be taking her for her last car ride in the middle of a winter storm. *She should be surrounded by sunshine and daffodils*, I reflected.

I glanced across the handful of people, all dressed in black, who sat stoically listening to the words of some dreary hymn. My aunts (Aunt Lois looked so much like Grammie), parents, brothers, cousins, and other relatives I'd only met at funerals stared straight ahead as a minister stood to pray for my grandmother. *You're too late*, I thought, concentrating on holding back my tears. *Too late.*

Two ministers conducted the funeral service: Dr. Harold Mitten from Brunswick Street Baptist Church, where my Aunt Lena, Dad's other sister, and my cousin, Heather, attended faithfully; and Archdeacon A. S. Coster, the Anglican priest who had married my parents.

How can you look so calm! I longed to shout. It was impossible to measure the amount of pain my relatives might be suffering by studying their faces. My dad's family had a long history of suffering in silence.

I stared down at my own black skirt and felt fury and resentment as the pallbearers carried the casket from the funeral home to the hearse outside. On the fifteen-mile trip to the graveyard I studied the snow as it began to blow into tiny white tornadoes along the way, and I imagined I could see Grammie Mills's smiling face along the edge of the cloudy sky above the dancing flakes. By the time we reached the gravesite, I was certain she wasn't even there, so I never watched as they lowered the casket into the ugly hole that had been hacked out of the frozen earth.

Many times since her death, at junctures when conditions appeared darkest, I have felt Grammie Mills's caress on my cheek. One night, about six months after her death, I was sick with the flu. I awoke to see her standing at the side of my bed. I began to cry and she reached down and touched my cheek. Her fingers were warm. When I closed my eyes and opened them again, she had vanished, but her touch lingered. I have felt her presence five times since then, episodes that have sealed my faith in the afterlife.

OUT OF CONTROL

After Grammie Mills's death, I felt angry most of the time. I despised who I was and hated everyone around me. Even my writing provided little distraction or release. I turned my back on trying to be the *good girl* simply to win the approval of others. I'd had enough of home and wanted to leave. The old-fashioned Christian laws that ruled my house allowed me absolutely no leeway. I felt as if I were being suffocated, especially now that it was summer and I was around my parents more than usual. If I was even a few minutes late coming home, I was accused of plotting an escapade with a boy. It was time to run my own life. I had it in my mind that I wasn't going back to school. I'd had enough of school, enough of everything from my past life.

To hide my true intentions, I told my folks I was going to visit Judy, my cousin in Fredericton. My parents didn't like the idea, but they couldn't do anything about it. I had made up my mind. I guess they reasoned I would be away only for a short while. They had no way of knowing I had shut my mind to them and was never coming back.

I showed up on my cousin Judy's doorstep and asked if I could stay with her for a few days while I searched for a job. She wasn't surprised to see me. I often popped in unexpectedly. Two days later I was working at a lunch counter in the Queen Street Zellers in Fredericton.

I met a new, exciting crowd—most of them at least four or five years older than I was—and began to experiment with hashish and uppers. The first time I smoked hash I felt sleepy and hungry, nothing more sensational. I never liked it. But I did like the uppers. After living with the chaos of my mom's and grandfather's drinking, I'd promised myself I'd never let alcohol touch my lips.

Three weeks into my stay in Fredericton I was smoking hash with a few hippie friends in a run-down rooming house on Regent Street when one of the guys, an educational student at the University of New Brunswick, suggested we all go to a dance at the KP Hall a few blocks away. I'd never attended any functions there, but I'd heard it was a pretty rough place. Everyone seemed eager to go except me, but I would never have admitted I was afraid. The stone from the hash made the venture seem even more severe. I didn't want to go anywhere near anything dangerous. I just wanted to sit still and be mellow, let my eyes melt and worm my way into some soul-smoothing music. But the others kept insisting, so I came up with a legitimate excuse. "I'm only sixteen," I quietly offered.

"That's no problem," Steve said. He was twenty, slim, handsome, and of Italian descent. I appreciated the fact that he was an older man and I knew he'd had his eye on me. He'd told Judy that he'd like to take me out. "I can get you in."

"You sure?" I asked, my wavering fear slowly overcome by the heady anticipation of being with a guy as good-looking as Steve. I licked my lips and watched his eyes, trying to figure out his intentions. Was he really interested in me or not?

"I'm sure. C'mon," Steve said, signalling for everyone to get ready. We were all sitting on the floor, listening to the Rolling Stones.

Outside, the air was sweet. I felt my feet moving, but I was totally stoned, shifting at the wrong speed. Everyone was chattering about strange things and laughing at the slightest hint of humour. Before we knew it, even though it seemed like forever, the six of us arrived at the dance hall. There was something happening in the parking lot. Violent noises and movement. A scuffle. Two men in their thirties were punching each other, while a young woman stood nearby screaming at both of them. It seemed by what she was shouting and by her position in the confrontation that they were fighting over her. Onlookers stood leaning against the dance hall, watching with mild interest or uneasy concern.

"I don't think…" I started to protest, but Steve hooked his arm in mine, his bare skin brushing me. I almost melted with the pleasure, with the seemingly illicit nature of that simple touch.

"I'll take care of you." Steve grinned, then winked, leading me around the brawl as one of the men went down and hit the pavement hard. *What new world is this?* I thought. *What screwed-up world?* My heart was beating faster. But I let Steve lead me while the others followed, casting glances back at the brawl.

When we reached the entrance, Steve whispered something to the burly, muscle-bound guy ushering people into the dance. The guy looked me up and down and I tried not to be nervous, but my eyes kept darting here and there. When he was done inspecting me, the bouncer smiled and made a sweeping gesture with his hand, graciously allowing me entry.

The hall was filled with people. The smells of stale cigarette smoke and sweet liquor provoked memories. I imagined those parties in my parents' kitchen, but this was my party now. This was my turn. I could break free and have fun on my own. I felt at home in the dimness with the loud music cutting off thought. Music, that was what I wanted. Steve took my hand and led me to the packed, smoky dance floor. Soon, I was dancing to the beat of "Memphis," a Johnny Rivers tune.

When I was through, Steve shouted over the music, "What d'ya want to drink?"

"I'll try a beer!" I yelled back. I'd never actually drunk beer before, but it seemed to be the beverage everyone was having. I'd tasted wine from the bottles in my room as a child and some other malty liquid my father had made once, but this was a new experience for me. After only one gulp, I was comfortable with the taste. I started to experience the same warm, safe feeling I'd felt when drinking wine as a child.

As the evening wore on, I consumed several more beers, revelling in the boozy lull that loosened me up and made me feel as if I truly fit in, that the night was there for me to take full advantage of. We danced for hours and I became a new person, healed, not needing to think about anything, a creature reincarnated exclusively for pleasure. When Steve decided we should go to a party, I agreed.

The party was at someone's house about ten minutes away. The quieter atmosphere was a big change from the hall, but I was feeling bubbly, so it didn't matter that much. I was interested in checking out the interior. The house was a suburban bungalow, bigger than anything I'd ever lived in. It was all new to me.

"You sure can hold your liquor," Steve said as we settled in the living room, which was clean and full of nice furniture.

I smiled with genuine pride.

I thought there might be more people in the house, but there were only two other couples. The man who owned the house was short and dark and not very attractive. In fact, he was almost ugly and seemed to have few friends. He'd have anyone around. That was why we were there. He told me he drove a milk truck. When he asked me what I would like from his liquor cabinet, I had no idea what to say. I'd never been in the presence of sophisticated drinkers. A tall bottle with dark green liquid caught my eye, so I pointed to it.

"How do you want it?" the man asked, unscrewing the bottle and holding the tip over a glass.

I sat in silence.

"On the rocks?" he asked.

Not knowing exactly what "on the rocks" might mean and feeling the eyes of everyone on me, I said, "I'll just drink it like it is." And so I did. I drank until I was liberated beyond belief. I drank until I was wobbly and barely still in my body. I drank until there was no more to drink. I finished off the entire bottle.

Things slowly became a blur after that. I found the company astoundingly interesting. I soaked up the conversations and laughed when I was supposed to. I kept sipping and loving the taste and loving my new friends until everyone was confusing to me and I felt my body move on its own. I felt it lean sideways even though I wasn't leaning. I'd have to catch myself to stay straight. I felt the room begin to spin. Deep inside, my body was turning against the air I was breathing, turning against gravity, turning crookedly against itself.

The next morning I woke in a place unknown to me. I was in a small bedroom on a single bed. My waist-length hair was covered with something sticky and thick. I caught a whiff of a pungent odour and knew it was vomit. The pain in my head became unbearable as I shifted my body. I leaned forward, cringing, and held my head, fearing my brain would crack in two.

Eventually I managed to get up to search for a bathroom. When I entered the living room, I realized I was still in the same house. The guy who owned it was passed out on the couch. All alone.

After that wild night, I slipped easily into a lifestyle of drinking and partying. The hangover soon went away and the booze kept me at a safe distance from myself. For a few months I drifted from job to job and lived wherever I could find a bed for the night. Sometimes it was with female friends, other times with male friends, known or unknown to me. I had no contact with my parents even though they lived only twenty miles away.

One night, in a bar, I met up with a girl who had been in my class back in Geary. Linda was married to a soldier, a guy named

Doug. They lived in Lincoln, halfway between Fredericton and Oromocto. Linda walked into the bar bathroom and found me crying because I'd just lost another job, this one in a candy store. I'd been late too many times and was finally let go. I had no place to live and wasn't even sure where most of my clothes were. Linda offered to help. She told me I could come stay with her and Doug. I accepted the offer, desperately in need of some sort of permanence, having no idea I would soon meet my first husband in Linda's home, and finally embrace the menacing instability that would nearly kill me.

STAN

When I moved into Linda's house in Lincoln, I made a firm commitment to get my life back on track. I even decided to visit my parents so I could let them know I was alive and doing well.

"Oh, Eva, you're all right!" my mother said, running to the door to greet me when I arrived. She wrapped her tiny arms around my back and held tightly, starting to cry.

I couldn't believe my eyes. Mom had lost weight and looked ill.

"I was so worried," she wept into my cheek. "I prayed every night."

I returned her hug, held on tighter, and burst into tears. *She loves me*, I thought. *She really loves me.* "I'm fine, Mom."

My father wasn't home from work yet and my brothers were at school, so I sat and waited with Mom as she filled the kettle for tea and set a plate of cinnamon rolls on the table in front of me.

She smiled. "One of your favourites. Eat."

I raised a cinnamon bun to my mouth as I studied my mother. She had definitely lost weight, more than I had first observed. "Are you okay, Mom?"

She sat in the chair across from me, her eyes sad and happy at once. "After you left, I just couldn't seem to eat much. We didn't hear from you. I was sure something awful had happened."

"I'm sorry. I didn't have a phone."

She nodded. "You're fine, though."

"Is Dad mad at me?"

"He was worried, too." Pausing, she watched me chew a bite of cinnamon roll. "He'll be glad to see you. He even called the police once. And I checked the hospital."

"I didn't think you'd be worried."

My mother stared at me as if remembering something distant and uncertain, then the kettle began to whistle.

When my father came home from his job as janitor at the Oromocto Shopping Centre, he didn't say a word. He just laid down his silver lunch pail and put his arms around me, gently patting my head.

My brothers were excited to see me. They eagerly chatted about what was happening in their lives.

I stayed with my family until Linda's husband, Doug, picked me up that evening around ten o'clock. I couldn't remember when I'd ever felt so loved. Leaving the house in a blissful state of reassurance, I even promised Dad I'd try to make it to church the following Sunday. We were opening up to one another and expressing our feelings. My mother was worried to the point of weight loss, to the point of sickness. Was it possible we could finally be at peace with each other?

That night back in Lincoln, Doug and Linda invited a friend of theirs over to meet me. It was a blind date of sorts, although I knew I was being set up. Linda told me the man's name was Stan and he was stationed with the Black Watch Regiment, just like Doug, at CFB Gagetown, a military base housed primarily within Oromocto town limits. When Doug mentioned Stan was also a Mohawk from Deseronto, Ontario, I grew even more eager to meet him.

Stan was three years older than I. He was a big, imposing man over two hundred pounds and as solid as a mountain. But his shyness and boyish face made him seem like a gentle giant. This time it wasn't only the dark skin and eyes that attracted me. It was also his deep, soft-spoken voice, so low he practically mumbled, and the way his fingers moved across the neck of his Gibson guitar. He carried his guitar with him everywhere he went. Music was becoming another of my addictions, and I was easy prey to the soothing, resonant pluck of a guitar.

Stan and I didn't talk much that first night. He spent most of his time singing country songs while we all enjoyed a few glasses of ale. I'd decided to lay off the heavy stuff and stick to beer for a while.

I knew the words to most of the songs Stan sang: old country ballads by Hank Williams and Marty Robbins, love songs by Jim Reeves and Buck Owens. When Stan started to sing "Crystal Chandelier" by Charlie Pride, I joined in and realized immediately that our voices blended seamlessly. There was a natural harmony between us. I was embarrassed and deeply touched at the same time.

"You have a nice voice," he told me with a timid smile that showed off his full lips.

I smiled back, feeling a growing fondness toward him. "So do you."

He stayed overnight at Doug and Linda's. I slept in my room and he stretched out on the couch.

Over the next couple of weeks I saw Stan frequently. When he revealed truths about his lonely childhood, how he'd been cared for by grandparents until he started school because of his mother's drinking, I felt a bond of suffering between us. As he talked about his father who had died when he was still a boy, I saw a profound sadness in his eyes.

"No one has ever really loved me," he professed, not looking at me. We were sitting in Linda's living room. It was 1967 and we were watching *Bonanza*. Stan believed Lorne Greene was a Mohawk from Ontario and therefore felt a special kinship with the actor. "Thank you for being so kind," he told me.

In the light of this meekness I vowed to try to help alleviate some of his pain. For now my own troubled past was forgotten. I would mend someone else's pain.

Just seventeen, I was hoping to have my own home and break free from the authority of my parents. Stan had never been a regular churchgoer, but said he'd be willing to attend my church. *That should please my parents*, I thought. So I followed Stan home for Christmas to Ontario to meet "the family" barely two months after we started dating.

The eighteen-hour train trip was accompanied by a forty-ouncer of Silent Sam vodka. I'd decided that this particular occasion called for something stronger than beer. We found a comfortable spot on the train on a bench across from a couple of guys with guitars. Between sips from my bottle, which I shared with Stan and the guitarists, I joined the trio to sing every country song we could think of. The other passengers appeared to enjoy the free entertainment. A few even sang along.

The vodka and musical camaraderie made me forget any misgivings I had about meeting Stan's relatives. By the time we reached Belleville, I was pleasantly intoxicated and ready for a new adventure. Even Stan was well lubed and much more talkative than usual. When we started out on our journey, he'd been unusually quiet. I suspected he had mixed feelings about his mother. He'd told me she'd never been easy to please.

Stan's cousin, Melvin, was waiting for us at the station. He was a small, wiry man in his mid-thirties who didn't have much to say, but he did have a welcoming smile that put me at ease.

Afraid of not impressing Stan's mother, I wore a dress, a ridiculous silver sequined full-skirted thing that should have been reserved for New Year's Eve. I had an eye for the gaudy, craving all the attention I could get. By the time I stumbled off the train in Belleville, the dress looked as if it had spent weeks hiding in the bottom of my clothes hamper. Shrugging, I downed the final drink of vodka from my cup. That last gulp of Silent Sam took the wrinkles out of any imperfections I might have felt about my appearance. We headed for Melvin's car, the click of my red high heels resounding through the parking lot.

When we arrived on the doorstep of Stan's mother's house, I was teetering slightly. A white woman came out to meet us. She smiled at Stan but made no move to embrace him. Her eyes shifted to me and I could sense the instant hatred. A snarl actually cut through her features. No one else came out to meet us, so I assumed this was Stan's mother, Loretta, though I couldn't remember him telling me his mother was white. We entered the small green bungalow, located in the town adjoining the Tyendinaga Reserve. It was packed with ornaments. I'd never seen so many ceramic figurines. There were animals, birds, men and women, and salt and pepper shakers on every shelf and table. While there seemed to be no particular theme to the collection, I noticed they were mostly white. Loretta's husband had died years ago and she was alone and bitter. We were two women vying for Stan's affection. Being white herself, maybe she knew exactly what it was that attracted me to Stan and despised me for it.

The day after we arrived other family members came to call. They were polite and attentive. The trip became an endless round of visits and introductions. Everyone who met me stared with interest, but few spoke except to each other in Mohawk. They would point, openly sizing up my large, firm breasts and wide hips with obvious approval. On a few occasions I had to stop myself from offering my teeth and gums for inspection.

Stan's paternal grandparents came for a visit. They lived only a few streets away from his mother's home. They, too, had moved off the reserve many years earlier. They were sweet and kind and went out of their way to make me feel comfortable. They were from old

Mohawk stock; no white blood had dared trickle through their veins until their son married a woman whose ancestors hailed from Scotland. Stan had been the only cross-breed from that union, and I am sure they hoped he'd get back on track and marry one of his own kind before the blood got too diluted and they all faded away.

Stan was plenty dark. You couldn't tell he had white blood in him. When I first met him, I thought he was Mexican or Spanish. His grandparents appeared more like the Indians I'd seen in history books.

"This is my little white squaw," Stan said when he introduced me to his grandparents with a wide grin. They laughed when Stan started calling me Little White Squaw occasionally, and I laughed, too, thinking it was an honour that would prompt my acceptance into the community. One of Stan's cousins had accompanied Stan's grandparents. He called me *yakonkwe*, with the *k* pronounced like a *g*. I liked the way it sounded and decided it must be something special until I learned it was simply the Mohawk word for *woman*. Little White Squaw sounded much more romantic, I decided. I was proud of my new Native title. I never dreamed it would condemn me to a limbo between the aboriginal and white cultures.

I devoured everything I could find about Mohawk history. One story that stuck in my mind was the journey of displaced Mohawks from New York State who had crossed the border to arrive in what later became the Province of Ontario. In 1784 they settled beside the Bay of Quinte. When the Mohawks lost their homeland during the American Revolution, the British Crown promised the small group of survivors a new homeland. A mere twenty families, approximately a hundred people, made it through the slaughter by the Americans.

Captain John Deserontyon, a Mohawk serving in the British army, led the surviving Indians to the spot that was eventually named Deseronto, where they settled and became known as the Mohawks of the Bay of Quinte. Stan, along with more than six thousand others, was a direct descendant of these brave people who were called the Keepers of the Eastern Door. I wasn't sure what that meant, but it certainly enhanced Stan's legendary appeal in my mind.

CHILD BRIDE

When Christmas holidays ended, I stayed in Deseronto with Loretta. She said she'd like some company and knew a place where I could find work. Keen to win her friendship, I agreed. Stan went back to Gagetown to rejoin his Black Watch unit, which was soon renamed 2RCR. By this time we had decided we'd tie the knot that coming March, and Stan believed it would be good for me to get to know his relatives and keep his mother company.

Loretta silently tolerated me for a while, but it didn't take long before I bore the brunt of her bad moods. She drank whiskey or beer daily and never stopped complaining about how hard her life had been.

"No one helped me out when I met Stan's father," she said. "You're lucky you've got a place to sleep. Nothing good ever happened in my life and nothing ever will."

I'd be washing dishes or dusting one of her ornaments while she sat at the kitchen table in her nightgown and curlers, complaining for hours. In the midst of such acrid regret I realized how kind my mother had actually been in comparison.

I would make sporadic attempts to persuade Loretta to like me; I'd offer to style her hair or fix her up with some makeup, but she'd just wave me away. She seemed so unhappy that I actually felt sorry for her. In a drunken stupor, when she accused me of being interested in her boyfriend, Rollie, a skinny truck driver who visited every couple of weeks, I gave up and simply tried to stay out of her way. I'd hardly even spoken to the guy. He gave me the creeps.

I spent hours writing poetry in my journal and jotting down

general happenings.

It didn't take long for me to grasp the great difference of opinion on skin colour between the Native men and women. White was definitely *in* with the males from the reserve (the Mohawks preferred to use the word *territory* instead of reserve). And they liked a woman "with a little meat on her bones," too. I became a popular item, and I was thrilled, basking in all the attention. I never imagined white meat would be considered such a delicacy.

The next month brought a flood of calls—from Stan's friends and cousins, all strangers to me—ranging from polite chitchat to outright sexual offers. One very short, overweight cousin asked me if I missed my nookie. He told me he'd take care of me if I was up for it. I told him he'd never be up enough for it and to go straight to Hell.

One of the younger men, a childhood friend of Stan's, was especially friendly and I enjoyed talking to him on the phone. His name was David and he patiently related to me several Mohawk legends. My favourite was the one about a deity named Peacemaker who summoned eagles to act as lookouts for signs of danger so the Mohawk people would be forewarned and could escape before they were harmed. I often wondered if the eagles had been there in New York State before the American Revolution, but I never asked David. He hated to be interrupted in the middle of weaving his tales.

Of course, the women didn't see me as the treasure I felt I had become. They were quick to indicate they considered me tainted goods. Cold, silent stares in the grocery store and heavily accented curses over the phone were frequent. "Why don't you stay where you belong?" they'd say. "Stop hanging around our men."

Within two months I returned to New Brunswick, devalued again, driven away by racist hostility. I found myself back with my parents and brothers in the little house in Haneytown. Back in a predominantly white community there was no chance of standing out because I was too pale. Back in a place where my boyfriend, Stan, who was still living on the army base, was the oddity.

Stan and I started attending church with my parents. Stan took to the hard preaching and lively music right away, and I was reassured to note that my mom and dad appeared to like him. Even before I said anything to my parents I told a couple I'd been baby-sitting for, Frank and Deana Thomas, that I was considering marriage. The Thomases endeavoured to talk me out of it, but one Sunday night after service, I told my father we were planning to wed and he seemed relieved. He suggested we talk to our minister, so I did.

A few days later Stan and I made an appointment to see Pastor Foster. We sat in his study in the Pentecostal church in Geary and I outlined our plans. Stan sat beside me without uttering a word.

The pastor looked at Stan, then me. "Have you considered what this marriage might be like for any children you have?" he asked, speaking patiently, deliberately. His searching eyes never left my face until I bowed my head. Stan continued sitting in silence, hands on his lap.

"Well, yes," I finally mumbled. "What difference could it make? It's not like we're black and white."

"No, but there are bound to be problems. People can be cruel. And then there's the difference in customs, traditions, things like that."

"But Stan never even lived on the reserve," I said. "He lived beside it."

"A culture is a culture, Eva," the minister said. But I wasn't listening. I didn't care what prefabricated words the pastor tossed at me. My mind was already made up. Even if he was right, what major problems could possibly arise just because two different cultures had decided to unite?

Mom didn't say much about my forthcoming union with Stan, but she did grow more excited as she helped me plan the wedding.

Nobody ever suggested I might be too young, even though I was just seventeen. My parents were probably happy and appeased that I'd finally accepted my predestined role in life. Both my parents firmly believed no one should interfere in a marriage no matter what might be going on. Whatever happened was between the man and woman.

As the novelty of the wedding plans wore off, I began to have real doubts about this particular calling. I did *care* about Stan, but I couldn't picture spending the next ten years with him, and certainly not a lifetime. I began to doubt my motives for this union. I wasn't really sure I wanted to give up dating other guys. When I talked to my mother about the way I felt, she reminded me reassuringly, "All brides-to-be have those feelings." But I was worried my doubts might be more severe than most. I kept quiet about my lingering attraction to other men. I thought about Ray Stewart all the time. That would have doomed me for sure.

On March 31, 1967, I drove in my dad's car to the Geary church where I was to be married. There was a chill in the air that settled in the pit of my stomach. I couldn't get warm, as if a frost had seeped inside and coated my veins.

As my father walked me down the aisle, the small Pentecostal church in Geary, the same one where my parents had first converted to Christianity, was packed with family, other church members, and a few of my friends like Donna and Beryl. Photos of that exercise resembled a funeral procession. Neither of us smiled. Stan was the only one who appeared genuinely happy. My smile was nervous and strained.

The tears in my eyes weren't tears of happiness but of trepidation. I figured it was too late to run. We exchanged vows and rings, and Stan kissed me before accompanying me back down the aisle. The entire ceremony was shrouded in a dreamlike quality. Nothing felt real.

Outside, after the ceremony, wet snow pasted confetti to my

short satin wedding gown. Flecks of confetti were still stuck to the dress when I stuffed it in a garbage bag a few years later and put it out with the trash.

LITTLE BURNT SQUAW

I became more dissatisfied than ever with my white epidermis. So I spent that summer trying to bake, broil, and fry myself in the blazing hot sun. I simply had to have dark skin in order to fit into the place I assumed I belonged. The darker I became, the better.

I spent practically every sunny morning at my favourite spot in the woods, lying on large sheets of tinfoil, dripping baby oil, while praying for rays like a hungry sun worshipper. I was slippery all over, covered in sweat and oil, eyes clamped shut beneath the fiery, oppressive ball of fire in the sky. It was an endurance test. Me against my body. My body against what I really wanted to be. And, yes, hallelujah, I did manage to turn a bit darker. I was delighted, despite the fact that I spent a fortune on jars of Noxzema to heal the peeling skin and blisters.

At one point I became so badly burnt that I was forced to visit the hospital. I waited in the emergency room, tenderly shifting in my seat, trying not to let my scarlet-pink skin stick to the vinyl. When my turn came, the doctor informed me that what I had managed to get for all my trouble was second-degree burns.

The doctor was curious to know what I had been doing to suffer such injury. Had I fallen asleep in the sun? Was I too close to a heat lamp? Reluctantly I explained about the tin foil and baby oil.

"Are you crazy?" the doctor asked, exasperated. "You could actually fry a fish like that."

Later that night I lay in bed with chills, shivering, sick to my stomach with heat stroke, my tender skin stinging, burning a hot electric-pink.

MY FIRSTBORN

When I was eight years old, my dog Pal was hit by a truck. I'd sat heartbroken in the arms of my apple tree, mourning the death of the small black furry spaniel that had been my solitary friend for more than a year. Tearfully I asked God to let me grow up so I could have children to love and who would love me in return. My perfect children would be cherished, adored. They would be given everything they desired. They would be treated gently. I wouldn't force anything down their throats. We would have an understanding between us. I don't think I even asked about a husband—what would I need one of those for?—but I knew I wanted to have at least four children. That way I'd never feel lonely again, and my babies would be treated right, everything would be made better.

As soon as our marriage vows were exchanged, I set my mind and body on becoming a mother. The first year with Stan was the honeymoon. We were happy most of the time, and I loved taking care of the tiny house we rented on Smith Road in Geary three miles away from where my parents lived. My old school friend Donna lived less than a mile away, and Beryl, my longtime childhood friend who I had lost touch with during my courtship with Stan, lived closer still. We got together for coffee from time to time, gossiping and trading news. Life seemed good, even though Stan and I had started drinking a little too much. We drank every weekend and we stopped attending church. Often there would be parties at our home.

One Saturday night Stan got drunk and picked a fight with his army buddy, Ron, from the base. Stan accused him of trying to hit on me when I asked Ron if he wanted a fresh beer from the fridge. I tried to intervene, but Stan was wild. He threw me against the living-room wall. All of the ten or so people present suddenly went quiet.

"Get out of here!" he snarled through clenched teeth. The look in his eyes hit me harder than the shove. I ran outside and hid, crouching behind a lilac bush. As the tears ran down my cheeks, I watched the fray through the window and heard the men's voices trying to calm Stan. I was wondering what I'd done to make my husband angry.

A few minutes later everything settled down and the party began to break up. The next morning Stan cleaned the entire house and made me breakfast in bed. After that the gatherings at our house were confined to Saturday-night card games with close friends.

Within weeks of the wedding I discovered I was pregnant with my first child. I felt nauseated whenever I saw food. I never thought of pregnancy. I suspected I had an ulcer and decided I better see my doctor. He could tell as soon as he examined me. An in-office pregnancy test proved him right. I burst into tears right there in my doctor's office. I was overjoyed. I had my heart set on having a regular, loving family.

Stan was just as excited as I was. When I told him, he cried, too, and wore a proud smile for days. He said he knew he'd be a good father, and I had no reason not to believe him. We both decided to start attending church regularly again. With a new baby coming we agreed we'd need God's help. The drinking and smoking stopped. We sang duets in church, mostly country gospel pieces or songs written by my father, while Stan played guitar. I was sure the future would be golden. The weekends were no longer party events. When we weren't in church, we spent time with my parents or my old friends, Frank and Deana, who had determined it was better to support my decision than to lose me as a friend. Often we just went for long walks on a country road, or Stan would play his guitar and I would sing.

As Stan became more involved in the dogmas of the church, I perceived a shift in his behaviour. He seldom joked anymore. He showed little emotion except at church, and he began questioning my every move. Sometimes he'd stare at me for hours without uttering a single word. There would be a deadness in his eyes, as if any light of recognition had been suddenly extinguished.

Then, without warning, a brightness would wash over him and he'd start talking cheerfully. He had been off somewhere and didn't even seem to know it. These episodes sent shivers up my spine. There was new danger here I hadn't anticipated.

One morning, as I was getting dressed, Stan grabbed my arm roughly. "Where'd you get that bruise?" he demanded, nodding at my bare thigh.

"I bumped into the door under the sink," I said. "I forgot to close it when I cleaned the bathroom yesterday."

He gripped my shoulders and shook me so hard I thought my neck would snap. "Don't ever lie to me!" he spit, his face merely inches from mine.

I could barely speak but managed to say, "I'm not lying, Stan, honest." Then I started to cry.

Just as abruptly as he had seized me, he let go and left the room. Later he acted as if nothing had happened.

I tried hard to be a dutiful wife. After I found out I was pregnant, I was no longer interested in sex. I felt little physical attraction to Stan, but I seldom said no to his advances. Sometimes I was actually quite fond of him. He was a great help around the house and often cooked me wonderful meals like chicken cacciatore or dried corn soup, a Mohawk dish I particularly enjoyed. And he was good company on those long nights as I anticipated the birth of my first child.

While I was pregnant I tried to do all the right things. I quit smoking and drinking and walked for miles, but my morning sickness often lasted all day and nearly the entire nine months of my pregnancy. Creamed mashed potatoes and canned sardines became my main fare. I craved so much fish I was afraid my firstborn might pop out squirming with gills and fins and a gasping fish mouth.

Like most first-time mothers, I was terrified something might go wrong. I became self-consumed, oblivious to anyone else's needs or desires. It was only me and my baby. That was all that mattered. I went to church more frequently and prayed for a healthy baby.

Six days before my eighteenth birthday, on December 8, 1968, I went into labour with my first child while at a Sunday-night service in the same church where Stan and I had been married. My mother insisted we come home with her. I was so excited when she assured me it wouldn't be long before I would be a mother. My dad drove Stan and me to the same hospital where I'd been born. Every two minutes Dad would ask me if I was all right. When my water broke as I was climbing out of the car, I suspected Dad would pass out.

The entire labour lasted five hours. At the time I thought, *Ahah! I guess good hips do pay off, after all. I am a fine squaw. Yes, I am.*

All seven pounds, five ounces of my firstborn was delivered into this world healthy and intact. My baby girl was astonishingly beautiful. *Perfect*, I told myself as I tickled her dimpled cheeks and rubbed the thick black hair on her little round head. She was so tiny and soft, so vulnerable. I could never have loved another human being as much as I did the moment the nurse placed her in my arms.

I named the baby Heather JoAnne as a special favour to my mother-in-law who had always longed to have a daughter. I felt sorry for her and hoped this gesture would make her treat me better. She told me she'd had the name picked out if Stan had been a girl, and since I had a cousin I liked with the same name, I agreed. But, secretly, I longed to give her some exotic name, a Mohawk one like Otsitsya, which meant *flower*. But, after all, Heather was a sort of flower, too, so I reasoned the name was just as fitting.

For days, lying in bed or sitting in the kitchen, I stared at Heather, astonished by how tiny and flawless she was, this wonderful being who hadn't existed in the world a short while ago. I felt over-whelmed in her presence. It was a spiritual tugging that must have been pure love. She was mine to care for, and my heart seemed newly complete and blessed.

TAUGHT A LESSON

Bright and early one morning when Heather was about three months old, while I was preparing breakfast, Stan approached me with unexpected news. "God wants you to stop listening to music on the radio. It's my job to make sure you stop listening."

A few weeks later I was given further instructions. I was to refrain from wearing shoes with high heels. They were created to tempt men to lust. They were the tools of wanton women. While I agreed that women and men should dress modestly, I couldn't see all the commotion about open-toed shoes or dresses that exposed arms. I never questioned Stan because I wasn't prepared to provoke the wrath I knew was building inside him.

These proclamations soon multiplied and intensified. One day Stan slapped my face when I told him the church should pay as much attention to gossip among the congregation as it did to women's clothing. I soon realized, with dread, that I was caught in a worsening cycle of oppression. Stan had tightened his hold over me. He was controlling my every move, questioning my every action, carefully analyzing each word I spoke for a treacherous double meaning.

For a while Heather became the centre of his existence. He seemed happy when he was around her, although he remained suspicious of my actions. The only time he appeared at peace was when he sat outside on our picnic table and played his guitar. Now he played only Christian songs; country and western was strictly forbidden by the church.

Our second child was born on a snowy Christmas morning in 1969. It had been a long, painful labour that lasted eighteen hours, but Jody Lee was as beautiful and perfect as his one-year-old sister. He looked like a miniature of his father. There was no mistaking his heritage. Same black hair, same full lips, same Mohawk skin tone.

Stan seemed more interested in the baby boy when we arrived home than he had in Heather. It was as if he finally had an ally in the home already stacked with two females. He would sing to his son and hold him for hours. He even lightened up after the birth, as though a huge burden had been lifted. I knew he was as proud to have a son as I was, and maybe that pride made him feel better about himself, more capable to have fathered a son. He was eager to help out at home and rarely questioned my activities. It was as if the mistrustful stranger who had intruded upon our lives had disappeared completely. The shy, gentle Stan I'd first been attracted to was back.

My husband started acting strange once more just a month after Jody's birth. That was the second time he hit me. I was tired and lost my patience when he didn't respond to my request to help carry laundry in from the clothesline. When he ignored me, I screamed at him. He rose out of his chair and stormed toward me, raising his hand and slapping my mouth so hard my lip cracked and began to bleed. From then on things grew steadily worse. The slightest show of insolence on my part always brought a slap or shake.

It was 1970 and Stan was away a great deal on manoeuvres with the army. It was the year the FLQ crisis took place in Quebec, granting me a reprieve when Stan was assigned there as a peacekeeper.

That was when Kevin came into my life. I noticed him one day at a service station where we stopped for gas. I hadn't seen him since I was thirteen years old, but I'd always considered him handsome.

Kevin had grown up only five houses away from mine in Haneytown. When he was a boy, he was well built and black-haired with rugged appeal. He was five years older than I was and had a reputation for trouble and pulling pranks on the other kids. He reminded me of Marlon Brando. After finishing school, he'd spent time in prison for car theft and was certainly the same bad-boy type I'd constantly hoped to save. Only this time he was responsible for saving me.

I ran into him again a few days later at the shopping centre.

"You're sure looking good," he said when he saw me in front of the grocery store. "Still got that beautiful long hair." He reached out and touched my hair.

I was tongue-tied, so I just smiled and asked him where he was living. He told me he was staying at his mother's house in Geary and wondered if he could call me sometime.

"I'm married," I said.

"Then you call me," he replied. A few days later I did. I'd been seriously considering suicide as the only way out of my abusive marriage. I'd be in the kitchen, doing the dishes or cleaning up, my mind in a grey haze as I wondered about the ways to end my life. The same monotonous chores every day, the same swell of anger and subjugation. Plain deadness in my heart. No heart at all.

When Kevin came along, I knew he could tell I was an easy target for his advances. He had a reputation for courting discontented wives, but I didn't care. The few stolen hours when I could manage a baby-sitter were my lifesavers. I savoured every minute spent with him driving over back roads, laughing at his outlandish stories, parking under the stars, or being passionate in the grass. It made me forget the prison my home life had become.

I carried the guilt of the affair with me, but I knew without Kevin I probably wouldn't have survived. I also knew Kevin would have killed Stan if I'd told him about the abuse. As it was, Kevin was soon out of my life. He had another girlfriend who wasn't married, so they drifted out west when the police started harassing him for a string of unsolved break-and-enters in the area. But an important part of him remained with me. I had become pregnant again.

Shortly thereafter, we moved into a row house in Oromocto provided by the base. We had grown out of the small two-bedroom house in Geary. The new dwelling had three bedrooms, a full basement, and a spacious backyard. There were children next door for Heather and Jody to play with, and one of my neighbours invited me over for coffee the same day we moved in. I was a nervous wreck by this time because I wasn't sure who Stan would allow me to talk to.

About a month before my due date in March 1971 I felt a desperate need to get out of the house. I'd been cooped up for days with two active toddlers and was bloated and uncomfortable from the pregnancy. I asked Stan to baby-sit so I could walk to the mall, and he readily agreed.

Before leaving the house I made certain two-year-old Heather and Jody, who was just over a year, were dressed and fed. I didn't want them making too many demands on their father. They looked so much alike, with their big brown eyes and thick black curls. There was no mistaking their kinship. As much as I adored them, I was relieved to take a much-needed break from their constant needs and steady demands for attention.

"I won't be long," I promised, pulling on my coat.

I experienced such relief at being able to round the aisles at the grocery store without Jody tearing open and eating half the order while Heather indiscriminately threw in bags of cookies and potato chips she wanted to gobble down for breakfast. The supermarket was like a pristine dreamworld. There was freedom amid the brightly coloured boxes and packages; everything was neat and immaculate, the refreshing air was so clean, and not a single person clung to me. Despite my hulking, quite-pregnant carriage, I felt light, unburdened, invigorated by the time I could spend exclusively with myself. Browsing through the magazine section in the market was as blissful as a vacation in Florida.

Done with my soul-lifting sojourn, I headed off on the gloriously silent walk home. The weather was springlike, even though I knew we'd be hit by a few more winter storms yet.

Stepping into the house and crossing the back-door threshold with my bag of groceries, I felt a peculiar tension in the air. I was about to call out "Hello," but the word caught in my throat. Both of the children were screaming upstairs and my husband was sitting in the kitchen reading the Bible as if he didn't hear a sound. I dropped the groceries and ran through the kitchen into the living room. Clutching the bannister, I bolted up the stairs as fast as my bulky body could carry me. When I threw open the door to the children's bedroom, Heather and Jody were holding each other in manic fright, tears streaming down their faces.

"Mommie, it hurts," Jody sobbed. He cried openly as he held out his chubby little fingers. "Hurts, Mommie. Hurts."

Heather had a facecloth wrapped around her hands.

"Oh, my God!" I gasped as soon as I saw their fingers. Blisters covered Heather's palms; Jody's were almost as bad. Fear weakened every part of my body, my head rushing with torrents of confused, broken thought. I stood stunned in a tingling, unreal world, unable to make sense of this. Did Stan know the children were hurt? Was there fire somewhere? My eyes darted around for matches as I sniffed the air and raced into the bathroom for ointment.

"What happened, baby?" I asked upon returning. My hands were trembling as I uncapped the tube of cream. I was trying to appear calm, but inside I was screaming and shivering at once. It took every bit of willpower I could summon to force a reassuring smile as I applied thick ointment to my babies' burns. Both children were whimpering, their chests throbbing with the remnants of crying fits, so I knew I had to remain calm. To press for an answer would only bring on another outburst.

I moved them both into Heather's bed and covered them with my special blanket—a pink-and-white quilt with roses stitched in the corners that had been made by my fortuneteller grandmother, Grammie Brewer, decades ago.

Kneeling by the side of their bed, I kissed the tears away from their hot, smooth cheeks. I pressed my lips together, fighting back tears of my own, then began singing:

"Jesus loves the little children.
All the children of the world.
Red and yellow, black and white.
They are precious in his sight.
Jesus loves the little children of the world.
Jesus loves the little children..."

After three rounds of song, a soothing sleep stilled their sobs. Not once had their father checked to see what was transpiring.

As soon as I was certain the children were settled, I went back down the stairs, fury mounting with each step, blood pounding in my ears. Stan had moved from the kitchen and was now sitting on the couch. Unlike most Natives on the reservation, he wasn't a staunch Catholic. He had converted to a charismatic evangelical movement. His Bible lay open on his lap and he watched me without the slightest trace of concern.

I snatched the Bible from his hands, threatening to hammer him with it. "What in hell happened?" I demanded through clenched teeth.

"There's no need to swear."

"I'll swear if I want to," I challenged, trying to keep my voice down so as not to trouble the children. "What did you do to the kids?"

"I taught them a lesson." His voice never rose one octave. He remained seated and stared through me, eerily peaceful.

"What kind of a lesson?"

"They were playing with the lamps. Turning the light off and on. I warned them." He nodded once.

"How'd they get burned?"

Stan said nothing.

I stepped closer, raising the Bible higher. "Did you see their hands?"

"I told them they'd get hurt if they kept doing that. Only one way to teach a child." His eyes shifted to the Bible I was holding. "The Bible says that. Spare the rod, spoil the child."

"What do you mean? What did you do?"

"I wet their hands and held them on the bulb so they'd see what I meant."

"Oh, God!" I heard something thump against the hardwood floor. Looking down, I saw I had dropped the Bible, the golden cross against black. My stomach rose in my throat. Gagging, I held it in, turned, and ran for the stairway, again clutching the bannister, racing for the upstairs bathroom. Tossing up the lid on the toilet, I fell to my knees and vomited.

When I managed to pick myself up, my limbs were powerless, my eyes damp. Feebly I wiped my mouth. A sob trembled in my throat as I glanced in the mirror, not wanting to see myself, hair in disarray, eyes bloodshot, face splotched red, loathing my reflection for having allowed harm to come to my children.

I took my time going downstairs, one hand on my belly, the other on the bannister. When I reached the living room, I stood in silence, pausing at the sight of Stan back at the kitchen table, patiently turning the thin, crisp pages of his Bible, devoutly reading.

The following Tuesday morning, after Stan left for work and the children—done with their breakfast—were playing in the living room, Beryl showed up for a visit. She hadn't heard from me in months, not since I'd moved back to Oromocto. I was gradually shutting down, withdrawing farther into myself in a futile attempt to contain the abuse.

Beryl was worried for me. When she gave me a big, warm hug, I felt emotion surge from deep inside. I broke down and cried, confessing about Stan's insane behaviour, about the incident with the children, about my constant and immediate fear.

"You should leave now," she insisted, holding me at arm's length and looking directly down into my eyes. "Right now. Bring the children to my place. You need time to think."

I didn't argue. I just gathered up some clothes and let Beryl help me throw them into a bag. Anxiously loading the children into Beryl's Volkswagen, I told them we were going for a visit. I glanced around the street, hoping Stan wouldn't show up all of a sudden. With everyone safely in the car, we headed for the trailer on Waterville Road in Geary where Beryl and her husband lived with their two small children.

It was another warm day, unusually mild for late February. I turned a bit giddy when I realized the snow was actually melting. I felt that way inside: the frost was dissipating, a change forthcoming from the release, the promise of spring.

We were barely settled at Beryl's when, later that night, the telephone rang. It was Stan. I'd left him a note in spite of Beryl's insistence that I leave without letting him know where to find us. He pleaded for my return, mustering all the wounded emotion he could manage. I resisted, telling him I wouldn't come home, that he couldn't treat the children the way he had.

His voice was quiet, despondent. "If you don't come home, I'll kill myself."

My heart sank at the possibility. After all of the pain, after everything he had done to me and the children, I still felt compassion for this damaged man who couldn't help himself.

"I *will* kill myself," he softly insisted "Without you I've got nothing to live for."

I hung up and sat still. The image of Stan killing himself wouldn't leave me. The liberating wind had been taken out of my sails. I did not want to be responsible for his death. I didn't want more guilt.

Two days later, hounded by images of Stan's imminent suicide, I gathered the children and their clothes and called my husband to come and collect us. Maybe things would be different. Maybe Stan was sincere in his regret. Maybe he'd been taught a lesson and knew better now.

Back in our home, I was apologetic for leaving. I was convinced Stan would change, having seen I was capable of abandoning him, of taking the children away with me. It seemed as if everything might take a turn for the better. I had made my point and Stan had called, whimpering, tail between his legs, begging for my return. Over the next few days Stan remained calm, seemingly reasonable, but sometimes I would catch him glancing at me in a way that suggested I was far from forgiven.

MORE BABIES

Reunited with Stan, old wounds were eventually clawed at, and home life quickly deteriorated. Hostility hovered over our relationship. It became a steady battle of words and fists. I wanted him out of the house. I wanted him gone. When Stan was called out of town for a military exercise, I thanked God for the reprieve.

My third child, another daughter, was born on March 19, 1971, and I was horribly sick. The pregnancy had been difficult. I was toxic, my nerves were shot, and I was physically exhausted from caring for two small children. Regardless, I wanted to name the newborn myself, for her to be the only one of my babies for whom I chose the name. My mother suggested Irene, but I wanted a name that reflected our Slavic heritage. We compromised on Sonya Irene.

Our home was like a war zone. Without the escape into Kevin's arms or into a bottle, I had to face the fact that I couldn't stand the man I had married. Instead of holding my tongue during his rages I would make things worse by refusing to submit. On top of that, I slipped into a crippling postpartum depression. I would watch my new fair-haired baby, this new life that had come into a world that was killing me, and hate her. I couldn't handle three children. Simply coping with day-to-day chores became an oppressive hardship. I desired nothing except to die. I grappled with an indescribable weight that drained my will. When I visited my doctor, he prescribed antidepressants. I was in such a state that I would sometimes nod off in the middle of feeding Sonya. I'd wash my face in cold water and try to sit up on the sofa so I wouldn't fall asleep, but nothing worked. I just wanted to stay in bed forever. Stan brought a young woman named Judy in from our church to help out with the care of the children and the housework.

Along with the antidepressants, I began taking Valium. For months I lived in a shadow world that prevented me from knowing or properly bonding with my new daughter. I knew Sonya would suffer because of this, yet I couldn't pull myself free from the void of drugs and depression. I was just too sick to give Sonya the attention a newborn required. More and more I felt dead inside, my spirit hardening to black lead, my mind shrouded in impenetrable darkness. Nothing mattered to me. I only wished to sleep, to lie down, shut my eyes. Simply standing, moving one foot in front of the other, became a defeating thought that knocked me farther back into myself. Grammie Brewer's predictions of almost seven years earlier came back to taunt me. How had she managed to foresee the situation I now found myself in? *I see a man with very dark hair and dark skin in your future.... Be careful, Eva. He is not a good man for you.*

Snuffing out my existence became a compulsive preoccupation. I was nothing more than a burden that would spread sickness to my children. I'd try to plan how I could safely transport my children to Beryl's house before I killed myself. I knew Beryl would make certain the children were okay. She'd let them know I loved them. After dropping the children off, I'd return home and write a note to Stan. "It's your fault," the note would read. Then I'd swallow an entire bottle of Valium, lie down on my bed, and wait for the sleep that would relieve me of the selfless ache that was my life.

Sometimes I'd consider using poison, but I'd heard that could be painful. My wrists ached terribly when I thought of doing away with myself. I was on the brink of a complete and absolute breakdown. Only my fear of going to Hell, and the obscure notion that my babies might need me, kept me from plummeting completely over the edge.

If it hadn't been for another pregnancy, I might have remained in that disassociated netherworld forever or, worse, passed beyond. When I discovered I was pregnant for the fourth time, I feared I'd never be able to carry another baby full-term. My bladder was in need of repair from the strain of multiple childbirths in such a short period. Sometimes I'd hemorrhage between my normal periods, and there was often a severe pain in my right side that indicated I might have a cyst on my ovary. I was only twenty years old and already had three children under the age of three and a home that felt like a concentration camp. I was totally exhausted, both physically and mentally. My spirit was dying and the pills I was taking were aiding in my self-destruction.

In addition to the problems I was experiencing with bleeding and pain, my doctor found a small growth on my uterus. The gynecologist suggested I consider abortion; however that was out of the question. I asked my doctor to wean me off the antidepressants and stopped taking Valium as the baby grew. When I felt the new life stirring inside me, a glimmer of my old optimism returned.

I called my mother to tell her the news. "Well, it doesn't look like I have an ulcer, Mom."

"That's a relief," she said. "Did the doctor say what it could be?"

"As a matter of fact, he told me I'm pregnant."

"You're expecting again?" she asked, a mixture of surprise and concern in her voice.

"Yes, I just found out."

"Well, I was going to wait a while to tell you, dear, but so am I."

"You're what, Mom?"

"I'm expecting, too. In June."

Mom was nearing menopause so this wasn't a planned pregnancy, but even at forty-two, she was excited by the prospect of new life. We were both due to deliver in June 1972. Mom had learned through a friend that her firstborn daughter, who none of us had ever met, was living in Moncton and was also due to have a baby the same month. *It must be a sign*, I assured myself. *A sign that life will get better*.

Mom delivered her fifth son on June 5, 1972. They named him Steven. My baby, Jennifer Ruth, arrived ten days later in the same hospital in Oromocto. She resembled Stan, but her hair was curly and a rich brown with auburn highlights, like mine. I burst into tears when I held her for the first time. Not only was she my baby, but she was a symbol of new hope. I just *knew* she was a special angel sent from God to help me. In spite of the doctor's warnings, she had arrived safe and sound. And I was feeling happier than I had in months. If I hadn't promised Aunt Lena I'd call her Jennifer, I would have named her Hope. Three days after Jennifer was born, Mom's first child, the sister I'd never met, had a baby girl named Anya.

While I was still in hospital the doctor performed a tubal ligation because I was hemorrhaging off and on. No more babies for me.

When I left the hospital, I required extra help because of the surgery. Stan was attentive and reassuringly calm. Mary Westall, the mother of the girl, Judy, who had helped out before, had taken care of my children while I was in the hospital. When I came home, Judy took charge of the domestic duties again for a couple of weeks. There was no postpartum depression this time and no mind-numbing pills to interfere with offering my children the love I felt for them in my heart. I spent most of my time with my babies—all of them—and tried to give Sonya just a little bit more time than the rest to make up for our rough beginning. She was the most inquisitive about the new baby. One day, thinking Jennifer was a doll, Sonya tried to drag her out of her carriage. Jody and Heather spent most of their time playing together. Sonya was the odd one out.

After Judy left us, I found it hard to cope with housework and four children, but Stan assisted a great deal. And there were no angry outbursts for a while. I wondered if we might make it as a family, after all.

Six months following Jennifer's birth I hemorrhaged so badly I was rushed to the hospital. An emergency hysterectomy was the only solution to my life-threatening condition. I was only twenty-one. No more babies for sure. I stayed in bed and cried for days.

SOOTHING THE SAVAGE BEAST

Shortly after Jennifer's birth, Stan decided to leave the armed forces and take a civilian job. He went to work for a company that manu-factured eyeglass frames. We moved out of our military house and into the top-floor apartment of a home in Oromocto West. It had a huge kitchen, a small living room, and three modest bedrooms.

Fortunately some of the congregation at the church were willing to lend a hand with the care of the children or I'd never have been able to manage. As it stood, Sonya spent a great deal of time with Mary Westall, the jolly mother of six children, including Judy. She adored babies. Mary attended our church and was always supportive.

Stan was a little easier to get along with after he changed jobs. On Sundays we would often go for drives to Crabbe Mountain just to take in the magnificent scenery or down to Burton to visit Frank and Deana. We ate at fast-food restaurants often. The playrooms gave us a chance to have coffee in peace. Stan sometimes took the children to Wilmot Park in Fredericton to splash around in the wading pool. During those times, there was absolutely no sign of the menace I'd been living with for almost five years.

We were eating supper one evening and Stan was watching Heather and Jody, making certain they ate every scrap off their plates. He would force them to eat everything, even if it made them sick. He wasn't as hard on Sonya or Jennifer because they were still considered babies, but for some reason Stan expected Heather and Jody to act older than they actually were. I was watching him, feeling sick in my heart, tired of the heated, confrontational mood at each mealtime.

"Stan," I finally blurted. "Why don't you just let them eat?"

He stared at me, desperate affliction in his deep brown eyes. "Be quiet," he snarled.

I ate another forkful of casserole, checking the children.

"I'm full, Mommy," Jody said. Recently turned three, he was a quiet little boy who seldom uttered a word.

"You eat," Stan barked, stabbing a finger at Jody's plate. "All of that. Eat."

"That's okay, Jody," I said, rising to my feet. "If you're full."

Bolting up, Stan turned on me. The arm he had been pointing with swept down to whack me soundly across the face. I staggered back but didn't fall. Jody went berserk. Uncharacteristically he leaped from his chair and started screaming at his father. He ran over and pounded Stan's leg with his little fists.

"Leave Mommy alone!" he yelled. "Leave Mommy alone. I'll kill you."

Stan was so surprised, so astounded by this show of retribution, that it took him several moments to react. When the outrage finally sank in, he grabbed Jody by one arm and flung him across the room. Our son crashed against the bottom cupboards and collapsed onto the floor.

I ran to Jody and swooped him up. He was weeping chest-deep sobs. I glanced back at Heather's shocked face. She was terrified, unable to move a muscle. With tears in my eyes I glared at Stan, but I couldn't say a word. All of us remained still, as if frozen in a family portrait.

Every waking minute became focused on planning a way to escape for good. I was plagued by the questions facing a woman forced to flee a dangerous household: *Where will I go? What about the kids? What will we do for money?*

I suspected I was a prisoner who would never be free of the torment. I was convinced one of us would have to die and I didn't want it to be one of my children. I saw no way out except for pills. I hated asking my doctor for tranquillizers, but if I didn't I knew I'd crack. I would take smaller doses this time, I bargained with myself. Valium became a soother, a protector, a means to detach and smother the fear and rage.

When I spoke to my doctor about the stress I was under, I was too ashamed to tell him the truth about the abuse. What sort of woman was I to stand for such denigration? Regardless, I'm pretty certain he knew. Bruises and split lips were common decorations. An occasional purple-ringed eye could be hidden behind makeup and sunglasses. These were merely superficial signs of the near-fatal wounds inflicted upon my spirit. A prescription for Valium was easy to obtain. Doctors handed out the drug like candy. I took the pills only at bedtime. They helped to a slight degree, but it was becoming more apparent the children and I would be in greater danger if I allowed the pills to further deaden my senses. Stan's moods were totally unpredictable.

Some nights I'd wake in a groggy haze while the bulk of a man rolled off me, his gratified moan like a growl reverberating deep in my head. Unconscious, I was of great use to Stan. Nothing woke me when I swallowed those tiny white pills. But my very real paranoia soon overtook my waking hours. Questions constantly plagued me: *What if he started on the kids? What if he decided he should kill me to deliver me from evil?* I knew I had to give up the pills if we were ever going to escape, but how could I manage, how could I extract myself from the hopeless darkness that spiralled around me?

Then a thought occurred to me: *Why don't I put Valium in Stan's evening coffee?*

I tried it that night, nervously crushing the pill with the back of a spoon while Stan waited for his cup to be delivered. Quietly sweeping the powder in, I listened for his possible approach, each tiny sound magnified. Rattling the spoon, I stirred the coffee.

My heart pounded wildly as I faithfully delivered the coffee to my husband. Handing him the cup, I was relieved to see he paid no attention to my trembling state, familiar with how I was persistently in a lousy frame of mind. Perhaps he was even gloating over my unsteadiness, revelling in the power he had over me. He took a sip and nodded his approval. I smiled like a good wife and walked away.

For months I continued spiking his coffee. It ensured I'd have a proper night's sleep and never need to take another nerve pill to put me under.

While Stan slept his drug-induced sleep, I sat in the living room, clearheaded, planning our forthcoming departure.

DEATH ON THE BRIDGE

My next attempt to break away from Stan nearly ended in my death. I had pledged to get out of that house, but no one wanted to take in five penniless visitors being chased by a crazed 250-pound Mohawk Black Watch soldier. No one could possibly be that charitable.

Fortunately my suspicions were disproved when Mary Westall, who was almost as big and could be nearly as mean as Stan, offered to let us stay with her and her six children. She cornered me after Sunday School one morning when I tried to sneak out unnoticed.

"Come live with us," she insisted, her eyes trying not to focus on the bruise around my eye. "Until you get on your feet. Sonya's already used to us." She even agreed to baby-sit while I sought employment.

"We're not going to have to live with Daddy anymore," I told the children one afternoon. Heather clapped her hands and started to sing: "Jesus loves the little children, All the children of the world…" My mind drifted back to that spring day when I returned home from a walk, only to find Heather's and Jody's hands burned by Stan. I'd comforted them with the same song. The rest of the kids joined in. Even baby Jennifer babbled along, not having a clue what we were so pleased about.

A week after I moved in with Mary I managed to secure a job working at a local motel restaurant as a waitress. I was feeling at ease, genuinely content for the first time in years. A monstrous burden had lifted from my heart and I was sure life would be better now. The noise of ten children in a three-bedroom apartment never even bothered me. It was a luxury to be free of constant, belittling intimidation. Compared to the quiet punches and whispered threats, the noise from the children sounded like a heavenly choir.

For the first time in years I found myself looking toward the future, and I'd even catch myself smiling with a faint hint of promise. I had a life again. A life that was mine. Surprisingly Stan hadn't chased after me and I was encouraged by his sensible reaction.

Perhaps he had accepted that things would never be right between us. I didn't miss him at all. I was even starting to flirt a little with the cook at the restaurant where I worked. The attention he paid me was heartening.

On a Saturday, two weeks after I began my new job, I was at the motel preparing to work a supper banquet when Stan stormed into the dining room wearing an old pair of green army fatigues, his imposing body rigid with anticipation. I was standing on the opposite side of the room setting one of the tables. When I saw Stan, the silverware I was holding dropped to the floor with a riotous clang. The coldness in his eyes sent a cascading shiver throughout me.

Stan didn't say a word to anyone. He walked over to me, grabbed my waist-length hair, and turned toward the door, pulling me along. Stumbling, in pain, I screamed at my co-workers, "Call the police!" I struggled against Stan, attempting to break free, stinging tears in my eyes. Desperately I tried to twist out of his grip, yanking my own hair in the process. "He's gonna kill me!"

Two other waitresses and the manager were standing in the banquet hall, watching the scene with detached disbelief. No one moved as Stan hauled me out the door and shoved me into the passenger's side of his small Toyota. My heart was beating so hard I thought people in the motel could hear it above my screams. Stan was still clutching my hair. Terrified by the certainty that I was going to die, I prayed for help, but no one, not one single person, bothered coming to my rescue.

Stan never opened his mouth. He slammed my door shut and walked unhurried around to the driver's side, confident I wouldn't run from him, secure in his hold over me. Once settled in his seat, he turned to me and smiled. "Why'd you think you could leave me like that?" he asked, calmly starting the car.

"I...I...didn't mean to."

"Well, you won't be leaving me anymore. We'll always be together." He shifted gears and raced out of the parking lot, heading for the ramp that connected to the Princess Margaret Bridge.

"Where we going?" I asked, unable to control my wavering voice.

"Over the bridge," he said, stopping for a tractor trailer that was gearing down. I glanced at the door handle, thought of yanking it and bolting away.

"What?"

"Over the bridge," he repeated. "Together, into the water."

"Oh, God, no, Stan. I'll do anything. I love you. I need you."

Slowly he pulled out and looked over at me. I was babbling anything that came into my head, desperate to live, thinking of my sweet children back at Mary's apartment. Their faces, their laughter and gentle mannerisms, filled my head. I believed I would never see them again, and tears rimmed my eyes as the car sped up.

"Please forgive me," I begged. "I'll never go anywhere. Not without you. Please, Stan, just give me another chance."

We were zooming across the bridge, Stan not giving me a glance. I was expecting his arms to thrust the steering wheel sharply one way at any second. I anticipated the erratic swerve of the car, the crash of metal before the gut-lifting plunge into the Saint John River far below. Trapped in a car, sealed in a tomb and sinking under water. Numb and sinking. Drowning.

"Staaannnn, no, please!"

His eyes were fixed on the windshield, his foot jammed against the accelerator. I watched his strong arms, his hands tight on the wheel, the veins rising. My eyes flitted ahead to a view through the windshield. The end of the bridge wasn't far away. We were almost across. If I could just make it. Hold on. Keep him from doing it.

"We can be together again," My eyes flicked from Stan to the road, the end of the bridge only sixty feet in the near distance.

"You get the children," he said.

"Yes," I agreed. "Yes, I'll get them, Stan. Let's go there now. I'll get them."

The car raced out from under the green steel trusses. We had made it across and I felt so relieved, thankful to be alive yet, in a matter of moments, vilely defeated.

"You just get the children," he said.

"Yes, Stan, yes."

An hour later, against Mary's harsh protests, I packed all the children into the back seat.

"Mind your own business," Stan snapped at her from inside the car. "It's a sin to come between a husband and a wife. God don't like that."

"Well, He don't like men who beat their wives and molest children, either," she retorted as he slammed the car door shut. Mary stayed right where she was, with her kids, all of them staring from the steps of the apartment building as we drove away. There was nothing they could do.

When I looked at the frightened faces of my four babies, I couldn't meet their eyes. In shame I turned away from them, fixing my gaze ahead through the windshield, studying the road and bitterly wishing I'd let Stan kill us both. At least with our deaths the children would be free of us.

ONE LAST ATTEMPT ON NEVERS ROAD

When we arrived at our old apartment in Oromocto West, boxes were stacked inside the door and furniture was sitting outside in the corridor. Entering the kitchen with Jennifer in my arms and the other three toddlers trailing silently behind, I found more boxes. Some of them were half full of dishes or linens. It was as if our lives had been disassembled.

"What's going on?" I asked.

"We're moving," Stan replied solemnly. "We're buying a mobile home. I want us to have our own place." He watched me with sorry eyes. "We're going to be happy."

My heart plunged and softened at once. I knew Stan meant

what he said. He really did want us to be happy.

"I'm so sorry," he said, tears streaming down his face. The children started to cry, too, as their father sobbed uncontrollably. I reached out automatically to comfort all of them.

That night we slept on mattresses on the floor. The beds had already been taken apart. When we woke in the morning, we continued packing. Boxing up our belongings and throwing out the garbage gave me great satisfaction. Within a week we were settling in our new mobile home in Avalon Trailer Park on Nevers Road. The park was in Lincoln, not far from the Trans-Canada Highway, halfway between Oromocto and Fredericton.

We were happier than we'd been in years. It was the first time we'd owned our own place, and there was ample room for everyone. Stan seemed proud that he could finally provide an adequate home for us and spent all his spare time fixing it up.

The children were looking forward to Christmas that year. Stan was tranquil, seldom even raising his voice. He was trying hard to make things work out for us, trying not to contaminate the sanctity of our new home. He'd built shelves in the shed to store our extra belongings. And he was working on a large wooden play box for the children. Even though he was drinking again and seldom attended church, he appeared to be at peace.

In 1972 baby Jennifer had her first Christmas. Jody turned three. Heather was four, Sonya nineteen months. I had recently celebrated my twenty-second birthday on December 14. Mom had invited us for supper—her special homemade chicken pie. As Dad snapped a picture of me blowing out the candles on the carrot cake Mom had baked, Stan and the children sang "Happy Birthday."

Christmas morning was a whirlwind of excitement for everyone. Our Christmas tree was covered with silver tinsel and red and white bulbs that were plentiful mostly at the bottom. The children helped with the decorating, and I didn't have the heart to change a single thing.

Trucks, cars, teddy bears, sleds, colouring books, pajamas, nuts, and candies—the living-room floor was carpeted with treasures to delight any child. That year Stan had gone out of his way to make sure the kids received special gifts. Stan's mom had sent a large parcel from Ontario: dolls dressed in Native costumes for all the girls and a bow-and-arrow set for Jody. Because it was his birthday, Jody received another gift, a toy tool set he used later to try to saw the legs off his bed.

After a large turkey dinner, I ventured outside with the three oldest children so they could try out their new sleds. I even went for a downhill ride. Stan stayed in with Jennifer while she had a nap. By evening I was exhausted in a pleasant way.

Although I usually woke early, around 7:30 a.m., I slept in on Boxing Day. It was almost nine o'clock when I woke to the sounds of children laughing. Usually the children jumped in bed with me as soon as they awakened. *They must be enjoying their toys*, I thought, grateful for an extra hour of sleep. Stan was still sound asleep beside me. I lay on my back, making a mental list of the chores to take care of that day. I knew I needed to do a wash for certain.

Eventually I got up and made my way to the bathroom on the other side of the master bedroom, carrying my eyeglasses with me. When I stepped onto the cool linoleum, my bare toes touched down on a powdery substance. Quickly I fitted on my glasses.

Flour! What was flour doing on the bathroom floor? I spun around, moving rapidly through the bathroom door that led into our hallway. I couldn't believe my eyes. There was flour everywhere.

I paused and listened to hear giggling coming from Jennifer and Sonya's bedroom. Tiny footprints led in that direction and I followed them.

When I opened the bedroom door, there stood baby Jennifer

completely covered in the white powder. Her long curly hair was totally grey. Only her big brown eyes were clearly visible. She laughed with a wide-open mouth as she threw handfuls of the flour into the air. The flour on the floor was at least an inch deep.

"What's going on?" I yelled. "Who did this?"

There stood my three other children, covered in varying blankets of flour, dark eyes wide with fear, all pointing at their little sister.

"She did it," Heather said. "Jenny did it. Her."

By this time Stan had joined us. I felt him come up beside me. "What in heaven's name?"

I was so angry I couldn't trust myself to speak. I grabbed Jennifer and carried her to the bathroom, yelling back at the others, "Start cleaning that up *now*."

I turned the water on warm in the bathtub and plunked Jennifer into the tub. She splashed around, stirring up a fine paste. Within minutes she was a gooey, messy dough baby. When I saw what I'd done, a smile broke through my anger. I started to laugh and couldn't stop. Gazing up at me, Jennifer bit a piece of dough from her hand and started laughing, too.

I was sure Stan and the kids thought I'd lost my mind. Stan even helped the children clean up as best they could. We didn't own a vacuum cleaner. When Stan and the kids finally peeked into the bathroom, I was sitting on the floor with a towel-wrapped Jennifer, trying to comb bits of dough out of her hair. I looked up at Stan, bit my lower lip, and shook my head. There was no way I could stay mad at the kids. And I was thankful Stan had taken everything so calmly.

By the time breakfast was over, the children were back in my good graces, but it took weeks to get all the flour out of the trailer. To avoid further temptation, I moved my flour tin from the bottom cupboard to a high shelf over the broom closets, far away from curious little fingers.

STAN'S BLEEDING

After Christmas, when Stan stepped up his attendance at church, the rigid, unpredictable tyrant soon revisited us. In fact, his inquisitions grew worse than ever. I couldn't do anything without being confronted with a litany of questions. One evening, when I came home from having coffee with a neighbour, I was greeted by the barrel of his rifle.

"Don't ever do that again," he said, taking aim. I felt all the strength seep from my legs and grabbed a kitchen chair to keep from falling. For a few seconds I held on to the back of the chair as Stan lowered the rifle. I stared into the eyes of the stranger I called my husband.

I didn't even try to argue. I walked around him and went to bed without a word, grateful the children were already asleep. The next day, after Stan left for work at the factory where they made eyeglass frames, I called my brother, Nelson, and asked him to come and disable the rifle so Stan couldn't shoot me.

It had been about two months since I'd taken Valium or used it in Stan's coffee. I still had a half bottle tucked away in an old purse hidden in a box filled with books, so I started taking half a pill in the afternoon just before Stan got home. Subdued by the drug, I wouldn't do or say anything that might set him off.

One of Stan's male friends had come to visit and was staying overnight. I was in such bad shape that I couldn't even remember the friend's name.

It was late in the evening. The children were all tucked in and sleeping soundly. Stan was at home, completely sober. His friend sat in a chair, watching us from the kitchen. I was sitting in an old wooden rocker with a padded dark green seat cover I'd picked up at a yard sale.

"You're thinking about leaving again, aren't you?" Stan said on the couch across from me.

"What are you talking about?" I answered cautiously.

"You been spending a lot of time over at Jackie and Lyman's."

Jackie and Lyman were the neighbours directly across the street. Lyman's brother, Laural, occasionally baby-sat for us.

"They're just friends, Stan. Don't be so paranoid."

It was true I'd been thinking about how to get away from Stan, but I was denying it. Stan stood up and walked into the kitchen without a word. *Something isn't right*, I thought. Becoming more and more agitated, he paced back and forth, then rushed to the cutlery drawer and yanked it open, pulling out a butcher knife.

"I'm going to kill you," he said, running his fingers along the blade, pressing harder, drawing blood. "And the children. That way you won't leave. We'll leave together."

Stan's friend jumped out of his seat and fled the trailer. I prayed he would call the police.

"No, Stan, don't…"

Staring at me as if he were talking to someone he'd never seen before, my husband seemed to see beyond the trailer and this world.

"All of us are going to Heaven," he whispered.

Backing away from him toward the outside door, I glanced at the children's room, but there was no sign of them. When Stan noticed my movement, he took a step forward.

"Please!" I shrieked, scurrying in reverse. I could sense the blade about to rip through me at any moment. My back struck the wall behind me. "Stan, please…"

"It'll be better there," he insisted, stalking closer, the tip of the knife mere inches from my throat.

"No, no…" I blinked the tears from my eyes, trying not to see the point of the butcher knife, attempting to look into Stan's eyes instead, to get past the blank certainty. "We don't need to die." I wanted to raise my hands and shove the blade away but feared my hands would be slashed.

Stan loomed nearer. His lips tightened and his eyes lingered on the children's bedroom doors.

I thought of snatching the blade. Now was the time. I eyed it, but my nerve was unsteady, useless. Stan was just too big. I yelled as the door to our trailer was flung open and men came storming in, heavy boots clumping on the floor.

"Put down the knife!"

Three RCMP officers advanced toward Stan. Two of them grabbed him while the third tried to pry the butcher knife from his hands as his own blood pooled on the kitchen floor. Stan clutched the blade harder as the officers worked to twist it free, but he wouldn't let go. He grasped the keen edge until it cut deeper into his hands.

It took a few minutes for the police to wrestle him out of our home. The noise was terrible. I glanced back at the children's room and saw Heather's sleepy head peeking from the half-open door of the second bedroom. I rushed back to her and whisked her into my arms.

"It's okay, honey. It's okay." Holding her close, I then tucked her into bed and whispered for her to go to sleep. "I'll be back in a few minutes," I promised, then checked Jody and saw he was still sound asleep.

None of the other children had woken during the scuffle. They were used to our fights, and this time neither Stan nor I had even raised our voices.

But then I thought Stan might have already visited my babies. I recalled the lost look in his eyes while he stared at their bedroom door. Earlier, while I was talking with Stan's friend, Stan might have sneaked in there and killed them. I hurried toward Sonya and Jennifer's bedroom door and flung it open. Kneeling beside Sonya's and Jennifer's beds, I touched their cheeks. Warm. Perfect, warm faces. I watched the covers for signs of my babies' bellies rising in breath. They were sleeping peacefully, but they could have been dead.

We all could have been dead.

Stan spent six weeks under observation at Centracare, the Saint John mental hospital. I went to visit him once out of some deep-rooted sense of matrimonial loyalty. The minister at my parents' church said I *had to* stay with Stan. It was what God wanted. We were united. Beryl told me God couldn't be that mean.

I was nervous when I went to visit Stan at Centracare. It was an old stone structure on top of a hill beside Reversing Falls in Saint John. Once inside, I was obliged to sign in and a large male nurse led me through a labyrinth of corridors. At the end of each hallway we reached a new unit where people in varying stages of mental illness roamed freely. Two units in, a young woman, not much older than I, stared at me intensely, then walked toward me. "Do you know where my baby is?" she asked before the male nurse brushed her off and we continued on. At various times throughout the years some of these patients had escaped and turned up in the waters of Reversing Falls. Each unit was locked and barred. When we reached the unit holding Stan, I noticed the patients were secured in rooms.

"He's on suicide watch," the male nurse told me. "He's been sedated."

As I entered the sterile white room bare of everything except a bed, I couldn't believe the change in Stan. Barely recognizing me, he was unshaven and wore blue pajamas. He gave me a slight smile that made him seem like a child happy to see his mother, but he didn't move from the bed.

I felt a lump in my throat. Where I had feared for my safety all the way over, I was now overcome by pity. Quietly I sat beside him and put my hand on his shoulder. He tried to say a few words, but they made absolutely no sense.

I stayed for ten minutes, not knowing what to say or do. Then, checking for the male nurse who was watching through the opening in the door, I signalled it was time for me to leave.

Stan was declared sane and sent out of the province, back to Ontario by train. The psychiatric examination revealed a childhood of abuse. Without intense therapy he would never be a safe partner. And I wanted my children to be safe.

Ten years passed before the children and I saw Stan again. The next time it was on my terms.

ECHINACEA

PART TWO

1975-1990

FIRST TIME IN LOVE

It was the spring of 1975 and I had been hibernating in my trailer in Lincoln after finally freeing myself from Stan's abusive hold. Although my husband had been shipped back to Ontario, I still feared stepping outside the door, thinking he might show up at any moment seeking revenge.

I was going stir-crazy, growing lonely in front of the television once the kids had been put to bed. The TV shows were getting on my nerves, sitcoms that mirrored nothing of my life, but there was little else to do. I had started to write again, mostly long, dark poems about my struggles with life, but it was a satisfying purge of all that had happened in the past few years. Because I'd taken a stand against my minister's wishes, my ties with the church were severed, too.

I was twenty-four and craved the companionship of other adults. I hadn't been out for a social drink in months, and it had been years since I'd kicked up my heels at a dance. I'd never been inside the local Canadian Legion, so when Anne, my baby-sitter, mentioned her parents were members and would love for me to join them at one of the regular Saturday-night dances, I seriously considered it. I had only met Anne's parents once, but they seemed nice, and so it was decided we would go.

Tonight's the night. My stomach knotted at the thought of walking into a strange place, of having to endure the scrutiny of people's gazes.

I called Anne. She was free, but her parents had already left for the Legion. At first I decided to stay home and continue with my usual boring routine. But something was nagging me—a part of me wanted out. So I pulled myself together and decided to go for it. When I called Anne again, I told her I'd changed my mind and she should come over. I was going to have a night out on my own and have a good time even if it killed me.

As soon as Anne arrived, the children ran to her and started climbing into her arms. All except Sonya. She stood sulking in front of me, her *Goldilocks and the Three Bears* book held out in one chubby hand accusingly. I called a cab, anxious to leave before I changed my mind again. While I was waiting for the taxi, Anne contacted the Legion and asked her mother to watch for me so I could be signed in. *Signed in?* I didn't even know what that meant.

The kids were ready for bed, fresh out of their baths. The smell of sweet baby powder soothed my trepidation as I kissed them all good-night. I noticed Sonya still waiting, looking up at me, holding her book.

"Anne will read to you, Sonya," I told her. "C'mon, don't do this now. Mommie needs to go out. I'll bring you back some candy."

Sonya's eyes brightened with anticipation and instant forgiveness. Her blond hair glistened in the lamplight as she turned and quietly trotted her book over to Anne without giving me a second glance. As long as treats came her way, Sonya was content. I'd been dismissed.

I watched my children with Anne, off away from me like that, and felt horribly guilty. For some reason deciding to go out and have a good time was akin to abandoning them, betraying them, leaving them unprotected against every measure of ill will that might possibly drift their way.

Geared up for a night of adventure, new faces, possible romance, the touch of a man's comforting hand, I wore a black cotton belly shirt tied in front with a pair of tight white jeans and black sandals. My hair, shiny and sweet-smelling from the perfume I'd sprayed on my neck, hung over my shoulders and reached my waist in the back. I wore little makeup, just a touch of blue eye shadow and mascara.

"You look great," Anne said.

Heather reached out to hug me. "Pretty Mommie."

My ego bolstered, I headed for the door. My bed was a big, lonely place. I craved a simple cuddle. Not sex, just a touch that would revive pleasure, make me feel I was human again.

Arriving at the Legion, I paid the taxi driver and met Anne's mother, Jean, at the door. The place was packed and there were plenty of approving stares from the men as I walked up a flight of stairs to the dance floor. But my heart sank when I walked into the hall and scanned the crowd. *They're all old people.* The throb of music was welcoming and eventually, clutching a cold beer in my hand, I felt a little more at peace with the partyers. I even suspected I might actually be blending in. The people weren't all that old, I assured myself, taking another big swallow of beer.

Like a prisoner on parole realizing the true extent of her freedom, I enjoyed myself more by the minute. No matter who asked me to dance—young, old, homely, or handsome—I accepted and gave myself fully to the beat of the music. Months of tiredness disappeared as I jived, twisted, and waltzed to the sounds of Black Jack, a five-piece country band.

Later in the night a tall, handsome Native man asked me to dance. Nervously I refused. I couldn't help but think of Stan, of that darkness. I was speechless. Finally, summoning the courage to respond, I shook my head, excused myself, and hurried to the washroom to calm the frantic thumping of my heart.

It wasn't until the band's last set of the evening that I recognized someone I actually knew from long ago. During the dance, I'd been seated at the front of the crowded room, close to the band. The man had been sitting toward the rear. But when I went to the back bar for another beer he spotted me and stood, his eyes following my every move.

"Don't I know you?" he asked, walking up beside me.

I recognized Bob immediately. He was the same small, well-built man with brown hair and cool blue eyes who had dated a friend of mine years before. We had actually met—for the first time—when I was about fifteen. One of Bob's sisters had been my classmate in Geary. I'd had a bit of a crush on him, but he never even looked my way back then. He had a reputation for fast cars and fast women. I'd always thought he was cute. The four beers I'd drunk had tipped me into a generous mood.

"You're Bob!" I shouted above the music. "Diane's brother?"

He nodded and smiled slowly, sexily.

"What are you doing here?" I asked foolishly.

"Looking for a good-looking woman like you."

I laughed. "Then why don't you ask this good-looking woman to dance?"

Bob followed me to my table and we set our drinks down so we could join the crowd as it moved to the beat of Bob Seger's "Old Time Rock and Roll." We danced every dance until last call. During the final waltz of the night, Bob quietly asked if he could take me home. Without giving it a second thought I agreed.

After the dance, Bob bought us both fish and chips from the diner next door to the Legion. We talked about the past and laughed quite a bit while we hungrily downed every scrap of the greasy fare.

On the way home in his car Bob turned up the music on the radio. Creedence Clearwater Revival belted out "Bad Moon Rising" as Bob held my hand for the first time. I felt a tingle throughout my whole body. I wanted to ask him to come home with me, to lie down in the dark and embrace him, but I wasn't sure how the children would react to Bob's presence. He told me he was staying at his parents' home. His first marriage, like mine, had just broken up.

Before he dropped me off at my place we parked on a side road. Bob took me in his arms and kissed me in a way that set off intense emotions. My body responded to his advances at once and we continued kissing. I felt a hunger so consuming I wanted to make love to him right there. As he continued to kiss me, I moved my hands up his back, working the shirt free from his waist. His lips moved down my throat, as my fingernails dug into his back. I'd never felt such ecstasy. Then I froze.

"What's the matter?" Bob asked, trying to catch his breath.

"I have to go. It's late. I promised the baby-sitter."

Bob kissed me again. "Okay," he simply said, starting the car.

It was extremely hard to go home after that. I was vulnerable, but I had to force myself not to go too far, to show restraint for once.

When Bob dropped me off, I stood with a smile plastered on my face and watched him drive away.

Bob and I saw each other often. He came to my home for supper about a week after we met. The kids were all over him the minute he walked in the door, and although I'd told him I had four children, I was afraid their energy would scare him off. I needn't have worried. He was great with kids.

Bob was a carpenter who hailed from a warm French family. The Donelles lived down the road from our trailer park in an attractive bungalow Bob's father had built. His dad was also a carpenter, a man who had a fondness for the bottle. His mom didn't drink, but she was passionate about dancing. And they all seemed to laugh a great deal. I always enjoyed spending time at their tranquil house where the biggest problem was nothing more than what to cook for dinner. I adored them all immediately because they were kind to me and accepted me for who I was. At last I felt as if I belonged somewhere.

My four children quickly grew to love Bob, especially Heather.

He won her heart, and maybe mine, about a month after we started going out together when he sat up one night and rocked Heather for hours to ease the pain of an earache.

When summer arrived, the kids and I moved from the trailer back into an apartment in Oromocto. I couldn't afford to keep the trailer up on my own and it had too many bad memories to make me feel attached to it. The apartment was sparsely furnished because the furniture in the trailer had to be sold with the mobile home to satisfy the bank loan.

I was penniless. There was only one place to turn—the welfare office. A friend told me I could find help there to rent an apartment. The thought of going on welfare filled me with shame and regret, but I had no way of feeding my children unless I went out and begged in the streets. I didn't have a job and my parents were barely managing to provide for their own children still living at home. I figured I could find employment, maybe with the newspaper again, if I were in Oromocto. The welfare people told me I could supplement my income by working part-time until a full-time job came along.

Feeling certain God must care about the well-being of my children, even if He was mad at me for parting company with my husband, I prayed to Him to guide me toward opportunity. Almost immediately my prayers were answered. A week after we moved into the apartment a new office opened up down the hall in my apartment building. It turned out the office belonged to a new weekly newspaper, the *Oromocto Monitor*. They were advertising for someone to work part-time as a reporter. When I handed in my application, I told the receptionist I wouldn't have much trouble getting to work on time, regardless of the weather. I could ensure this. I was hired the same day by Al Nonovitch, the owner/editor.

Bob was genuinely happy for me when I informed him about my success. He was always telling me I was smart, and that made me feel worthy. I thought he was the most wonderful man I'd ever met. I'd read stories about being *in* love. Now I knew exactly how it felt.

A few months after Bob and I started dating I began experiencing bouts of dizziness. I made an appointment with my doctor and he suggested I might have diabetes. I would have to be tested. When I told Bob, I could see the news deeply affected him. He was so shaken he had to sit down.

"When will you know for sure?" he asked gently, taking my hand and patting it. "When's the test?"

"The test's tomorrow morning," I told him. "Dr. Roxborough says I should know in a couple of days."

"Well, I know you'll be okay. I'll do anything I can to help."

I learned later he went to church that night—a place he reserved mostly for Christmas, Easter, funerals, and weddings—and lit a candle for me, offering it up with hope for my good health. All the roses in the world couldn't have touched me more. Here was a man who cared for me. I wasn't used to such devotion, and it felt so healthy and charitable.

When the news came that I wasn't diabetic, Bob brought over takeout fried chicken for supper to celebrate.

My mother's father died that year. He was one of the men whose unwanted caresses had plagued my childhood. I had mixed feelings about his death. For obvious reasons I wasn't as close to him as I was to my grandmother, but I was saddened that he had to die in an old folks' home alone.

I don't remember much about the funeral other than the hymn, "What a Friend We Have in Jesus," sung by my cousin, Heather. I questioned my grandfather's prearranged choice for a musical selection. Had he ever really considered Jesus to be his friend? I'd certainly seen no sign of it while he was living. But when I heard someone say my grandfather was finally free from alcohol, I supposed the hymn might have been fitting, after all. Even dirty old men needed friends, I thought, feeling the same kind of pity I'd felt when I visited Stan in Centracare.

IN A STRANGE APARTMENT

Bob and I lived together for three years before we decided to marry. Those years were like heaven compared to the rest of my life. I finally had a man who was a true partner, a man who loved me and all my children. We were a family. Convinced I was in love, I turned a blind eye to my first failed marriage and heedlessly tied the knot for the second time.

The wedding was a quaint little ceremony solemnized in the Oromocto Baptist Church on September 17, 1977. Quite appropriately that church was later turned into a funeral parlour. But that late-summer day it was bristling with the excitement of the living.

All of my children participated in the ceremony. Heather was a junior bridesmaid; Jody, junior best man; and Sonya and Jennifer fought their way up the aisle as flower girls, stumbling over their pink-and-green cotton gingham gowns. Bob's sister, Judy, took the role of maid of honour, and my brother, Allison, stood as best man. It was one of the happiest days of my life.

After the ceremony, we hosted a reception on the army base, where Bob was working as a civilian carpenter. It was a lively evening with fine music provided by our DJ friend, Wally, and plenty to drink. For the first waltz Wally played Dr. Hook's "A Little Bit More," one of our favourite songs. Bob held me tightly in his arms as we danced to the familiar words: "When you think I've loved you all I can/I'm going to love you just a little bit more."

Unfortunately everyone drank too much, and I spent my wedding night sitting up nursing a bottle with my brother while my new husband snored in the motel bed beside us. Until the wee hours of the morning Allison and I talked about movies and songs we'd both enjoyed. My brother was crazy about science fiction, animated fantasy, and documentaries that dealt with the paranormal. He had a brilliant, analytical mind and was also a talented writer but lacked the confidence to pursue a career in writing.

"You should go to university," I said. "You're so smart."

"I don't have time," he said, obviously wanting to change the subject.

I studied his features in silence as I took another sip from my drink. None of my brothers really resembled me. For one thing, they all had much lighter hair, and two of them even had blue eyes. Allison was tall with sandy brown hair and a moustache. His eyes were brown, like mine, but a shade lighter.

When there was no booze left to drink, I crawled into bed with my new husband, and my brother passed out in the hotel-room chair.

My kids were impressed by the idea of gentle hands that could give a pat on the head without tightening into a fist. Bob became the only real father they'd ever known. For a while we were a proper family.

Bob made physical fitness a priority. He jogged and worshipped every sport known. His eyes would light up quicker for a hockey game than any new outfit I might model for him. He always made sure we had lots to eat and he never once hit me.

After the wedding, we settled into another apartment on Gilmour Street in Oromocto. There were only two bedrooms. The four children slept in one big room in two sets of bunk beds. It was crowded but cozy. Bob's two sisters, with their four children, lived directly across the hall, which was convenient. I was working two part-time jobs, and one of his sisters often baby-sat for me when I left for work at Steinberg's, a grocery store in the Oromocto Mall. Bob was usually home when I went out to gather information for the features I was still writing for the local newspaper.

During our relationship, Bob often encouraged me to go back to school. I took six months off work to attend a community college in Fredericton. There I completed the academic subjects required for me to attend university. Once again I was at the top of my class. When one of the instructors noticed my writing, I felt a renewed interest in it again. I was actually beginning to get my life back on track.

Christmas was a precious time during the eight years Bob and I were together. We would gather for large helpings of mouth-watering pork pie laboriously baked each Christmas by my sister-in-law, Myrtle. She and her husband had three boys and lived next door to her parents on Nevers Road. We'd wash this down with egg nog or a glass of wine. Then, with full bellies and contented smiles, everyone would head for midnight Mass.

I often sat and basked in the serenity of those nights. I never let the skeletons from the past, or my apprehensions, cloud my gratitude. It was a time of enchantment. Maybe, I thought, God really did love me, and this was the marvellous payment for having endured my hellish past, my trial by fire.

Every summer we would all take a vacation. Usually we'd head for Nova Scotia to visit Bob's relatives. I was always surprised by how they made me feel so welcome. I was convinced someone would eventually think Bob was crazy for marrying a woman with four small children. But no one ever made me or the children feel like imposters. It was as if we had always been part of the family.

Bob's maternal grandmother became one of my favourite relatives. She was shorter than I was, which was no small accomplishment. She stood under five feet but in no way lacked the confidence or assertiveness I found so hard to muster. The first time I met her was in Joggins, Nova Scotia. She was cooking dinner when we arrived and immediately stopped everything she was doing to give her grandson a big hug. Then she turned to me and said in a strong French accent, "So you Bob's woman? I hear all about you. Nice-looking woman. Nice-looking kids. Come in, sit down. We gonna eat." She came toward me, and I didn't know what to do until she opened her arms wide. Quickly she hugged me and all four kids and was on her way into the next room with our coats in tow. She was in her mid-seventies but moved faster than I did in my mid-twenties.

Bob and I were totally devoted to each other and to the children. We had a routine that began building my confidence and instilled in me a sense of security. We both worked and, in our free time, attended the kids' plays, ball games, and swimming events. Bob watched all the hockey, baseball, football, and basketball games on television—every single game he could set his eyes on. And I did my chores around the house, had coffee with one of Bob's sisters or my friends from work, or spent time dabbling in fortunetelling. Gaining more and more confidence, I reached out to one of the few areas of my past that I found intriguing. I started reading tarot cards. Once in a while I'd interpret tea leaves for a friend, but my real fascination was with the cards. I began by using a regular deck. I studied in a book what the different cards represented, but mostly I just analyzed the people. I would get a "feeling" I couldn't explain and tell people secrets about themselves and events that were about to happen. My predictions were usually accurate and people started referring to me as the Gypsy Lady.

I never told Grammie Brewer, who was living in Fredericton at

York Manor, that I was telling fortunes because I knew she'd have been upset. She'd given it up for good when she began attending Baptist church services, and she'd warned me years before that playing with the "other world" could only summon bad luck in the end.

For entertainment Bob played baseball on the Black Watch field and hockey at King's Arrow Arena. He was a great ball player, and I remember feeling proud to be his wife as I watched him slide into home plate to score the winning run or leap to tag a man out on second. He played hockey in the Industrial League with his two brothers and that was a rough division. Often there were fights on the ice and frequently Bob was part of them. Sometimes the fights would spill over into the stands.

When Bob's team played the club from the reserve, altercations in the stands were guaranteed. The guys from the Oromocto Reserve were crazy on the ice. Most of them would rather scuffle than skate. And the fans in the stands weren't much different. Reserve girls were thrown out for attacking other fans in the bleachers. I would yell and cheer Bob's team, but when they played the reserve team I sat a safe distance away and kept my mouth firmly shut.

Bob and I bowled together on a team and we attended dances at the Oromocto Legion with Bob's family every Saturday night. On Sundays we took the kids for a drive and stopped off to see Bob's mother and father. It was a schedule I could count on until Bob's drinking started to worsen.

In the beginning Bob drank on weekends. He usually passed out and was never violent, so I didn't complain much. When he began to drink after work and failed to show up for important events, like Jody's Father and Son Bowling Banquet, I became unnerved, fearing the imposition of the past.

Our regular Saturday nights at the Legion soon started earlier for Bob. Without me he played shuffleboard in the morning, steadily downing bottle after bottle of beer. By the time I joined him, dressed up for the evening, he would be ready to sleep it off.

Before long I was drinking just as much as Bob. Parties and week-nights at the Legion displaced some of the regular family routine. The tender, caring man I had married slipped away as the bottle beckoned for more and more of his attention, and I mourned for his return. The mourning took the form of resentment. I resented Bob for showing me the good times, then robbing me of them. Inside my head, under the influence of a dozen or more beers, I believed I might be settling some score by encouraging other men to take notice of me.

At first it was just casual flirtation. I sought the attention, the compliments. I was feeling empty again and despised that sickly feeling.

The black hole inside me since childhood, which I had partially filled with Bob's attention and now with alcohol, grew painfully larger. I needed constant diversion to keep me from being submerged in the old pain. Men encouraged that darkness to overshadow my life, I reasoned. But men were also the most logical choice to fill it again. I didn't know any other way to feel adequate.

One night, after drinking myself into a reckless state, I woke up in a strange apartment, next to one of my husband's friends. I couldn't even remember leaving the hotel lounge where a group from work had been celebrating the forthcoming Christmas holidays.

Panic seized me as I thought about Bob and my kids. *What time was it? Was this a weekday? Did I have to work? Did he? Oh, God, what would he say? What could I tell him?*

I checked my watch. It was 7:00 a.m., Saturday, December 23. I had time for an excuse.

Dressing quickly without waking the man beside me, I looked at him and was overwhelmed with nausea. I hurried into the bathroom and threw up, cursing myself all the while. How could I stoop so low? What was wrong with me?

I needed a drink, some toothpaste, a coffee. My hands were shaking, and I was trying to reason how I could get out of this mess without Bob walking out on me. I found a phone on the wall in the kitchen and called one of my girlfriends from work who had been with me the night before. Her groggy voice answered after four long rings.

"Cindy, you've got to help me," I said, huddling close to the receiver.

"Eve, what's the matter?"

"I can't talk now, but please, Cindy, will you tell Bob I spent the night at your house if he calls? I'll explain later."

"Sure, sure, Eve. Are you okay?"

"No," I said, and hung up.

When I arrived home by taxi, Bob was sleeping on the couch, three empty beer bottles on the coffee table beside him. I crept into the kitchen, shocked by the reality of seeing my children up and eating cereal.

"Where were you, Mommie?" Jennifer asked. "Daddy was awful mad."

The older ones stared at me accusingly but didn't speak.

"Mommie was at a friend's house," I whispered, praying Bob wouldn't wake up until I had my alibi down pat. "It was late." I went to the tap for a glass of water, my throat sawdust dry. "I didn't want to come home and wake you up. What did Daddy say?"

"He said he was going to leave." Tears began to stream down Heather's cheeks. I drank the glass of water, unable to look my daughter in the eye.

It took a lot of promises over several days to calm the waters. Bob disappeared but only for one night. He got drunk and slept at a friend's house. I was so worried I couldn't sleep. When he walked into the house the next morning just before lunch, he wasn't talking. Revenge, I figured, and that was the way it went from then on.

As the drinking increased, so did my disregard for our marriage vows. I began hanging around with a different crowd. I was thirty years old and most of the people in my new gang, comprised of both whites and Natives, were younger than I was and had one goal—partying.

FORTUNETELLING

My mother called to let me know that Eunice, the half sister she'd told me about, had surfaced unexpectedly, wanting to meet her birth mother and siblings. She would be coming to visit in two days. Far from being disturbed by the idea of her past returning to haunt her, my mom seemed delighted with the news.

"I've prayed for this day for years," she said.

I had no idea.

"The people who adopted Eunice changed her name to Shirley," Mom explained. "She's living in a suburb in Moncton and she's coming here to meet us."

Since Mom had only ever told me, and not the boys, about having another daughter, she had her work cut out for her in the next day or so, because Eunice/Shirley planned to visit in two days. Mom had to let my brothers know they had another sister before she showed up on the doorstep.

When I finally met Shirley, who came to my house with Mom, I was amazed to discover she was a fortuneteller, too.

Shirley pointed at two amethysts on a small table. "I like your crystals. I *use* crystals, too." The way she said the word *use* prompted me to ask what she meant.

"I use them for positive energy while I do my readings," she replied matter-of-factly. As she continued with her explanation, I discovered she had been telling fortunes for much longer than I and had a regular clientele. She even worked with the police, helping them to find people. They'd approached her to locate an elderly woman who'd gone missing in her area. She'd been able to give them an idea where to search just by studying the woman's photograph. I was blown away by the news.

Shirley didn't resemble me much, other than we were both only five feet tall and had long hair. But hers was blond, while mine was dark. I thought I detected a bit of Sonya in her. Shirley had three daughters, like me, but no sons. When she showed me a photo of her girls, I noticed her daughter, Brenda, shared a likeness with me.

After our first meeting, we decided to see each other again. Shirley suggested Bob and I visit them in Moncton. We spent time getting to know each other. I talked about growing up, leaving out most of the painful parts, and Shirley spoke mostly about her children and fortunetelling.

I made a few more trips to Moncton, and although I was eager to build on our relationship, it soon became apparent Shirley was no longer interested. During one visit, she just shut down. Her voice and mannerisms were cold. I was confused and hurt by the change in her. I hated rejection. She kept in touch with my mother periodically but made it plain I held no special place in her family. The only contact we had after that visit was initiated by me, and my advances were usually met with cool indifference.

After learning of Shirley's success at making money fortunetelling, I decided to put out a shingle, as well. People would often ask me to read their cards, so I started booking them in at seven dollars per reading.

Most of the time I would spend an hour with each client. In my new role as fortuneteller I began to attract a particular kind of crowd: enlightened women who drank freely and thought their marriages were holding them back from their true potential. Marlene was a New Ager before the term was popular. She'd been married to one of my husband's friends and was always trying to boost the excitement in her life. She liked tarot cards and loved a good time. Pretty soon her adventurous nature caught me and I decided to break loose and have some fun. I deserved better. No more Legion and taverns for me. I was moving upward. I wanted nightclubs and parties, wild gatherings where drugs were as common as booze.

Bob and I never indulged in much conversation, but now we never talked at all. Our communication seemed to exist only in bed, and that had changed, too. Where there had once been an intimacy consummated by eager bodies, now there was an angry spark of desire fuelled only by desperation. We didn't even hold each other afterward anymore. Bob would just tumble into sleep and I'd usually get up and listen to George Jones moan out the words to "He Stopped Loving Her Today" or "I Ain't Ready Yet."

At this point Heather had successfully sung in a few talent contests in Oromocto. She adored being onstage, but even around the house she was constantly singing. Heather was also involved in competitive swimming and always looked forward to school. But all of a sudden she was having trouble with her studies. And she was getting sick—stomachaches, headaches, and fevers.

Three years earlier, at the age of nine, Heather had begun bleeding uncontrollably. The doctor had determined the bleeding was the start of menstruation and that her body lacked the progesterone required to keep her cycles regular. Sometimes she would hemorrhage. Other times the flow would be closer to normal but would last twenty days or more. After a visit to a gynecologist and exploratory surgery, the doctor decided to give Heather hormone shots and put her on the pill.

A little later, at the age of eleven, she was sexually molested by a stranger early one evening on the way home from a school event a block from where we lived.

"You have to do something!" I had screamed at the RCMP officer who had showed up on my doorstep, responding to my call. "She's just a kid."

"We suggest you take her to the hospital to see if she's okay physically first," the officer suggested.

"Of course, she's okay physically. The jerk ran away when he heard someone coming."

Heather was in my bedroom lying down. She'd cried herself to sleep as Bob held her. The officer took a report from me, but I refused to wake Heather. In the end, nothing came of it. The police told me it would be difficult to find the man responsible for the attack. And Heather refused to talk about it after that night.

Heather's body continued to manifest signs of her chaotic emotional state. Ear infections, severe headaches, a ruptured appendix, and bouts of pneumonia plagued her adolescence. I tried to care for her, to soothe her, but after so much stress I couldn't handle any more illness. Instead of dealing with the problem, I went drinking. There were worry-free times in a bottle, and I wanted more of them.

Sonya had always been the real free spirit. She was a fine dancer, often swirling around the house or turning cartwheels. Her inherent sense of grace made her a talented gymnast, and she was happiest when she was in the water. She could swim for hours without touching the beach.

Now she seemed unhappy all the time. Instead of dancing she often sat for hours in front of the television, saying nothing.

Even Jody, my mild-mannered son who had begun showing real potential as an artist, and Jenny, my kindhearted baby who wrote poetry every day, bickered and fought more. The house was falling apart as the children gradually absorbed their parents' sickness.

Bob and I no longer went to Saturday-night dances. In fact, we rarely went anywhere together. I hung around with my crowd and he went with his. Our relationship was muted. I'd even started hanging around with some Natives from the two Maliseet reserves—St. Mary's in Fredericton and Oromocto First Nation, or Wellamooktook, as the older Natives called it, attached to the town of Oromocto. Despite my resolve to stay away from Native men, I felt a familiar attraction growing once more. I wanted a dark man to take control of me, wound me, destroy me. I'd failed at my marriage, a union that had started out so blessed, and I figured I should be punished.

On a Sunday morning in May 1981, while the kids were at Sunday School, I decided to confess and put an end to the charade. Bob was watching TV when I asked him if we could talk. He wasn't surprised about my affair with Rodney, a co-worker in the grocery store where I was still working. He already knew. But he cried when I told him I was leaving.

"There's just no sense in trying anymore," I admitted.

"Do you still love me?" Bob asked.

I hung my head so he wouldn't see my tears. "I don't know."

My kids cried for a long time afterward, too.

"But why, Mom?" Heather pleaded over and over. "He's our dad."

I told her she would understand when she got older, then locked myself in my bedroom where I, too, sobbed for hours.

It was a decision I lived to regret. In the end, I was the one who wept the longest. I was running away instead of working things out. It was this mentality that further encouraged my self-loathing and perverted descent into booze and drugs.

My children never really recovered from that loss of stability. Hurt by my cold rejection, Bob retaliated by shutting the door on me, but worse yet, on my children. He never visited or called. It was a hurt that deeply scarred Heather. She kept his picture by her bed and sometimes tried to call him but could never reach him. Everything around me provided reason to sink deeper into the bottle. With all this additional guilt and shame, I convinced myself I was completely useless. I couldn't do anything right, not even for my children, the ones I loved most.

In a matter of weeks, approaching my thirty-first birthday, I graduated from problem drinker to binge drinker, a common variety of full-fledged alcoholic.

THE FIRE

The next two years were spent working, drinking, and struggling to hold my family together. I was employed at Steinberg's about thirty hours a week and still writing for newspapers. Off and on I worked on a book about the life of a young woman I'd met through fortunetelling who had been sent to prison for robbing graves. She'd also been involved in a notorious ring of people practising witchcraft.

A great deal of my energy was siphoned off trying to cover up my growing addiction, especially when I went out into the community to cover stories for *The Daily Gleaner.* We were forced to move again when I received a notice to vacate the row house that was still in Bob's name. This time we moved into a third-floor apartment on Lanark Street directly across from where I worked as a grocery clerk. The pace was hectic.

The affair with my co-worker ended days after I made the break from Bob.

At a party one night I met a man eleven years my junior who could hold his liquor even better than I could. His name was Doug and the party was at his brother Wade's house. Wade and his wife, Cheryl, lived in a row house near where I had lived with Bob. The party was a rocking event with about thirty people, most of whom I already knew. I felt like a queen bee when two guys started competing for my attention, stumbling over each other to bring me drinks or offering a cigarette or toke of marijuana. When I spotted Doug, I forgot all about them. He was seated at the kitchen table, tapping a set of drum sticks in sync with the tunes blaring from a ghetto blaster nearby. April Wine. Van Halen. AC/DC. He kept beat with them all. When he paused to take a drink from his beer, he noticed me looking at him and invited me to sit down. Doug had shoulder-length brown hair, a trim build, and the sexiest eyes I'd ever seen. I found out he didn't have a steady job so, once we became more intimate, he spent a great deal of his time at my place.

One night in my apartment I read his tarot cards for him and saw a dark-haired woman in his future. I assumed it was me and convinced him of it. Two weeks later he moved in with me and the children. I tried to hide Doug's presence from my father, who was now working as a janitor for Oromocto Property Developments, the company that owned the apartment where I was living. But one morning, when Dad was in the building, he stopped by to say hello and met Doug face-to-face while I was still sleeping on the pullout couch that Doug and I shared in the living room. Dad never stopped by again after that.

Doug was heavily into drugs. He mostly smoked hash, but he'd do anything that was going around—cocaine, acid, or magic mushrooms. I was interested mainly in booze, so I did my best to lean him toward the bottle. He was fond of tequila. It was a full-time job keeping up with him, and my relationship with my children suffered greatly because of my obsession with this charismatic young man. I spent so much time with him that we did little as a family anymore.

I still made certain my children ate nutritious food and wore clean clothing and I continued to attend all their school functions, but I knew I wasn't supplying them with the home they really needed. During the week, I was a dutiful mother, but I lived for weekend parties that often turned into violent fights between Doug and me. When we were both drinking, which was usually every weekend, one of us would get jealous. I did my fighting with my mouth; Doug liked to throw things or punch holes in the nearest wall.

I was still telling fortunes, and soon found out my children, especially Sonya, were gifted "readers," too. One day Sonya picked up the cards I'd laid out for my friend Marlene and pretended to read them. "You're going to marry a dark-haired man you already know," she explained.

Since Marlene hadn't divorced her light-haired man yet, we all laughed at the absurdity of the assumption. However, a couple of years later the prediction came true.

My children and I often practised sending messages telepathically. Making a game of it, I'd think of a number or a colour and get them to concentrate and see if they could pick up what I was "sending." Jody was most often correct when it came to "receiving," but Sonya was by far the best "sender." When she concentrated on a number or a colour, I'd usually discern it right away. Heather had been able to communicate that way for a long time. I could usually sense when something was wrong with her even when she was miles away. Jennifer was the least interested in our games. She opted for the practical explanation, figuring there must be a scientific reason. But when spooky things started to happen around us she changed her mind.

One night, while I was getting ready to step out for the evening, Sonya came into my room. I watched her in the mirror while I checked my hair. She was staring at me.

"What's up?" I asked.

"A man is going to try to hurt you, Mom."

"What?" Amused, I turned to her. I tried to laugh it off, despite feeling the hair on my arms stand at attention.

She moved closer to me. "Please don't go."

"I'll be fine, sweetie. I'll be with Marlene."

"No. Please don't go."

"We'll watch out for each other." Doug was away, and Marlene and I were going down to the club, a five-minute walk from our apartment building.

Sonya continued to protest. "But you *will* be by yourself," she insisted. "You don't know this man. He'll hurt you."

Eager to get away before I was totally spooked, I told Sonya I'd call her in a couple of hours to let her know I was okay. She was still concerned, but she shrugged and gave me a hug.

Marlene was waiting for me outside. We decided to walk. When we reached the club, we picked a table away from the dance floor and ordered a couple of beers. We knew a few people at the club, so we spent the evening talking and sipping. Nothing out of the ordinary. At around ten o'clock I glanced at my watch and remembered my promise to Sonya. I excused myself and went to the pay phone near the front door of the club.

When Sonya came to the phone, I told her I was fine. "I'll be home by midnight. You go on to bed. I love you."

I hung up and returned to the table to find Marlene talking to a man we both knew as Dave. Marlene had told me she was interested in this guy, so I decided to mingle and give her some privacy. After a few drinks, Marlene infomed me she was leaving with Dave. Fortified by alcohol, I felt perfectly fine. What harm could come to me? I could take care of myself.

A half hour after Marlene and Dave left the club I decided to walk to the Oromocto Hotel and check out the lounge before heading home. The hotel actually faced the side of my apartment building so it was in the right direction. When I arrived at the hotel lounge, I joined a table full of people I knew from work. Everyone was in high spirits, celebrating someone's birthday, so I ordered a beer. Two good-looking guys I'd never seen before were sitting at the adjacent table. Interested, I kept my eyes on them, then noticed one was watching me. After another beer I motioned them over.

They told us they were construction workers from a northern New Brunswick French community. They were in town to finish a contract job. When one of them invited me to his room for a drink after the bar closed, I saw no harm in it. I could handle another drink, I thought. I'd been sipping all night, and there was nothing else open at that time. I wasn't interested in sex; I only wanted another drink. I was always game for another drink and was too insulated by the glow of the last Jack Daniel's I'd just consumed to feel any fear.

I followed the man across the threshold of his dim hotel room, a neat single with faded brown carpet, and the door was shut behind me. The man let me know what he had in mind right away by beginning to unbutton his shirt. By his gruff gestures, I decided he wasn't interested in foreplay. He made a lunge for me, grabbing my hair and pulling it hard.

Gasping, I jerked toward the door. The man raised his fist and I jammed shut my eyes. I felt the blow, not to my face—I was prepared for that—but to my chest. I crumpled forward but he straightened me, grabbing my breasts so roughly I thought I'd collapse from the pain. When I shrieked, he let go for a second, perhaps wondering how to silence me. In that split second I scrambled for the door and raced down the hallway, not stopping until I was inside my apartment building. It took me a few minutes to calm my shaking body. I sat on the bottom step of the stairs leading to my floor and lit a cigarette. My hands were trembling so much it was a difficult feat, even though I was completely sober now. I felt like bursting into tears, but I held it in so I could trod upstairs to my apartment and give the impression nothing had happened, in case one of the kids was still awake. I'd left thirteen-year-old Heather in charge and was hoping everyone would be in bed.

And I was lucky—everyone was asleep. I headed for the bathroom, desperately needing a shower. Standing there topless, I surveyed the damage. My breasts and arms were already covered with ugly purple bruises.

Next time I'll listen, Sonya, I thought as I flicked on the shower and stepped under the hot, soothing spray. *Next time I'll listen.*

The following day an old friend, Claudette, stopped in to have her tarot cards read. She was the only one I ever told about the incident. She insisted I call the police, but I wanted to put the violence behind me. For everyone else who saw the bruises, including Doug when he returned, I concocted a story about tripping and falling on a discarded bicycle on my way home from the club. Everyone seemed to believe me except Sonya.

In the summer of 1983, fourteen-year-old Heather asked if she could visit her grandmother in Ontario. Stan had been in contact with the children, and I had talked to both him and his mother, Loretta. She had been sober for years now, and Stan didn't drink anymore, either. He sounded like a different man and Heather kept asking to see him. I didn't feel secure about the idea of Heather being near Stan. I refused to allow her to go.

"If you don't let me go," she told me, "I'll run away."

So I gave in with the understanding that she was to call me or my parents if anything felt uncomfortable, and a bus ticket would be paid for at this end.

Jody was thirteen and dependable, so he stayed with his sisters to keep an eye on things when I worked. He was drawing steadily then, creating his own world with his art. What he showed me were black-pen sketches of animals and birds. What I later found under his bed were accomplished drawings of nude women. It was surprising because they were much better than the animals. I guess his heart was in it and he was more interested in those details.

Doug was a fine artist and encouraged Jody to explore different mediums like charcoal and pastels. I'd given Jody an art kit for Christmas 1982, and he'd been drawing on a regular basis ever since.

On July 8, I was standing at my post in front of the cash at Steinberg's with my back to the large store window that faced my apartment building when a group of teenagers ran in yelling, "There's a fire across the street." I was talking to a customer, so it took a few seconds for the words to register.

When I turned, a crowd had already gathered at the windows and everyone was talking excitedly. Hurrying over, I pushed my way through for a clear view and saw a bunch of people standing near my apartment building. Frantic, I sprinted out the door, across the parking lot, and up a small grassy hill to reach the street in front of my home. Sighting smoke billowing from the building, I started to scream and ran into traffic, ignoring the oncoming cars.

As I neared the edge of the crowd, a hand reached out and touched me.

"It's your apartment, Eve," one of my neighbours said.

"Where are my kids?" I pushed the neighbour away and pressed to get closer to the building. "Where are my kids?" I screamed louder.

My father caught me. He'd been working in my building that day and had been the one to call the fire department after smelling smoke.

"They're all right, Eva," he assured me, holding my sobbing body in his arms. "They're safe."

Within minutes three of my children were at my side. Panicky, I searched for Heather. "Where's Heather?" I asked before remembering she had travelled to Ontario.

"My hamster's in there," Sonya said, tears in the corner of her eyes. "They wouldn't let me go get him."

I put my arm around her and gave her a squeeze. I didn't know what to say about the hamster trapped in the fire, burning up. We stood together and watched in distant horror as the glass from our living-room window suddenly blew out with a percussive bang. Black smoke poured through the gaping hole where our kitchen table had once stood.

What am I supposed to do now? I wondered, completely lost. *Everything must be destroyed.* I checked the crowd, wondering, *Where's Doug?*

Thirty minutes later Doug finally arrived. I'd forgotten that he'd been painting a house to earn some extra money.

"What happened?" he asked, out of breath and startled. "Is everyone okay?"

"The kids are okay. I don't know what happened. I just don't know."

That night Bob agreed to take Sonya for a few days. Jody went to my parents' home, and Jennifer stayed with one of her friends in the next apartment building. Doug and I headed for Wade and Cheryl's. Although the fire had been contained, leaving the building intact, there was nothing much salvageable in our apartment. All the new furniture and clothing I'd worked so hard to purchase lay buried beneath the black soot. All my photographs, my letters, the newspaper clippings of the articles I'd written, my books and even the manuscript about the girl who robbed graves that I'd been working on for over a year, were gone. I didn't have house insurance. I couldn't afford it.

The next day the local newspapers carried the story. My supervisor at Steinberg's, Marg Granter, and my co-workers, Karla and Tina, established a fund at the local bank to which people could contribute. Donations of clothing poured into the Oromocto firehall. Friends at the local tavern, wanting to help the children get over the loss of their pet hamster, took up a special collection to buy a new one, complete with a cage and all the accessories.

I was overwhelmed by the generosity of the Oromocto people, strangers freely coming forward to help us. It was unimaginable to me. One day at work I was ringing produce through my cash for an older gentleman when a soft-spoken lady in her early forties approached my checkout.

"Are you taking a break soon?" she asked. I'd met Mary Ward while covering a school-board meeting for *The Daily Gleaner*. Something about her gentle smile, the way it enlivened her sparkling eyes, gave me a feeling of importance and made me suspect she might be a Christian.

"I'm off in a few minutes," I said, ringing through the last of the older gentleman's items.

"Can I speak with you in private?"

"Sure."

When my break came, Mary followed me to a small room in the back of the store where the grocery pallets were stacked.

"When I was praying," Mary said, "God told me to give this to you." She reached into her purse, took out a piece of paper, and handed it to me. It was a cheque.

"Thank you," I said without peeking at the amount, thinking that might be rude. "That's so sweet of you." People had been popping up from everywhere to hand me ten- and twenty-dollar bills, and I was grateful for the help.

Mary gave me a kind smile and began to walk away. I glanced down at the amount on the cheque—$2,000. Surely there were too many zeros.

"Wait a minute," I called after her. She was halfway down the soup aisle, so I had to run to catch up. "Are you sure about this?" I touched her shoulder.

She turned, calmly looked at me, and smiled again. "Yes, I am. God bless you."

"Thank you so much," I whispered tearfully, touched by her kindness in the name of God.

Thank you, too, God, I said silently.

Altogether more than $4,000 was donated to help us start over. We also received more clothing than we knew what to do with. In fact, a truck from the Salvation Army was filled to overflowing. And we had to store the extra pieces of furniture and household goods that had been dropped off for us at the fire station, in Wade and Cheryl's basement, and on their front lawn covered with tarps.

All we lacked now was a place to live. We'd been staying with friends and relatives for weeks, shuffling from one place to another, homeless.

One day my mother received a call from the mother of my brother Nelson's best friend. Faye Tidd, a real-estate agent who later became the mayor of Oromocto, wanted to talk to me. She was disheartened to hear about my misfortune and told my mother she had some news that might interest me. Faye had a deal on a small bungalow on Branch Road in the far end of Geary, seven miles from Oromocto.

I only needed $2,500 for the down payment and an additional $500 for the lawyer's fees. I could manage it, thanks to people like Mary Ward, who had donated their hard-earned cash to help out a homeless mother and her four children.

By the time fall rolled around, we were living in our new home with four finished bedrooms and enough space for everyone. Doug had joined us. Something substantial had come out of our loss, after all.

The fire marshall never determined the cause of the fire. My tarot cards had been among the many items that had burned. I remembered my grandmother's warning and swore never to replace them.

OROMOCTO FIRST NATION

I had made a few friends on the Oromocto Reserve during the past couple of years. I'd met them at the local tavern and invited them to my new house for parties. Some of them became regular visitors after that. Heather was back from Ontario. Both she and Sonya were hanging out with girls from the reserve. That was how I learned from one of their Maliseet friends that Stan had been involved with a woman there years before while we were married. The woman was only too happy to let everyone know so the information could be passed on to me.

One Maliseet couple, Norman and Jeanette, would often sit and drink with me at the Downhomers. Through our conversations I learned that Norman was a craftsman who made guitars. The notion intrigued me so much that I wrote a feature story about him for the *Oromocto Monitor*. Doug had no hangups about race, so he didn't care who we partied with as long as we partied.

Shortly after our apartment fire, the land claim of the Oromocto First Nation was making front-page news in all the newspapers. Naturally I wanted to be the one to cover it. No other reporter had my connections with the Native community.

The man who was making the headlines agreed to my request for an interview. His name was Emmanual Polchies. He had been a U.S. Marine and had extensive knowledge of the Oromocto First Nation's history and its strained relationship with the Canadian Armed Forces.

It was a story I was intent on doing fairly. Polchies indicated that some of the other reporters had already twisted his words to make him look like the "bad guy."

Polchies was the chief at that time and had fought long and hard for compensation for seventy-two acres of band land surrendered to the Department of National Defence to establish CFB Gagetown in 1953. It was the first claim to be settled in Canada under a specific claims policy, and Polchies was a "vigorous worker," according to Audrey Stewart, negotiator for the Office of Native Claims. He landed the Oromocto Band a whopping $2,550,000. Polchies was often referred to as "Billy Jack," the legendary movie hero of the time. The name suited him. He wore a black hat just like the film character and fought hard for his people. I covered the facts as they were presented and admired Polchies.

The claim was a landmark occasion for everyone on the reserve, even for winos like Old Nubby, a man who had spent his entire sixty-four years on the reserve. The only time he ever left was to go to the liquor store in the mall ten minutes away. Most of the time he'd walk up and down the streets on the reserve, looking for people to pass the time with. His small, slanted eyes would light up the craggy hollows in his face when someone invited him in for a cup of tea. He'd tip his dirty Boston Bruins cap, scratch his prickly scalp, and say, "Don't mind if I do."

Once in a while he would travel with relatives to another reserve, but that was usually to celebrate at someone's wake. He lived a simple life: sleep, visit friends, eat a little, and drink Challenge wine. All that changed drastically in 1983 when he was handed a cheque for $10,000 for the settled land claim. Many

Natives had never seen a sum larger than their $60 biweekly welfare cheques.

When I covered the story of the land-claim settlement, I felt some animosity at first, considering I'd just lost everything in a fire and here were people who'd never worked a day in their lives throwing away thousands of dollars on booze and vehicles they drove into the ground. There were only about 170 band members, and I was sure most of them had never heard of the improper land surrender. I resented watching the tavern's profits shoot through the ceiling while my ceiling was blackened by ash.

For Old Nubby, and most of the other residents on the Oromocto Reserve, the issue wasn't particularly important. It was the payoff that most interested them. When people heard about the money, Chief Polchies became everyone's best friend. Natives would stop him on the road and tell him what a great guy he was, how they'd always known he would be an excellent chief. However, it didn't take long for them to forget about his struggle on their behalf when he and two councillors were charged with misappropriation of funds four months later. As their money vanished, so, too, did their support. Chief Polchies fought most of that battle alone.

Local businesses capitalized on the settlement. Wood Motors even opened a temporary car lot in the town to accommodate the sudden surge in automobile sales. Ken Hill's Towing made a killing pulling new cars out of ditches and, in some cases, out of the river.

But Nubby didn't bother with a car. He headed straight to the shopping centre with his newfound wealth to stock up on his favourite wine—cases and cases of it. I watched the clerks who had once snubbed him carry the purchases out and pile them on a bench with a smile, probably the first flash of white teeth they'd ever turned his way. They regarded the cases, then scanned the parking lot, searching for his mode of transportation. Old Nubby had no way of transporting the cases home.

I was at the shopping centre picking up groceries that day and watched Old Nubby stand and scratch his head as he stared at his treasure. He gave a cheerful smile, looking younger than he had in years, and turned his attention to the parking lot, taking in the small strip mall adjacent to the liquor store. His eyes noticed a bright red ride-on lawn mower displayed in front of the hardware store across the lot. Suddenly his dark, old face brightened and he headed for the hardware store while anxiously checking over his shoulder to keep his booty in view.

"Gimme that machine," he barked at the clerk as he turned to eye his stash.

"What machine?" the clerk snapped, then scowled, not wanting anything to do with another drunk Native.

"That thing," Nubby answered, pointing to the mower and pulling a roll of one-hundred-dollar bills from his pocket.

I was delighted to see Nubby in control for a change. Usually security would chase him out of the mall for loitering.

When he saw the wad of cash, the clerk uncurled his lips and smiled toothily. "Why of course, sir. What exactly would you like?"

You hypocrite! I thought.

"I want that machine to take home. Load it up."

"Load it up?"

"Load it up with my bottles." He pointed toward the liquor store bench where his goods were piled.

"Oh, your bottles, of course."

I watched, along with several others, as the clerk rushed around to fill up the lawn mower with both gas and cases of wine so Nubby could drive it home.

When Nubby mounted the vehicle, he resembled a knight on his shiny new steed. He started the engine and headed off, negotiating through the parking lot without spilling a drop. I felt like cheering but kept silent when I heard two women talking beside me. "Those Indians don't know how to handle money," one said to the other, who nodded in agreement.

Nubby probably didn't really care about the money or the vehicle. The ride-on lawn mower never cut a blade of grass. Someone told me it was abandoned the same day and wrecked by teenagers who had nothing better to do.

Nubby's party lasted at least a month before he became too sick to keep it up. By that time I'd lost any malice toward the Natives. I was living in my new home.

FOR THE RELIEF OF PAIN

A year later Doug finally found a full time job and the parties abated for a while. Then he dumped me for a girl closer to his own age. Ours had been a relationship based on mutual love of Jack Daniel's and the scalp-tingling kick of bennies.

After putting up with his rages and supporting him when he was jobless, being dumped was the final humiliation. I felt like a discarded bedroom slipper. And I felt too tired to start over again at thirty-three. Too tired to resume all the bothersome games that went with courtship.

I wanted Doug back and went out one warm autumn night to beg him to come home, even if just for a short while. Desperate for companionship, maniacally searching through the bars, I found him at a tavern in Oromocto. He was beside a big, buxom blond with an exaggerated smile and easy, steady laugh. Doug was laughing, too. He couldn't see me where I was standing in a corner on the other side of the room, but I had a clear view of him.

Doug was apparently oblivious to any hurt he'd caused me—a wrenching pain that rapidly strangled my will to survive. He wasn't aware or he didn't give a damn. I chose a table, alone, in a dark corner in the upper deck of the club and nursed three tall glasses of coffee brandy while studying how they were reacting, how they seemed happy in a way we never were. They appeared to have a special chemistry. I watched them for as long as I could stand it. A half bottle of tequila sat at the bottom of my purse. I'd taken it out of the back of my fridge where it had been stashed for a special occasion. Now I went to the club's bathroom and choked down a big mouthful before wandering outside to hail a cab.

I told the taxi driver to take me to Burton, a small community not far from the Oromocto Reserve, and stumbled out of the cab a few houses before the entrance to the Burton Bridge, which spanned the Saint John River.

There was one thought in my mind as I staggered ahead: *I have to end this*.

Leaning over the bridge railing, I stared down at the cold black water far below. A big full moon hung in the violet sky, and the late-September chill cut right through my clothes.

I climbed onto one of the railings, my toes poking into empty space. Looking around, I noticed the taxi driver hadn't left the spot where he'd dropped me off. I was too bombed and too upset to care.

Swaying back and forth, I considered the fall, imagining it in my stomach, the deadweight descent. I shut my eyes and leaned forward into nausea, teetering, my fingers growing numb. I didn't know if they were still clamped onto the girder or not. Then I heard a voice call out. It belonged to a man. I thought it might be Doug. Opening my eyes, I glanced down behind me. An RCMP vehicle was parked next to the taxi, and an officer approached me, holding out his hand.

"I want to help you," he said. "Let's go somewhere and talk about this."

"You don't understand!" I shouted back. "No one understands."

"If you tell me, I might understand. Why not give me a chance?"

I was cold and I needed to pee. My bladder was aching. The policeman sounded kind. He took a careful step nearer. "Come on down," he said. "I care."

That was enough for me—the words *I care*. They softened me, permeating my desperate self-consumption. A male voice was beckoning to me, telling me he cared. And he sounded as if he really meant it.

Slowly I edged off the railing. The officer grabbed and held me while I cried. For those few minutes I thought I just might be okay. Genuine human warmth in my arms. I sobbed and hugged him tightly. He was a strong man in a uniform. A protector. I never wanted to step beyond that moment of safe enclosure.

Then the officer's partner, who seemed vexed with me, briskly led me to the police car and took me to Oromocto Hospital, where I was admitted for my own protection. I was required to stay for a few days until I managed to convince my doctor I was sane, that I was a happy, well-adjusted person who wasn't going to try to toss her life away again. I knew a lot of the nurses in the hospital. I had been a patient before. Sonya and Jennifer had been born there and later had their tonsils taken out. It was the same hospital where Heather had had her appendix removed. Since there was no psychiatric ward, I was placed on the surgical floor in a private room and sedated. I slept for two days.

After hearing about the suicide attempt, Doug came to see me while I was in the hospital. He told me he'd keep an eye on the kids. When I returned home, he was there, acting glad to see me, but I knew he was still dating the other woman. He seemed to be more interested than ever in partying, and I just didn't have the energy to keep up. My children knew I was on the verge of slipping away from them. No one told them about the bridge incident. They assumed I was in the hospital for my nerves. They knew I cried most of the time. I sat and wept for what seemed like no reason at all, never able to explain why when my children inquired what was the matter.

At thirteen Sonya was more in control of the house than I was. Often she'd write out the grocery list or decide what we would have for dinner. All of the girls were great housekeepers.

Eventually Doug left for good. This time I knew he wouldn't return. Nothing was the same anymore. Nothing.

"You're no fun," Doug told me one day. "At least my new woman can make me laugh."

I started to drink even heavier. I figured I'd find someone else to make me forget Doug, so I frequented bars every chance I got. Still, there was no distraction from the pain. Even when I held it together during work, I felt a black desperation gnaw at me. It was next to impossible to smile and pretend nothing was wrong. I was a different person, a cheap fake.

One night I sat on the ground behind the Oromocto Shopping Centre, watching the river while sipping my bottle of Yukon Jack, a brandy-like liqueur. It was after midnight and the ground felt damp and cold, even though it was an unusually warm November. I'd been to the lounge in the Oromocto Hotel, but I couldn't stand the noise. I wanted to be alone to think, to figure out what to do. I watched the wide, slow-moving river and sipped from the bottle until it was gone. Then, tossing away the empty, I stood there for a long time, alone and still.

I drove home feeling practically sober. Sonya was sleeping over at a friend's house. Heather was in Oromocto Hospital recovering from a kidney infection. I guessed that Jody and Jenny were in bed sleeping. Going to the bathroom, I quietly removed a full bottle of painkillers from the cabinet.

In the kitchen I pulled two bottles of beer from the fridge and carefully shut the door. I felt nothing as I walked down the stairs to my bedroom in the basement. I couldn't even sense my footsteps. I was hollow and filled with grey lead. Jody and Jenny slept in the upstairs bedrooms, so they wouldn't hear me.

I never hesitated.

The label on the plastic bottle said "For the relief of pain," and I was convinced that it was a specific message to me, a sign from God. This was the way to numb the anguish eating away at me. I uncapped the bottle and eagerly swallowed the pills, four and five at a time, helped by gulps of beer. I felt the hard pills push down my throat.

When I was finished, I decided to call Frank and Deana Thomas, who had helped me when I was a teenager. I had no idea why I chose to phone them. I hadn't talked to them in quite a while, but their home number was etched in my brain.

After a few minutes, I felt myself pull away from my body, as if I were floating. I saw colours and thought I could hear people talking. Then I saw a woman. She looked familiar, but I couldn't figure out who she was or why she was smiling. After a while I rose from where I was sitting. I was going, gone... The faces of my children drifted in the air, disembodied.

When I opened my eyes, I was in a white place and felt an ache that I suspected was my body. Hard tubes were stuck in my nostrils and in my arms. I was in a white bed in a white room. It was the closest thing to Heaven, a place of earthly crossover.

I had almost died, I learned from a nurse. But I had been held back, so badly did I need a cleansing, to be gutted of all the bitterness and hurt.

Although I had no recollection of it, I discovered I had actually talked with Frank and Deana Thomas. They had called an ambulance and had saved my life.

Somehow Heather heard I was in a room upstairs from her in the hospital, so she came to see me. I wished I had died when I glimpsed the look in her eyes, a mix of terror and contempt.

How could I have been so stupid? I asked myself. *Why hadn't I thought about the children?*

"I'm sorry, Heather," I said, holding out my arms to her. She put her head on my shoulder and cried while I stroked her shiny black hair. "I won't do anything like that again."

In the next few days I made the same promise to Jody, Sonya, Jennifer, my parents, my friend Beryl, and even the Thomases when they came to see me in the hospital. They were all very kind and gentle. Except Beryl. She was mad at me. She paced back and forth at the end of my bed. "When are you going to stop punishing yourself and all the people who love you?" she demanded. She told me her husband, Tom, refused to visit. "He says he isn't going to watch you destroy yourself any longer."

There was nothing I could say. I was just grateful Beryl cared enough to be there.

When I was released from the hospital, I went home, determined that things would be different. Stan had been talking to my parents. He told them he planned to visit Oromocto, claiming he wanted to speak to me, to make amends. He stayed at my mother and father's place. I agreed to meet him as long as my brothers, Carman and Robin, were present.

"I don't expect anyone to welcome me with open arms," Stan said as we sat at a table in the restaurant at Woolworth's in the Oromocto Mall. "I just want a chance to get to know my kids, if they'll let me."

He had come to clear away the wreckage of his past, to let me know he was sorry.

I listened to what he had to say without comment. I felt relieved to be free of the fear I'd carried for so long. Stan didn't look like much of a threat. His eyes seemed tired and he'd put on weight. He told me he had been diagnosed with diabetes. Perhaps that explained some of his earlier behaviour. The reasons were irrelevant at that point. Still, I felt uneasy being around him and told him it was up to the children whether they wanted to get to know him or not. He stayed at my parents' place for a few days, and the kids, I figured, visited out of curiosity. I never asked them any questions and they never volunteered any information. Then Stan went back to Ontario.

It was the summer of 1985, and Heather was beginning to get into trouble for drinking. I'd been called to pick her up at a couple of school dances the year before because she was drunk and had started a fight with one of her female schoolmates. Now she was sixteen and pretty much leading her own out-of-control life. Once she took off with friends to party and disappeared for a week. When I called the police to look for her, they told me there wasn't much they could do because she was sixteen. I drove around and questioned all her friends, but no one seemed to know where she was. Then Doug came across her at a party in Oromocto. When he found her, he carried her out over his shoulder, kicking and screaming. As he was leaving, he warned everyone that Heather was only sixteen.

"If I catch anyone feeding her booze again," he said, "I'll call the police myself." He delivered Heather to me. She walked in, sat on a chair in the kitchen, and put her head on the table. She looked as if she hadn't slept in days. There were dark circles under her eyes when she glanced up at me.

"Heather, do you realize how worried I was?"

"I'm sorry, Mom."

I went over and sat beside her, putting my arm around her as we cried together.

Jody had decided to hitchhike to Ontario to visit Stan. My budding poetess Jennifer was still devoted to me in spite of my transgressions and was usually close to home and eager to help with chores. Sonya, having decided she didn't like me much anymore since becoming a teenager, hung out most of the time at the Gardners' place across the street. She missed having a father figure and was particularly fond of Robert Gardner.

Gail Gardner was a hospitable woman about five years younger than I was. Her husband, Robert, or Bubba, as most people called him, was a big, rough-spoken man who doted on children and motorcycles. He was the brother of my childhood heartthrob, Norman Gardner. I hadn't seen Norman in years. Gail told me he was living in Prince Edward Island but visited Geary occasionally. His friends called him Stormin' Norman because he drove his Harley Davidson with a fury in all kinds of weather.

One day in June I was sitting on my step having a cigarette, watching my German shepherd, Wizard, playing with a smaller white dog from next door. Often I would sit on that same step and talk to Wizard as if he understood what I was saying. I'd tell him how I wanted my life to change, how I planned to stop drinking and get on with my writing career, and he'd look at me with big black eyes free from condemnation. When I cried, he even licked away my tears.

I treasured my little white house with the green trim, too. I especially loved the large weeping willow that stood about ten feet from my living-room window. There were lilac bushes at the side of the house and ornamental trees around back. I could smell the unique blend of all these exotic scents as I waited to see my childhood boyfriend.

Norman was coming back to Geary for a visit; Gail had told me the previous day. I surveyed the street and gave brief notice to a few passing cars until I heard a distant buzz like a far-off lawn mower. The sound grew nearer and louder. I watched the chrome shining in the sun as a Harley Davidson motorcycle roared into my yard. Norman looked as if he'd just driven off a poster for *Easy Rider*. The dark, slim boy was now a burly man weighing at least

250 pounds.

"How ya doing?" He grinned as he stepped off his bike. His smile was the same—perfect white teeth set against brown skin. He was darker than any Native I knew, but I'd never heard him talk about aboriginal ancestry. He was wearing heavy leathers, pants and jacket, and a full-faced helmet. The patch on his jacket said CHARLOTTETOWN HARLEY CLUB.

"Oh, my God, Norman!" I jumped up and ran over to greet him.

He ambled toward me and gave me a big hug. By this time Jennifer, hearing the commotion, had joined us. Heather and Jody were both away and Sonya was listening to music downstairs.

"This is my baby, Jen," I told Norman. Jennifer had been inside cleaning the bathroom for me. She still had the rag in her hands.

"What a pretty baby," he said with a hardy laugh. "Come to Papa." He reached out and wrapped his big arms around Jennifer, who gave him an embarrassed smile.

"You've changed a bit," he said, checking me over. "What've you been doing with yourself?"

"Not much."

"No?"

I smiled. "Come in and have a beer." I'd been restricting my drinking to weekends again. Fortunately it was a promising Saturday morning. Norman followed me and Jen in through the doorway.

"You look a lot like your mother used to," Norman said to Jen as we entered the kitchen.

"I do?"

"Would I kid you?" Norman laughed again and ruffled Jennifer's hair as he lowered himself into a kitchen chair.

I could tell by the way she smiled that Jennifer was pleased. Most of the time people said Heather and I looked like sisters.

When Sonya came up from downstairs, she was a bit standoffish, not unusual for her. She liked to take her time getting to know people.

I called Gail and told her Norman had arrived. Within minutes she and Bubba were at my door.

A half hour later we were all on our way to the tavern for steak and eggs. Both Sonya and Jennifer had jobs baby-sitting for the night, so I kissed them goodbye and said I'd be over at Gail's later if they needed to contact me.

When we finished at the tavern and went back to Bubba's, there was already a number of people gathered there, prepared for a party in honour of Norman's homecoming. The night went relatively smoothly. There were no fights and I didn't get depressed. Norman was at my side all night, and I felt happy and secure.

Although Norman kept in touch by telephone and I saw him whenever he came to visit, I soon found out he lived with a woman on Prince Edward Island. So my anticipation of a rekindled romance was short-lived.

BLACKOUT

On Easter Sunday morning, 1986, I was sitting on the floor of my bedroom in Geary listening to hymns on the radio. The dirty brown carpet was littered with discarded sweaters, jeans, and socks that hadn't managed to find their way to the clothes hamper in the bathroom. Even though I was mostly in my own broken world, I still wrote occasionally for local newspapers and had managed to hold down a receptionist position at Process Technology in Oromocto for more than a year. But I wasn't sure how much longer I could hide my problems. Bills were mounting and I knew the house would be gone soon if I couldn't find a way to meet my delinquent mortgage payments. I was too exhausted, too defeated, to care. I couldn't cry anymore. My half-empty bottle of Asti Spumante wouldn't kill the dreadful pain in my chest and I didn't want to face the accusing looks of my children when they woke.

Heather had moved out. She'd decided to do something about

her drinking and started going to Alcoholics Anonymous meetings where she met an older man named Vince who wanted to assist her. She was living on Grand Manan Island, working part-time at a store and living with Vince and his wife and family, who were helping her cope with being sober. The rest of the kids were home, still in school, and doing okay.

As if operating on automatic pilot, I attended meetings during the week to gather information for news reports that had to be submitted the next day. Whenever there was a special event at the school or interviews with teachers, I was there. Most people had no idea about the double life I was leading. On days when I didn't drink, I thought maybe I'd simply imagined the other woman who couldn't handle her life.

Alone, the demons from my past and present haunted me. I felt so much guilt for all the mistakes I'd made. I'd let down my kids, my parents, and the God I once professed to love. It was a heavy load to carry. And I'd started having terrible dreams that brought the faces of my abusers back to me so vividly I dreaded going to sleep. The memories were so intense that I couldn't go for long without medication of some kind. The weight of emptiness that pressed at me from inside and out was heavier than anything tangible.

As I listened on the radio to "What a Friend We Have in Jesus," my grandfather's favourite hymn, the same grandfather who had betrayed my childhood trust in him, I thought God might take mercy on me and help me in some way. Sitting in a clump on the floor, my hair unwashed, my clothes dirty, I bowed my head and tried to pray. As I shut my eyes tightly, I was plagued by visions of my life as it had been the past three years. I saw endless rounds of parties and men I didn't respect but whose company I sought so I wouldn't be alone. I didn't know who I was anymore. I loved my kids so much, but knew I was damaging them. I felt powerless and lost.

Instead of the face of a saviour I saw the dark sad eyes of my children.

I took another drink and crawled into bed for some useless sleep. It would be another year before God finally answered my prayer and showed me mercy and deliverance.

On New Year's Eve 1987 I stayed at home and didn't drink. Alone, I wrote out twenty-two resolutions for the year ahead that I hoped would change things for me and my children. I was only working part-time now for the newspaper since I'd been laid off from my job at Process Technology. *Go to university* was number five on my list of resolutions. *Control drinking* was right at the top.

The night of April 4, 1987, started out like any other evening on the town. I was at a country bar in Fredericton with Stormin' Norman and some of his friends. Norman was in town for a week and eager to party. I was eager, too, even though I was virtually wiped out from a busy day at work. The handful of black beauty uppers Norman gave me soon fixed that. When we arrived at the Country Corral, I was flying high. I was raring to dance as soon as we entered. I tried to drag Norman onto the dance floor, but he pushed me gently but firmly toward the shooters bar. After the first whiskey shooter, which I drank in one gulp, coughing when it hit its mark, I forgot about the dance floor, too. Norman was paying so I kept drinking. After five or six shooters, I couldn't remember a thing.

Four days of drinking and popping amphetamines followed, days that came back to me only in snatches—shooters at the Country Corral, chugging beer with bikers at an outdoor party, screaming at some big, ugly bouncer, stealing a bottle from some-one's fridge, being thrown inside a black van, clothing torn, bloody feet shoeless, running, running, so much blackness and another naked stranger next to me. I honestly couldn't fit the pieces of this bizarre puzzle together. I'd been blacked out most of the time.

If it hadn't been for Norman's intervention, someone probably would have killed me. I heard I'd made quite a few enemies: women ticked off at me for flirting with their boyfriends, a bouncer I'd badmouthed when he refused to serve me more booze. I honestly couldn't remember, no matter how hard I tried, and that terrified me. Norman was the one who filled in the details. As he told me what had happened, it was as if he were describing a movie he'd seen, one I hadn't even heard of.

I could have killed someone and had no recollection. That thought distressed me more than the excruciating pain in my belly as I went into withdrawal from the booze and pills.

Finally I surrendered. I let go of everything and emptied myself, begging God to help me. This time He answered at once.

THE WILDERNESS CLINIC

I didn't check into an institution for detoxification. My institution became the wilderness. I spent most of my time in the woods near a favourite stream, the Brizzley, about four miles west of my house on Branch Road. I sat by the stream and watched it flow. So much life drifted by in the currents: tiny abundant forms of life that existed without knowledge of human complications and corruption.

Walking out behind our house to Fox Hill, I sat there for hours on a stump, staring at the thick, sturdy pines, listening to the soothing whisper of the wind. The scent of the woods was medicinal, lush with the aroma of cure.

I had always equated the woods, brooks, and wildflowers with peace. I had learned that from my father very early in life. When I was young, I often watched him leave for a night in the forest, just to get away from the pressures of daily living.

Once I asked him, "Aren't you afraid to stay there all by yourself, Dad?"

"There's nothing to fear in the woods," he replied. "It's the rest of the world you have to watch."

Sometimes I'd lie full-length against the ground and let my tears run onto the grass. I pretended the earth was hugging me and listening to my confused thoughts, untangling them, exposing them to the healing warmth of the sun that beamed high above the enclosing treetops.

I talked to all the life around me, and it felt perfectly right and exact, this acceptance of growth, of all natural living things.

The sight of an ant carrying a heavy load of food home to his children could keep me transfixed. Such pristine visions brought me near to happiness. In this insect paradise I was no one but myself observing things as they were meant to be.

The first few weeks I spent sober were surprisingly peaceful. I had been a binge drinker—mostly weekends—so I had championed getting through the weekdays by keeping busy. Now I focused on doing the same on weekends and steered clear of old drinking buddies and hangouts. I had more time on my hands because I'd decided to leave my writing job. I was too confused to write about events that held little importance to me now.

My hours in the woods allowed me to think freely, cleanly. In all that splendour I realized how lucky I truly was. *I'm still young and healthy. I have four beautiful children who should hate me, but they love me. They need me. I'm not alone. How could I be so stupid? I can do this. It's not too late.*

A few days after I'd quit drinking I called Heather in Grand Manan. "I've got some good news for you, Heather," I said, smiling into the phone. "I've quit drinking."

"I knew you could do it, Mom," she said. She, too, was trying to kick alcohol and drugs. Sadly she'd had to leave her own screwed-up home to do it. "I've been dry over two months myself."

"I'm so sorry for all the times I wasn't there for you, Heather." I trembled as I spoke, my voice wet with tears. "I was such a bad mother."

Heather's tone was warm and reassuring. "You weren't a bad mother. You tried, Mom. You did the best you could."

"Can you forgive me?"

"You have to learn to forgive yourself."

I couldn't believe how grown-up she sounded. Had I ever been that adultlike at seventeen?

A couple of weeks later Heather came home. Vince, the AA member Heather was staying with, dropped her off on the way to Fredericton where he had business. It was a tearful reunion for everyone, but it held special significance for me and Heather. Our mother-daughter bond had grown even stronger. We were sisters in recovery.

That night we ordered Chinese food from the Chopsticks Restaurant in Oromocto and sat around reminiscing about good times, and even some of the bad ones that we could laugh at now. Like the time a bunch of my drunken friends had set out to steal me a goat because I'd complained about not having a lawn mower. Or the morning I'd awakened to find a horse hitched to the weeping willow in my front yard. We'd had a party and I'd told one of the guys I'd love to have a horse, so he'd found one somewhere down the road. When we discovered him, the friend was lying on the front lawn, passed out, like a tired cat beside its prize mouse.

My children helped me regain my sense of humour—a valuable weapon in the battle to recover—and they helped me see all the times I'd been a fit mother, like the night I stayed up all night to make a costume for Sonya's play because she'd forgotten to give me the notice two weeks before, or the many other nights I'd baked cookies or made fudge for school events.

Heather asked if I'd tried any twelve-step meetings. I told her I'd checked out some Alcoholics Anonymous discussion meetings in Oromocto. When she asked me to accompany her to a speaker's meeting in Fredericton, I was troubled by the idea, but I agreed to go.

Walking to the old Catholic church on Westmoreland Street in Fredericton where the AA meetings were held, Heather reached over and took my hand. I felt my knees weaken, tears glazing my eyes. She knew I was nervous, and I think I might have backed out altogether if it hadn't been for the proud smile she'd given me when, earlier that day, she had called a friend from AA to announce that her mother was coming to her first speaker's meeting.

As I entered the meeting room in the basement of the old church, I had no idea what to expect. I was afraid I would face a room full of old men in oversize trench coats leering at me when I turned the corner. But what I saw were men and women of all ages, nicely dressed, most of them laughing and talking to one another. I thought I was in the wrong place. When one of the men, a short little Frenchman named Mark, rushed up to shake my hand, I almost hit him with my purse. Heather, catching my reaction, laughed and gave the grinning man a hug.

"This is my mother," she told him.

"She looks just like you, Heather." Mark's smile widened as he offered his hand again hesitantly. This time I accepted it.

As I stood there, people rose from their seats and approached me, friendly hands reaching out to shake mine and pat me on the back. I recognized Lois, a woman I'd met in Oromocto while working at the mall. They all understood what I had been through. They knew because they had been there themselves. There were so many people wanting to shake my hand and offer me kind words that I thought I'd just won the lottery. And, as it turned out, that wasn't too far from the truth.

MY FIRST YEAR IN RECOVERY

I made genuine friends in AA. They were men and women of all ages, people who would go out of their way to ensure I felt accepted. People who made a point of caring for my well-being.

The twelve-step recovery program taught me how to live with the reality of my condition. Everyone assured me the first step was the one I had to be utterly convinced of if I wanted a new life: *We admitted that we were powerless over alcohol and our lives had become unmanageable.* I had no problem whatsoever making that admission. And I'd already accepted steps two and three: *Came to believe that a power greater than ourselves could restore us to sanity* and *Made a decision to turn our will and our lives over to the care of God as we understood him.* I firmly believed that alcoholism was a soul sickness and I was certain no human power could relieve it.

My childhood reverence for God once again filled my heart. But the reverence had taken on a new light. I came to know God as a friend who was always with me and who loved me in spite of my trespasses. That was a far cry from the threatening, unforgiving judge who had stood ready to punish my every wrong thought when I was a child.

Of course, life never stopped happening. Sometimes it was pretty awful. Eric, a guy I'd been dating off and on before I quit drinking, wasn't ready to lose a drinking partner. I'd broken off the relationship for good when I realized he had no intention of leaving his bottle behind just because I had decided to quit.

Eric retaliated by showing up at my house and scaring me to death. "What're you doing?" he screamed the minute he walked through the front door.

I was folding clothes in the kitchen a few feet away, and was shocked to see him. "That's no way to say hello," I said with a slight chuckle. I wanted to humour him. He'd never hurt me before, but I'd heard he'd beaten up a former girlfriend when she tried to leave him.

"I wanna talk to you," he said, coming into the kitchen with the tip of his index finger fixed on my face.

I didn't want the kids to get upset. Jody and his friend, Linden, were in another room watching tv. The girls were downstairs cleaning their rooms, ghetto blaster blaring some raunchy tune by Nazareth.

"Calm down and let's talk," I told Eric as I gestured him to follow me to the only private room in the house—my bedroom.

Once inside, Eric grabbed my arm and threw me onto the bed.

"Please, Eric," I pleaded as I landed on the mattress. I muffled my cries, speaking in a whisper. "You don't want to do this. I do care for you. It's the drinking. I can't take anymore."

"Like hell it is," he snarled, staring down at me. "You've got another man." He knelt on the bed and pinned my sides with his knees, his face coming close. I could smell the stale booze on his breath and saw the menace in his eyes as he leaned even closer and tightly grabbed my arm, forcing his lips against mine. Then his hand was struggling with the waistband of my jeans. I knew it was useless to resist, so I lay there, quietly pretending, the way I had done so many times before when I was younger. I pretended I was somewhere else.

A few days later, my dog, Wizard, went missing. I never found the dog, but reliable sources, men who drank with Eric, told me he finished his revenge by shooting Wizard in a field down the road from my house.

Again I had been humiliated and devastated, driven to the brink of negating myself in a bottle. To keep strong I thought of my children and my friends. Lois, an AA member I'd known for years, welcomed me into her home until I felt comfortable enough to return to Geary where my children held the fort in my absence. Lois convinced me it was time I cared enough about myself to stand up to my abusers, no matter how much I might feel sorry for Eric. So I pressed charges and Eric went to jail. We didn't even have to go to court. Eric pleaded guilty to common assault instead of sexual assault, and I agreed to the reduction in charge so I wouldn't have to suffer through a trial.

No sooner had I finished dealing with the court and Eric than another crisis hit me. I arrived home from work one day to find a fire truck parked in my yard and neighbours running around with buckets of water. The little white-and-green bungalow that had finally become a real home was burning. I saw Jennifer standing there crying and ran up to her. "What happened?" I asked.

"I smelled smoke," she said. Being so frightened by the first fire she was in, just two years earlier, she'd run out of the house immediately and phoned the fire department from next door. "The smoke was coming from your bedroom, Mom. It must've started there."

As I watched the smoke and flames, my heart ached horribly. I recalled the previous fire that had brought me to Geary to live. Fire had driven us here. *Surely it wasn't time to move on yet?*

As it turned out, there wasn't a great deal of damage to the structure, mostly smoke and water. No one was hurt, and this time I was insured. However, as with the first fire that had destroyed my apartment, no explanation was found for this near disaster.

"I have my own theory about the cause," I told the firefighter.

"What's that?"

"I think it's a dark spirit following me."

"A ghost?"

"Something like that." I thought it might have to do with the occult practices I'd been involved in.

I handled the event with relative calm. Instead of despairing over what had happened, I looked upon the incident with gratitude because we still had our home and no harm had come to my family.

At AA meetings I often heard people talk about how the program taught the importance of accepting life on life's terms. They said it was a lesson that usually took a long time to learn. We were always ready to blame someone and to punish them and ourselves by drinking.

Eventually Heather slipped back into a cycle of self-abuse. She telephoned me one night at about one in the morning from a phone booth in Fredericton. I could tell by her voice that she was drunk and angry. She'd had a fight with another girl over some guy they'd both been eyeing.

"Come pick me up?"

"It's late, Heather. I have to work tomorrow."

"Please, Mom," she begged, vaguely frightened. "I can't stay here. That girl's after me."

I thought about leaving her there to deal with her own life, but I couldn't say no. "Okay, okay, I'll be there in a half hour." I told her to walk to a coffee shop near where she was and stay put.

She didn't say much in the dark car after I picked her up and neither did I. I assumed she'd be staying with me, if only for a few days.

Heather's addiction now went beyond alcohol. That same year she became hooked on cocaine. Standing by her hospital bed as she struggled for life after swallowing a bottle of prescription sleeping pills, I felt gut-wrenching pangs of guilt. *If only I had shown her a better way to cope.* I knew it was useless to look back with regret. I was learning this creed myself and had to stick with it. *Yesterday was gone. It can't be changed.* I heard it over and over in the AA meetings, and so had Heather. *We only have today. One day at a time.*

I studied Heather in her hospital bed. She was extremely pale, but otherwise might have been sleeping. She looked so peaceful. But the IV attached to her arm, pumping saline into her dehydrated body, reminded me she wasn't out of the woods yet. *One day at a time*, I told myself. *One day...*

When Heather left the hospital, she agreed to check into the Ridgewood Rehabilitation Centre in Saint John. So we all breathed a touch easier for a while.

I knew little about the dynamics of having an adult male friend, so I became suspicious of all men. To me men were abusers who only took advantage of women. In their brutish, greedy lifetimes they wanted nothing more than to use up as many women as possible and discard them.

Ironically it was a man with a reputation for the ladies who actually became one of my best friends and played an integral part in helping me learn about forgiveness.

I didn't like Miles when I first met him because he often made sarcastic jokes about other people. He had been sober four or five years more than I, and his wife at that time was active in Al-Anon, the sister program for relatives and friends of alcoholics. I'd met them both at one of our Round-Ups in Fredericton, a convention attended by hundreds of recovering men and women. The meetings, held around the clock for two days, featured guest speakers with inspiring messages of hope and perseverance. All of this offered compelling fortification, a gush of honest and positive energy to soothe the gash in my soul.

Dances and banquets were held in conjunction with the Round-Ups. The one in Fredericton even included a Friday-night hootenanny where musicians and singers would entertain the audience. It was during one of these social events that I met Miles. He was a very thin, well-dressed man with a mischievous glint in his eyes. Miles was playing in the backup band at the hootenanny, and I saw at once that he was a capable rhythm guitarist and fiddle player. Miles backed me up the first time I sang in front of an AA audience. I stood onstage singing "It Wasn't God Who Made Honky Tonk Angels," an old Kitty Wells tune from my childhood days. When I was done, Miles whispered, "Good job," as I walked past him off the stage. Later, in a designated smoking room, he said, "You've got a great voice for country. You sounded just like Kitty."

After that night, I often saw Miles at AA meetings, but it wasn't until a few months later when I bumped into him at a local coffee shop that I spoke to him in any detail. This was the place where many people who attended AA in Fredericton would meet on a daily basis to guzzle vast quantities of caffeine, working to quench any thirst for stronger refreshments. During my first two years of recovery, I was a regular patron, and I could drink with the best of them, sometimes fifteen cups a day that would leave me jerking in a fit of nerves at the slightest unexpected provocation. Of course, being a nervous basket case was better than going back to my old ways. I'd asked to be laid off from my job at the grocery store shortly after it changed hands, and I'd stopped writing for the newspaper so I could better concentrate on my recovery. Being on unemployment insurance gave me lots of free time to socialize and try to figure myself out.

"Hey, Miles, over here," I now said, smiling and waving when I saw him come through the door. There weren't any other AA members in the shop, and I was keen to talk to someone about my latest "spiritual awakening."

Miles nodded, grabbed a coffee, and joined me.

"How ya doing?" he asked, sitting down. As usual he was well dressed, sporting beige pants and a dark brown shirt that accented his tan.

"Just great. I'm getting ready to do my fourth and fifth step." I took a slow sip of coffee. "I know it's time." These two steps dealt specifically with looking clearly at the mistakes of the past and why they had happened. Taking responsibility for your actions in front of another person was an important part of emotional healing.

"You don't need to worry about that," Miles retorted with a scowl. He glanced around the shop, dismissing my comment. "Just go to the meetings."

"Didn't you do them?"

"Why should I?" he asked, staring straight at me and grinning. "I've been around a lot longer than you and I'm sober, aren't I?"

I felt the pink cloud I'd been riding give way beneath me. *You arrogant bastard*, I thought, but I didn't say a word. I just sat there and listened to Miles rattle on about the popularity of the most recent hootenanny.

"A lot of people commented on my guitar playing," he said. "They liked my singing, but I didn't think I'd done a good job. My throat was bothering me."

I wasn't deep enough into recovery to read the obvious signs, that his pompousness was the manifestation of deep-rooted insecurity. I just thought, *Time you did some of those steps yourself, my friend.*

"It was a pretty good time," I said, finishing my coffee. "I guess I'd better get home."

"Yeah, me, too."

We both stood, headed for the door, and climbed into our separate vehicles. I watched him drive off. He had darkened my mood, snatched the wind from my sails. *Next time,* I assured myself, *I'll talk to a woman.*

I didn't speak to Miles much over the next year. Then I began dating another musician. This one had a voice like Merle Haggard's. His name was Bill, and he and Miles always seemed to be in competition. Soon after I started a new one-year-contract job with Positive Heart Living, an organization that promoted balanced lifestyles. I worked with two other women to develop a manual about the risk factors associated with heart disease. We would also produce a short video to accompany it, and I was looking forward to venturing into scriptwriting. A local company, Atlantic Media Works, trained the three of us. The prospect of learning new skills was exhilarating. I'd never even held a video camera in my hands before.

Horror stories abound in the rooms of AA. Stories about the messes people have made of their lives due to years of destructive alcoholism. There were men who had beaten and killed their wives or children while in an alcoholic blackout, women who woke up in strange hotel rooms stripped of their dignity and their cash after selling themselves for a few extra drinks, upright employees who turned to embezzlement to finance their out-of-control habits, and good Christian girls who once hoped for a chaste life but grew to wish for a quick death.

People from all walks of life, backgrounds, ages, religions, and races attended AA. They told their harrowing stories, then explained how their lives had been turned around since quitting the bottle.

I could sit for hours and listen to Larry D. talk about how he'd found a higher power after coming to AA. Larry was a counsellor in private practice who once spent much of his time in jail. Marg W., a charming older lady, made me break down and cry practically every time she spoke. She disclosed how her drinking had damaged her daughter and her relationship with her first husband. As usual, when hearing such stories, I harkened back to my own children and the ruin that had been exacted. Marg had sobered up the same year I was born and was still attending the meetings. And Ray G., an attractive Maliseet entertainer, could put a crowd in stitches when he spoke of his recovery. He'd turn the most tragic stories into jokes, which helped me believe that maybe someday I, too, would be able to laugh at my past misadventures.

"There's great healing in laughter," he told me one day. There was nothing truer. You either learned to laugh or you crumbled into dust.

These people were so different, so individual, yet there was a camaraderie, a sense of union unsurpassed by any other organization I had encountered. That feeling of oneness, of bonding by being marred in the same way, replaced the barroom fellowship that drinkers often mistook for understanding and acceptance.

AA taught me that as soon as I admitted defeat, as soon as I had been broken, I became a winner. I listened intently to the members' messages of hope—Mary S., who won back the respect of her family who once hated her; Bill W., who had dropped out of school in grade eight and went on to graduate from university; Jen R., who had attempted suicide five times and was now a counsellor at a detox centre; Bob P., who had learned to read and was off the streets and living in his own apartment for the first time in ten years. Reunited families, new self-respect, healed relationships, happiness, and freedom from the compulsion to drink as a coping mechanism gave me a foundation to face life without the need to be perpetually numbed.

During that first year of sobriety, I was so euphoric I couldn't believe it was actually me living inside my skin. I felt I was seeing the world for the first time. The word *rebirth* surfaced in my mind, however tainted it had become by crazy images. That was precisely what it was like—a rebirth, a freshness that lent the world a fault-less, sparkling quality.

I continued to date Bill. During the day, he drove a delivery truck, but most nights he attended AA meetings. He was a dynamic entertainer and his singing won him many admirers. The first time I heard him perform a Merle Haggard song at an AA dance he snagged my interest. He was a small man with thick, bushy brown hair tinged grey. Even his eyebrows were bushy, and when he smiled his eyes lit up. He was incredibly charming; women often sought him out to ask if he had time to talk after a meeting. It was obvious he was fond of the attention. He lived to socialize and was popular with all kinds of people.

Ours was no great love affair, but a pleasant relationship all the same. Bill escorted me to AA conventions and meetings throughout the Maritimes, places I'd never had the chance to visit on my own. We spent hours talking to newfound friends, extending the net-work of support that I've maintained to this day.

Although we were seldom physically intimate as a couple, we were a solace to each other, and I learned that someone might want me for more than just my body. There was real worth within this skin of mine that someone might actually find interesting.

Trying to help Heather stay in recovery was a full-time job. I took her "slips" personally. She was living at home, but her periods of sobriety were sporadic. I wasn't that surprised when she told me she would be having a baby that November. Heather had been sexually active since she was fourteen. The father of her baby—a young man of Chinese-Canadian parentage—was a drummer in a local rock band.

I'd just returned from an AA meeting in Fredericton and was sitting at the kitchen table making a list of bills that needed to be paid the following day when Heather came in and pulled up a chair beside me. "I got something to tell you, Mom. Now don't get mad."

I looked up at her and saw the truth in her eyes. "You're pregnant."

"How'd you know?" she asked incredulously.

I shrugged. "I figure it had to happen sooner or later."

"You're not mad?"

"Why should I be?" Actually I wasn't angry at all. "It's not like you killed someone."

Heather appeared relieved as I took her hand and asked about the father. "It's Minto, isn't it?"

"He only wants to stay friends." Heather shrugged and didn't seem that upset, so I remained calm.

"That's okay," I said, stroking her long black hair. Inside, I felt dismal. I wished my mixed-up child could experience a little of what I was feeling before she had to cope with a baby on her own. Yet I was determined not to preach, so I simply said, "I'll be here for you," and hugged her.

Heather held on tightly, and I rocked her in my arms until she let go. "Thanks, Mom."

The discovery of Heather's pregnancy prompted me to talk with Sonya. She and her boyfriend, Harry, had been going together for a few months and he often stayed at my house, sleeping in Jody's room or on our couch. I thought it was my duty to remind them about contraceptives. It was time for a mother-daughter talk.

One morning, while the rest of my children were still sleeping, I cornered Sonya as she came out of the bathroom.

"I've got some coffee on in the kitchen. Come have a cup with me."

Sonya enjoyed coffee as much as I did. She poured herself a large cup, added two spoons of sugar and some milk, and sat across from me at the table.

Without any preliminaries I started. "You know, Sonya, that a person has to be careful these days," I broached the topic carefully, trying not to provoke her. She might be laughing and talking one minute, but if someone said something she didn't like, she'd clam up and no one could coax her to speak.

"What are you talking about, Mom?" Her forehead crinkled above her narrowed brown eyes. I realized she'd been pretty cranky for the past few days. Maybe I was picking the wrong time to talk about this.

"I just want to talk."

Sonya looked at me, waiting.

She's such a beautiful child, I thought.

"Are you and Harry using anything—you know—for protection? You're both young. You don't want to make any mistakes."

Sonya stared at me as if I were from another planet. It was almost a minute before she said, "You're too late, Mom."

All I could say was "Oh."

After the shock of the two pregnancies wore off, I gradually became excited about being a grandmother. I would only be thirty-six when my first grandchild was born. People would stop me and admire my grandchild and say, "My, but you're so young to be a grandmother." I figured I'd enjoy the babies on my terms, play with the children for a while, then hand them back to their mothers. *Sweet revenge,* I thought, chuckling. *You can have the diapers and the late-night feedings. I've done my time.*

Heather decided she wanted to live on her own. She called the welfare office and was told it would offer assistance. She found a small apartment on Union Street on Fredericton's north side. I was comforted to learn that her next-door neighbour, Sue, was an AA member.

SONYA'S CRASH

One day in the summer of 1988, on my way to the Oromocto Mall, I noticed a crowd at the entrance of a road about a quarter mile from my house. *Must be a fight or something,* I thought as I slowed to catch a glimpse. I recognized the teenagers on the fringe of the crowd. They were friends of my son. I stopped the car on the edge of the highway that led into Lavina Road. Like most people, I was curious to see what tragedy had occurred. Plus my writer's brain was interested in all the gory details. One of the teenage boys saw me sitting behind the windshield and came running up, shouting something and pointing. It took a few moments for the words to register. He was saying "Sonya, Sonya's hurt!"

Later, I couldn't remember leaving the car or even turning it off. Before I knew it I was on my feet, the crowd was parting, and I stepped ahead to witness a twisted motorcycle and a body lying on the rough pavement. The body, which wasn't moving, wore a full-face helmet that had shattered when it hit the pavement. *That can't be Sonya,* I thought. *She never keeps still.*

Confused, I searched around for Harry, but he was nowhere in sight. I ran to where my seemingly lifeless daughter was lying.

As I knelt, I discovered blood soaking one leg of Sonya's jeans. It was slowly seeping across the ground, the only thing moving.

Finally I snapped out of my stupor. "She's pregnant," I told the white uniform beside me.

Then I was inside the ambulance, trying to keep my eyes off the white bandage on Sonya's left leg that was quickly changing red to match her sweatshirt.

Why do you always insist on being colour-coordinated? This insane question tripped through my brain. Sonya hadn't regained consciousness, never once opened her eyes to indicate she could hear my whisper, "I love you. Hang in there, baby." But her pale pink lips, framed by the oxygen mask, parted once to expel a small plastic gob of blue bubble gum. *It's a sign,* I assured myself as I grabbed the attendant. "You could have choked on that," I babbled to Sonya. "How many times have I told you bubble gum's no good for you?"

The ambulance ride to Oromocto Hospital should have taken ten minutes yet seemed to last hours. Crisis disabled time as we sped through daylight in the screeching white vehicle. I prayed that this wasn't the end, that Sonya and her baby would survive.

When Sonya was wheeled into the emergency room, my knees gave out as I surrendered the stretcher I had been clutching. Turning toward the nearest seat, I crumpled into it and implored God for strength to be there for Sonya. For once I hadn't wished for the unfeeling effects of alcohol or downers during a major crisis. I prayed and experienced a fortifying serenity. There, in that hospital, in the middle of this horrific disaster, I felt healthier than I had in years.

"Eve, are you all right? What's going on?"

I opened my eyes to see the concerned face of Ted H., one of my AA sponsors. He was sitting in a wheelchair with a homemade bandage wrapped around one of his legs.

"Oh, my God, Ted, what happened to you?"

He chuckled. "I got into an argument with my axe and I guess it won. What about you? What's going on?"

"Sonya, my daughter, has been in an accident. She's pregnant and unconscious." Hearing the bold truth spoken aloud, I broke down and sobbed.

"She'll be okay," Ted vowed. "The Big Boss is watching out for you." He barely had time to wink before his wife and the nurse whisked him into a room to be stitched up.

I drifted back down the hall to the room where the ambulance attendant had taken my daughter. The doctor had asked me to wait outside until a nurse came for me, but I desperately needed to know what was going on. As I entered the room, I had an odd feeling that Sonya and the baby would be okay, even before the doctor said anything. Sonya, I was told, had a concussion and would have to be observed for twenty-four hours. Already she had started to wake up and complain of a headache.

"The skin on the top of her left leg was scraped off," the doctor informed me. "It has to be treated like a burn. She'll probably need skin grafts."

There was a large cut just above her knee that would require forty stitches and leave a scar. All things considered, she would be fine. As far as the doctor could tell, before an ultrasound, the baby was unharmed.

I considered the baby and Sonya's boyfriend, Harry, then turned to see him hobble into the room. He had a sprained ankle and a few bruises. Other than that he was well, yet worried sick about Sonya and the baby. There were tears in his eyes as he grabbed her hand.

When Sonya opened her eyes and said, "Get me out of here, I want a cigarette," we all burst into laughter.

From that day forward I knew there would never be another reason to drink. My faith in God flourished. Even in hardship I could become peaceful as long as I turned fervently to prayer. I didn't have to visit church and get down on my knees. God heard me wherever I was. All I had to do was ask for help and the inner turmoil would shift to a warm, sleepy feeling that reminded me of the times my grandmother sang me to sleep or covered me with a thick pink quilt.

I dealt with life one day at a time, sometimes one hour at a time, one minute at a time, and convinced myself I was never alone.

In September 1987, when my youngest daughter, Jennifer, missed two periods, none of us even suspected she might be pregnant. She was only fifteen and had never been out with boys as far as we knew. I took her to the doctor to have her checked. With Heather's history of bleeding, I wasn't taking any chances. When the doctor called to inform me of the results of Jennifer's examination, I wasn't there, but Sonya, now back at home and almost fully recovered from her accident, pretended she was me and found out for herself. She then contacted me at work to break the news. Shortly thereafter, Jennifer called and asked me to come and get her at school. The doctor had gotten in touch with her there. I told her I already knew.

Jennifer was my baby. She still had dolls displayed in her room and she was determined to be a marine biologist. I didn't think she even liked boys.

I raced to Oromocto High School. The sight of Jennifer, with a book bag slung over one shoulder, head drooping, broke my heart.

As she settled into the front seat, she looked at me and struggled to speak, but her mouth merely hung open. Tears filled her eyes. "What are we going to do, Mom?" she finally asked.

She was so scared, so young and unprepared for motherhood. I felt rage and swore to kill the boy responsible for getting her pregnant. Taking a deep breath, I forced myself to concentrate. *God, help me say the right thing*, I silently prayed as I held her hand. "Right now we're going to Heather's. It'll be easier to talk."

"I'm scared, Mom," she said, squeezing my hand.

"Don't you worry, baby. We'll figure something out."

My baby was going to have a baby, I thought. It just wasn't fair, but I was determined she would never feel alone. I tried to stay calm and be strong for her.

Heather had fixed her apartment up nicely. There were flowers in vases everywhere and the place was spotless. She certainly had my mother's talent for keeping house.

"I know a girl who stayed in school and had her baby," Heather pointed out. "Welfare helped with her expenses."

Heather even joked that all three sisters were pregnant at the same time. She was very affectionate toward Jennifer, rubbing her back, offering to make her a cup of tea and suggesting she could share some baby clothes. By the time we left, Jennifer seemed to feel better.

Later that night, alone in my bedroom, I let the tears seep into my pillow, stopping only to blow my nose as quietly as I could manage. I didn't want Jennifer to feel any worse.

Sonya and Jody were surprised and angry. Jody threatened to have a talk with the guy who had gotten Jennifer pregnant. Sonya's boyfriend, Harry, said he'd go with him.

"I want to go, too," Sonya piped in. "And I'll be doing a lot more than talking."

It took a great deal of convincing on my part to stop them from turning into a vigilante crew.

Jennifer's grandparents were also shocked. My mother broke down on the phone when I told her. "The poor little thing," she said between sobs.

Apparently an older boy had taken advantage of Jennifer's childish crush on him. It was the only time I ever considered that an abortion might be a solution, might reinstate her innocence, her life. But deep down I knew an abortion could harm her, as well. There would always be the guilt of terminating a life.

Even so, it was me who hesitantly brought up the subject. It remained an option that had to be weighed and considered. "You know there are other choices, Jen," I told her the morning after we received the news.

"What d'ya mean?" she asked. Jennifer had stayed home from school that day and I had called in sick at work so we could deal with the situation. It was early, about 7:00 a.m. Jody, Harry, and Sonya were still in bed.

"Well, there's always adoption and maybe even abortion. You're young and I think the doctor might—"

"No way!" she cried, putting her hand up to signal she was dead-set against it. "No abortion."

I was actually relieved to hear she felt that way. I didn't believe in abortion, either, but I couldn't picture her raising a child at her age while she finished school. I knew I'd be little help. Getting my own life on track and coping with day-to-day events drained most of my energy. I couldn't picture raising another child. I needed time to heal, and I was honest about that.

My contract at Positive Heart Living was nearing an end. I had to concentrate on finding another position.

"I wish I could help more, Jen," I told her one evening before bed. "But I need to work and I need my AA meetings. I won't have time to baby-sit."

"It'll be okay, Mom. I have faith."

"You're such a sweet girl," I said, kissing her cheek. I was relieved she was no longer afraid and I knew that her siblings had much to do with that.

When a Christian couple, Dwight and Debbie Palmer, who attended my parents' church and lived down the road from us, heard about Jennifer's pregnancy, they immediately offered help. The Palmers were friends of my mom and dad, and were also registered foster parents. Debbie called Jennifer to come visit and told her they'd heard through my mother that Jennifer would need someone to care for the baby while she attended school throughout the week. They were willing to do that. The provincial government had a program at the time to assist young mothers in this exact situation. Health and Community Services would send Jennifer a monthly allowance while she lived at home. It would also pay for her baby-sitter and any medical expenses.

That seemed like a fine alternative, but neither Jennifer nor I were sure it would be the best option for either her or the baby. I sensed that adoption was becoming a sounder solution in Jen's mind, and I started to think maybe she was right. We talked about the child and the possibilities. We talked about what would be best for the baby. We discussed all the alternatives.

In the meantime I had two pregnant teenagers, Jody, and Harry under one roof in our house in Geary. It was a zoo! Everyone woke at different times. Jennifer, Jody, and I rose the earliest because we all left the house at approximately 8:00 a.m. Sonya and Harry, who had their own room now, slept in.

The moods of two pregnant females and a recovering alcoholic didn't always blend harmoniously. One afternoon Jennifer was helping me prepare the evening meal. A country song was playing on the radio. Harry and Sonya began arguing loudly in the living room beside Jody and his friend Ronnie who had just turned up the volume on the TV so they could ignore the other noises. I lost it! I turned, rushed out of the room, and threw the bowl full of lettuce, tomatoes, and celery I'd been preparing on the living-room carpet.

"That's it!" I yelled. "I can't take this." Heading for the door, I grabbed my package of cigarettes on the way and stomped to the end of the driveway, head buzzing, eyes darting up and down the street. Then I took a deep breath and decided to calm down.

I paced back to my steps, sat down, and smoked three cigarettes. When I reentered the house, the radio and TV were off and the kids were busy cleaning up. Harry, who had picked up the vegetables from the carpet, held the bowl out and grinned. "Would you like some tossed salad?" he asked.

Eventually Jody became overwhelmed by the domestic chaos. It was 1986 and he had left grade eleven the previous year, ignoring my protests. I couldn't do a thing about it. It seemed as if the only activities he enjoyed doing were drawing, playing video games, and talking to girls for hours on the phone. He was eighteen and eager for adventure. Soon he decided to spread his wings and try his luck in the world. Taking off, he hitchhiked to Kingston, Ontario, where he'd made friends while visiting his father in Deseronto.

That year, along with his Christmas and birthday gifts, I sent a huge box of condoms. I was determined to have my advice work for someone, anyone. I felt like standing on the street corner and tossing condoms at passersby, shouting, "Beware, beware. You're next."

When Jody wrote back and said not to worry, that he was considering the priesthood—thanks to his sisters—we all had a great laugh, even though we weren't Catholics. The family that had spent so much time in tears together was beginning to learn to laugh. My relationships with my children were growing stronger. The pregnancies had bonded us. We watched programs on TV about expectant mothers, and I told them all the positive experiences I could remember about my own child-bearing. There had been good times, and I could still recall with clarity the thrill of feeling the first movements of each of my children.

It was around this time that my relationship with my parents also began to transform. They no longer dreaded hearing from me. No doubt they noticed the changes in my life, and I could only imagine how relieved they must have been to be free of the fear of receiving another call from their drunken daughter contemplating suicide.

My parents hadn't visited my home, even to have a cup of tea, for more than five years. In the past, when I was deep into the bottle, any get-togethers took place in my parents' home. Such occasions usually coincided with someone's birthday, and I stayed only long enough to drop off a present and quickly escape.

Sober for five months, I was startled to see, through my living-room window, their brown Dodge pull into my driveway one October afternoon. At first I feared something must be terribly wrong. I hurried to the door, but when I saw my mother's grin that dreadful sinking feeling vanished. Even Dad had a smile on his face.

"We've come for a cup of tea," my mother said, a plate in one hand and a plastic bag in the other. "I brought you some coffee squares."

Reaching out to take the plate, I said, "Come on in." They followed me into the kitchen, casually checking out the place on the way. "It's so good to see you," I told them, knowing things would be different from then on between us. I still felt bitterness for mistakes my parents had made while raising me. But I knew they loved me and had done the best they could. I knew because I loved my own children fiercely, in spite of all the mistakes *I* had made as a parent.

After seating herself at the table and taking a quick, appraising look at her surroundings, my mother pulled a scrapbook out of the plastic bag. "Nice kitchen," she said. "I love that china cabinet. Look, dear," she said to my father, "it's built right into the wall."

"Yes, that's nice, isn't it?" he commented as Mom handed me the book.

It was an oversize emerald-green scrapbook. No clippings protruded from the edges, attesting to my mother's consummate neatness. I opened the cover to see an article I'd written for *The Daily Gleaner* years before. Mom had kept all of my published writing, and I was deeply touched. Tears welled up in my eyes. There was no mistaking her pride in my accomplishments. Dad, too, smiled and said, "I guess you'll have to be the real writer in the family."

My mother was so proud of my change in lifestyle that she often bragged to her friends I was going to AA. Anonymity wasn't important to her. She was grateful to have a daughter who had survived.

My father and mother hugged me when they left my house. Mom paused on the doorstep to say, "I love you." Dad did the same while patting the top of my head, the way he used to when I was a child.

LITTLE WHITE HUNTER

My brothers, Nelson, Allison, Robin, Carman, and Steven, were all adept hunters and fishermen. When I was younger, I took great delight in trailing behind my father in the woods through the thick alder bushes of southern New Brunswick, seeking out a brook where trout were jumping. Fresh trout, pan-fried with onions and diced potatoes, was one of my favourite meals.

When my children were small, I often took them to French Lake, five miles from Geary, to fish under the bridge for pickerel. I never ate pickerel myself, but Stan liked it. I just enjoyed fishing. Pickerel were heavy fish, often weighing three to five pounds. They could put up quite a fight before they were reeled in, and that was the fun of it. Jody was the most successful angler in the family. Heather hated to get her hands dirty, and Sonya thought worms were "yucky," while Jennifer enjoyed watching me cut the fish open.

Now sober, I was beginning to recall some of the pleasant times in my own past. Before I stopped drinking I'd often sit in the tavern in spring and talk about fishing with the guys as we downed a few ales. We'd make plans to go the following week, or month, but I never got there. When I took up fishing again in 1987, it had been at least ten years since I'd actually sunk a hook in the water.

I had been moose hunting on a few clandestine night excursions when I drove drinking buddies out for the kill. At the time they didn't have licences, but we didn't care. We'd chug beers while heading down a road where we knew there would be moose and deer.

Sooner or later we'd catch a set of shiny eyes in the headlights. One of the guys would lean a .308 rifle out the window, drunkenly steadying the barrel while popping off a few shots. I'd never fired at anything other than a paper target, even though Eric, my boyfriend at the time, had given me pointers on how to track moose and deer. But I loved moose meat.

My first year sober I phoned in my name for the New Brunswick moose draw. Only so many licences were handed out. A couple of months later I saw in the newspaper that I had been successful. What delighted me most was that three of my brothers had applied for a licence, but none of them were lucky enough to score one. It was an omen to me that *the times*, as singer Bob Dylan once said, *really were achangin'*.

The three-day hunting expedition was planned for the end of September. It took a month of preparation. People in the area fell over backward to be my guide. If they didn't receive a licence, then this was the way to secure some meat and a permit. Every week I followed my guide of choice. Claude was a tireless, stocky man in his late twenties who always wore a baseball cap and a red-and-black plaid jacket as we checked the woods on the army base training area for signs of moose. I imagined the moose stacked as steaks in my freezer for the long winter. Working only part-time for the *Oromocto Post*, I needed meat to supplement the often meagre provisions in my cupboards.

Claude knew about a roost built high in a tree overlooking a bog where we thought moose might come to drink because we had seen tracks nearby. On these scouting expeditions Claude and I would sometimes hike ten miles through the woods, bog, and logging roads. I cherished every minute of it, even though it was hard for me to keep up with Claude. I never wanted to stop, each step deeper into the woods filling me with excitement, invigorating me, bringing me back to life.

The night before the season was to open officially, Claude and I settled into a roost as soon as it began to turn dark. I was wearing my green army fatigues, an orange hunter's jacket, and an orange baseball hat. Claude was in his standard red-and-black lumber jacket. Both of us had on black rubber boots. We had climbed a wooden ladder to settle on the platform twenty feet above the ground. The platform had three half walls all the way around and was open in the front. We laid our sleeping bags on the wooden floor. Carefully I set my loaded Remington .308 next to my sleeping bag. Claude took out his horn made of birchbark and blew into it, calling for the moose. It was the only sound in the night. After that we settled into our sleeping bags. I had plenty of questions to ask, but Claude told me to be patient and, more important, to remain quiet. He went to sleep fairly fast, but I stayed awake. I didn't feel safe up there. The platform wasn't well constructed, and I had an uneasy, hovering-above-ground sensation. It was a long way down without a parachute.

I was sure we'd wake up the next morning and spot a big bull moose basking in the water. An easy shot even for a rookie like me from the vantage point we had. Finally, after listening to bird sounds in the night that I couldn't identify, I fell asleep with a chilled nose.

When I woke before dawn, Claude was shaking me and whispering, "Wake up." Eagerly he sat up on the platform and made another moose call. We waited, holding our breath, but didn't hear anything. Gradually everything around us began to lighten like a developing photograph, but there was no real sign of the sun yet. We waited some more. My heart was beating fast. I was expecting any minute to see a bull moose storming across the bog. Sometimes when the moose heard these calls they'd come charging forward with hair standing on the backs of their necks.

We waited and waited, sitting at the front of the platform where the ladder was, our eyes fixed on the ground. Nothing. Claude pointed down and headed for the ladder. I followed him and we searched around, treading slowly and listening. But we didn't find a single moose.

After the second day, I was beginning to tire. My feet ached because they had been wet for so long. All of my woollen socks were soaked, and I was fed up with sleeping suspended above the ground. I wanted a bath and my own bed. But I stuck with it. Again, on the second day, there was nothing. Where were the stupid moose?

For three days we'd been walking, climbing, and driving around the forest roads in Claude's four-by-four. We even canoed Mersereau Stream. The only moose we spotted were those on the backs of other vehicles. I became extremely discouraged and began to ask God to help. I desperately needed moose meat.

On the final day of my licence, around 7:00 a.m., we discovered an abandoned roost deeper in the woods in a place we hadn't visited before. I followed Claude up the ladder. As soon as we both settled, a bull moose walked out of the woods in plain sight. It was about fifty yards away. A clear shot across a field. But I didn't even get a chance to shoot. "Give it to me," Claude said, grabbing my rifle with both hands. I didn't mind so much because I was shaking with the thrill of it.

Quickly Claude raised the rifle and fired once. The moose dropped, legs going up in the air as it hit the ground. Claude looked out from behind the rifle, pausing to see if he needed to give it another shot. But the moose didn't stir.

We climbed down, and Claude hurried across the field toward the moose. I was right beside him. Nearing, Claude hesitated and raised the rifle, thinking the moose might get up and charge us with its massive antlers. When we were a few steps closer, we realized the moose was dead, and laughed with delight and relief. Claude slapped me on the back, then we hugged each other.

Bending down, Claude put his finger on the wound. There wasn't a lot of blood. He rubbed his finger gently over the bullet hole, then stood, reached over, and stroked his blood-tipped finger on my left cheek. "Now you're a real hunter," he said. Then he looked back at the moose. "Here's where the work starts. Hook his hind legs over your shoulders."

I stooped and sensed the blood drying on my cheek while I gripped the moose's hind legs. Struggling to raise them over my shoulders, I stumbled a bit. The smell of the moose was awful. Claude showed me how to hold the legs, then slid his hunting knife from its sheath at his waist. He opened the moose's belly with one swipe. The sack of intestines bulged and steam rose in wisps.

Standing there, with the belly of this huge animal open before me, I felt more alive than I could ever remember. This was nature at its best, what we were meant to do. Out in the woods killing our meat, not pretending to be civilized in office buildings, engaged in all the complex scenarios we had created just to put meat on the table. Everyone should be out doing this, I thought, instead of working for pay cheques so they could visit the frozen-meat section at the supermarket. I was on a rush like I'd never experienced before. But when I regarded the moose's head, hollow eyes and protruding tongue, I began to feel remorse for taking the creature's life. I stared at the expanse of sharp antlers, the rack that could cause so much damage. I was grateful that it was a bull and not a cow. I would have felt much worse if it had been the latter.

I thanked God for answering my prayer and thanked the moose for giving up his life so my family could eat.

And eat we did. Even after I gave Claude and several friends and relatives a share, the 460-pound bull lasted for four months. By January I was trading moose for chicken with anyone who would oblige me.

GRANDCHILDREN

Heather was still addicted to alcohol and cocaine, but when she was six months pregnant, she quit everything in anticipation of her baby. As she felt the child grow inside her, sensed it moving, she began to sound more confident, more excited about life and the prospect of becoming a mother. She was happier than I'd seen her in years, and we started attending AA meetings together again.

Cedric, a soft-spoken man in his early fifties, took it upon himself to help newcomers in AA. He was a retired soldier who puttered at woodworking when he wasn't out providing taxi service for someone in trouble. He went out of his way for my family. Not only was he there for me if I needed to talk, but he often helped out by fixing something broken in my house or by giving Heather a drive when I wasn't able to. When he announced he wanted to organize a baby shower for Heather in his mobile home in Maugerville, on the northern outskirts of Fredericton, I was blown away. It wasn't that I didn't expect such a kind gesture from Cedric; it was just that I'd never heard of a baby shower given by a man. I called Heather to tell her, and she was ecstatic.

It was a baby shower like I'd never seen before or since. Cedric had invited everyone who knew Heather in AA, and I'd invited all her other friends. The trailer was crammed to capacity with men and women of all ages. Even Old Don, an elderly man who had lost his family many years before because of his drinking, came with a carefully wrapped gift of pink and blue booties.

"I'm betting on a girl," Old Don said.

We noted his choice with amusement, then took a poll from the rest of the group. The majority agreed with Old Don.

My boyfriend, Bill, took out his guitar, and Heather, who had always loved to sing, led us in some country songs before we stopped to dine on everything from takeout to egg-salad sandwiches. And we all guzzled coffee. In no time we went through five large industrial-sized pots that Cedric had borrowed from the local Lions Club Centre.

On November 27, 1988, my first grandchild was born in the Dr. Everett Chalmers Hospital in Fredericton. Aleshia JoAnne—seven pounds and five ounces—was adorable, with dark chubby cheeks and thick black hair. Because Heather had been using alcohol and cocaine during the first six months of the pregnancy, the hospital team had been on the alert for signs of withdrawal in the baby, but she was completely healthy. I knew there were many others praying for the baby's health.

I stood and watched as the miracle of birth unfolded. My friend Gail Gardner was with me. We were both clad in green hospital gowns and masks. Gail had agreed to be Heather's coach, so I was free to watch the entire scene without trying to remember when to breathe. I was having a difficult enough time preventing myself from hyperventilating.

Heather's face lit up as she held her daughter. The nurse had placed Aleshia in her arms as soon as the baby was breathing correctly. In spite of the obvious pain she'd been in, Heather smiled warmly at her new infant. "I'll be a good mother," she vowed, looking at me, her voice filled with weakness and wanting.

"I know you will," I told her.

I held Aleshia when she was only ten minutes old. She was a tiny, perfect cherub and felt like a cloud in my arms. *This is life*, I thought. *You're so beautiful, little angel. We'll show those macho guys we girls can hunt.*

I was determined this child would have the best start she could possibly have. She would reap the benefits of my hard-won knowledge. I figured that would be one way of making up for my failures as a mother to Heather. I couldn't repair the past, but I could influence the future.

As I tickled Aleshia's tiny upturned nose with the furry stuffed moose I'd found in a gift shop, I smiled. It was a funny promise I'd made perhaps, but my first moose-hunting expedition was only a month or so behind me, so the two special moments seemed to fit.

Both represented natural victories.

I knew I'd be able to give this baby what I had never been able to offer my own children at that age. I had often failed miserably as a mother, but I'd be a good grandmother, the best there ever was. I wouldn't screw up this time.

When Heather took Aleshia home to her apartment in Fredericton, everything was ready. Heather had carefully prepared for her baby. Clothes were neatly folded and placed in a newly painted dresser. The crib was made up with yellow blankets, just in case the prediction of a girl had been wrong. The entire apartment was shiny clean.

Stan came home for a visit that Christmas. He stayed at my parents' place, but I invited him out to see us a couple of days before Christmas. Stan wanted to meet his first grandchild, and I decided Christmas might be a good time for me to practise a little forgiveness. I didn't believe Heather felt comfortable about it. She never said much, but before she went out for the day, leaving us to baby-sit, she told me, "Make sure you're there when Dad holds Aleshia."

All of my children were present for Christmas dinner and Aleshia was the star. Even Jody couldn't hold her enough. She looked like a Native princess in her white lacy dress, moccasins, and headband.

On Christmas night Heather asked us to watch Aleshia while she went out to visit. I had an uneasy feeling she might be getting ready to drink. "Don't you think you should be here with your baby?" I asked her.

"I'll only be gone a couple of hours," she assured me. "I need a breather."

Two days later she showed up without explanation.

Within a week Heather was struggling to keep her addiction at bay. Barely recovered from giving birth, she was once again drinking practically every day. Heather tried to take care of Aleshia, but it was too much. She couldn't muster the energy to rise for feedings while she was nursing a terrible hangover.

"I'm losing it again, Mom," she told me one Monday morning. "I've got to get back on track for Aleshia. I love her so much." Her voice failed. "But it's hard."

"Maybe you just need some help," I suggested.

The first week of January she called Child Protection and requested assistance. A female social worker came out to visit and placed Aleshia in temporary care where Heather could continue to see her and still find time to work on recovery. I agreed with her decision and was there for her, helping her pack up some of Aleshia's things before the social worker arrived.

When it was time for Aleshia to leave, Heather changed her mind. She held on to Aleshia and didn't want to turn her over. "Maybe I should give this more thought," she said. "I love her."

I had to coax the baby from her, saying, "You're doing the right thing. It's just for a while till you get better. And you'll still be able to see her."

But Heather, staring at the baby, wouldn't let go of her.

"She *will* be able to see her, won't she?" I asked the social worker.

"Of course," the woman answered. Turning to Heather, she added, "You've made a brave decision, a good one, Heather. You'll both be happy you did this one day when everything's better."

Slowly Heather handed Aleshia to the social worker, tears streaming down her face. I rushed to the baby for one last kiss. As we walked together to the car, I studied Heather's face when she waved goodbye. Aleshia's chubby face broke out in a smile, but Heather's features were filled with loss and worry.

Aleshia was placed with Roger and Flossie Enman, a Christian family, and Heather visited regularly. I never had the opportunity to visit because I was suddenly busy with my second grandchild. Brittany Jessica arrived on January 2, 1989, in the same hospital where Aleshia had been born less than two months earlier. Harry stayed with Sonya through the long labour. The rest of the family waited for news in the waiting room usually reserved for fathers only. By this time most of the nurses recognized us.

Brittany Jessica weighed six pounds, twelve ounces and was absolutely perfect. Long and lanky with hair so light and fine it looked as if she had none at all, she reminded me of Sonya as a newborn. Brittany squirmed the first time I held her. I couldn't have felt any prouder as I congratulated Harry, who beamed with pride. He was a sweet guy with a twisted sense of humour and he adored Sonya. I thought he'd make a good father. It certainly seemed as if life was finally coming together for them. Sonya, Harry, and Brittany Jessica would make a wonderful family.

· ALESHIA

I was working part-time now in the accounting department of a safety supply house in Fredericton, anticipating the birth of my third grandchild, due in six weeks. Heather was still struggling to get her life in order so she could bring Aleshia back to live with her. In the meantime she was also having a lot of physical problems.

For years Heather had suffered irritable-bowel syndrome. As she matured, the disease worsened and she began experiencing bladder and kidney problems. One of these very painful conditions—interstitialcystitis—was correctly diagnosed only in her mid-twenties, although she'd endured it most of her life. She'd been drinking almost steadily now for five years. Drugs had become part of her life about two years after the drinking started. Her body had done what it could to keep up, but by the time Aleshia was born Heather was falling apart. Still, she hadn't given up yet on getting her life back together. Against all odds, she longed to be a dependable mother.

On January 20, 1989, Heather was admitted to the Oromocto Hospital with a kidney infection. I was at work two days later when I received her call.

"Oh, Mom!" Heather gasped, crying so hard I could barely make out what she was saying. "Aleshia's dead, Mom. She's dead." Then I heard a long, inhuman wail.

"Stop it, Heather!" I yelled. "Stop talking like that." I threw the telephone receiver onto the floor and started to scream.

My boss, a Jewish man who was usually quite intolerant, ordered the supervisor, Joanne, to pick up the phone. I sat in the chair beside my desk and began to rock back and forth as tears poured over my cheeks. I was trying to take myself to that fantasy land I'd created as a child. I didn't want to hear any more.

Joanne obtained the whole story. That morning the foster mom had prepared Aleshia's bottle and gone to the baby's bedroom. When she arrived at the crib, she knew right away something was wrong, even though Aleshia looked as if she were sleeping. She was too still, and when the foster mom touched her, the baby was cold.

A frantic attempt to revive Aleshia by mouth-to-mouth resuscitation proved fruitless. My granddaughter was pronounced dead on arrival at the same hospital where she'd been welcomed into life only two months earlier.

The hours that followed that phone call were as hazy as any of my alcoholic blackouts. The difference was that I knew there were things to do. I did them automatically without recollection, but I did them right. Before joining my grieving, heavily sedated daughter, I informed the rest of the family. It was up to me now to take care of everything. Joanne hugged me after she hung up the phone and reminded me that my daughter needed my strength. As I headed for the back door holding Joanne's hand, I repeated the Serenity Prayer:

God, grant me the serenity to accept the things I cannot change
The courage to change the things I can
And the wisdom to know the difference.

Heather and I decided that one night at the funeral home would be enough for all of us. My daughter had been discharged from the hospital but remained heavily sedated. My other children were fully in this world but were taking the death hard. Heather had opted to stay with the parents of a young man she'd started dating around Christmastime.

I refused offers of tranquillizers. God and my friends would get me through the crisis. I couldn't fully accept the death and instead concentrated on what needed to be done for others. I contacted everyone, including Stan who was still living in Deseronto with his mother, and let them know what had happened and when the funeral and visitations would be held. I talked to the funeral director, picked out a tiny white casket, and gathered the burial clothing— a white lace dress Heather had chosen, an undershirt, a diaper, and the leather moccasins her grandfather had given her at Christmas.

Heather had asked me to bring a snowsuit, too, because it was winter. I did these things in as businesslike a manner as I could manage, resolving to keep my crying to a minimum, reserving it for later. But I came close to losing this determination at the funeral home the night before the funeral.

Even though Heather was taking Valium, her pain couldn't be numbed completely. At the funeral home she hardly left her daughter's side. She stroked Aleshia's tiny hands, her cheek, her hair, then straightened her dress and talked to her as if the baby were still alive.

Most of my family showed up, even my brother, Carman, who had been distant toward me over the past few years. That night he told me he loved me.

Then I saw Stan and didn't know what to do. It was difficult at first to have him around, but he stayed out of my way and tried to be helpful. That was the first time it dawned on me that I would have to find a way to forgive him. In the light of death all excess baggage became unbearably heavy.

Heather, Aleshia, and I were all born Sagittarius, the Gypsies of the zodiac. And Gypsies adored their jewellery. For Heather it was silver. It used to be the same for me, but at some point my preference shifted to gold.

Heather had always wanted a silver birthstone ring, and I had given her one when she was sixteen, which she lost shortly afterward during one of her drunken escapades. I told her I wouldn't give her another ring until I was certain she was going to pull her life together and stay sober. That happened on her birthday when Aleshia was only twelve days old. I knew it would mean a lot to Heather, and it did. The ring symbolized new hope.

That was probably why she placed it, as well as she could, on Aleshia's tiny finger that night, the baby's finger never able to fill out the ring. I knew what that gesture meant, and I broke down and sobbed. The people who offered me comfort didn't know I was actually grieving for Heather.

MY FIRST GRANDSON

Two months after Aleshia's death Jennifer went into labour. She'd asked my boyfriend, Bill, to be her birthing coach, and since he'd never had children of his own, he felt honoured. He was as excited as a child at Christmas. Even though Bill lived in Fredericton, he and Jennifer attended prenatal classes held by the Victorian Order of Nurses in Oromocto.

Jennifer was asleep in my house in Geary when she was suddenly awakened by the onset of labour. Her water broke while she was asleep with her three-month-old niece, Brittany, sprawled comfortably over her belly. Sonya and Harry were sleeping in the next bedroom. Heather was still living in Fredericton, and Jody was spending the night at his friend Ronnie's house. I had stayed in Fredericton for the night at Bill's. It was 7:30 a.m. on April 2, 1988, the day before Easter Sunday, when the phone rang to break the news.

Bill lifted the receiver, listened sleepily, then grunted something and dropped the phone as he leaped out of bed to search for clothes. "It's Jennifer," he said. "I've got to get to the hospital."

"What's wrong?" I asked, snatching up the receiver and talking into it. "Is Jen in labour?"

"Yes, you better hurry up" came Sonya's panicky voice. "We're on our way." She hung up.

I set down the receiver and tossed my legs over the bed. I couldn't help but grin at Bill as he frantically hurried around, hunting for a clean shirt.

"Well, this is it," I told him. "Are you ready?"

"I sure hope so," he said as he fumbled with the buttons on his shirt and ran to find a coat. He was out the bedroom door before I could tell him he'd taken his bathrobe by mistake.

"You might want to change your coat," I said, chuckling as I followed him into the kitchen.

He gave me a questioning look before he realized the mistake. We both broke out laughing.

"I think I should drive," I wryly suggested.

Bill and I were at the hospital before Jennifer arrived. They had to travel from Geary. Bill and I were just downtown. And Harry and Jennifer had to drop Brittany off at Harry's mother's house along the way.

When Jennifer walked in with Harry and Sonya on either side, I had to stifle a laugh. Jen looked as if she had a giant diaper on. She'd hurriedly stuffed a large bath towel under her jogging pants to keep from flooding the car. Smiling with delight, she wasn't even in pain. Sonya and Harry appeared much worse than she. So did Bill. He was white and shaking.

Upstairs in the labour room Bill went in with Jennifer after slipping on his sterile hospital greens. Harry, Sonya, and I took our familiar seats in the waiting room. The nurse told me it would probably be a while since this was Jennifer's first child. We knew the drill. Harry went out for coffee. Bill, clad in his hospital greens, rushed out and said, "Get me an extra large."

About an hour later Jennifer started having pain. Bill appeared, out of breath, and told me I'd better get in there. Everything went very quickly after that. My first grandson was born at 2:39 p.m. that afternoon. He was named William (in honour of Jen's beaming birth coach) and Vincent (after one of her favourite teachers, Vincent Smith). Billy made his debut, healthy and handsome, with thick brown hair just like his mother's. His skin was darker by far than any of the other babies, and so were his penetrating little eyes. I could swear he recognized me the first time I held him.

I can't let Jennifer give you up, I thought. *But can we do it?*

When I laid eyes on my first grandson, my rational, levelheaded talks of "alternatives" flew out the window. A tiny new life, inherently connected to my life, lay there before me. An inexplicable attachment was triggered. *A linking of the generations, ancestor to ancestor*, was how Stan's Mohawk grandfather, long gone by now, would have explained it.

I needn't have worried. As soon as I saw Jennifer, she told me she could never part with Billy. "He's beautiful, Mom."

Jennifer chose to keep him and she never looked back.

SOBRIETY

I attended AA meetings two or three times a week. An unconditional love grew between me and my new AA friends, particularly my two new sponsors, Ted and Faye. Sometimes their help took the form of a few extra groceries or a drive to a doctor's appointment when my car refused to start or had run out of gas and I couldn't afford a fill-up. Once, Ted even bought me a cupcake with a lit candle in it, personally delivered to my office on a day I was ready to give up and head for a bar.

I couldn't believe how caring strangers could be. Faye, Lois, and Cedric called constantly to make sure I was doing okay, and all around me I felt an almost physical shield of altruism, no matter what was happening in my life. I actually began to *do* things instead of merely talking about them. I went for walks in the woods, began writing short stories, and enrolled in a ceramics class.

Day by day everything appeared more vivid, greener and bluer, in the forests and streams I rediscovered. The flowers boasted brilliant, saturated colours, and the sun felt warmer, nurturing, friendlier.

I began to fish, scouring brooks for trout, and continued hunting, for partridge this time, on the back roads of Minto where I four-wheeled through the mud with friends. I felt like a kid again, only now I wasn't afraid. In AA they called this rediscovering of natural joy "pink clouding." Heaven on earth.

In AA, members celebrated every important milestone of their sobriety. Since the first year was so difficult for many, these milestones were broken into three-month intervals. Members who reached these particular milestones without drinking were congratulated at the meetings with a round of applause and given a small keepsake, usually a coloured poker chip or sometimes a key chain, to remind them of their achievements. After one full year of sobriety, and at all yearly intervals thereafter, a special celebration was planned, often complete with cake and candles.

The night in 1988 when I celebrated my one-year AA birthday I was so nervous I could hardly put two words together. I was overwhelmed by emotion when I considered the hopeless state I'd been in only a year earlier, and how optimistic I had remained in spite of all the tragedies I'd had to face. It had been a nerve-wracking year, and I hadn't touched one drink or pill to help me through it.

The celebration was held in the basement of St. Anthony's Church on the north side of Fredericton. Usually our group—named the 3RS to represent Reliability, Responsibility, and Recovery—drew a crowd of fifty to sixty people, but when I entered the basement there were over a hundred people. I was astonished by the show of support and felt like crying but maintained my composure.

"All I can say is thank you for helping me get back my life and the respect of my family," I told the AA members, then thanked my family for being so supportive. That was all I could say when during the meeting I was finally overcome with emotion and cried. But for once they were tears of joy.

My parents showed up, along with Heather, Jody, Sonya, and Jennifer, and my buddy Gail Gardner. I had selected the AA readers and speakers for the night, people who had been particularly helpful to me that year. It was so hard to choose one person over the other. There were only six spots to fill, and I figured I could have assigned sixty.

Faye and Ted presented me with a medallion and certificate to keep as a souvenir of that night. My children carried out a huge homemade carrot cake—baked by Cindy, another AA friend—with a single candle on top. After I blew it out, each of the kids gave me a hug and everyone applauded wildly.

Then Jennifer turned to the audience and said, "Thank you for giving us back our mother."

I shook my head, tears in my eyes, and cast a glance at my mother. She was crying, too. In fact, there didn't seem to be a dry eye in the place.

"We're proud of you," my mother told me after the meeting. "You're a good girl." Both of my parents hugged me, and Mom handed me a birthday card that congratulated me on making a new beginning. That night I received more than forty cards. I felt higher than a kite.

LEAVING THE NEST

My kids started leaving the nest for good in 1988 when I was thirty-seven. Sonya and Harry married on September 3, a beautiful full wedding in the same church where I had married Stan twenty-one years earlier. Jennifer was the maid of honour. Jody, Heather, and I sat together and looked after nine-month-old Brittany. Even Stan was invited. He travelled from Ontario to New Brunswick by bus. Sonya had decided it was the right thing to do, inviting Stan. He'd lost some weight and was sporting a full beard now and sat quietly beside my parents. But it was my boyfriend, Bill, dressed in a new navy sports jacket and grey pants who walked Sonya down the aisle. She was a queen in her long white gown and veil. She and Harry seemed to radiate happiness.

Sonya and Harry, with the financial help of Harry's parents, Clem and Bertha, and grandmother, Constance, bought the small mobile home Robert and Gail Gardner had lived in. Harry began working for a trucking company, and Sonya took a job at the Geary Kwik Mart. Within a few months they owned a new mini-home on the same piece of property.

Around this time Heather started dating Tony Nolan, a dark-haired young man from Chipman, a small country village forty miles away. Tony had a history of violence and had been incarcerated for car theft. He worked for a roofing company and looked like the bass guitar player in the rock band Mötley Crüe. In fact, with similar hair, eyes, and slight build, he and Heather resembled each other, so much that some people mistook them for brother and sister. Tony was a construction worker with an artistic side. He could draw anything from memory.

Heather never had more than five or six weeks of sobriety since Aleshia's death and she was often depressed. But I later learned when Heather came to visit after a fight that had left bruises on her arms and back, that both she and Tony were dabbling in the drug scene. She told me Tony used cocaine, but what she didn't tell me until months later was that he sometimes liked to "bang it"—inject directly by needle—instead of snorting. So Heather was introduced to shooting intravenous drugs. They decided to move to Hamilton, Ontario, to try life in the *faster* lanes. Tony's brother, Johnny, had moved there, and he told Tony he'd have no problem finding a job that paid more than $7 an hour.

The following year Jody relocated to Kingston, Ontario, with his friend Ronnie. Bill and I broke up when his former wife decided she wanted to give it another chance. I had no real warning. Bill left for Nova Scotia to see his parents, and a week later he was packing his things to settle back in with the wife he'd already divorced. I wasn't sure what I was supposed to do with the diamond he'd given me. I knew things would never work out with his wife. They had already split once. He'd want me back and I'd have already moved on. I told him so and turned out to be right. In the end I sold the diamond to buy a new dress.

That left me with Jennifer and Billy, who was less than a year old. Another friend, Peter, who I sometimes sang with at AA events, was looking for a place to board, so I offered him a room downstairs. Then, in the spring of 1990, Jennifer mentioned finding a place for her and Billy in Oromocto. She and her friend Lana, who also had a small son, were working as waitresses in Oromocto and decided they could pool their money and share an apartment. I figured I didn't need a house anymore. I spent most of my time in Fredericton and was still working for Carleton Safety Supplies as a bookkeeper, doing a bit of freelance writing, and accepting the occasional shift as an attendant at the Victoria Health Centre, the local detoxification unit. Most of the AA meetings I went to were in Fredericton and so were many of my friends. I was finding it difficult to maintain my own place. I barely knew how to replace a blown fuse, let alone swing a hammer. I figured I'd probably end up skulling myself with it. So I talked to my boarder/friend Peter and put up a FOR SALE sign. He told me he'd still board with me if I rented a place in Fredericton, so that helped sway me.

I'd never been to a university, not even to visit. Ten years earlier I had taken courses at the local community college where I'd completed my grade twelve, but I had always dreamed of being part of a university campus crowd, finding people with whom I could talk on my level. I would constantly read biographies, history, and psychology books but I never had anyone to share these ideas with. I was hoping university would introduce me to individuals of like mind.

Now that my kids were gone, I decided to get on with my life. The first day I visited the University of New Brunswick I was overwhelmed by the lushness of the campus. The grounds and buildings exuded civility and ancient wisdom. *Everyone looks so young,* I nervously thought. *And smart.*

When I entered the university's registrar's office there was a lineup of kids in front of me. They were wearing new clothes and they all appeared clean-cut and privileged. I considered retreating before anyone realized I was there, but I remembered something I'd heard at one of my AA meetings. *All things are possible if you stay sober one day at a time.* I kept repeating that to myself like a mantra. Then I took a deep breath and stepped up to the counter. The woman who greeted me was friendly and I almost blurted, "All things are possible if you stay sober one day at a time." But I bit my tongue. When the woman smiled, I relaxed a little, took another deep breath, and told her I was thinking about taking a course. She handed me a brochure with course listings and some other papers to fill out, then directed me to a small table across the hall. About a half hour later I was signed up for a business management course that would commence in two weeks.

I was trying so hard to pump up my self-confidence, but I was still convinced I'd fail. I couldn't get clear of my own insecurity and self-loathing.

Still, I was looking forward to the first night of the course, meeting new people, buying new books. There were about fifty of us in the class, even a couple of students who were much older than I was. The course was tough. I had no problem grasping the theory, but when we delved into anything that required mathematical calculations I was utterly lost. I'd always had a mathematical deficit. The section on corporate businesses was the most difficult for me. I was forced to read my notes over and over. I had a hard enough time simply balancing a cheque book, for goodness sake! I guess I'd thought about having some kind of business of my own someday. A guy I knew had told me this course would be suitable and I'd believed him. I was determined not to quit.

I studied every night, curtailing my coffee time after AA meetings, and finished the course. I tried not to wonder about the results. I'd blanked out for a while at the final examination, but I'd done my best. When the transcript finally arrived, I pulled open the envelope, saw my B+, and whooped with joy. I'd done it! With that victory under my belt I started to feel I could go a little bit further. It might take time, it might take a lot of work, but I was sure I'd return to university to complete a degree. Faithfully I kept a journal and resumed writing feature stories, this time for the *Oromocto Post*.

Heather moved back to Fredericton without Tony early in 1990. I hadn't heard from her in over a month and had spent a great deal of time on my knees imploring God to keep her safe. When she showed up, she was thinner than ever before, not more than a hundred pounds. When she told me she was pregnant, I was deeply disturbed. Heather had been heavily involved with drugs in Hamilton, so I was worried about both her and the unborn baby. She and Tony had developed a daily dependence on cocaine for a couple of months and often chose to administer the drug with needles.

They fought violently, often kicking and punching each other, Heather told me. Tony's temper almost always led to physical beatings, and when Heather was stoned she wouldn't back down, not even for her own safety. Still, Heather missed Tony. He called me the day after she arrived.

"Is Heather around?" he asked.

"Is this Tony?"

"Yeah, how ya doin'?"

"I'm okay. What about you?"

"A lot better. I'm off all the junk now."

"Heather's doing better, too. I don't want anything to screw her up."

"I just want to talk to her."

I passed the receiver to Heather without comment. I'd learned a long time ago that words were useless against a junkie's love or lust.

When Tony followed Heather back to New Brunswick a few weeks later, my daughter welcomed him with open arms. They moved into a new apartment on the north side of Fredericton and vowed to quit drugs and drinking so their unborn child could have a better life than what they had been living.

Their vow was quickly broken. After a night of partying, Heather called the next morning to tell me they had trashed the apartment.

"Were you using?" I asked.

"We were only snorting, Mom."

She went on to say they'd been drinking whiskey, too. From then on their situation was unpredictable. Often they'd go weeks without using drugs or fighting. Then Tony would accuse Heather of plotting against him, or she'd freak out because she saw him talking to another woman.

When Heather was seven months pregnant, there was a particularly violent argument. Tony lost his temper and kicked Heather in the stomach. The police were called, and Tony was taken to jail. Heather was sent by taxi to hospital for observation. Luckily, after being examined, it turned out she had nothing more than bruises. Miraculously the baby was fine. I had asked God every morning and every night to send an angel to guard that unborn child.

Tony went to jail for six months.

After she was released from the hospital, Heather moved back with me until her baby was born. She attended meetings of Narcotics Anonymous, stopped drinking, and started making new friends who wanted to help her.

On June 27, 1990, I drove Heather to the Dr. Everett Chalmers Hospital, the same place where Aleshia had been born three years earlier, the same maternity floor where all my grandchildren had come into the world. Heather was in hard labour and had been drug-free for less than two months. Her pains had started while we were visiting with a friend on Brunswick Street in downtown Fredericton. I was deeply concerned and had been praying for the baby's safety for quite some time.

Dear God, please protect the baby and help Heather. Please forgive her. Let the baby be born normal.

Now, just concentrating on my driving, I didn't say a word, though I did pray during the entire ten-minute trip to the hospital and held Heather's hand. My daughter was in obvious pain. She kept clutching her protruding middle with her right hand.

I stayed with Heather and continued holding her hand throughout the labour, but I had to leave the room when they examined the newborn baby. I was scared and wanted to see Sonya and Jennifer, who had arrived at the hospital during the seven-hour labour. I needed to remind myself of the normalcy of my other daughters' lives. I wanted to be braced by them.

The doctor came out of the room and joined us in the corridor. "She's one lucky little girl. No signs of withdrawal. She's perfectly healthy."

Sonya, Jennifer, and I breathed sighs of relief.

"And Heather?" I asked.

"She's exhausted. She'll need to rest for a while."

Sasha Alexandra Thompson looked like a white china doll with chubby cheeks and curly black hair. Thankfully Heather had come through the ordeal without complications. She called the superintendent at the Kingsclear Reformatory so Tony could be made aware of his new daughter. He'd been attending anger-management sessions and AA meetings and was allowed an escorted visit to the hospital. A uniformed corrections officer accompanied him, and I was there when he arrived.

"Can you take a picture of the three of us?" Heather asked, reaching for the camera on the nightstand beside her hospital bed.

When Heather signed out of the hospital a few days later with Sasha, she was determined to turn over a new leaf. She'd even told Tony she was giving up drugs so she could take care of Sasha. She would be staying with a friend, a former schoolmate who also had a baby only a few weeks old. Again I was optimistic that Heather's life of drugs would soon be nothing more than a bad memory.

I was anxious for my house to sell so I could take an apartment in Fredericton. I was ready to venture into the unknown. I would be living sober and alone in my own place. Jennifer and Billy were happy in their apartment in Oromocto with Lana and her little boy, Cody.

The house sold within two months, and I was left with $8,000 after I paid what I owed the bank. I celebrated by having dinner with Peter and toasting the sale with ginger ale. Then I paid off my bills, gave each of the kids $300, and rented an apartment on St. Mary's Street in Fredericton.

GIVING SOMETHING BACK

Now that my house was sold and I had moved into a new place, I decided to treat myself with a trip to Alberta to visit my friends,

Beryl and Tom, as well as my brother, Nelson. While there I took in a rodeo, toured the Rocky Mountains, visited Drumheller and the hoodoos, and even made a brief foray up to Fort McMurray and the tar sands. When I returned to Fredericton, I felt rejuvenated and ready for anything.

For a few more weeks I worked at the Victoria Health Centre, holding down twelve-hour shifts as an attendant and requesting information from patients when they registered. I'd learned how to check for pulse, respiration, and blood pressure in a training session, and I kept records of these vitals on each patient who was newly admitted. I had a weak stomach when it came to cleaning up vomit or human feces. Most of the time, though, I enjoyed helping others who were suffering from the same disease that I had.

I felt as if my life had new purpose, and for the first time in a long while I didn't have to worry about what was going on with my children. Sonya had returned to school to complete grade twelve and now had a keen interest in working with the police force. While studying she was offered the chance to participate in a ride-along program with the RCMP. The next thing I knew the little girl who had once taken my car for a joy ride at the age of fourteen was training to be a corrections officer. She, Harry, and Brittany moved into a beautiful new bungalow. Jennifer and Heather were still living in Oromocto with their children, and Jody was staying with friends in a small apartment in Fredericton.

Recovery from using alcohol to deaden my senses was made more bearable by the fact that I loved sobriety. There was still anguish I had to deal with; the booze had often increased the suffering, not deadened it. With the alcohol gone I had to face the source of my pain. Recovering from addiction was relatively easy, but how could a woman recover from hating herself?

181

Even when the drinking was no longer a problem, living often was. For me the guilt of failing my children weighed on me constantly. No matter how much my life changed, how much I struggled to make amends, or how long I remained sober, I couldn't forgive myself. The nagging thought that life for my children could have been so much better if I hadn't succumbed to the bottle tormented me endlessly.

I had started to see a counsellor, a beautiful, gentle woman named Gloria Gallant, because I knew I needed all the encouragement I could get. She was the person who finally convinced me I had done the best I could do as a mother.

"You were a child yourself," she pointed out. "You had your own demons to face."

She told me repeatedly that I should focus on the things I'd done right and understand that I wasn't responsible for the choices my children made. The latter concept was harder to accept.

I also spent hours talking to Ted Spencer, an Anglican priest who was a friend to many AA members. He was my spiritual mentor without ever *preaching* at me. Still, most of my support in those early years was found at AA meetings.

I was at an AA meeting in St. Stephen when a woman began talking about her strained relationship with her eldest daughter. She said it had taken her five years to realize that family members didn't heal simply because you stopped drinking and made a few new promises.

"Don't make amends," she said. "Live them. And if you can't help the ones you love the most, if they don't want to accept your apologies, then help someone else for the time being."

I felt as if she was speaking directly to me. The devastation reaped by addiction was a communal problem. I'd been struggling with the growing guilt and frustration I felt when Sonya refused to let me talk about the past so I could seek her forgiveness.

At the end of my drinking Sonya had assumed much of the

responsibility for our household. With her sisters' help she had made certain the house cleaning was completed when I was too ill or tired to do it. She fielded the calls from work if I was too sick to go in, and she brought me the glasses of ginger ale or tomato juice I needed the morning after a night out on the town. Sonya took care of me. When I sobered up, I no longer required that same kind of support. It was an unsettling change. At one point when I tried to bring up the past she surprised me by saying, "I don't know what you're talking about. You never drank that bad, anyway."

I realized then that it wasn't the right time to push for absolution. What I had to do was rechannel my own need for forgiveness toward helping others and thus alleviate my guilt. That was when I went overboard and pledged to save the world.

I wasn't used to living alone, and Peter was seldom around, so I decided I might be able to help someone by taking in another boarder. Jim H. had been in and out of detox more than fifty times in his forty-two years. Everyone said he probably wouldn't make it but, of course, I knew better. What he needed was someone to believe in him, to encourage him. Someone like me, blazing with my newfound purpose.

Jim was looking for a place to board. He said he'd never stay sober sleeping at the Emergency Shelter, and he only received $438 from Income Assistance each month. I had an extra room, so I decided he could stay with me and I'd only charge $200 a month for room and board. I could also give him a hand staying sober. Because I had made it through the fire myself, I could remind him of the teachings of AA and be there for him.

The first couple of days worked out just great. Jim settled in and we talked about recovery in a practical way. He was eager to attend meetings and often asked me for advice. And I felt the positiveness of the experience begin to boost me. I was actually helping some-one get their life back on track.

Jim lived a quiet life. He went to plenty of AA meetings and spent hours drinking coffee with his friends or walking along the riverbank. He was appreciative of my patience in waiting for his cheque to arrive. All was well.

On the third day of Jim boarding with me I found my front door ripped off the hinges when I returned home from work. It appeared to have been kicked in. As I cautiously started up the steps to my apartment, I smelled alcohol in the air. My anger mounted as my pace increased. When I entered the living room, my mouth was already open, ready to shout my disapproval, but there was no one there for me to berate.

A half-dozen empty wine bottles were on the floor in front of the chesterfield. Cigarette butts littered the top of the coffee table. I sat and tried to calm myself by saying aloud the Serenity Prayer: "God, grant me the serenity to accept the things I cannot change..." I kept repeating the words, averting my eyes from the bottles and butts.

Then I heard rowdy voices downstairs, outside the broken door. One of them belonged to an extremely inebriated Jim.

Springing to my feet, I lurched to the top of the stairs and stood there, furious, as Jim and his associates—two filthy older men I recognized from the same detox centre Jim had left a few days ago—began to stagger up, their voices drunkenly loud. Jim had obviously cashed his cheque. He had a full bottle of wine in his hand.

"Hold it right there!" I shouted. "You and your friends get out. Now, before I call the police."

Jim wavered slightly, his eyes narrowing as he glared up at me. "You stupid bitch," he snarled.

I saw him pull something out of his shirt pocket that resembled a knife. Not waiting to find out for certain, I spun, bolted for the rear door, and ran down the back stairs to a neighbour's to call the police. Two officers were there within five minutes. Jim and his friends didn't even resist. They were sitting on the front step sharing a new bottle of Golden Nut wine and singing a Merle Haggard classic, "The Green, Green Grass of Home," when the policemen arrived to take them away.

I didn't press charges, but I never listened to Jim's apologies, either. I shivered when I thought about how I'd mouthed off at neighbours before I sobered up. If I'd kept drinking, I might have come to this end myself.

Jim moved back into the shelter, and I vowed to spend my time trying to save women instead.

One rainy afternoon I bumped into Miles in the Fredericton Mall, and he invited me to have dinner with him. He was nothing but skin and bones under his tailored black shirt and tight white jeans. There were none of the welcoming wisecracks I'd come to associate with this lighthearted man. I detected none of the arrogance that used to leave such a bitter taste in my mouth. In fact, he wasn't smiling at all. Being off the bottle for a while, I wasn't as touchy and defensive. It was easier for both of us to get along. We were merely two human beings struggling to recover, trying to move forward. I could tell from the tone of his voice that he wasn't about to hand out any seemingly expert negative advice, and I needed to commiserate with someone in the same emotional boat.

This time the talk over coffee and dinner at a local restaurant was much more subdued, more imbued with human feeling. Miles shared his hurt over the breakup of his relationship. His partner had left him for someone else, and he was struggling with that loss. I listened intently. He was quick to comfort me when I told him about my disastrous attempt to reform Jim.

"You have to be careful," he said, using his hands as much as his mouth to make the point. "Not all men are as trustworthy as me." He rolled his eyes and I laughed.

"That's a good thing," I joked back.

For a few weeks we spent a lot of time talking. We met almost daily for coffee. Sometimes we'd get together at the local coffee shop, or Miles would bring coffee to my place. Other times we'd drive out of town to enjoy different scenery. I even took him to meet the rest of my family. He already knew Heather from AA and had a great deal of compassion for her plight. When I commented one day on her track record of sobriety, he said, "Don't worry. She'll make it. It just takes longer for some than others." Neither one of us was ready yet to acknowledge that a romance might be budding, but a solid friendship was definitely developing.

In spite of the affinity that was growing between us, Miles gradually drifted off when another woman in AA started flirting with him. I teased him about it at first because I didn't think he'd actually do anything about it. But when he told me one day he was going to a dance with the woman, I realized a bond was forming.

"What's wrong with me?" I asked, a little put out by his choice.

"You won't sleep with me." He laughed, but I could see he was serious.

I was too confused at that point even to consider sleeping with Miles, so he did what became standard practice for him. He found another woman to help him forget the last one who wouldn't conform to his standards.

I saw no harm in staying single for a couple of months.

In October 1990 I heard about a job opening at Child Find New Brunswick with their street outreach division. They advertised for an on-site street worker to supervise disenfranchised teenagers.

The idea of helping young people in need was appealing, so I applied and was called in for an interview. When the executive director, Claudia Bradbury, phoned a few days later to tell me I had the job, I was walking on air. I called everyone I knew to share the news.

It was my duty to maintain files of missing children and oversee the day-to-day operation of the street kids who stopped in for our services, which included everything from setting up doctor's appointments to providing lunch and dinner to arranging reunions with parents or relatives. The kids came from all kinds of backgrounds and arrived in various states of dress. Many drifted in from larger cities like Toronto or Montreal. A few were local youths whose parents had either given up on them or were too busy with their own problems to care where their offspring were. In many cases the teens were running away from some kind of abuse.

With my natural inclination to be everyone's mother, I soon became personally involved in helping some of the kids get their lives in order. I hadn't learned yet how to detach from the pain of others, and most of these young people were suffering, even the ones who tried to hide behind profanities and outrageous wardrobes.

Bailey was a sixteen-year-old girl from Montreal. She was quite petite, even shorter than I was, and probably weighed about ninety-five pounds soaking wet. Her curly dyed blond hair framed a baby face with huge brown eyes. She had just had an abortion when I met her and was running away from the baby's father, a cruel bouncer in a strip club.

"Where are your parents?" I asked her one day.

"My mom's a hooker. I don't have a father."

"Your mom must be worried sick."

"I doubt it. She threw me out when one of her boyfriends hit on me."

"But surely someone's wondering where you are?"

"No one but René."

René was the ex-boyfriend who'd paid for her abortion when his beating hadn't accomplished the job.

"Well, you can't go back to him," I told her. "We'll find a new life for you here."

Bailey became my special project for a while. I was determined to help her turn her life around, even going as far as to suggest she move into my apartment, despite the protests of my friends and family. I even agreed to allow another homeless girl named Carrie who had befriended Bailey to sleep on my couch.

Both of them had problems with booze and drugs, so I carted them off to AA meetings every night. And I provided them with an ample supply of literature from both AA and NA. I went out of my way to serve the sorts of meals my mother cooked for me.

I made arrangements for Bailey to enter a long-term treatment centre in Bangor, Maine. Carrie didn't think she had that much of a problem. But both girls agreed to talk to a counsellor when I set it up. Later I took them to visit Heather and Sasha so they'd have a larger network of acquaintances. They both began playing with five-month-old Sasha as soon as they saw her.

Within two weeks Bailey, with Carrie in tow, was gone, running back to Montreal and the dangerous René. They stole food and the $50 I had stashed in a ceramic piggy bank. A note left on the kitchen table simply stated: "Sorry. I'll pay you back when I get to Montreal. Love, Bailey."

I never saw either of them again, and it took a long time to deal with my failure to shelter and transform them adequately. The money I'd lost meant nothing to me, and I'm sure I would have continued to take in other street kids had it not been for a new policy at work that prevented me from doing so.

My position required that I be qualified to meet the needs of the young people I worked with, which meant more training. I was ardent in my desire to pad my knowledge. When I wasn't at the centre in Fredericton, I was studying—family mediation, suicide prevention, dealing with sexual abuse, addiction, and teenage pregnancy. I even learned how to detect and respond to youth involvement in Satanic cults through a series of workshops presented by Pam Harquail.

Tracking kids who might be involved in cults was a high priority for some board members and one particular policeman. A sign of such involvement, according to Harquail, was obsession with occult symbols like pentagrams. Often the kids who came to the centre scribbled these symbols on paper or even carved them on buildings. Now, instead of accepting the graffiti as the distasteful art of bored and unhappy youths, I was told to keep a special eye on those who did it. If they exhibited other signs, such as interest in music with Satanic lyrics, I was to note it and inform the board. Since most of the music kids listened to at that time—Ozzy Osbourne, Black Sabbath, Wasp—could have been considered suspect, I figured I'd have to list most of the street kids who dropped into the centre. I thought it was ridiculous. But, just to be sure, I decided I'd better not tell anyone about my fortunetelling days. Even my involvement with Native ceremonies came under suspicion when one of the directors told my supervisor to keep an eye on what I was telling the kids about sweat-lodge ceremonies or any Native rituals for that matter. Regardless, I never met any serious Satan worshippers, even though I was certain the Devil had a hand in some of the homes these kids were fleeing.

THE SPIRITUAL SIDE OF THE PROGRAM

At AA I was introduced to the significance of pursuing a spiritual source of help and serenity, but the construct of that source was never dictated. If I'd been told it entailed anything remotely connected to organized religion, I would have probably opted for diving back into the bottle and doing laps. I didn't want any more sermons. I didn't want preachers shouting at me. I had been through a lot in life, more than any preacher could ever hope to understand. I was all grown up and the words of certain preachers I recalled seemed aimed at naive children.

These deliberations put me in a tight spot when two of my dear AA friends, Arnie and Helen, invited me to Cursillo, a spiritual retreat sponsored by the Anglican church. After discussing the idea with a few friends, I decided it might be a possibility. I knew I wanted to deepen that part of my life, but I was more than a little disquieted. The Anglican faith wasn't one of those charismatic religions, I reasoned, and the retreat wasn't being held in a church building. Cursillo would take place at Circle Square Ranch on Snyder Mountain in Sussex, an hour and fifteen minutes south of Fredericton.

When Arnie told me I would be picked up and dropped off as I wouldn't be needing my car while I was at the retreat, my confidence eroded and I almost backed out. It was just the excuse I needed to stay away, retreat into myself instead of into Cursillo.

"What if I get sick or have to leave for some reason?" I asked Helen and Arnie after an AA meeting in Fredericton. "What if I don't know anyone and I hate it?"

"You will know someone, Eve," Helen assured me. "Lynn and I will be there." Lynn was a friendly, soft-spoken French woman I'd met in AA.

"I'll pick you up if you get sick or anything," Arnie promised.

I stamped my feet like an angry child. "I'm not getting stuck up on some big hill in the middle of nowhere with a bunch of Bible-thumpers!"

Arnie put his big hand on my shoulder. "Cool down, kid. No one's trying to take you hostage."

"I'm not really sure about this church thing," I confessed.

"You'll like it, Eve," Helen insisted, patting my back reassuringly. "I was never one for church, either."

"Listen, I wasn't even sure about this God thing a few years ago," Arnie explained. "Look at me now. I'm a full-fledged Bible-thumper." He gave me a huge grin.

I'd never known Arnie to push the Bible on anyone. All he ever did was share his story about how he was a "rotten drunk" who went from being an atheist to being happy and satisfied with his life. I surveyed Arnie closely. It had obviously worked for him.

"Okay, I'll give it a try," I agreed. "But if I want out of there, you'd better be ready to come and get me."

"I'll be at your beck and call," he said. In fact, he even offered to drive me to Cursillo.

I packed a bag, choosing the plainest outfits I owned—Anglicans were quite conservative, I thought—and left for my weekend adventure, a little more confident now that I might have a good time. The drive to Snyder Mountain took about an hour. More like a big hill than a mountain, it was a pretty place surrounded by forests.

When we arrived at Cursillo, Arnie carried my bags to the door of the ranch-style building and gave me a hug.

"You're on your own, kid. Enjoy."

I was anxious as I walked through the door and entered a large reception area, but everyone was so friendly that my fears were soon dispelled. I was even more relieved when I ran into Helen and Lynn a few moments later. I believed they'd been watching for me.

The first evening I sat by myself in an armchair by the fireplace. I was feeling out of place and dislocated. My heart was racing and I was thinking about calling Arnie when an older silver-haired woman came up to me and said, "Hello," then settled in the chair beside me. We started to talk, and she learned of my hesitation about joining the others.

"I was nervous the first time I came here, too," she said, extending her hand. "My name's Bonnie."

"Hi, Bonnie," I said, shaking her hand. Touching her, I noticed her fingers were bent and twisted.

"Rheumatoid arthritis," she explained when she caught my eyes lingering on her fingers. "I look forward to these retreats now," she said with a little smile. "They give me strength to cope."

She spoke of her battle with the crippling disease and how God had given her courage to face the pain.

"God is wonderful," she admitted. "I'd never face a day without His strength. Sometimes I physically can't get out of bed."

"That must be a burden."

"But what about you?" Bonnie asked.

I acquainted her with my story of alcoholism and the pain it had caused. I told her that what I'd been through was nothing compared to the damage that had been inflicted upon my children. I admitted I still carried guilt and that I wasn't comfortable in a church setting.

"I used to be mad at God when I first came down with this disease," Bonnie said, shaking her head slightly. "But I soon learned things could be much worse." She paused for a moment to search my eyes. "I'd like to pray for you. Prayer is very powerful. Would that be okay with you?"

I didn't flinch when Bonnie placed her crippled hand on my shoulder. "Dear Lord," she said, "please let Eve find peace in this world. Please let her find peace with her past. And help her children cope with their hardships. Amen." Her eyes remained shut and her hand never left my shoulder. Two women walked by, but they appeared not to notice us. I figured prayer was a normal pastime here.

While Bonnie began to pray again, I felt a sterling warmth come over me. "Dear Lord, please allow Eve to forgive herself for the mistakes she's made. She knows she was wrong. She's suffering and she needs your love." When Bonnie was finished, she leaned forward and gave me a big, warm hug. She even touched my cheek briefly the way my Grammie Mills used to. Then she rubbed my back with her crippled hand and leaned away from me. "I'll be keeping an eye on you this weekend," she said with a wink. "You don't need to feel alone."

Our conversation was cut short by a call for the evening meal. "I need to make a fast trip to the ladies' room," Bonnie said. "I'll see you later."

Over the next three days, Bonnie and I stopped to chat often, and she continued to focus on the positive in my present life, instead of dwelling on past blunders.

"Remember, your children see your strength," she pointed out one evening when we were sitting just outside the chapel. "They're affected by the courage it took for you to face your mistakes and correct them as much as they were affected by the bad choices you made in the past." Her smile was so kind that I suspected she might really be an angel. I'd always believed there were angels on earth. I'd even read somewhere that everyone had one of their own.

"I'm sure they're really proud of you," she continued. "You're doing something important with your life and the best is yet to come." I appreciated hearing the words, but I was nowhere near the stage of recovery where I actually felt proud of myself.

I was surprised to find myself enjoying others' talk concerning certain passages in the Bible that helped them deal with obstacles in their lives. The scriptures were pure poetry containing beautiful and often stunning reflections and sentiments. Bonnie particularly admired the verse from Philippians 4:13: "I can do all things through Christ which strengtheneth me." I was fond of that creed, too, and made a mental note to write it down on the cover of my AA book so I wouldn't forget it.

When they offered Communion on the last day of the retreat, during a simple service, I participated with the others. But I still felt I wasn't actually part of the community. I felt like a fraud in God's eyes. I was a guest among these devout Christian women, a guest at the banquet who didn't deserve to eat.

Returning to Fredericton, this time with Helen and Lynn, I attended a few of the follow-up meetings, but the destitution inside me hadn't abated. This wasn't the religion for me. It wasn't helping, so I soon stopped attending meetings altogether.

A few months later, when Arnie died unexpectedly from a heart ailment, my association with that religious community expired, as well. Helen and I attended the funeral together. So did many of his AA friends and several people I recognized from the retreat, including Bonnie. She lived in Saint John, about an hour away, and she told me I was welcome to visit as we both tearfully said our final good-byes to Arnie. I knew I'd miss Arnie's encouragement and the humour with which he faced life's challenges.

A DAY TO BE PROUD

I often listened to men and women in AA express gratitude for sobriety's special gifts. I'd experienced several of these gifts myself: being there to see my grandchildren born, being able to support Heather and keep myself from falling apart when Aleshia died. These were gifts that drinking would have never allowed me. It was important to know I could be dependable. Even more important was the ability to take part in my children's successes.

The day that Jennifer graduated from high school was one of the proudest moments of my life. I couldn't let go of the thought that she was my baby. She'd endeavoured to take care of her son, Billy, and still keep her marks up while others would have dropped out. She'd thought about throwing in the towel many times, she later told me, but I'd never seen any hint of that.

Jennifer was one of more than two hundred students scheduled to graduate that day, including my youngest brother, Steven; Jennifer's best friend, Angie Noble; and Jennifer's boyfriend, Fred. June 20, 1991, was extremely hot—thirty-three degrees Celsius. And the heat seemed even worse as I entered the packed gymnasium of Oromocto High School. I hadn't been in the gym since 1967. Curious, I looked at the bleachers and stackable chairs arranged on the floor. There were blue and gold decorations on the walls, the school's colours. Sonya and Heather were with me. Mom and Dad had come along to celebrate the accomplishments of their son and grand-daughter. I'd thought about bringing Billy, but I finally decided it would be no place for a three-year-old, so he stayed with Debbie and Dwight, the couple who helped Jennifer after Billy was born.

I'd had my hair done for the special occasion and I was wearing a new green-and-white polished cotton suit. It was a stroke of luck that I'd chosen a cool material. The gymnasium felt like a sauna and the air was stifling. There were numerous parents and grandparents present.

I waited for Jennifer's name to be announced. They were being called out alphabetically. Patiently I sat there, sweating and blowing air up at my face, fanning myself with the program the school had provided. I was growing more and more grateful Jennifer's last name started with a *C*.

Finally I heard her name called and my eyes were fixed on my daughter as she marched to the podium in her long blue gown with gold trim. I beamed with satisfaction at the charming woman she'd become. Her beauty went far beyond the delicateness of her features or her long, thick auburn hair. She had the heart of a saint, always trying to help and comfort others, even when she was distressed herself. When she took the diploma in her hand, tears spilled from my eyes.

After the ceremony, Jennifer and Steven met us outside. Dad insisted on a few hundred snapshots.

"You look beautiful," I quietly told Jennifer. "I'm so proud of you, baby." I looked at my youngest brother. "And you, too, young man," I said, patting him on the back. He was at least a foot taller than I was.

I was even more delighted when they both left for a safe graduation party, free from alcohol or drugs.

LITTLE ORANGE SQUAW

It wasn't until the fall of 1991 that I took up with another Native man. My marriage to Stan was almost eighteen years behind me, but not entirely forgotten. I'd become good friends with Irene, a tall, dark-skinned Mi'gmaq woman from the Lennox Island Reserve in Prince Edward Island. She had moved to Fredericton to attend university. I met her at an AA meeting.

I also first met Elijah at an AA meeting. In a room full of conservatively dressed men and women, he stood out with his braided, waist-length black hair and bright beaded headband. My eyes kept shifting toward him during the evening. There was a sensuousness about him, an aura of mystery. After the meeting, Irene introduced us as we were leaving for the coffee shop. Elijah had been sober for only a few weeks, he told me when I inquired. I invited him to join us for coffee and he said yes. He was a soft-spoken, gentle Mi'gmaq from the Red Bank Reserve. Irene already knew him from one of the Native gatherings she'd attended there.

At the coffee shop Elijah sat across from me and Irene. He spoke few words but smiled plenty. Elijah didn't take his eyes off my face, and he listened intently to my every word. When I paused to take a sip of coffee, he gazed directly into my eyes.

"You're very beautiful," he said. I was self-conscious and excited at the same time, so I let the compliment slip by without any response.

Elijah seemed to have a gentle spirit and his mood was soothing. When he asked for my telephone number as we were preparing to leave, I didn't hesitate. I often gave my number to AA members who might need a friend. It was a common practice at AA. The idea was to phone someone if you felt you were heading for a bottle. All too often, though, the calls came afterward, when the member was already drunk.

"Make sure you use this *before* you drink," I joked as I handed him my number.

"I always call pretty women," he replied, again looking directly into my eyes. *He has eyes like an eagle*, I thought, laughing off his compliment, then heading quickly to my car to hide my red face and pounding heart. Irene rode with me in my car.

"I think he likes you," she said.

"You're crazy," I kidded.

"You wait and see. He'll be in touch all right."

I shook my head but hoped he would, feeling like a teenager again. I dropped Irene off at her apartment in Forest Hill and headed across the Princess Margaret Bridge to my place. I was hoping Peter might be around so I could tell him about my meeting. But, as usual, he was out. I seldom saw him anymore, except when he paid his board. Our schedules were so varied.

When I woke the next morning, a Saturday, Elijah's compliments from the night before were fresh in my thoughts. Later that day the phone rang.

"I was thinking about drinking some more coffee," Elijah teased when I answered. "Can you help me?"

"Well, I suppose I could make a twelve-step call," I quipped, then agreed to meet him at a coffee shop in an hour.

That day we each drank four cups of coffee and went for a walk on the green beside the Saint John River. We talked and strolled, finally settling near the train bridge. After that we began seeing each other practically every day.

"Close your eyes and picture the eagle," Elijah whispered one day as I lay on the rug in his apartment. "He's letting the wind carry him higher and higher. You're floating with him. Let yourself feel the breeze. Float with him."

After some practice, I could put everything out of my head by concentrating on one of my favourite animals, usually an eagle or a black bear. Elijah told me the bear was my spirit helper, and that notion made me feel relaxed enough to put worry and fear out of my mind for short, rejuvenating periods.

Our friendship was based on curiosity. Elijah was intrigued by my experiences as a fortuneteller, and I wanted to know more about Native spirituality. Since we were both lonely, we were a comfort to each other in a time of immense spiritual need. Elijah couldn't seem to make his meditation techniques work for himself for long. Alcohol and drugs often proved too powerful for his best intentions.

In December he went home to visit his kids and fell off the wagon. He said he'd tried to block out everything he felt when it came time to leave them. He even prayed to the Creator and asked his spirit helper to guide him. He got drunk, anyway. When he told me the turtle was one of his protectors, I suggested he should switch to something a little more agile since he was having such a battle. That made him laugh, but I was deadly serious.

Elijah became one of my teachers. There was no great passion between us. I simply helped him examine his worth and he helped me define mine. I'd spend hours talking to him about such things as acceptance and forgiveness. He told me he'd been sent away to a residential school in Nova Scotia when he was a child. There he had been beaten for speaking his mother tongue. He was angry with the priests who had been his tormentors. I shared with him some of my experiences of abuse.

"I understand your frustration, Elijah," I told him one afternoon as we sat by the river. "But until you release that, forgive them, they'll always take up space in your head. They don't need to be there. They're harming you still. That space could be given to something much more worthy, like your paintings."

Elijah nodded in agreement.

I made sure he attended AA meetings, and he made certain I took time out for fun. We attended AA dances and even went to one hosted at the New Brunswick College of Craft and Design where Elijah was studying.

Elijah had been deeply scarred by his childhood. He said he came from a mixed-up family. He wouldn't talk about the details, but there was no mistaking the pain in his eyes. When any subject was too painful for discussion, Elijah lapsed into complete silence and became stone faced.

He often spoke about the limbo world created by the clash of cultures. "It's hard to know who you are when your skin is brown and mostly everyone else around you is white," he said, referring to residential school. "I spent my whole life feeling different. They made me feel it was wrong to be different."

Elijah helped instill in me a sensitivity for the plight of Native children raised in white homes.

"You need to know who you are to feel whole," he told me. "If you're an Indian, you're an Indian. No matter where you live. It's not a choice. It's not like a Catholic turning Protestant and learning to adjust. And most white people don't see that."

I could relate to some extent from my time in Tyendinaga. Elijah was the first one to explain to me why certain Natives were called *apples* or *born-again Indians*. I'd heard Calvin, a Maliseet friend of Elijah's, refer to a mutual acquaintance, another Mi'gmaq, in this manner.

"He grew up with a white family," Elijah said. "Now he wants to learn about his real ancestors. He's red on the outside like us, but on the inside, his ways, he's white. And that makes for one screwed-up Indian." We were sitting in my living room getting ready to go to a meeting.

Elijah cited the case of Canadian Prime Minister Jean Chrétien's adopted son, Michael. He told me Michael Chrétien had been born in Inuvik, Northwest Territories, the son of an Inuit woman named Anne Kendi who, at the time, was struggling with alcoholism. The boy went into a local orphanage where Michel Chrétien, the prime minister's brother, discovered him while working as a medical volunteer. When the boy was eighteen months old, he was adopted by Chrétien and his wife and grew up in the same household as his new, lighter-complexioned brother, Hubert, and sister, France.

"They probably thought they were doing a good thing," Elijah pointed out, rising to make a pot of tea. "He certainly would have everything money could buy. How could they know what it would be like stranded between the red and white paths?"

Elijah said Michael became an *apple.* It was easy to see he was part of the red race, but he was living in a white world and learning only white ways. Elijah had read somewhere that Michael was a troubled boy. "And it can only get worse," he said with certainty.

Elijah was a gifted painter and jewellery maker who worked in many forms: birchbark paintings, oil paintings, beaded earrings, necklaces, and wood carvings. As long as he stayed away from the bottle, his steady, patient hands carved art out of anything. He crafted me a leather vest with an eagle painted on the back. The eagle, recognized by all North American Native people as the creature closest to the Creator, was meant to be my protector.

He also gave me a walking stick, the handle shaped like a wolf head, beads and fur attached. "This will protect you for sure," he told me. "If you use it right, it could pack quite a punch."

I laughed as I thanked him. His generosity and compassion definitely had a positive influence over me. He was a true gentle man. I had never met a man quite like him before, nor did I suspect they even existed. Even my second husband hadn't been so generous, though he, too, was quite gentle.

Surrounded with gifts from an admirer, I was no longer anyone's "little white squaw," a name I'd come to associate with "doormat." I was just a positively happy woman.

During this period, I encountered many women of colour on my travels to Native gatherings and special events with Elijah. Some of these women also visited my apartment. Stepping back into the Native community, after having gone through a failed Native marriage, made me feel even more like a pale relation. My concerns about my pallid skin colour resurfaced. Maybe Elijah would start to notice our differences more. Maybe no one would accept me.

This time I decided to be a little more practical. I was certain colour wasn't worth the risk of being afflicted with skin cancer, so I opted for the colour that came in a tube. I'd heard about women on the rez using sunless suntan lotion to darken their skin. So I went to the local drugstore and walked out with a half-dozen tubes of sunless tanning cream guaranteed to toast my body golden brown overnight.

I was attending a Native conference in the morning at Saint Thomas University on the other side of the river. One of the guest lecturers was a woman from Nova Scotia who was scheduled to talk about the criminal justice system and how it adversely affected Natives.

For the conference I wanted to be dark. So the night before the event I stayed home to prepare. I laid the tubes of cream on the night table, placed a large multicoloured towel on the floor beside the bed, and sat down. I started with my legs and wondered, as I spread the cream evenly over the front, whether I should use as much for the backs of my legs. And what about my feet? Did I apply it there? The soles, too? I figured I should probably do the tops anyway. Smearing the cream on my face was the most diffi-cult task. How close to my eyes should I go? I wondered. And what about my ears? The instructions said: "Coat evenly. Avoid the eyes." A wealth of information. I was left to use my best judge-ment. The entire slathering process took about an hour.

Carefully I laid out towels to protect the sheets on the bed, under and around me, before settling in that night to dream of the new, darker me. Elijah was working late on a project at the college, so I'd suggested he stay at his apartment. He lived on the opposite side of the Saint John River. This would be a surprise for him. I smiled confidently to myself as I lay on the towels, my arms slightly out at my sides to make certain I didn't smudge my coating. Lying in the darkness, I felt as if I were trying to obtain a tan from an invisible sun.

The next morning, when I awoke, I couldn't wait to catch sight of my new skin in the mirror. With glasses in hand I stumbled to the bathroom to view my Native transformation. Fumbling the frames onto my face, I saw all too clearly. I studied my reflection in awe, my jaw slowly slackening.

There I stood in all my glory—a sickly orange-brown amid paler streaks of white and beige. I was dumbfounded. My heart dropped to my knees as I quickly took stock of the damage. The only positive aspect I could come up with was that, fortunately, my face was evenly coated. Regardless, I looked as if I was done up for Halloween.

After the first few waves of dread shuddered through me, a simple enough thought offered itself: *Well, I definitely managed to get my own unique colour!* I burst out with a chuckle. What a mess I'd made of myself.

I had no choice but to attend the conference the way I was—with an orange face and a stern expression that dared anyone to pass comment on my amazing metamorphosis. *Just let someone make a comment*, I thought. *I'll tell them where to go.* But no one even mentioned it. *Amazing what new skin colour can do for your attitude.*

When I returned home that evening, full of intriguing information from the conference, I immediately tossed the remaining tubes of lotion into the garbage. I'd already had a shower that morning, but I had another, praying the soap and water would wash away my cosmetic transgressions. No such luck.

When Elijah came over later, his eyes widened the instant I opened the door. He tried not to laugh. I was striving not to smirk, as well, but Elijah couldn't hold it back.

"Don't you dare," I warned him, but he laughed his head off and soon I joined him.

"Zebra," he called me as he entered my apartment. "Why aren't you satisfied with your own colour?"

"I don't have one," I joked, but as my response registered I felt there was truth to those words.

With each day that my skin lightened, I breathed a little easier. I spent so much time in front of the mirror that I thought I was actually willing my skin whiter.

Later I learned from Irene that she'd heard a white woman in Red Bank say there were much more effective brands available than the one I had chosen. She told me this in case I wanted to give it another go. But, no, I'd sworn off the Native tan in a tube. Never again. I had learned my zebra lesson.

When Elijah went home to visit his children and their mother again, he ended up getting drunk once more. He called me long-distance to come and get him. My friend from the spiritual retreat, Helen, went with me to collect him and bring him back to Fredericton. When we drove into Red Bank Reserve, Helen headed for the house where his children lived. She had grown up in a village nearby so she knew almost everyone there. Elijah was waiting for us with his suitcase beside him. His usual neatly braided hair hung loosely over his shoulders. He smelled like stale beer.

Elijah proclaimed he was glad to be coming back to Fredericton, but things would never be the same between us. Elijah missed his children, and I suspected he still loved their mother, his second wife. When he left his studies and me in March 1991 to return to Red Bank, I wasn't that surprised. He'd been steadily withdrawing from me and had stopped attending AA.

Irene offered comfort by inviting me out to dinner. Miles and I had coffee, and he assured me I'd find someone soon who was right for me, whatever that meant. Miles was dating a woman in AA named Marg and appeared happy. He told me he was even thinking of tying the knot again.

I missed Elijah, so I decided to submerge myself completely in AA and my job with the street kids. My own children were busy with their lives, and I could find plenty of work to keep me occupied.

FIDDLEHEADS

PART THREE

1991-1993

MY FIRST SWEAT

In 1991, when I was forty-one, I met Chuck, a Native from Oromocto First Nation. He was five feet, six inches and slightly built. Agile like a cat, he possessed great discipline and was a successful hunter and fisherman with alert eyes that seemed to see as sharply as any hawk. I considered him handsome, with his thick curly black hair and matching moustache. Neat and clean, he was a skilled woodsman with a vast knowledge of survival under the most adverse conditions. As a child, he'd learned all about the wilderness from his father, and he was fiercely proud of his Maliseet heritage.

When I met Chuck, I had been sober for four years and honestly believed I had my life together. I was living on my own and still working for the street outreach organization. My own children were all living independently. Heather was in Oromocto. Tony was released from jail and stopped by to see Sasha a couple of times. One night, while drinking, he and Heather got into another fight. Fearing the repercussions of violating his probation, he took off to parts unknown to avoid going back to jail. Heather continued to drink, but Sasha remained with her whenever she could stay straight. Child and family services were monitoring the situation at Heather's request. Whenever she slipped into addiction or became sick and ended up in hospital, Sasha spent that period of time in foster care. That bothered Heather and it certainly weighed heavily on my mind. No doubt we all remembered what had happened to Aleshia while in foster care. Heather was finding it harder and harder to control her cravings for alcohol and cocaine since the death of her first child two years earlier.

Jody had returned from Kingston and was living with his girlfriend, Terri Lynn, in an apartment in Fredericton. It was his first major romance. He was working as a short-order cook at a fastfood restaurant. When he and Terri Lynn eventually broke up, Jody was devastated. To turn his mind from the heartache, he decided to hit the road yet again, this time with his friend, Dennis, and headed west to see the world. His road trip, in one of the worst storms that winter, caused me great concern, but I needn't have worried. He was a clever young man. If there was anything I'd taught him, it was resourcefulness and faith.

Dennis and Jody finally arrived in Cranbrook, British Columbia, a few weeks later, after being forced to abandon their worn-out car in Winnipeg. It quit on the highway. Luckily for them there was an emergency telephone down the road. Dennis searched through the Yellow Pages and found a number for a towing service. When the tow truck showed up, the driver told Dennis and Jody the car probably had a cracked engine block and suggested they sell it for scrap. He knew a nearby junkyard. Jody and Dennis went along with the plan. After they paid for the towing fee, they had just enough money left to buy coffee, potato chips, and two bus tickets to Calgary.

Arriving in Calgary, they sought out the local welfare office and applied for emergency funding to book them a room for the night, a meal, and two tickets to British Columbia where they planned to bunk with friends who had moved there from the East Coast. This would tide them over until they could find work. Jody remained in British Columbia for two years, working at odd jobs and finally attending Kootenay College to study business administration.

Sonya and her husband, Harry, were living in Geary and expecting their second child. Harry had recently passed his tractor-trailer test and was lucky enough to land a well-paying local job. At the time their daughter, Brittany, was two.

My baby, Jennifer, was still living with her son, Billy, in an apartment in Oromocto. I continued sharing my apartment with Peter, who was home more these days, playing his guitar at nights and singing. He had a soft country voice, so we often sat around and sang together. We'd performed a couple of times at AA events. Another girl, Shawn, a tiny woman with glasses and a pixie face, would join us when she visited, and before long we decided to try our luck as a trio. We called ourselves Second Chance and had our first gig singing at an AA convention in Fredericton. We sang three highly different sorts of songs: "The Rose," made famous by Bette Midler; "Peaceful Easy Feeling," an Eagles classic; and "Don't Close Your Eyes," a new country song by Keith Whitley. We were far from professional, but several people told us they liked our harmony. I found great solace in singing, so I looked forward to our practices. For a while they became the highlight of my life.

After that we sang at a few more local benefits until one day Shawn received a call from a man at City Hall, asking if our trio would be interested in performing. The mayor was having a special celebration on the tourist attraction riverboat *Pioneer Princess*. It would be our first and last paying gig.

The night before our scheduled performance Peter got drunk, started mouthing off at someone, and ended up with a stunning black eye. When I saw him the next morning after he woke up and wandered out to the living room, I asked, "Peter, what happened to you?"

"I had a close encounter."

"You can't go like that to our concert." I sat him down at the kitchen table and applied makeup to his eye. It just made him look worse. I knew it was hopeless.

"It's just as well, anyway," Peter said. "I probably would've screwed up."

I left him sitting there and called Shawn to break the news. She was really ticked off. "I should've known," she said. "I should've expected as much from him." She told me she'd call the organizer and explain one of us was sick.

Peter still boarded with me, but our trio was disbanded. And though he continued to drink off and on, we were able to maintain our friendship.

Theresa, a woman I had sponsored in AA my second year sober, had become a close friend and confidante. We were both Sagittarians, cared deeply about people and our spiritual growth, and had always been attracted to men who were bad for us. Theresa was four years younger than I was but had an unusual number of health problems. She walked with a cane when arthritis made it difficult to manoeuvre and frequently suffered excruciating outbreaks of shingles. Somehow she seldom complained. Irene, my Mi'gmaq buddy, and I still spent a great deal of time together at her place or mine as she patiently taught me about her culture, its ceremonies, and belief system. Occasionally we'd attend special events, like Native awareness days, at the university.

Life seemed to settle down, and I began to feel better about myself.

Shortly after I met Chuck, Irene invited me to a powwow in Nova Scotia. It was to be held at the Millbrook Reserve in Shubenacadie. Chuck heard us making plans one night at the coffee shop and asked if he and another friend, Bobby, could join us. I agreed.

It was one of those warm, lovely spring days when we set out from Fredericton in my old silver Ford station wagon. The back was stuffed with our bags, Chuck's guitar, and a cooler filled with sandwiches and soda. I had an Eagles tape blasting away in the car stereo. Irene and I sat up front loudly singing along with the familiar refrains of "Hotel California" and "Life in the Fast Lane." We knew them all and had sung them countless times before while driving around Fredericton en route to meetings or coffee get-togethers. Occasionally I'd hear Chuck and Bobby joining in from the back seat. Irene had a Native drumming and chanting tape with her, and we listened to that for a while, as well.

About halfway to our destination, in Sackville, steam started pouring from the front of the car. "Abandon ship," Bobby hollered as I pulled over to the side of the road near a sign that said: WELCOME TO SACKVILLE. I was convinced it couldn't be anything serious. We all got out of the car, and Chuck checked under the hood.

"Radiator," he said to me. "Rusty as hell. No way of doing a patch job."

I looked at him, then at the steam billowing from the engine.

"She's shot," Chuck said, suddenly scowling. "What're we going to do now?"

I wasn't sure, but I didn't appreciate his sour mood. The rest of us were smiling, trying to remain optimistic. There had to be another way to get back on the road.

"I knew I shouldn't have come on this trip," Chuck mumbled, glaring at me accusingly.

"There's always the bus," I suggested, ticked off with him. I wanted to tell him to take his things and leave, but he apologized with a sheepish smile and suggested we call a tow truck. We all searched for a phone. Luckily there was a small roadside motel a hundred yards down the road. Bobby offered to go make the call.

The man from the towing service delivered my car to a garage that wouldn't be open for two days. He left it in the lot, then dropped us in front of the same roadside hotel where Bobby had used the phone. We decided to pool our money, rent a room, and worry about sleeping arrangements later. Bobby and Irene barely knew each other, and I hadn't planned on sleeping with Chuck.

We sat on the hotel bed, feeling out of place. Our mission had been abruptly terminated.

"What next?" I asked Irene. She'd just come out of the bathroom after freshening up. It was nine o'clock on a Friday evening.

"I think we should eat," she said. "Yeah, let's eat." So we all headed for the dining room attached to the motel. We only had a small amount of money left. Noting breakfast was served all day, we decided to order bacon and eggs. It came with coffee and was the cheapest item on the menu.

Back in the room, Irene called her brother in Shubenacadie and left a message on his answering machine, informing him where we were. Chuck turned on the TV, but no one watched it. We joked about our circumstances. Even Chuck seemed more agreeable with a full stomach. Shortly after midnight, Irene's brother called back and told her he'd have someone pick us up in the morning. It was welcome news. Everything was back on track.

Tired from the eventful day, I settled quickly in one bed with Irene while Chuck grabbed the other one.

"I ain't sleeping with you," Bobby told Chuck with a laugh. He snatched up a pillow and blanket and stretched out on the floor.

I fell asleep almost immediately. I was too exhausted to think.

Early the next morning two Native men in their twenties pulled up in a white van. Irene had given our room number over the phone, so they came directly to our door as I was getting out of the shower. Our rescue party had arrived from Nova Scotia. They had driven the extra distance to retrieve us, even though neither of them had met any of us before.

I remember listening to the Traveling Wilburys singing on the radio: "It's all right, even when your car don't drive. It's all right as long as you've got someone to love." Everyone thought that was pretty funny and started singing along. All I could think about was the broken car radiator and the idea that I was penniless. I had less than $10 now and a bank card that could get me another

$20. That wouldn't go far, though.

"What a mess," I said to Irene, but she wasn't having any of my grief. She just laughed and sang louder, a little off-key.

"How are we going to get back?" I asked, my thoughts already pulling me toward the safety of home. "We don't have any money." I wondered what my kids were doing. Sonya was due to have her second baby. Why hadn't I stayed home to be with her? I was beginning to regret my escape, feeling selfish and unworthy.

Irene kept singing.

"How?" I repeated.

"Just relax and have fun. It'll be looked after."

I studied her big, cheerful brown face and wondered how she did it. Nothing could dampen her spirits. My mood had turned bitter, and her cheerfulness only increased my desolation.

"Come on," she implored, slapping my leg. "Sing."

One of the other men—who said his name was Billy, like my grandson—backed her up. "It's better than crying," he said.

Soon the party mood kicked in and began to win me over. By the time we reached the gathering, my throat was sore from singing and my heart had lightened in anticipation of a weekend of ceremony.

The aroma of the fresh bread was a welcoming scent as I entered the recreational centre, a high-ceilinged building with rows of tables at one end. There must have been more than a hundred people—mostly Native—standing around talking to one another. Dozens of happy children ran back and forth, playing what appeared to be a game of tag. I'd never seen so many bright costumes outside of a masquerade: brown and tan leathers, the colour of coffee with cream, decorated with multihued beads and feathers; shirts and skirts of all tints with satin ribbons; and bright shawls draped over braids and vital brown skin. The energy in the place lifted my spirits in no time.

I didn't know a soul, and when Chuck and Bobby went off visiting people, I stayed close to Irene, but she was soon rushing to hug old friends and family members who laughed heartily when they saw her. I was being introduced and hugged along with my travelling companions, welcomed into the gathering, not as a stranger, but as one of them.

Soon we were drawn to the food. Plates laden with warm fry bread and pots brimming with corn soup covered one long wooden table. Large kettles of tea and coffee, paper cups, sugar and milk, and bottles of juice crowded another smaller table. We were told the ceremonies would begin soon. I knew from hanging around with Irene that *soon* might mean a few minutes or a few hours. We were on Indian time now. Schedules and watches were useless at a powwow. Things happened when they happened.

Irene said the Grand Entrance, a march-in of special people with the elders at the lead, marked the opening of the powwow, but it had already taken place before our arrival. An elder had smudged the food with the purifying smoke from burning sweetgrass. Now we were waiting for a local drum group to arrive so the dancing could commence.

When the drummers appeared, a very tall Native man dressed in leather, the master of ceremonies, invited everyone to join the intertribal dance. That meant all tribes and nationalities, including whites, were welcome. In one corner the children danced around the drummers and chanters. Babies tapped their tiny moccasins on the floor beside their mothers and fathers. Elders, hardly able to stand on their feet, seemed to find new life as they slid one foot in front of the other, giving themselves over to the invigorating drumbeat.

With large steaming mugs of tea in hand, we all found a place to sit so we could watch the dancers. Men in regalia—beaded leather costumes with feather headdresses—had gathered around the drummers in the centre of the hall. Slowly they began to dance in a graceful march. Some carried wooden staffs with animal heads carved on the tops. Others shook hand-carved rattles that hissed an accompaniment to the drums.

As the drums grew louder, the dancers' pace increased, taking on a methodical bounce, the movements of their bodies blending seamlessly with the beat. Soon they began to spin, gyrating in rhythm with the loud chanting that filled the room, ricocheting off the walls and mounting toward hypnotic intoxication.

Irene leaned toward me, then nodded at the floor in front of us. "C'mon."

"Are you crazy?" I gasped.

"Never mind that, Lone Ranger. Just get up."

She rose, grabbed my arm, and hauled me to my feet. I didn't protest. I followed her and hid on the inside of the circle beside Irene, who was almost a foot taller than I was. I didn't think I could pick up the rhythm and didn't want anyone to notice my bumbling steps. But the steady, pulsating drumbeat soon loosened the muscles in my legs. The resounding chanting transcended the confines of language and further enraptured me. This surreal experience prompted a sort of weightlessness. My sneakers moved as evenly as the moccasins around me. I was no longer self-conscious. The music filled my head, resonating deeper, touching me spiritually as I danced. Contained within this limitless circle, within the ancient beat and rapturous chanting, I discovered an acceptance, a purity that surmounted human want or longing. It was as if I were flying.

Chuck and Bobby spent most of their time talking to people they knew from the various Native communities. Bobby was from Eel Ground, New Brunswick, and recognized others from the same community. Chuck was the only Native from Oromocto, but he knew several people from Membertou on Cape Breton Island and Woodstock First Nation in New Brunswick. I wasn't sure if they even danced at all. I was too caught up in the music.

After the dance, I felt grounded in a disoriented way. The four of us headed out to spend the rest of the night at an elder's house, a five-minute walk from the centre where the festivities were being coordinated on the Millbrook Reserve.

When we arrived there, women were already seated around the kitchen table talking about plans for the morning. There were to be two sweat-lodge ceremonies, one for the women and another for the men. When Irene suggested I join the women for the sweat-lodge ceremony, I leaped at the opportunity. I was still high from the evening of dancing, the pulse of the drums still beating in my head. I was sure the sweat-lodge ceremony would be equally exhilarating. If the ceremonies were going to make me feel this good, then I wanted to be fully indoctrinated.

Perhaps, by being a part of this ancient sweat-lodge ceremony, I'd come closer to melding with the Native community, closer to understanding the Native people who had been, and still were, such an important part of my life. I was fairly certain Chuck and I were headed for a serious relationship, and I wanted to know more about his Maliseet ancestry and the lifestyle from which he had descended.

The sweat-lodge ceremony for the women was scheduled for sunrise the next morning. It was after 2:00 a.m. when, fully clothed, we finally settled into our sleeping bags on the living-room floor of Elder Libby's house. She had put up twenty-two people in her small three-bedroom bungalow. Because it was so late before the conversation ebbed, I suspected everyone would sleep in, forget about the sweat-lodge ritual, and do it a little later in the day.

I dozed peacefully, pleasantly exhausted and enriched by my new experiences. It was a clean, sweet sleep that held no threat, the delightful repose that can only be appreciated by a fatigued mother.

What seemed only moments later, I felt someone roughly shake me. Grumbling, I hesitantly opened my eyes to see another one of

Irene's huge, undefeatable grins only inches from my face. I squinted groggily at my watch. It wasn't even five o'clock! I moaned and shut my eyes.

"Are you gonna sleep all day?" Irene demanded. "There's work to do, *dus*."

Reluctantly I sat up and tried to get my bearings. Then, standing, I made my way to the bathroom.

"Put on your nightgown for the ceremony," Irene called after me. "And hurry."

I reached into my small suitcase, still perched on a chair by the bathroom door, and retrieved a red flannel sleeveless gown and my toothbrush. I washed, brushed my teeth, threw on the nightgown, then sat in the kitchen beside Irene. There was a plastic container filled with tobacco on the table next to several lengths of coloured cotton. Irene nodded at the container.

"I don't smoke, remember?" I mumbled sleepily.

"It's not for smoking, stupid!" Irene laughed, and so did the other women sitting with her. "It's for making tobacco ties for an offering. For the sweat."

"Oh." I wasn't sure what she meant, but I obediently followed her lead. Before long I was clumsily braiding different coloured pieces of ribbon with small clumps of tobacco tucked inside. I had a hard time getting the knack of it. Elder Libby sat beside me and patiently showed me how to hold the material in place so I wouldn't lose most of the tobacco on the table.

"The harder your work, the better your prayers," the old woman told me. "Just watch what I do."

I didn't quite understand the symbolism, but I went along, meticulously following her directions. Soon the kitchen was full of women engaged in some sort of activity; most of them were dressed in cotton nightgowns. The men were still all sleeping. *How nice for them*, I thought, feeling cheated.

"Hard work being a man," a middle-aged woman with a blue

robe said, as if reading my thoughts.

"Hey, we're the lucky ones," a massive Mi'gmaq woman in a flowered flannelette nightgown replied. She had a red bandanna tied around her head and exuded a heartening strength. "Women have the power, you know." She must have tipped the scales at more than three hundred pounds and looked as solid as a mountain.

Irene seemed amused by my silence, chuckling and peeking at me while she went about her duties.

When we stepped outside, the air was early-morning cool. It was almost completely dark. We walked together down a quiet reserve road that led toward a wooded area. With the shadowy, predawn landscape around me, I began to question my readiness for the ceremony. These thoughts multiplied, vaulting out of control, and I began to get scared.

What am I getting into? I asked myself. *What would my Christian parents think if they heard about this? What does God think?*

My thoughts were frenzied, but before I could decide to back out, I noticed everyone had stopped in someone's backyard. It was growing lighter, but it was still difficult to see. It appeared we were at the sweat lodge, a simple dome covered with blankets and tarps, the kind my brothers used for shelter in the woods when we were fishing or hunting. It was nothing like what I expected. Quiet. Unassuming. *How can fourteen women fit in there?*

A few feet away tiny orange tongues of fire danced among thin spirals of smoke rising from a shallow pit in the ground. Rocks peeked through the gaps in the thick wooden slabs that had been arranged specifically to keep them from catching fire. They were used to cover and contain the heat.

"Those rocks'll be carried inside the lodge," Irene explained, "to another shallow pit where they'll be covered with water to make steam."

As my eyes adjusted to the burgeoning light, I discerned we were on a street surrounded by several bungalows, most of them painted green. Behind the line of houses there was a thick wooded area. *We must be on a back street*, I thought. I was startled to see a man with bushy black hair standing eerily beside the fire with what I guessed was a pitchfork. I almost yelped and bolted.

Irene put her arm around my shoulders. "That's the firekeeper. A very hard job. He's been here for hours preparing this for us. The fork's to carry in rocks."

"Oh" was all I could manage to utter as Irene giggled. Her laughter, plus the fact that I now understood I wasn't about to be skewered by the pitchfork, helped ease my tension. A few of the women had already started to duck into the sweat lodge.

"We have to smudge with sweetgrass," Irene said as we moved closer to the flames beside the firekeeper. She continued with her explanation while we shifted in place around the rocks. "Offer tobacco and prayers to the fire before we enter." I followed her lead. Continuing to circle, we threw tobacco, picked from a nearby bowl, into the flames and paused to pray, bowing our heads and silently offering our requests to each of the four directions—north, south, east, west. I didn't really grasp the meaning of the entire process, but I followed diligently out of respect, a sense of spiritual awe, and fear of making any mistakes that would paint me as more of an outcast or a spy. The tobacco ties we'd worked on were hung somewhere else, Irene told me.

When the firekeeper was convinced everyone had been washed by smoke from the burning sweetgrass, he nodded and we headed for the lodge door. Removing our shoes, jewellery, and eyeglasses, we handed them to the firekeeper, who now stood beside the open canvas flap. His unsmiling face did nothing to reassure me that I would be all right once inside the lodge. I dragged my blue towel with me like a security blanket. Irene's was wrapped around her neck.

As the sun began to rise behind us, golden fingers pointing into the eastern door of the sweat lodge, Irene dropped to her hands and knees to crawl inside. I watched her white nightgown go before me, then I fell to all fours and quickly inched close behind her, not wanting to stray from her side.

Inside the lodge we crept to the left of the fire pit as far as we could go and squeezed in. I was already feeling warm and they hadn't brought in the first rock yet. It was quite dark, even with the door flap still open, shadowy in a way that made everything unreal. I was beginning to feel uneasy again, but the heady smell of soft, spongy cedar boughs that carpeted the floor soothed me slightly. That and Irene's reassuring pat on my shoulder.

Thank God, I'm right beside the door, I thought, eyeing it, planning my escape. But just then two latecomers entered and pushed me deeper toward the middle. *Now I'm trapped!* When the lodgekeeper, Judy—Irene's sister-in-law—called for the rocks, I began to pray in earnest: *Please get me through this one, God. I believe in you. That's not what this is about. I just want to know, to see, that's all.*

As each of the first seven rocks was brought in and placed in the hollowed-out section of ground near the door, it became hotter and hotter in the cramped lodge. The air turned denser, sweat beaded on my forehead, and I found it difficult to breathe. *I'm suffocating! I'm going to pass out.* My eyes darted around, but everyone else looked fine. When the firekeeper passed in a bucket of water to the lodgekeeper, I was tempted to stick my head in it.

The firekeeper closed the door flap, making sure no light was visible. I was certain I'd collapse in a ball of sweat and fear, then jumped about five inches off the ground when a loud hiss of steam rose from the rocks. Enveloping clouds of heat enshrouded my entire body as I covered my face with the towel. Streams of sweat poured down my back, between my breasts, and onto my legs. I was melting and I couldn't breathe. *I'm going to die,* I thought. *I'm melting and I'm going to die.*

As the steam subsided, my breathing became less laboured and I made a conscious effort to relax. I recalled the meditation techniques

Elijah had taught me and tried to picture an eagle flying in a cool breeze, and it worked for a while.

The first round of prayers was about to begin. The lodgekeeper explained this for the benefit of newcomers. Holding out hope, I tried to see in the dimness, make out images. Once I thought I saw the shape of a bear hovering above the pit. A woman's voice began to pray in Mi'gmaq. When she was finished, she said the words *all my relations*, which were equivalent to *amen* in my mind, and another woman took her turn. Some of the prayers were exceedingly long, and because it was so dark inside I had no way of knowing how close we were to the end of the line. I only knew Irene would pray before me. Then there were only two other women to pray after me before the door could be opened for a few precious minutes of fresh air. Sweat stung my eyes, and I wiped it away with my towel. By now, it was flowing freely down my back.

The prayers were mostly in Mi'gmaq, so I had no idea what the women were praying for. I was told by Irene that to pray for good health and happiness was the best prayer you could offer for yourself or anyone else. So that was what I decided to do. I would pray in my own way, tapping into the sentiment of the ethereal verses being chanted around me. And I would add a special prayer for Sonya and the grandchild who would soon be born.

I was trying to keep track of the women by counting after each one prayed, but I grew shakier, my knees weakening even though I was sitting. I lost count. My undisciplined body knew I would never be able to make it through three more rounds of cleansing. I wasn't convinced I'd survive the first one. I might fall over at any moment. I wondered if that had happened to anyone before. I was pretty sure it had. There must have been women dropping like flies in these things. I wished there was room for me to lie down. I stuck it out, though, and when Irene completed her prayer, I said, "I pray for good health and happiness for all my children, my grandchildren, all my family and friends, and for myself." That was enough for me. With sweat streaming off every inch of my body, I towelled my face, mumbled "All my relations," and waited for the other two women to be done.

When the door flapped open, following the completion of the first round of prayers, I again mumbled the respectful "All my relations" as I crawled out. In addition to being spoken at the end of prayers, the phrase was also used by all traditional Mi'gmaqs and Maliseets when they entered or left the sweat lodge. It acknowledged that the individual realized she was connected, not only to all the other people in the lodge, all creatures, rock, mineral or animal, but also to all ancestors and the generations unborn.

I made my way outside as quickly as I could navigate on trembling arms and knees. As the fresh air hit my face, I felt invigorated but my self-perceived weakness disappointed me. *I let my fear win,* I ruminated, breathing the cool air deeply. *They're all probably laughing at me.* As soon as I felt strong enough to manoeuvre, I stood, walked over to a log where some women were already seated, and plunked down.

"It's your first time, *dus*," Irene said, joining me on the log. "You did good." She held out a bottle of cold water. I took it and drank, the chilly fluid rushing to my head, rejuvenating me with a natural high.

Another woman, with long, straight blue-black hair, approached and handed me a small wooden bowl holding blueberries. "Have some," she prompted, nodding kindly.

I took a handful and popped two of the fat berries into my mouth. They were juicy, sweet, and cold, like the water.

"Don't be upset," the woman said encouragingly. "I only lasted two rounds my first sweat. It gets easier." She smiled and walked over to the firekeeper to offer him the berries.

"Are you going back in?" Irene asked. The lodgekeeper had reentered the sweat lodge. "It's time for the second round."

The words, "Not on your life," almost slipped from my tongue, but instead of withdrawing, I reconsidered and, with a puff of bold breath, said, "Okay, I'll try again."

On my way toward the sweat lodge, the firekeeper came up to me and held out his hand. I didn't know what to do.

"Sage," he said. "It'll help you breathe better when it gets too hot inside."

I reached out and took the sage from him.

"Throw it on the fire," he said, making a swift and steady tossing movement with his arm.

"Thank you."

Moments later I was once more settled inside the lodge. With the flap down it was pitch-black again, but I found comfort in it now. I held on to the sage, a talisman against failure. The second round was a little easier. Because I knew what to expect, I could gauge my breathing to take in the warmth slowly and allow the heat to caress and cleanse me, instead of fearing and fighting off its advancing waves.

Again the women prayed, and the songs became endearing. I was actually able to join in and concentrate on what I was doing. Meditating, I prayed earnestly for my children, for their safety and future peace in our lives as a family. Bathing in the sensation of purification, feeling that, yes, I might be a part of it, after all, I smiled contentedly as the sweat poured off of me, carrying away years of hardship and spiritual poison.

It wasn't until near the end of the second round that I finally threw my handful of sage into the fire pit. The sweet smell prompted a woodsy familiarity that reminded me of my recent journeys into the forests at home.

When I left the sweat lodge, I felt like a new woman, a very hungry new woman. We headed back to Elder Libby's house for a feast prepared by her son and some of the women in the community. I wanted to sample everything, even the smoked eels I swore I'd never touch.

Before anyone could eat after a sweat-lodge ceremony, food had to be offered to the wood spirits to ensure their blessings. One of the women departed with a plate. We waited until she returned to signal we could dig in, and that was what we did. I never saw women enjoy their food so dearly. We all ate as if we hadn't eaten in days.

In the midst of devouring my meal, I discovered that some of the women at the house hadn't attended the sweat-lodge ceremony. I asked Irene why and she explained that some of them were on their *time*—their menstrual cycle—and all women were forbidden to touch any object to be used in a ceremony. They were also forbidden to enter the sweat lodge.

"Is that because they're unclean?" I asked.

"No, not at all. It's just the opposite. When it's a woman's time, they're considered *too powerful*."

I liked the sound of that.

Then, inquiring about Chuck and Bobby, I was informed they were already at a sweat-lodge ceremony for the men. I was anxious to share my new experience with Chuck.

Later I met an elder who had travelled from Woodstock, a Maliseet community sixty miles from Fredericton. His wife, Nadine, was white and exuded an aura of strength. Something in her blue eyes said, "Don't mess with me," even though her smile and handshake were warm and accommodating. She was the sort of well-rounded woman I admired. Her husband, Ervin, had met Chuck before, so the two of them spent a great deal of time talking while I followed Irene around.

Just before the closing ceremony of the powwow, I asked Irene again what we should do about getting home. The events would soon be over and the worry started to kick in. I hadn't considered the difficulties of our return during the two days when we'd been engaged in the ceremonies and socialization with other participants.

"We'll talk about that after the giveaway," she said as we seated ourselves at a table inside the hall where the final ceremony would soon commence.

"The giveaway? What's that?"

"It's how we close our gathering. Everyone puts something in and everyone takes something out."

"Like presents?" I asked.

"Yes. Everything from jewellery and clothing to electric appliances. Whatever people feel like giving."

"I didn't bring anything." I began to fret. What could I possibly offer?

"How about that pretty silk scarf in your suitcase? Or those earrings you're wearing? Doesn't matter, as long as you give."

"Oh, okay." I decided to offer my blue silk scarf with the butterflies on it. I figured since I'd only worn it once it was the best choice. Besides, the earrings had been a gift from Elijah and I wasn't ready to part with them yet.

The conclusion of the powow was held in the community centre. I couldn't believe it when I saw all the beautiful gifts stacked neatly against one wall. There were paintings, jewellery, ornaments, toys, even a set of dishes. Irene and I added our gifts to the collection. Chuck contributed a leather belt he'd brought, and Bobby gave a beaded choker.

When the drummers began, the elders marched around and picked presents from the pile. The rest of us lined up to follow, even the children. Everyone was smiling more than usual and talking excitedly. It was like Christmas. When it was my turn to pick from the stock, I quickly retrieved a pair of delicately crafted earrings made from porcupine quills and tiny white and green beads shaped to resemble an eagle.

There were still a number of items left even after everyone had a gift. When the music ended, the elder from Woodstock held his hand up and all present stopped speaking and admiring one another's gifts. A short, stocky, middle-aged man beside him called for the group's attention.

"We have some people from New Brunswick who need our help," he said, pointing to where Irene and I were standing. "They need money to get home and pick up their car. We're going to have a blanket dance to help out, so dig deep."

I couldn't believe my ears. "What are they talking about, Irene?"

"I told you not to worry," she said with a kind smile. "Just stand here and be thankful."

A young man brought out a grey woollen blanket and signalled for three other men to join him. They spread the blanket and each grabbed a corner in one hand. The drumming and chanting began again as the men circled the floor with the blanket. As they passed, each person threw money onto the blanket—pennies, quarters, loonies, five-dollar bills, tens, even a few twenties. After they made a full circle, they walked back to where I was standing and passed the blanket to me. The tingling I had been feeling peaked and tears welled in my eyes. I nodded and whispered, "Thank you," then said it in Maliseet—*"Wo-li-won"*—out of respect for the elder who had initiated the blanket dance.

We received close to $200; the car repairs would cost $150. The men who had picked us up in the white van offered to drive us back to Sackville so I could retrieve my car. Elder Libby packed us a lunch for our journey home.

"Take care of yourself, *dus*," she said as she hugged me good-bye. "Make sure you come back."

"I will," I told her. "Thank you so much for everything. I'll remember you in my prayers."

When the four of us arrived safely back in Fredericton, we were all in excellent spirits. My heart felt incredibly light. When I called to see how Sonya was faring and was told I had a new grandson, I cried out with joy, a triumphant whoop much like I'd heard at the powwow.

Mitchell had made his debut on May 4, 1991, at 5:04 a.m. in

the Dr. Everett Chalmers Hospital in Fredericton. He was a healthy seven-pound, one-ounce bundle of bliss and had come into this world the same time I had awoken for my very first sweat-lodge ceremony in Nova Scotia.

CHUCK

Chuck was especially charming to me. The fact that he was considerably articulate made him all the more appealing. He spoke of the importance of spirituality in life and explained how the Creator had intended for the Indian people—he always referred to himself as an Indian, never a Native—to care for the land and teach other races the way of doing so. He also related fascinating stories about supernatural beings.

One such narrative spoke of a time when an unknown man had been spotted in various places near the river, keeping sinister vigil over the Oromocto Reserve. "A lot of people noticed him," Chuck said, "but when anyone went to check, he'd be gone and there would be no human footprints in the soft mud on the riverbank. Only the imprint of hooves, like those found on a goat or pig."

Chuck said the man was seen four days in a row but vanished the same time one of the elders on the reserve passed away. Although I found this story intriguing, I didn't consider it strange. I remember my mother and my grandmother recounting tales of unfamiliar men appearing, sometimes coming to the door and knocking, before a relative or close friend died. I was well acquainted with accounts of "forerunners."

Chuck explained that he was a member of the Crow Clan. That meant the crow was his special totem. Since I'd always been fond of crows myself, I took this to be a sign we were made for each other. I never considered there might, in fact, be another ominous explanation.

Chuck knew a great deal about medicines and was more than

willing to pass on his knowledge. We often walked through the woods or canoed on the Saint John River near Jemseg to search for plants and herbs Chuck said would help convey healing. He told me that finding balance in life was what the spiritual journey was all about.

I grew fond of the pungent smell of burning cedar and sweetgrass. It reminded me of the grass fires we'd had each spring to clear the fields when I was a child. The only problem with burning sweetgrass was its close resemblance to the smell of smouldering marijuana. I sometimes received peculiar looks from neighbours who didn't know the difference. Undoubtedly they thought I was smoking pot. I discovered I was more peaceful when this wild brand of incense was burning in my home.

Sometimes, late at night sitting on a riverbank with Chuck telling me stories of animals sent to aid human beings, I felt close to heaven. His voice was melodic and hypnotic in a way that made me believe he was gentle. Yet his sensual charisma beckoned much baser desires. We made love often, sometimes naked in the forest under the stars with nature brimming around us.

I spent the next few years trying to prove this relationship was different, even though a dear Mi'gmaq friend, Elizabeth S., who I first met at an AA meeting, warned me I was destined for a hard life unless Chuck underwent a miraculous change of character. Elizabeth lived in the same Maliseet community as Chuck's first wife, and she had told me Chuck had a vicious mouth and roving eye.

When I met him, he was coming off the booze, learning to live life sober. Characteristically I attempted to redeem him, to encourage his recovery process through AA. For about a year he seemed to enjoy attending the meetings as much as I did. At my fourth-year AA birthday celebration Chuck read the 12 Steps at the opening of the meeting. Elder Ervin gave me a medallion and a print of a Native warrior, and Miles was my guest speaker. Again my daughters, including Heather, presented me with a birthday cake.

Chuck fell off the wagon twice after we got together, but that was it. Finally he stayed dry and became a drug-and-alcohol counsellor for the reserve. He had little training, but there was no one else who wanted the job who wasn't on drugs or alcohol themselves. In the past the position had been held by individuals who were using some mood-altering substance. At least Chuck was sober and knew firsthand about the positive aspects of AA.

He worked hard to save seemingly hopeless alcoholics and had limitless compassion for the sick and elderly. If he heard someone he knew was in the hospital, relative or not, he'd go out of his way to visit. He often brought gifts of moose meat or fiddleheads to elderly people in the Oromocto community where his mother resided.

I was still living in my apartment on St. Mary's Street in Fredericton when Chuck decided to move in with me. Not wanting to be apart any longer, we searched for something bigger and soon moved into a bungalow in Durham Heights, set high on a hill overlooking the Nashwaak River. It was about ten miles outside Fredericton off the highway heading north. I signed an agreement to make payments that would constitute a rent-to-own deal. Peter, who got along quite well with Chuck and who was in a serious relationship of his own by now, moved with us and rented one of the bedrooms.

Chuck and I had been dating for about nine months, and already it was a stormy relationship. I could never predict his moods. He was severely jealous, often accusing me of being interested in other men if I merely said hello to them. He would disappear for days at a time, then return without explanation. My children weren't happy about my liaison with Chuck, particularly Sonya.

"It's not that I don't like him," she told me one day when I was at her house for coffee. "It's just that I don't like seeing how he affects you. You're a nervous wreck most of the time. And half the time he doesn't even tell you where he is. What kind of a life is that?"

I knew she was right on a few of her points, but I wasn't ready to admit it. I already suspected my feelings toward Chuck bordered on addiction. I was miserable without him, but more and more I was becoming miserable with him.

Sometimes Chuck seemed to ignite with rage over the smallest slight—a car passing him in traffic, someone butting in line at the grocery store, a man or woman who failed to say hello when he went to AA meetings.

I remembered hearing something about his rebellious teen years from my brother, Nelson. They had mutual friends from Gagetown where Chuck grew up. Back then Chuck had a reputation for fighting. No intended or imagined insult went unpunished. In the 1960s he went away and joined the American army, as many Canadian Natives chose to do at that time. Perhaps it was during this stint in the army when he learned to perfect his disassociation from the world. Sometimes, when I talked to him, he, like Stan, seemed to be somewhere else.

My daughter, Heather, was constantly battling illness. She was plagued by bouts of pneumonia and infection after infection. Then an Oromocto doctor diagnosed her as HIV positive. Peter was with me when the news came over the telephone. The doctor told me Heather would probably only live another two years. I was horribly shocked.

When I went to see Heather in the hospital, she said she would have to give Sasha up. She just couldn't do it anymore, and now she didn't even know if she'd be around.

The tragic uncertainty of Heather's future prompted me to take my granddaughter, Sasha, to live with me. Sasha was in the hospital at the time with an ear infection and was being checked for the HIV virus, as well. I took her home with me as soon as she was released. It was December 1991.

"It's all a mistake, Mom," Heather called me excitedly one afternoon in January. "My tests are negative. It's all a big mistake."

The doctor had called Heather into his office to give her the results. He didn't bother to apologize. He had based his diagnosis on an anonymous phone call telling him Heather had been examined by an insurance company when she lived in Ontario. He'd never given her a test before. We found out that a woman who was angry at Heather for exposing some of her indiscretions to a mate had made the call, posing as an insurance agent, and the doctor hadn't bothered to verify the authenticity of the claim. "Mistakes will happen" was his justification.

My parents had even been badgered with phone calls because a rumour that Heather had AIDS was spreading through the community. The information had been leaked by someone working at the hospital.

I have often thanked God for my own physician, Vaughn Roxborough. He used to be Heather's MD once, too, but she'd sought new help when he refused to supply her with pain pills. He has been my family doctor since Heather's birth and is one of the kindest men I have ever met. Dr. Roxborough continues to take time to listen patiently to my complaints and fears after all these years of unrest. Doctors can play an important part in our lives as priests to our bodies, our minds, and sometimes our spirits. Mine was a positive force in helping me get through some rough situations. And he was the first person ever to confront me about my drinking.

Although the HIV diagnosis was wrong, Sasha stayed with me. Heather went to live on the Oromocto Reserve, and her dependency on drugs grew. There were no guarantees things would get better anytime soon, if ever, so I was determined Sasha wouldn't grow up around drugs and alcohol.

Chuck adored small children and was devoted to Sasha. He had infinite patience with her. He'd play with her for hours and take her fishing or on trips in the woods to teach her about plants and natural medicines. Chuck also had a special rapport with my grandson, Billy, and often brought him along, as well. He still spent a great deal of time with his own teenage twins in Kingsclear. He took them fishing, duck hunting, and hiking. When he was visiting his kids, he often stayed the night. It soon became apparent that Chuck's nights away from me weren't spent alone. He never tried to deny it.

"All men deserve more than one woman," he told me in a fit of anger one day, knowing I'd always take him back. He repeated this fact several times. I was trapped by my own genuine love for him.

THE DUCK INCIDENT

Irene, who was now living in Prince Edward Island, came to visit a couple of days after Christmas and stayed for two weeks. Sasha was visiting with her Aunt Sonya so I could have a little break after the festivities. Chuck had remained sober over the holidays, but disappeared the day I'd gone to pick Irene up at the bus station.

It was the afternoon of New Year's Eve and Chuck had been gone for four days. I knew where he was. I found out by calling a friend from Kingsclear Reserve who lived across the street from Chuck's ex-wife. Chuck had been seen coming and going. I was getting angrier as each day passed without a telephone call. I had no number for his ex-wife—it was unlisted—and I knew she'd have hung up on me, anyway. The only thing that kept me from going over to the Kingsclear Reserve was Irene. Her good-humoured company and satisfying cooking kept me home.

I was trying to maintain a normal routine so I wouldn't dwell on Chuck's absence. I was cleaning the bathroom sink, scrubbing my thoughts of Chuck away, when I heard someone barging in the front door. Irene was peeling potatoes at the kitchen table. A voice greeted her: "How ya doing, Irene? Happy New Year!" It was Chuck.

I was out of the bathroom before Irene had a chance to answer.

"And just what do you think you're doing here?" I screamed, clutching my cleaning rag. The pulse in my neck throbbed dangerously, like a bomb about to explode, and my cheeks were burning. I shook my rag at him violently. "I know where you've been!"

Chuck looked at me calmly without a hint of remorse or emotion. "I'm here to get the duck," he said with a sarcastic grin. He seemed completely sober. "Then I'm leaving."

"What duck?" I asked, confused. I'd expected penitence, a little display of contrition, flowers, a card, or a letter begging for forgiveness, like all the other times. But here he was smiling, talking about a duck. I wanted to kill him.

"My duck," he said as he walked over to the freezer and yanked open the door. He reached in and rummaged around, pulling out a frozen duck complete with all its plumage. He'd shot it in October, stuck it in a plastic bag, and tossed it in the freezer without cleaning it. Neither one of us had bothered with it since, except to shove it in deeper when the turkey arrived for Christmas.

"And where do you think you're taking that duck?" I lurched toward him.

He moved out of my way. He wasn't going anywhere with that duck. It was mine, even though I hated it.

"I'm giving it to my son."

"No, you're not!" I tried wrenching the feathered fowl from him, but it slipped from our hands and thumped to the floor. We both lunged forward, grabbing for it. Chuck got hold of it first, but I had a good grip on one of its legs and spent the next few seconds jerking the bird back and forth so hard that Irene swore later she thought it had been resurrected.

"I want that duck." Chuck snarled through clenched teeth. He tugged furiously, but I held firm.

"You're not getting it," I growled, yanking the duck toward me.

"Take the damn thing!" Chuck suddenly let go, and I flew backward, crashing to the linoleum floor on my back. I had one wing clenched in my fist. The rest of the duck roosted on top of my head.

I jumped up as Chuck ran out the back door. My eyes caught sight of a butcher knife on the counter and I snatched it up. Irene's eyes were as big as full moons when she saw what I was doing. I ran for the back door after Chuck.

Standing outside, I saw him scramble toward his grey Dodge. "You want the stupid duck, then here it is!" I yelled. Clutching the knife handle, I turned toward the house and slammed the bird against the door frame. Raising the knife, I plunged the blade into it, pinning it to the house, then continued screaming at the retreating car.

When I was finished and Chuck was out of sight, I spun and went back inside. Irene handed me a cup of tea. I looked down at the cup, barely recognizing what it was through my rage. My hands were trembling as I took it. Irene then picked a couple of black feathers out of my hair.

She laughed. "If you wanted a headdress all you had to do was ask."

I glowered at her but then felt the rage turn to hilarity. I shook my head and laughed until tears rolled down my cheeks, until my belly hurt more than my pride, until the tears turned colder and began to hurt more than my belly.

Irene hugged me and led me to the couch. She told me to lie down. I was totally drained and had no problem following her advice. She covered me with a blanket while I stared at the ceiling, wondering what I would have done with the knife if I'd caught up with Chuck. A shiver ran through me and then another. The blanket didn't do much to warm the chill away.

Chuck was back in two days, remorseful this time, with roses as usual. He had to make a lot of promises to get back in my good graces, and agreed to stay away from Kingsclear at night and to take me with him when he visited his kids. Even with the promises I made him sleep on the couch for a couple of days.

"Just like old times," Irene whispered with a chuckle on her way to bed in Sasha's room the first night I took him back.

The duck stayed pinned to the house until a crow ate the final remnants of its rotting leg.

CLAIM AN INDIAN ANCESTOR

Newly committed to each other, Chuck and I began travelling to Native gatherings. Elder Ervin and his wife, Nadine, who I'd met in Shubenacadie, often held powwows on their property in Woodstock. They had a huge home where they took in young people from other reserves who were struggling with addictions. We visited on a regular basis, offering to help and seeking counsel from them.

What often amazed me about First Nations gatherings and pow-wows was the large number of white people anxious to dress up like Natives. I sometimes wondered if they had failed to escape the cowboys-and-Indians period of their childhoods. Or maybe they thought they could reach a dizzying plateau of enlightenment by simply breathing the same air as Natives. Even more amazing was the creativity with which the majority of them could manufacture an ancestor from some ancient tribe. For reasons unknown to me, "Cree great-grandmothers" were the most popular relatives of choice in those circles.

I became so caught up in the claim-an-Indian-ancestor fad that I tried to join it at one point. Hadn't my father told me stories of his grandmother, Suzanne Chouinard, who had hailed from some-where in Quebec? Maybe she was Cree. The family used to refer to her as an Indian, especially when they told the story of her chasing off a bear single-handedly, waving her defiant fist in the air, but the closest we could come to Cree was Métis. This was a fashionable declaration at that time, so I stopped mentioning it.

Like most white women who lived on reserves or travelled in Native circles, I often wore silver and beaded jewellery crafted by Natives. I was especially fond of turquoise. And, for a time, I wore around my neck the small medicine bag given to me by Elder Ervin, usually concealed by whatever shirt I happened to be wearing. I didn't feel comfortable putting this sacred gift on display. It would be like a neon sign advertising my faith.

One could always tell the groupies from those who had actual connections to the communities. The imposters took everything with utter seriousness and figured all words and happenings were grand and ominous indications of something profoundly supernatural. I once sat in the corner and listened to the elders joke about those visitors who talked incessantly of their mighty visions. Some saw portent messages in dreams or signs of good or evil from the shape of clouds, rocks, or tree markings. Others would inquire whether they were cursed, asking if the gnarled tree root they'd stumbled over while out hiking might really be a spirit. I had no idea how some of the elders kept a straight face. They fielded some of the most ridiculous questions I'd ever heard, yet still preserved the dignity of the seeker by listening intently. Later the elders would unwind with one another, and because I often camped in the house at Woodstock where this chatter took place, sometimes in English, I was occasionally privy to their glorious humour.

"What did you tell the hiker?" one elder asked the other.

"You mean the guy who tangled with the killer roots?" the other answered. "I told him the truth. Sometimes a tree is just a tree."

"Did he believe you?"

"Sure."

"What did you say then?"

"I told him to pick another path."

The other elder nodded sagely. "Oh, yes."

"You don't like where you walk, pick another path."

They both began chuckling until they were laughing openly.

Of course, there were genuin mystical happenings or signs witnessed by people of all colours, and the elders agreed whole-heartedly with the presence of these phenomena. But most of the groupies who followed the powwow circuit were searching for something quite unlike a spiritual sign. Many of them were seeking a new identity or the acceptance they couldn't find in the white world. Some of them were there simply to meet people, or to pick up a hunter or an authentic Native woman. Elder Ervin's wife, Nadine, often spotted the women who were there to catch her husband's eye instead of his wisdom, long before he figured it out himself.

FIDDLEHEADING

Chuck was eager to include me and Sasha in his expeditions and willing to teach us more about living on the land. Fiddleheading—the harvesting of edible green ferns—was an important part of his culture, and he wanted us to appreciate the tradition as much as he did.

I had eaten fiddleheads many times since I was a child but had never picked them. Usually our family bought them in the spring at the local grocery store. Sonya and Jennifer had travelled with friends from the Oromocto Reserve one spring to Nova Scotia on a fiddleheading expedition, so I knew a bit about what was required to harvest the ferns. But this was a new experience the three of us could share. Two-year-old Sasha was thrilled when the outing was mentioned.

In late May most regular business on reserves halted for the picking of fiddleheads. Maliseets called fiddleheads *mahsos*, a word that signified a thing of great importance. Not only were they considered good eating, these ferns were also thought by some people to be magical symbols that provided protection from enemies. One legend stated the ferns were gifts from the Creator given to the little people who lived by the river for protection from predators. Others said the circles formed by the heads of the curled ferns were to remind Native peoples that the circle of life was endless. But the Mi'gmaq and Maliseets also used them as a signature decorative motif for baskets and clothing.

In spring, when the waters receded along the rivers in New Brunswick, these curled ferns stuck their fat green heads above the water line. The heads were the culinary delight. The first time Chuck, Sasha, and I picked fiddleheads together in Jemseg, we came away with seventy pounds of the rare treat. During the picking, we were devoured by mosquitoes, but that didn't hamper our fun.

There was a great deal of debris on the river that had gathered during flood season the month before. Each plant had a stubborn dry brown casing that had to be shed before it was fit to cook. That meant the fiddleheads required vigorous cleaning. Chuck, like most Maliseets, used a handwoven ash basket to pick fiddleheads and the same basket to carry out the cleaning. He gave me and Sasha one basket to share since we were novice pickers. Sasha actually tried to eat most of her harvest.

Chuck pretended he was doing a little dance while he patiently carried basket after basket of fiddleheads to the river to be washed. He'd swish the fiddleheads inside the basket, shake it, drain it a couple of times, and then transfer the cleaned crop to another container, usually a sack. He'd keep up the pretend dance for the benefit of Sasha, who always laughed. From the way she watched him, it was obvious she adored his attention.

When all the fiddleheads were washed and loaded into bags, we headed home, stopping on the way to sell three-quarters of our crop to a local road stand in Maugerville. Back in Fredericton, we had to wash the fiddleheads again at least three times in warm water before they could be cooked. Then they were prepared like any other green in a small amount of boiling water until cooked through but still firm.

That year I froze a load, about twenty pounds, for future use. I also bottled some with a hint of garlic and later found that I preferred the bottled ones over the frozen. Whatever way I prepared them, the plump, green ferns delighted the tongue when served with butter and vinegar. The first time I cooked them for Sasha she ate an entire plateful. Chuck smiled his approval as she shovelled them into her tiny mouth.

LORE AND RECIPES

I was only five when my dad used the cool dark mud from a brook to stop the pain from a bee sting in my swollen leg. My mother was always boiling friar's balsam on our wood stove to ward off colds and flu. Even my mother's father gathered dandelions to concoct a drink he professed could cure anything. The liquid resembled left-over dishwater, but the old man swore by it. I never questioned him, even when he seemed a lot sicker the morning after drinking it. I found it hard to believe it was actually wine, although my mother told me the difference. I was certain something that looked that bad had to be medicine. Unfortunately my grandfather was only interested in the flowers for wine. He might have lived longer if he'd realized dandelion roots contained a drug used to treat diseased livers.

Growing up in the country, I'd often collect gum from spruce trees. My tongue still curls when I remember the tangy gobs of sticky white resin we used to scrape from the rough bark. I'd chew it until all the flavour was drained, then pop another piece into my mouth. In spring and summer we had an endless supply of gum, and it didn't cost a penny.

The forest held all kinds of treats. I particularly enjoyed the minty freshness of wintergreen. The smooth green leaves exuded a sweet peppermint when chewed. I preferred the leaves to the tiny red berries they framed.

For a country girl the idea of using plants for medicines was basic common sense. In spring the silky white petals of the tired old apple tree gave off a fragrance that made me temporarily forget the imperfections in my life. This was my kingdom on high. Perched in the tree, I'd see my dad tramping into the woods when he was upset.

"I get rid of my anger by taking a switch and beating it on the ground," he once told me. "That way you never hurt anyone." I tried this procedure, but it never worked for me. I only succeeded in hitting my own thighs.

My brother, Nelson, built a small log cabin in the middle of the trees behind our house. Sometimes, when night fell and Dad hadn't returned from his stomp into the woods, we'd assume he was sleeping in Nelson's cabin. Sleeping alone, thinking, maybe writing poems in his head in the forest darkness.

"I feel closer to God in there," he explained. In later years he ventured there to pray and fast. Abstaining from food and drink, he sometimes spent up to seven days in that cabin. Fasting was an integral part of our Christian beliefs, although I rarely partook myself. Food was such a comfort in my life that I found it agonizing to give up eating for more than a day, despite the fact I believed, like my parents, that functioning without food cleansed the body and disciplined the mind.

My father would offer up his fasting to help strengthen his prayers for others. I saw it as a noble conviction, and I admired my father's dedication.

I think he missed that rough old cabin more than the house when he and Mom had to move to make way for a new highway.

In the summer of 1986, when Irving Oil offered my father money for his house and property, he didn't seem upset at all. He said the land had never been worth much, anyway. The rocky soil had hampered any efforts to cultivate a vegetable garden. Mom was certainly enthusiastic about getting a bigger place; four of my brothers were still living at home.

They all packed up and moved into their new mini-home in Waasis, another small community just nine miles from where they'd lived all their lives. For my mother the new home was a palace: four bedrooms instead of two, a spacious living room for the first time since they'd been married, and an ample bathroom where there had only been a flush in the corner of my parents' bedroom. The property was well landscaped with blue spruce trees, rose and lilac bushes, and a shed for Dad to store his tools. A few feet behind the mini-home there was a thick wooded area where Dad could wander and seek peace.

"How many of you ever seen a bald Indian?" Elder Charles Solomon had everyone's attention as soon as he opened his mouth. He was a short, squat man with an intense, probing gaze that made you feel unsettled until it was tempered by a grin. Small, wire-rimmed glasses that kept slipping down rested on a pug nose.

It was obvious that Elder Charles enjoyed entertaining people with his stories about plants and animals, and he appreciated a good joke. He could tell tales about Native heroes and history for hours, and his enthusiasm was contagious. Skillfully he mixed fact and fancy, suddenly breaking a serious mood with a humorous anecdote. Moving from tales of Native-type leprechauns to remedies for diarrhea through the use of common plants kept the listener charmed. He knew more about natural medicines than anyone I'd ever met.

Elder Charles was one of the guest speakers for Native Awareness Days in 1992 at the University of New Brunswick. Chuck had insisted I come hear the elder who stood out from the crowd, dressed in blue jeans and red sweatshirt with a full headdress of coloured feathers on his grey head.

"And you won't ever see a bald Indian, either," Elder Charles assured us. "'Cause he knows what medicine to use if his hair starts to fall out." He spoke about the magical healing powers of the bear and the use of bear grease to hold on to that manly head of hair.

I had my notebook with me for the lecture and wanted to learn as much as I could about medicinal plants and herbs. Many of the others, mostly white observers, had pens and paper ready, as well. I scribbled down everything Elder Charles had to say. I knew Chuck would expect me to remember what I had heard.

Native Cure for Balding

Bear grease—a gooey fat scraped off the hide before it is tanned—should be rubbed into the scalp to prevent balding. The grease should be stored in a cool, dark place—the bear likes his den. It can be used for all sorts of skin problems, including diaper rash.

My awe of Elder Charles mounted as he talked about further cures. I felt respect for, but also a sense of kinship with, the man who held such knowledge of natural healing abilities. He was like a magic man of old, and that appealed to my mystical side. Elder Charles made me think of a seer brought to life by my Gypsy fortunetelling grandmother.

He explained that both raspberries and blackberries could be steeped to make a tea that worked well to settle diarrhea. Since these berries were plentiful only in the autumn, he suggested keeping a supply of the dried fruit on hand. "And if all else fails, get some raspberry tea from the health-food store," he added with a chuckle.

When Elder Charles began to talk about muskrat root (*giew-hes-whas-eq* in Maliseet), I was in familiar territory. I knew this plant as the calamus root. It had been renamed by Native people in honour of the furry rodents that fed on them near riverbeds. Most Native people in Atlantic Canada used the dried root for sore throats. Chuck often talked about it, and I'd seen singers at powwows use it.

Elder Charles outlined how to make tea from the root. When asked if muskrat tea really worked, he shrugged and said, "You never see a muskrat with a cold, do you?"

When the elder took a break, I hurried over to the platform to tell him about my experience with muskrat root. Most everyone else, including Chuck, had left for a cigarette break outside or a cup of tea at the other end of the room.

"I've tried muskrat root for my sore throat before," I said.

"Did it work?" he asked.

"Not really," I admitted. "It made me gag when I tried to chew it. I almost vomited."

"How much did you take?" he asked with a frown.

"Just one small bulb," I said.

"One small bulb! Holy cow! No wonder you felt sick. You only chew a tiny sliver." He spaced his thumb and forefinger close together to illustrate his point. "Not the whole plant."

That gave everyone within earshot a good laugh. I blushed but took it in stride, knowing I'd never try muskrat root again. Small or big piece, it was too bitter for me. I would stick with a famously harsh brand of cough syrup. After all, it was made from pine tar.

When the lecture resumed, I continued to listen attentively. Chuck didn't appear as interested and went out for coffee halfway through. I was so engaged by the elder's voice I often forgot to write anything down. And when I looked at my notebook, I realized I had only recorded a few of his remedies.

Colds and Cramps

Calamus root is dried and made into a tea to treat colds and stomach cramps.

How to Make Muskrat Tea

Dig up the bulbous ends of the root and wash them. They are then pried apart and broken into pieces two to three inches in length. String up the pieces and leave to hang dry. When dry, steep to make a powerful tea that will alleviate cold and flu symptoms.

How to Make Black Cherry Tea

Black cherry bark (*wha-qua-mooz*) is used to treat a cough. When you add a little sugar, it doesn't taste quite so bad. Break a small branch off a black cherry tree and scrap the bark away. Allow the bark to dry. Steep for about an hour, strain, and add sweetener to taste. Recommended dosage: two tablespoons every hour until the cough is cured.

Sore Throats

Boiling wild onions will produce a syrup that is very effective in soothing sore throats. Honey can be added to the mixture to make it more palatable.

Elder Charles didn't appear to have any prejudice. He was just as thorough teaching white folk as he was with his own *skigin*. He often had people of all ages, from all races, travelling with him along the shores of the Saint John River to dig up muskrat roots in the fall or comb the beaches of the Bay of Fundy near Saint George in late summer to pick sweetgrass.

I knew sweetgrass grew close to salt water. Usually Irene would bring me some that had been picked near Lennox Island on the shores of the Atlantic in Prince Edward Island.

Elder Charles told his audience that sweetgrass was often referred to as Mother Earth's hair and was considered a sacred medicine. The grass, with its sweet haylike fragrance, was burned by Native people in North America to purify the body, mind, and spirit and to welcome new harmony.

Elder Charles explained that sweetgrass was usually harvested in late summer, bundled, and carried home.

"You can pull each of the tall blades apart to make three separate strands," he said. "You braid these together just like hair and tie up the ends with string. You do this when the sweetgrass is wet. Then you hang it to dry so you can use it to smudge later. The smoke from the burning sweetgrass washes the person or object so it can be cleansed."

It was fortifying to discover that so many of the trees and flowers in the nearby forest I frequented held cures for such things as blood poison, bladder infections, eczema, even arthritis. I was determined to learn all I could and was comforted by the possession of this information. It was so much a part of the past, of Stan's history and Chuck's history. It was a part of Stan I'd never really seen. He rarely talked about Mohawk tradition or earth medicines. In fact, he hardly talked about his childhood at all. And when he did the stories were usually about his white mother. But because Chuck fully embraced his Native culture, I learned something more about him every day by gathering knowledge of his heritage. A heritage he never denied.

MY THIRD WEDDING

Sasha, Chuck, and I continued to travel, visiting other reserves, often camping in our station wagon. Like any little girl, Sasha loved roasting wieners over an open fire, and Chuck and I both enjoyed cooking outdoors. We didn't need a barbecue. We carried an old oven rack for a grill and usually dug a fire pit somewhere secluded enough to evade nosy forest rangers.

Chuck was still running between me and his ex-wife in Kingsclear, but was spending the bulk of his time with me and Sasha, so I tried to blot out thoughts of his infidelity. I wanted to enjoy the times we had together. When I didn't complain, Chuck was usually civil to me. I was afraid of losing him, not only for my sake but for Sasha's.

In June 1992 Chuck went on a spiritual retreat in Woodstock where Elder Ervin Polchies held the fall powwows. When he returned, he told me the Creator had shown him in a vision that we should be wed. He said he thought things would be better for us if we were married. If he were my husband, he'd be able to stay faithful.

We took Sasha to a baby-sitter and drove to Maine the very next day to shop for rings. I didn't want to tell any of my children or friends because I knew they'd try to talk me out of it. They'd often warned me to escape the situation before it got worse.

"He's not going to stop running around," Sonya said when I visited with her one day in Geary. "You have to face that, Mom. Or live with it for the rest of your life. Can you really do that?"

My Mi'gmaq friend, Elizabeth S., who lived on the same reserve as Chuck's ex-wife, was also concerned that I would be stuck with a mate who was challenged by monogamy.

When we returned, Chuck phoned his mother and told her we would be married on July 17 by a justice of the peace. He hadn't informed me yet. Chuck had asked his mother if we could hold a small reception at her house on the Oromocto Reserve. When he hung up, he said, "She seems happy for us." I was happy, too, to hear these concrete plans for our future.

I didn't want to make a big fuss over this wedding. I knew most of my friends and family would be against it, so I only told them a few days before the occasion. Besides, I'd already had two big wedding celebrations and neither had done me any good. This one had to be different, smaller, more intimate. I even went to work at Child Find on the morning of the seventeenth to tie up a few odds and ends before I left for a two-day vacation.

The ceremony was brief and attended by about twenty people. Back at Chuck's mother's house we had refreshments, opened presents, greeted guests, and listened to my friend Beryl sing two songs in honour of the day: "She's an Eagle When She Flies" and "Leather and Lace." The latter, a Stevie Nicks song, seemed most appropriate to me. It spoke of how love bridged the gap between people from two very different backgrounds.

Chuck and I spent the night at a motel in Pocalogan, an hour's drive away near the ocean outside Saint John. Chuck sang along with country tunes on the radio as we drove and happily squeezed my hand, the one sporting the new gold wedding band.

The next day we returned home and life resumed its regular routine. Three weeks later my new husband headed out for a week-end hunting trip with friends. Lulled into a sense of security by Chuck's unusual attentiveness, I kissed him goodbye without any apprehension. The following day Chuck's sister called to tell me her brother was back with his ex-wife. She told me where they were if I wanted to go there and confront them. My mind raced over the options. If I went there, I couldn't be responsible for what I might do. But the bitter triumph of catching them in the act was tempting. In the end I chose to stay at home. I hardly slept that night. Alone in my bed, I felt my rage deepen by the minute.

When Chuck arrived home the next day, I was waiting for him and asked him where he'd been.

"Hunting," he said calmly, looking me straight in the eye as he stood in the entryway.

"You are a liar!" I cried. "A no-good liar! You were with Ruth in a trailer in Cumberland Bay."

When he saw I had more details than he'd expected, he laughed in my face and pushed me roughly out of the way. As I didn't want to upset Sasha, who had just come out of the bedroom from her nap, I opted for the silent treatment. I barely spoke to Chuck for a week, and he did everything possible to get back into my good graces: taking Sasha to the park, washing dishes, even cooking meals two nights in a row. When he massaged my tired feet one afternoon as I lay on the couch watching *The Price Is Right* on television, I felt my resolve finally melt. Sasha had just gone to bed for her afternoon nap. Chuck sat up and took hold of my hand, smiling with innuendo. I returned his smile, then he stood, pulled me from the couch, and led me to the bedroom. I was back in his passionate embraces as we reconsummated our marriage for the full two hours that Sasha slept.

GEOGRAPHICAL CURE

In late autumn 1992 I was laid off from my job at Child Find due to restructuring. Chuck had been spending more time with Sasha and me, and I still hoped we could have a future together.

We'd been having numerous problems with the house, particularly with the sewer system. On several occasions it backed up into our bathtub and we'd used a chemical cleanser to unclog the drains. Eventually the drain cleanser wouldn't work, so we called in a plumber. He told us it would cost at least $2,000 to repair, and that wouldn't fix it permanently. The little house that had seemed too good a deal to be true was indeed just that. It was falling apart around us. I bailed out of my agreement, losing a $1,000 deposit in the process. Chuck said the Oromocto Band would help us with the move and rent, so we took a bungalow in Marysville, another suburb of Fredericton on the north side of the Saint John River.

Soon we were settled in our new bungalow, I worked hard to ensure we would be a happy family, but Chuck was moody and hated living in the city. Three months after moving into the dwelling, we relocated once more—this time to the Oromocto

Reserve to share a house with Chuck's sister, brother, and nephew. I was grim about the arrangement, but Chuck assured me it would only be temporary and that we'd soon have our own house on the reserve. Happily, though, with all the adults in the house, Sasha got plenty of attention and, like any kid, she thrived under such conditions.

It was crowded, but I felt more secure having people around me. I thought Chuck would be less likely to take off to see the other woman in Kingsclear and was confident he'd never call me names in front of the rest of his family.

Within days of moving to the reserve Chuck became more temperamental than I'd known. He stayed away for longer periods and offered no explanation for his absences. The only improvement for me was that I had other adults to talk with, and Sasha had a new best friend—Naomi, a dark-skinned girl with very blond hair. Naomi was almost three, like Sasha, and lived across the street.

Jody returned home from British Columbia during this time. I'd really missed him. He was my only son, and although I was thankful to have my daughters close enough to visit, I needed the reassuring hugs that only a son can provide a mother. I worried about him being so far from family. He had been away for almost two years, and I was comforted to see he was well. Jody was still as handsome as ever and had filled out. He was now a wide-shouldered, solid young man. I appreciated more than ever having him around as an ally. When he told me he'd be staying in Fredericton with his old friend Ron while he searched for work, I was so ecstatic. I knew he'd be in my corner if I ever needed help. Besides, his First Nations ancestry was apparent in his look, lending further credibility to my place in the Native community.

I soon learned that other members of Chuck's family could be just as temperamental and unpredictable as he was. Chuck's sister,

Raven, maintained I should leave him, that he was no good.

"He's mean with women and he's faithful to no one," she confided in her kitchen one morning over coffee. "He took off with another woman the same night he married his first wife." She indicated Sasha and I were welcome to stay, but she didn't want Chuck around. They were often at each other's throat. Yet one day, when I attempted standing up to Chuck, Raven took his side. I'd called him a no-good bum.

"I don't want you talking to my brother like that, you lazy white bitch. This is my place, not yours." Then she turned to Chuck and shouted, "Get out, or I'll throw you out."

Chuck stormed from the house, slamming the door. Thank God Sasha was upstairs sleeping. There was no doubt in my mind that Chuck would head back to Kingsclear and his first wife.

A few hours later Raven apologized. "I really like having you around," she said. "I've got a headache. Must be coming down with something." She often came down with something when she didn't have any of the little white pills she took several times each day.

One afternoon Chuck showed up to talk to me. He'd been away for about a week this time. Raven wouldn't let him in when he stepped up to the door, so I went outside, even though I was hesitant. I asked her to keep Sasha inside.

Standing beside my station wagon, I waited for Chuck to speak. I started to fidget with the bottom button on my yellow cardigan.

Arms folded, head slightly bent, Chuck was perfectly calm.

"I'm miserable without you, Eve. I want us to be a family." When I didn't respond, he moved closer and reached for my hand. "I want to change," he pleaded. "I want to be good to you and Sasha. Please give me another chance."

I told him I couldn't live like that anymore and that I didn't believe him. "I'm not taking you back," I said.

"Please. It'll be different." He looked so despondent that I wanted to take him in my arms. I remained adamant, perhaps because his sister was listening from an open window upstairs.

"No way," I said, hands on my jean-clad hips. "That's it."

Chuck looked surprised at first. He took a slow, deep breath, then turned abruptly and walked back to his car. He was wearing a white T-shirt under a red plaid hunting jacket and a pair of faded black jeans. When he opened one of the back doors, I thought he'd made a mistake, or maybe he'd brought a gift for me as a last attempt to vie for my affection.

He leaned into the car, then backed out, straightened, and turned. I could see the anger in his eyes, and there was no mistaking what the steel tire jack in his hands was meant for. I ran as fast as I could into the house. Behind the screen door I watched helplessly as he smashed the driver's window in my car, then made his way around until every single piece of glass was shattered, except the headlights. Raven had taken Sasha upstairs so she wouldn't witness what was happening. I knew it was useless to call the police. They'd never arrive in time. Besides, I was still Chuck's wife; they wouldn't do anything.

I had the windows replaced the next day. My insurance company covered it. I told them some kids on the reserve had been playing hockey and gotten into a fight near my car.

Three days later Chuck showed up again in broad daylight and broke two of the newly installed windows, again with a tire iron. He didn't attempt speaking with me. He just yelled from the driveway until I came to the door. I called the reserve cop, but he did nothing more than promise to talk to Chuck. This time my excuses to the insurance company had me blame a nighttime vandal. They said I had to file a police report. I called the local RCMP detachment and told them the truth of what had happened, but never followed through on the charges and ended up paying for the windows myself.

That night, fearing for my safety, I called Elder Ervin and Nadine in Woodstock to tell them what was going on. Nadine urged me to call Fredericton Transition House for abused women and children.

"But he never touched me," I said, baffled. "I can't tell them I've been abused."

"You get on the phone and call them right now or I will," Nadine said, her voice loud and stern through the receiver.

I called the emergency number for Transition House and explained to the woman who answered what had transpired in the past few days.

"You need to get away from there immediately," she urged. "We can send a taxi to pick you up if you don't have transportation or if you're afraid to drive."

I agreed to check myself and Sasha in for a few days so I could meditate on what was left of my marriage. I didn't consider that I was in danger. After all, I'd been in much worse situations. Raven said my belongings were safe at her house. She indicated that the Oromocto Band would probably help me find somewhere to live when I figured out what I wanted to do.

THE TUMOUR

I had been at Transition House for a week when I woke one morning and realized my belly was hard and swollen. I had been going to the bathroom more frequently but didn't feel as if I had a bladder infection. I'd felt the burning sensation and accompanying chills from that particular ailment before. It was uncomfortable to lie on my belly when I was in bed, but I never gave it much thought, given all the other concerns banging around in my brain.

When I mentioned my symptoms to the nurse on staff, she suggested I call my doctor immediately. It took Dr. Roxborough only twenty minutes to return my call once I explained the situation to his receptionist. He asked me to come in that afternoon around three o'clock.

Transition House arranged a sitter for Sasha. They had a list of people who had been screened and deemed safe to stay with children when the mothers had appointments outside. Sasha took to the women at Transition House right away. They had an activity co-ordinator for children, who arranged everything from playing games and reading stories to taking walks.

The director suggested I take a taxi to the doctor's office. This would prevent Chuck from spotting my car outside the Oromocto clinic. She had one of the counsellors call me a taxi.

When I sat down to talk to Dr. Roxborough, he asked me how things were going. I told him about the events leading up to my temporary residence and familiarized him with the swelling in my belly.

"It's like I'm pregnant and it all happened in a few days," I explained. "Sort of an Immaculate Conception." I tried to make a joke to disguise the fact I was on the brink of tears.

"Well, let's take a look," Dr. Roxborough said. "You've been through tougher times. I'm sure you'll make it though this one." He smiled and gave me a reassuring pat on the shoulder as he pointed to the examining table.

In spite of Dr. Roxborough's gentleness, the examination was painful. When he was done, he gave me a few moments to dress and join him back at his desk.

"You have a growth, Eve," he said. "On one of your ovaries, I believe."

"A growth?" The room suddenly took on an unreal aspect as fear plunged through me. "What kind of growth?" I couldn't bear any more bad news and I couldn't, at this point, stop myself from crying.

"There, there, now," he said gently, clearing his throat and handing me a tissue. "Don't think the worst."

"Well, what is it?" I took the tissue and wiped my eyes. "What do I do now?"

"You'll need to see a gynecologist right away. He'll decide what to do. But I think we need to move quickly."

"Is it cancer?"

"There's no way to tell right now. That's why we have to deal with it immediately."

"How long will it take to see a specialist?"

"I'll have an appointment for you in a few days."

I left the office gripped by soul-numbing dread. Where I had feared for my life because of Chuck, I was now terrified of something inside me, something I couldn't even begin to control. If Dr. Roxborough was booking an appointment for me to see a specialist in just a few days, it had to be serious. I left the clinic and rode another taxi back to Transition House. Thinking of Sasha, I wept the entire twenty minutes it took to reach my destination.

Four days later I met with the gynecologist. He patiently examined me and, once finished, said I had a tumour that was probably attached to both ovaries.

"It has to come out," he remarked matter-of-factly. The tumour was growing rapidly and was now quite noticeable. I did indeed look pregnant.

"Is it cancer?" I asked.

"I don't know," he said. "I'll schedule your surgery as soon as I can fit you in." He inquired about my personal life and I told him where I was living. "It's obvious you're carrying a great deal of stress," he said, then went on to explain how tension often caused disease. "Women carry the brunt of their pressure in their reproductive system."

I thought it a strange comment for a medical specialist, but believed it to be true. I imagined the tumours in my ovaries to be caused by Chuck's poinsonous handling of me.

"When you go back to Transition House, it might be a good idea to take a few days to get things in order. There's no telling how it'll go or how long you'll need to recuperate."

I left the gynecologist's office carrying the burden of the world on my shoulders. Again I pictured Sasha and my children. I thought of Chuck and wondered if this news would make him feel bad for the way he'd treated me. Would the news make him more faithful now that I might be terminally ill?

At Transition House the counsellors went out of their way to help me plan what I needed to do. I sat with a counsellor named Sharon Cross and made a list while Sasha played with one of the many other children staying there.

"You'll be all right, Eve," Sharon assured me. "It'll come together, you'll see." She paused. "And as for Chuck, he's not capable of being who you need him to be. Right now you need people to lean on, and he's not one of them."

A couple of days later the doctor's office called and told me I was scheduled to enter the Dr. Everett Chalmers Hospital in ten days. There wasn't much time to get things done, and my belly was growing day by day, making it almost impossible to sleep comfortably or venture very far from a bathroom because of the constant pressure on my bladder. I suspected my belly might burst before they could operate. It would rupture and flood the place with the blackness I was carrying around.

With a deadline I was able to focus better. I prayed for strength, kneeling by the bed in the room I shared with Sasha. The more I prayed, the stronger I became.

When I called Ervin and Nadine in Woodstock, they offered to let Sasha stay with them while I had my surgery. Since Sasha was already familiar with the place and the people who lived there because of all the times we'd visited, I decided it was a wise choice. I knew Nadine, Ervin, and their daughter, Janice, would take good care of her.

When I spoke to my mom, she sounded upset, then started to cry.

"I'll be fine, Mom," I assured her, even though I didn't believe it myself.

When I told her Sasha and I would be going to Woodstock in a couple of days and that Sasha would stay there while I was in the hospital, she asked, "Why don't you come stay with me and your father after your surgery?"

"Okay," I agreed. "Thanks, Mom, I will. Then I'll join Sasha in Woodstock."

I talked to Raven by telephone and brought her up-to-date on the situation. "What's Chuck up to?" I asked her.

"He's in Kingsclear most of the time."

"Oh."

"He stopped in a few times for news about you. I told him I didn't know what you were doing."

I asked her to let him know about my physical condition but not to divulge where I'd be staying in the meantime.

"He knows you're staying at Transition House."

"I'm not there now," I said, lying so she could pass that information on, too.

The hardest part of the whole ordeal was talking to my children. I called a family meeting at Jennifer's Oromocto apartment. My children were so used to trauma and crisis that I don't think they were too concerned when I requested the meeting.

When I arrived, Sasha ran to give Heather a hug. Sasha still called Heather "Mommie" and I was "Mommie Eve" in Heather's presence. After a few minutes, Sasha joined Billy in the bedroom to fill in a colouring book.

My children appeared distraught as we settled in the living room. They had no idea what to expect. The four of them sat and listened to my explanation without asking a single question. I was wearing a white maternity top over black stretch pants. And I hated stretch pants! It was obvious from my swollen belly that something was amiss. Until that point my petite frame had been nicely filled out. Although I was never a willowy woman, I looked good at 140 pounds in spite of my height. My body was firm from all the walking I did, and although my waist certainly wasn't slim, there was no mistaking the new shape of my belly. It actually stuck out.

I told the children they should consider the possibility that something might happen to me. I could see by the pain in each face how difficult it was for them to accept this news. Speaking in an even tone, I tried to make it easier by showing no emotion, explaining I had an appointment with a lawyer the next day to make out my will. I could see tears in Jennifer's eyes. The others were shocked, their eyes widening as I talked about the will.

"It's just a precaution," I assured them, "something to be taken care of before I go in for surgery."

I reminded Heather of a conversation we'd had with Sonya when I first brought Sasha to live with me. At the time I'd asked Sonya if she could take Sasha if anything ever happened to me. She'd said yes.

Sonya and Heather were standing side by side, and I turned my gaze on them. "I need to know if that agreement's still in place today. It hasn't changed, has it?"

They both shook their heads.

"But nothing's going to happen to you, Mom," Sonya quickly interjected.

"Maybe not. But it doesn't hurt to have things in order."

I told the kids I'd be staying in Woodstock with Sasha until the day prior to the operation. Then I'd come back and stay with one of them before I went into the hospital. I asked if they could all try to be there when I went into surgery.

"Where's Chuck?" Sonya asked, sitting beside Jody on the chesterfield. "Why isn't he here?"

"We're not together right now."

"No loss," she said spitefully.

No one talked much after that. The room became unusually quiet as I called for Sasha to put on her shoes and prepared to leave. We all hugged and kissed goodbye before I left to catch a taxi back to Transition House. I'd left my car there so Chuck wouldn't know where I was if he were in town.

The following day I had an appointment with Allen Murray, a lawyer I'd attended school with in Geary, to draw up my will. I felt better afterward, knowing my affairs were in some kind of order for a change. I didn't want Chuck to have any claim to Sasha or my insurance money should the surgery take a turn for the worse. All he'd get was the rifle he'd given me as a gift and my guitar, which I'd intended to send to him, anyway, before I ended up in Transition House.

It was an inordinately despairing time for me, a period when I needed my husband most, but he couldn't give me what I desperately required. When I checked into the hospital, with Sharon from Transition House along for support, I was terrified. The whiteness of the place, the sense of impending doom, closed in on me. If only Chuck could come and tell me I'd be all right. I wanted him by my side, the way he was supposed to be.

Sharon helped with the arrangements to have Sasha picked up to go to Woodstock. Kissing Sasha goodbye without bawling was a difficult feat. My children did everything they could to console me, but my thoughts weren't rational. I kept thinking about death and asking Sharon, "What if I don't pull through this?"

The children stayed in my room, constantly reassuring me everything would be fine. But I was too fearful. In fact, the surgery was almost postponed because I was so distraught. The doctor told my children it wasn't wise for me to go into the operating room in such a mental state. It might add risk to the operation.

An hour before I was scheduled to go into the OR, Chuck walked into my room. He was dressed in his usual white T-shirt and blue jeans and wore a khaki army jacket. The children barely said two words to him.

"I prayed you'd come," I told him.

He bent near the bed and kissed my cheek. "How are you feeling?"

"Scared," I told him. When I reached out, he took my hand and gently pressed it.

"You'll be okay," he said. "I'll say a prayer for you."

A nurse came into the room and asked him if his name was Chuck. When he answered yes, she said there was a phone call for him at the desk from a woman named Ruth. His ex-wife.

"Tell her I'm busy," he said.

"Don't worry," Sonya briskly responded. "I'll handle this." She headed toward the nurses' station where the phone was located.

Chuck stayed for about ten minutes, not saying much, just holding my hand. Then he told me he had to attend a meeting with the band council.

"Will you be back?" I asked.

"Yes," he said as he released my hand. That was all I needed to hear. I was completely relaxed and at peace with my world.

Weeks later I found out that Sonya and Heather had been the ones to make certain Chuck visited. Sonya had told him he'd better get in and tell me he cared or she would find a way to make his life miserable. Chuck had always been intimidated by Sonya's confidence.

Waking after the operation, I gazed around groggily to see the pleasant face of a nurse. She went to the phone and called for my doctor who was still on duty. Sometime later, after I was wheeled back into my room from recovery, the doctor arrived. My kids had been there waiting for news.

The doctor placed a hand on my forehead. "How are you doing?"

I muttered something through my drugged stupor.

The doctor turned to my children and said, "We had to take both ovaries. But we removed all of the tumour and things look good." He went on to explain that the tumour had been sent to a laboratory in Saint John to be analyzed. He felt assured it was benign.

Very late one night after the surgery, I woke to see Chuck sitting in a chair beside my bed with his head in his hands, but I drifted off to sleep again, so we didn't talk. A few days later the doctor's diagnosis was confirmed. The tumour was benign.

My recovery was slow and painful. I developed a fever in the hospital that indicated infection, and for a few days I struggled to ward off pneumonia. My children and other family members visited the hospital often. So did friends from AA like Anne, Faye, and Miles, along with his new wife, Marg. Their love helped me mend.

I talked to Sasha on the phone and could tell she was happy. She'd chatter about the movies she'd viewed or the games she'd played with little Jonathan, Nadine's grandson. She'd always finish with "I miss you" before we ended our conversations. Nadine told me Sasha was fitting in well, playing with Jonathan most of the time and watching her favourite movie, *Beauty and the Beast*, so often that everyone was singing the songs around the house.

"Don't worry," Nadine said. "Just take care of yourself. We'll see you soon."

When I left the hospital, I spent four days with my parents at their mini-home in Waasis. My mother waited on me hand and foot. Dad tucked me in at nights and prayed for my health to be restored by laying a gentle hand on my forehead and saying, "Jesus, please heal Eva's body and take away all her pain."

I didn't have much interest in food when I first came home, so Mom coaxed it back with my favourite meals: creamed potatoes with tiny slivers of raw onion, fish cakes made from salmon, chicken soup with homemade bread, and an endless supply of ginger ale and cranberry juice. Before long my appetite was almost fully restored, even though my stitches still hurt whenever I shifted too quickly.

One evening my mother came in to cover me up and take dishes away. I'd been lying in bed thinking about Chuck and wondering why he couldn't be a faithful husband the way my father had been to my mother.

When my mother asked if I was feeling all right, I looked away and started to cry. "Why can't I find a good husband, Mom? I feel so alone."

"I know, dear. I know." She sat on the edge of the bed and leaned over to give me a hug, careful not to touch my belly where the stitches were.

"Try to get some sleep," she said, stroking my hair. "Don't think about anything right now. Just say a prayer and go to sleep."

Her voice and gaze were gentle and soothing. Her long grey hair was twisted into a small bun and bobby-pinned on the back of her head. She wore a pale green cotton house dress with a high collar and long sleeves. Mom never wore anything that showed her arms above the elbow and she always wore high collars. I realized her key to survival all these years, the creed she lived by was: *Just don't think about it and pray*.

Those few days I spent with my parents were priceless. I had a rare opportunity to revisit my childhood and view it through adult eyes now focused on the beauty in these two people who had always desired the best for me, even when I assumed they hated me.

In the evenings we'd sit around the wooden kitchen table, neatly set with a peach-coloured tablecloth that matched the peach-coloured curtains, drink tea, and have a little "lunch"—a piece of Mom's molasses cake or a sliver of her mouth-watering apple pie.

My mother is still the world's best housekeeper, I thought every time I sat in that kitchen. Nothing was ever wasted. When the left-over table scraps weren't enough for another meal, they became food for Mom's beloved wild birds. She'd throw bread and cake crumbs, tiny pieces of fat from bacon or pork, and seeds onto the roof of the shed. Then she'd watch with delight from the kitchen window as the birds gathered for a feast.

"Look, Eva," she called one morning, "there's my morning doves. They've been coming all week."

I looked out and saw a rooftop covered with various shapes and sizes of birds. I only recognized the chickadees because of the yellow on their breasts. I'd heard the doves coo, but I'd never actually spotted their sleek grey bodies until Mom pointed them out. She knew them all and could name every species. Then she saw a few black crows swoop in to land. She grabbed the broom and ran out into the yard. I watched her through the window chasing away the crows.

"They scare all the others off," she said, still annoyed when she returned. "I used to throw crumbs onto the ground for them, but the squirrels came instead. I even had a fox here once. I put the run to him, though, before he could eat my birds."

Sitting in the kitchen at night, Dad would talk about the "old days" when he was a boy on the homestead on Rifle Range Road, which the army had claimed long before I was born. He talked about the hard times when there was no food to eat.

"Sometimes I'd be forced to live with strangers," he said.

"Why?" I asked.

"Mother was in the hospital. She took a breakdown, and father was sick a lot."

Happy times didn't seem to exist. My father's sisters had to go out to work when they were still in their teens. When there was no money for food at home, the sisters often lived with other families, too.

Mom told me about the fights between her parents she'd witnessed as a child. She said they were always yelling. Her father used to run around with other women. He even brought one home with him once when he was drunk.

Mom had also lived with strangers for a time and said she'd seen a little boy locked in a root cellar at one of her foster homes simply for not paying attention. It was a common form of punishment, along with beatings with a razor strap. She never said she'd been abused, but Mom wasn't one to talk directly about anything that had happened to her, other than when she fell in love with my dad. She told me she thought he was handsome the first time she laid eyes on him. He'd asked her sister, Barbara, out first, but Mom quickly caught his eye. Despite the hard times they'd endured, there was still a special fondness in their eyes when they regarded each other. I recognized that look as love. It was the same expression Bob and I had exchanged the first couple of years we were married.

Those days with my parents helped me understand why they had never interfered with my life, even when they were aware of some of the abuse I was suffering. They'd been taught as children to keep a stiff upper lip. I was certain they'd hoped their children would be spared similar pain, but when it happened to me, they felt powerless to interfere, not out of any lack of love, but because they knew I had to rely on my own strength.

Chuck phoned while I was at my parents' home. My mother picked up the receiver in the living room. I was sitting at the kitchen table sipping tea and talking to my father about a children's story he'd written when I was a child. It was called "Clownsie and the Little Golden Bell," and the main character was Eva, the little red rose fairy. I was about to ask him a question, when my mother called out softly, "Eva, it's Chuck."

My heart beat faster as I rose and walked into the living room to accept the receiver from my mother. "Hello," I said cautiously, not wanting to show emotion.

"Look, I know you're probably mad at me," he said hurriedly, no doubt expecting me to hang up. "But I really miss you and I wanted to know if you're okay."

We talked for a few minutes. I let him know I was feeling better and he promised he was sorry for disappearing. He said he'd gone to talk to a priest and understood he'd been a jerk. He wanted to see me. We did get together to talk, until I realized he was more interested in whether or not I was still able to perform sexually after my surgery. I told him to get lost.

As soon as I was feeling better and had sufficiently recuperated, I drove to Woodstock to see Sasha and make plans for a new future. If there was one constant in my life, one thing worth getting back on my feet for, it was Sasha. I missed her completely.

Sasha and I returned to Raven's home. We lived there for three weeks before the Oromocto Band gave me enough money to rent an apartment nearby on MacDonald Avenue. That was one thing about Native communities: they took care of their own. Still Chuck's wife, I was considered the band's responsibility. I stayed in touch with some of his relatives and a few of the friends I'd made while living on the reserve. With her friend Naomi, Sasha continued to periodically join the reserve day-care program for preschoolers called Headstart. The Oromocto Band paid for her to attend.

The director of Headstart, Dixie vanRaalte, was white, like me. She was a petite blond with a wide smile and sparkling blue-grey eyes. I was registering Sasha at the day-care when Dixie walked over and put out her hand in greeting.

"Hello there, I don't think we've met before, I'm Dixie," she said all in one breath. "And who is this precious little one?" She squatted to get a better look at Sasha. "I hear you're a friend of Naomi's. I bet you like to sing, too, don't you?"

Sasha's eyes widened. She did, indeed, enjoy singing.

"Well, we love to sing here, too, Sasha. I think you'll like it." Dixie straightened and gave Sasha's brown curls a gentle pat. "You're welcome to stop in and see me anytime," she said to me. "And please feel free to call if there's ever a problem."

I thanked her and left the Headstart facility knowing I'd just made a new friend. In the months to come I did call Dixie and did get to know her. Sometimes I'd discuss the problems I was experiencing, such as being attached to a community that hadn't fully accepted me.

Dixie had her own problems with being embraced by the community. But she was a go-getter and regarded life as a challenge that, with the proper strategy, could be conquered. She once told me she'd survived breast cancer, a bad marriage, and single parenthood. After that she figured the rest was a piece of cake. She had a strong spirit. At times I felt as if she were the only person who truly empathized with what I was up against. When she left Headstart to accept another position with the Micmac/Maliseet Child Care Council, I felt as though I had lost my greatest ally. At the time I had no idea Dixie and I would connect again and build both a friendship and working relationship that would take us both even deeper into the Native world.

ACCEPTING THE BLAME

Chuck continued to call after I moved into my apartment, but I went out of my way to avoid him. I purchased an answering machine and always waited to hear who might be calling before I picked up. I was attending AA meetings with increasing regularity for support and often called on old friends like Miles and Theresa.

By the spring of 1993, I made a vow to try something different, to get out of the rut I was in. I'd received money from the Oromocto Band for the first couple of months, damage deposit included, but after that I was on my own. I had no choice but to turn to the white welfare system, which I loathed. After receiving only one cheque from social services, I signed up for a course at Saint Thomas University in Fredericton and applied for a student loan which I received and consequently withdrew from the welfare program.

Introduction to Philosophy was taught by Professor Frank Cronin, a patient, middle-aged man who smiled generously when he spoke, obviously enraptured with his subject matter. Every minute in class, listening to talk about Socrates and Aristotle, opened up new views of the world for me.

Once again I became a spirited child engaged by places and peoples I'd seldom heard of. When I argued with Dr. Cronin that it was unfair to stereotype the goats in an allegory based on sheep and goats, he smiled, not condescendingly, but as if to say, "Just think about it one more time, why don't you?" And I did. And I saw.

I devoured Jacob Needleman's *Heart of Philosophy*. When Needleman related his personal search for fulfillment, his investigation of religion and the occult, I was struck by the similarities to my own quest for personal worth. Needleman, too, had turned to other cultures and foreign philosophies only to find, in the end, the answer had been inside him all along. That simple conclusion came to him one day, an inner voice prompting him to delve within.

I was becoming stronger and enjoying my leisure time with Sasha. Often we would walk to the river and picnic. Sometimes we'd pick up fried chicken or hamburgers on our way. After eating we'd search for rocks to skip on the water, or we'd feed the seagulls. Sasha prized those birds. "Can we have one for a pet?" she'd ask. She couldn't understand why one wouldn't follow us home. She even laid out trails with the bread crumbs we brought along, trying to tempt one back to our apartment.

Chuck's calls persisted. Finally I agreed to meet him for coffee on campus while I was still attending my class at Saint Thomas University. I didn't think he'd have much power of persuasion now that I felt stronger in my conviction to move ahead with my life. I was ready to meet him on my terms but had to admit I missed him. So did Sasha. She never actually asked about him but often spoke as if he were still around.

"Daddy Chuck likes seagulls," she announced one afternoon as we sat by the river.

"He does?" I asked.

"Yes, he does and he really likes crows."

"Mommie likes crows, too, baby."

She smiled and crawled onto my lap for a cuddle. "And so do I!"

Over coffee Chuck told me he'd heard I was doing well at university and asked if I planned to attend full-time. The thought had crossed my mind, but I wasn't sure.

"I've been thinking about going to university myself," Chuck said, sitting across from me in the STU coffee shop. "I want to make some changes in my life."

"That's good," I replied evenly, not ready to jump back on his bandwagon yet.

"Look, Eve, I've done a lot of stupid things in my life and I know you probably hate me, but I miss you and Sasha." He stared at me, but I didn't return his gaze. I had the power now. "Is there any way we could try again? I'll even go for counselling."

"What about Ruth?"

"She's history. I never should have gone back there. I just felt guilty. She's the mother of my children. That's what did it."

"I need to think about it," I told him, venturing a look into his eyes. "I can't afford to get back into something that'll drag me down."

"Okay, that's good. Just think it over." He reached out and patted my hand.

"I will."

"There's a gathering in Maine in a couple of weeks," he said as we both stood. "Why don't you come with me? No strings attached. We could see how things go."

"I'll let you know." I glanced at my watch and picked up my philosophy text and notebook. "I've got to get home and study."

"Do you have your car? Can I give you a lift?"

"That's fine," I told him. "I have my car."

He walked me up the steps to the lot where both our vehicles were parked. "Would it be all right if I come and see Sasha later?"

"Not just yet."

"Okay, I understand, but tell her I miss her."

"I will."

I waved as I pulled out of the parking lot. Chuck looked despondent, and I couldn't stop thinking about him on my drive home to

Oromocto. As I entered my apartment, I knew I'd go back with Chuck. After all, I was still his wife. I believe he knew it, too.

It was difficult to study for my mid-term exam after that. I kept thinking about Chuck and the ease of reuniting.

While I felt ready to contact Chuck, I reasoned doing so too soon would make me appear anxious. As it turned out, Chuck called the next evening to ask me about accompanying him to the powwow in Maine. I told him I hadn't yet decided and I waited a week before telling him I would attend.

"I can't wait," he said. "Can I come see Sasha now?"

"Not yet," I replied before saying goodbye and replacing the receiver.

I didn't tell Sasha I'd been talking to Chuck or that we would be going away. I didn't want to raise her hopes.

I asked Sonya if Sasha could spend the weekend with her because I wasn't sure how Chuck and I would get along and I didn't want Sasha to be there for any fireworks. Besides, I was certain Chuck and I had romantic intentions. The physical attraction between us was overpowering.

The trip was more like a honeymoon than what we'd actually experienced after our wedding. On our first night back together, after three long sexless months, I let loose all that bottled-up passion. The sex was fresh and vigourous. We camped out under the stars and spent more time in each other's arms than we did at any of the powwow events. The first night neither of us slept a wink.

The next morning we joined the gathering and watched the dancers and singers, but then decided to tour the coast of Maine near East Port, stopping at a restaurant for seafood. After the previous night of passion, we were famished. I ordered baked haddock with mashed potatoes and baby carrots. Chuck had scallops and fries. After our dinner, we headed back to our camping spot beside a stream and grabbed a few winks after another ecstatic round of lovemaking.

Within a week the three of us were living together again on the reserve. This time it was in our own place—an apartment in a building that was once the old band office on MacDonald Avenue, down the street from my previous apartment.

I continued at STU. While most people in my philosophy class listened intently so they could simply pass their final exam, I searched for personal answers from ancient Greek philosophers, craving the wisdom that could be applied to my own problems. It was coming—channels were opening in my brain. With every further understanding, something clicked in my head, and I'd sit there, enthused, and think, *Yes, I see that*.

One sunny afternoon I was walking across a field on my way home, peacefully elated about my status as a university student. Being in a university gave me such an immense sense of worth. I was honoured to be there, but still had the nagging feeling I didn't belong. From this sense of dissonance it became clear my life choices had been centred around my childhood belief that I was bad and deserved nothing good. Any time someone treated me well, I was uncomfortable. It was so unfamiliar, and I'd sabotage the relationship the way I had with Bob, then seek out men who would treat me like dirt. I was partially responsible for the abusive situations.

By accepting some of the blame, I could begin to shift the inner geography away from "victim" toward "survivor." I could work to repair my distorted mode of thinking.

The next day, when I visited school to pick up my final mark, I felt more confident. The grades were posted on the professor's door. I scanned the list of student numbers and discovered that I had received an A+ on the philosophy course. A week later a letter arrived from the university, informing me I had been awarded a small bursary of $250.

I couldn't wait to tell Chuck.

St. Johnswort

PART FOUR

1994-1996

BACK ON THE REZ

Things were peaceful between me and Chuck now. He stayed home more often, spending hours wood-burning scenes on pieces of hardwood he'd collected. Sasha would often sit beside him and watch as he branded the patterns of coyotes, wolves, teepees, and eagle feathers with the tool. Once in a while he let her try it. She usually drew a happy face with a crooked smile. Sasha would scribble on paper or work in her Cinderella colouring book while he worked. Often the two of them watched movies together. Their favourite was a western, *White Buffalo,* starring Charles Bronson. On pleasant afternoons they would drive to a wooded area near the river where Chuck would teach Sasha about plants and animals. She was just over three when she picked her first bunch of muskrat roots. Sasha was thrilled, happy to have us together. She had laughed and run into Chuck's arms the first time he returned to our apartment. When she found out we'd all be moving back to the reserve, she clapped her hands and asked, "Can Naomi come over?"

Because I planned to go to university full-time in the fall, I wasn't working. I expected the Oromocto Band would grant me an allowance as it had previously. The housing was free and as long as we weren't working, so was our electricity. Chuck decided to attend university part-time. He received biweekly cheques from the Oromocto Band to cover expenses such as food, clothing, cable, telephone, and gas. My money was included with his, so I never actually saw any cash except what he gave me for groceries.

We spent most of the summer out-of-doors, often taking short trips to Jemseg or Crow Hill, north of Fredericton, to camp or fish. I didn't see my children or my parents much during this time. Chuck kept us pretty much to himself. Heather had started to date Chuck's nephew, Joe, so I did run into her here and there. She was still drinking, but there were times she seemed almost normal. During those occasions, she'd visit or take Sasha overnight to stay with her. She shared several different apartments with friends who tried to help her change her life and they were all willing to have Sasha spend quality time with her mother. It gave me a break, as well.

When Chuck actually enrolled at university, I wondered if he was doing it to keep an eye on me. I knew he had a great respect for knowledge; he often read books about Native history and treaty rights and could talk about those subjects tirelessly. It came as no surprise he registered for two Native studies courses.

I decided to pursue a degree in social work. I had already received a certificate in family mediation while working with disenfranchised youth at the local drop-in centre, and I'd trained in several other related areas. I was committed to helping others who were victims of poverty and violence. I'd attended training seminars and workshops on everything from healthy sexuality and AIDS to eating disorders, substance abuse, and caregiver burnout.

My work at detox had deepened my compassion for the suffering addicts. Watching them as they paced the floors in a sweat or lay on their beds shivering and crying in pain, I relived my own descent into the pit of addiction, and felt an even greater desire to help.

When I met Dr. Stewart Donovan, my plans to be a social worker were blown away. As soon as he started talking about *Gulliver's Travels* in my Introduction to Literature class, I experienced the thrill of voyaging intellectually into the same magical world of books that had sustained me as a child. This was the safe place where I had always thrived.

After reading a few of my writing assignments, Dr. Donovan suggested I enter the writing competition sponsored by STU. That was all the encouragement I needed. The Expository Writing Competition in Issues in Roman Catholic Theology was jointly sponsored by the Saint Thomas Chair in Roman Catholic Theology and *The New Freeman*, a Catholic journal.

Having limited knowledge of Catholicism, I opted to write about the "holy war" I saw taking place in Native communities between the staunch Catholics and those who were still practising their ancient ceremonies. I called my essay "The Spiritual Split":

What about the internalization of spirituality that Native peoples already possessed before Christianity ever crossed their path? Why is it that the people who had never laid eyes on a Bible had such reverence for life and the Creator and performed rituals not unlike those sanctioned by the Catholic Church? Could God-the-Creator have found a way to communicate to Native people without the help of the Church? After all, wasn't the burning of sweetgrass, sage, and tobacco much like burning incense? Couldn't sacred fire burn just as well from coals on the ground as it could from candles on an altar?

Chuck read my essay. I was interested to hear what he might say, but he offered no comment. Thinking I might have struck a nerve in him, I left it alone, confident I had approached the subject with diplomacy. Not waiting for his sanction, I entered the contest, delivering my essay to the registrar's office.

Two weeks later I was told I had won second prize. Chuck was more interested in what I planned to do with the $250. He said he was proud of me but appeared to be indifferent.

When I told Sasha that "Mommie Eve" had won a prize, she kissed me and said, "Happy Birthday."

Tension was again beginning to mount between me and Chuck. He was struggling with his course at STU, and I suspect he was jealous of the ease with which I had breezed through mine. I often helped him compose assignments.

"You think you're smarter than me," he said angrily one evening after supper.

"No, I don't," I replied defensively.

"Well, no one around here cares if you get an A," he snarled. "So don't think anyone's impressed."

I was hurt but didn't pursue the argument. I figured he was feeling bad about himself. It really had very little to do with my marks.

After the first semester, when it was time for me to sign up for a new course, Chuck suggested we take one together—North American Native Religions.

We attended our class with Dr. Thom Parkhill every Tuesday and Thursday afternoon. Chuck often sat across the room from me instead of beside me where I would have preferred. He said he could keep a better eye on me that way. "You seem to have a lot of male friends," he told me when we were driving home from class one afternoon.

I hardly had time to stop and talk to anyone that year. I was intent on achieving top grades. The only guys I met were in the classroom, and I hardly knew anyone's name, but Chuck insisted I was sneaking around behind his back. Pretty soon the insults resumed with no provocation. I couldn't figure out what had happened. "White bitch" became such a common greeting that I thought it must be my name. Most of the time Chuck saved his insults for me privately, but sometimes he'd even call me names in front of Sasha.

By January 1994, Chuck was away from home more than he was there. I knew he was staying in Kingsclear again. People had told me so and again he didn't deny it. He reminded me that Native men traditionally had more than one wife, so he couldn't see what

I was so upset about. He began to hang out with other Native students he'd met at STU, many of them female.

It was during this period, while still living on the Oromocto Reserve, that I began to experience the worst sort of prejudice. I'd walk into the band hall to talk to a counsellor or the chief about much-needed home repairs when one of the Natives would make a wisecrack about white people. "Looks like the honkies are coming to beg," someone would say, and the rest of them would laugh. I pretended not to hear.

I could never be sure who would turn on me. Friendly smiles and gestures often masked the ill wishes of gossipers wanting to smear my reputation. Several of Chuck's ex-wife's relatives resided in Oromocto, and they didn't approve of his new wife for reasons of allegiance. Others just didn't like my skin colour. And Chuck was the worst of the lot. He'd often joke and snicker with his friends or family members, speaking Maliseet as I sat beside him. I'd know by the tone of their voices and the few words I managed to store in memory that he was talking about me. One word kept coming up repeatedly while Chuck laughed and gestured toward me. It sounded like *del-oz-el*. When I asked my sister-in-law, Vera, about it, she sheepishly admitted it wasn't a nice term. She said it meant something like "dirty underwear" and indicated that she, too, had heard Chuck use that term when referring to me.

To keep sane and steady I clung to my successes at university, continuously assuring myself I was doing well and to keep at it. I wouldn't let myself be defeated by negativity. I knew by now that reuniting with Chuck had been a mistake, but I also knew I'd find a way out when the time was right. I had left him before and I could do it again.

At the end of my first year at university I had a grade-point average of 4.0. That was roughly equivalent to an A+. I was named to the dean's list and awarded a scholarship from STU for full tuition for the following year. I was also given the Kay Robinson Prize for

Scholastic Achievement and the Desmond Pacey Scholarship for my high standing in English. Finally I was beginning to feel as if I had accomplished something, as if I had succeeded in demonstrating my abilities. I didn't need Chuck's recognition to feel good about my intellectual achievements, yet I longed for his praise just the same.

Anxious to move on, I was determined to finish my four years of undergraduate study in three. In my second year I took six full courses and stayed in school during spring intercession for another credit. Chuck enrolled in two courses and we worked out a schedule so I could be home when it was time to pick Sasha up from Headstart.

Torn once again between my ambition and my desire to be part of the Native community, I strove to select the courses that would cover all this ground. I was interested in learning more about the culture into which I had married, and to which my children would always belong. So I chose a large number of Native studies courses. I was also being drawn toward courses offered by the English department, so I signed up for Women's Literature and Creative Writing, both taught by Dr. Patricia Thornton. I was surprised by the number of successful women writers and became immersed in the works of Alice Munro and Jamaica Kincaid.

The creative-writing class opened new perspectives for me. I'd always preferred writing nonfiction, but it was fun to experiment, using my imagination to describe a fictional character like an old woman waiting for a train on a cold December day or a hungry dog studiously watching his master in anticipation of dinner. I was stimulated through the creation of these fictitious worlds and submerged myself fully in them.

"You're very talented," Dr. Thornton told me one afternoon in her office. "Have you written much fiction outside this class?"

"Next to none," I admitted.

"Well, I'd try my hand at fiction for a while, if I were you," she said with a supportive smile.

For obvious reasons I also had an interest in psychology. I became fascinated with all forms of therapy but was particularly intrigued by books I'd read on narrative therapy. I began envisioning a way to fit all of my interests into a thesis.

My daughter, Sonya, enrolled as a part-time student at STU and accompanied me for one course that September. We took Introduction to Sociology and, as a course project, worked together to create a family tree. Sonya was always a bright girl with a great sense of humour, and we shared our dislike of the female professor who seemed to favour the young men in the class.

"I wonder which ego Ms. Marilyn Monroe will stroke today?" Sonya whispered as we entered the classroom one afternoon.

"I don't know," I answered. "But I swear if she ignores my raised hand again, I'm coming to class disguised as a man."

I put my heart and soul into the project and did end up with an A, which I thought should have been an A+. My final mark was B+, my lowest the whole time I attended STU. Sonya received a B, which was great considering it was her first course and she was an even more attractive female than I was. The deadline for the Expository Writing Competition in Issues in Roman Catholic Theology had rolled around again. I slaved to put the finishing touches on a piece called "The Kingdom of God" and kept my fingers crossed, hoping I might win something. This time my essay took the $500 first prize. The day I received the cheque I treated Chuck and Sasha to supper. We had pizza and Caesar salad, one of Sasha's favourites. Then we went shopping and I bought them new outfits. I picked myself up a black velvet dress I thought might be fitting for special occasions.

At the end of my second year I was on the dean's list again and was awarded another scholarship for the following year's tuition—money much needed. I also won the Kay Robinson Prize for Scholastic Achievement for the second year in a row. My grade-point average was 3.9, and I couldn't help but feel more confident than ever about my academic abilities.

Unfortunately Chuck didn't appreciate my growing self-assurance, and I had no real allies on the reserve. My days in the hushed corridors of university were my escape. They offered the reprieve I needed to continue living in the Native community without buckling under the weight of oppression.

SQUANDERING FEDERAL FUNDS

Living on the Oromocto Reserve was a real eye-opener for me. Being on the receiving end of prejudice was no surprise. As a white woman, I was an easy target. I became the enemy because of the pain Natives had accumulated from white people I'd never met or even heard about. Some of the discrimination I experienced had nothing to do with my skin. In addition to being regarded as a "honky," I could just as easily be dismissed as an outsider or interloper.

Yet I was unprepared for some of the things I saw going on in the community, especially the blatant squandering of federal funds by the band officials who ran the community. I'd heard about politics on the reserve, how the families of whoever was chief at the time would receive special favours or be hired to work on projects established to create jobs, but I was still naive enough to believe there was some kind of accountability, if not to the community, then at least to the federal government, which doled out the money.

Most people in the community, including Chuck's family, spoke openly of parties thrown using federal cash, especially near election time. One member of the community told me hookers had even been brought in before one of the elections by the incumbent chief and council. The hookers were used to buy votes for the chief and the family members he intended to have serve with him on the band council. The man, a relative of Chuck's, said there had been a party with free booze purchased with money earmarked for a community program. I was outraged and told Chuck it should be reported. He said everyone already knew.

"What about the federal government?" I asked. "Do they know?"

"They don't care as long as we don't leave the reserve," Chuck replied. I thought about how the people on the reserve had once turned against Chief Emmanual Polchies after the land-claim funds ran out. It didn't surprise me that money was still the prime motivator for most of the voters on the reserve. That was simply human nature for many people, regardless of their race. What irked me most was the sloppy way the federal government handled its affairs, and the fact that someone outside the chief's family would have to do without funding for education so the parties could continue. The incumbent chief was a serious drinker and made sure the people who stuck with him had their beer glasses filled.

When I persisted asking Chuck about the situation, he told me to mind my own business or I'd be sorry. I had enough trouble on my hands coping with his jealousy and prejudice, so I followed his advice. Even if I did keep my mouth shut, I never ceased to be amazed at the way money was freely handed out to people who used it for drugs like cocaine and alcohol, while others begged to scratch together a little extra money for groceries for their children, or to obtain furniture to replace sofas and mattresses with sagging or broken springs.

I learned firsthand how long it took to have any sort of home repair carried out if you weren't connected. I lived in a building that was filthy and run-down, barely fit for human habitation. It had taken five large bottles of bleach to clean the floors and the bathroom when we first moved in so I could feel comfortable enough to stay. Our laundry room still had a urinal on the wall from the days when it was a washroom at the old band hall. It hadn't been cleaned in years, and urine and feces were caked on the inside. I poured an entire bottle of bleach over the mess and told Chuck I refused to clean it. It was a man's job and he could take care of it. Eventually the urinal was removed altogether by a carpenter who worked for the band.

Some people lived in houses where floors were beginning to sag and mildew had overtaken the walls of their basements, while others lived in new homes with all the latest conveniences funded by the band. A few community members even used their own money for home improvements.

· If you were connected to the chief, then you could skip ahead on the long waiting list for housing. Far worse than the favouritism was the waste of funds paid for imaginary jobs. The fisheries sector was where the abuse was most prevalent. Many community members were paid high seasonal salaries so they could later collect premium unemployment cheques. They did so without working more than a day. Some "workers," like Heather's boyfriend, Joe, just showed up regularly to collect their pay cheques.

So much was out of whack on the rez. The turmoil was pervasive. There were drug and alcohol counsellors who threatened to kill their wives or who used narcotics and were heavy drinkers. There were counsellors in charge of education who had little formal education. There was a female counsellor who organized events for children but who frequented taverns and physically assaulted other women and sometimes even men.

I often asked myself: Where were the role models? Where were the traditional values so many of the Natives constantly preached as hallmarks of their distinct culture? In my estimation there were very few people on the Oromocto Reserve, while I lived there, who weren't angry or troubled. Those who seemed content with their lives were in the minority and kept to themselves.

In the three years I was connected to the Oromocto Reserve, there was a pitiful lack of healing in the community.

I used to pray that some kind of justice would prevail. Good people who were trying to live in peace should have been able to do so. I wanted to see the true Native spirituality that spoke of harmony, forgiveness, and balance infuse the community and especially the administration, chief, and council. Why couldn't a community that had turned its head for years while children were raped by their fathers and brothers take responsibility for the future of their children? Instead I witnessed the perpetuation of violence, hate, alcoholism, and drug abuse, all ignored by the supposed leaders of the community.

"Why doesn't someone do something?" I asked Sarah, one of my sisters-in-law, when we were talking about the growing problem with drugs on the rez. She was a kind woman who worked as a teaching assistant in an elementary school in town and had expressed concern about the children in her community.

"Nobody knows what to do," she explained. "Every time someone tries to organize a group to make things better, people don't stick with it.

I once asked the chief what he was going to do about the drug problem on the reserve. He looked at me as if I were telling a joke.

"Don't worry," he said. "I'll be looking at that. Things aren't that bad yet."

Each time I questioned any of these wrongs I was put in my place, which was beneath the Natives. By speaking out, I was in constant danger because leaders in the community were still part of the drug and alcohol culture. I ran the risk of being physically assaulted if I didn't keep my mouth shut. The only way to survive was to close my eyes tight to it all.

When a new chief, who was educated and seemed genuinely concerned about the addiction problem, was finally elected, I was hopeful some good might come of it. This chief was young and full of bright plans to improve the situation on the reserve. But one year wasn't enough to reverse the harm caused by decades of deceit and greed. When his term was up, the previous chief was reelected with a bigger majority than before.

THE TAX RACKET

The status card was a significant symbol of what divided Natives from non-Natives. These "tax cards," as they were most often referred to, granted the owners exemptions from provincial sales tax. When one considered all the rights the government had taken away from Natives over the years, the tax exemption seemed a meagre victory. Regardless, the status card was a much-coveted piece of paper, so much so that many non-Natives befriended Natives simply to use their cards for large purchases. At Christmas-time some Native cardholders would make two or three trips through a department store checkout in an evening to accommodate the shopping whims of their white friends. On a $200 purchase that could mean a saving of more than $20.

All of that came to an abrupt end in March 1993 when the provincial government, under the Liberal leadership of Premier Frank McKenna, announced that tax cards would no longer be valid as a means of dodging the eleven percent sales tax in New Brunswick. By doing so, McKenna hoped to raise a million dollars per year to apply to the provincial deficit.

That year no one was happy with the budget announced by Finance Minister Allan Mahar. Taxes were to be raised in the province. Student bursaries and prescription-drug programs were facing cuts. There was a great deal of grumbling in every corner, but none so loud as that from First Nations.

The first protest came the day after the tax-card announcement. Mi'gmaqs from the Eel River Bar First Nation in northern New Brunswick ignited a bonfire on Highway 134, dragging fir trees and an old telephone pole to fuel the flames and effectively block the road to traffic. Tempers flared, but overall the protest remained peaceful and was sanctioned by Roger Augustine, the president of the Union of New Brunswick Indians. The RCMP, not wanting to make matters worse, set up detours and pretty much left the protesters to their business.

Augustine called an emergency meeting as other Mi'gmaqs from the Quebec community of Listuguj (Restigouche) joined forces with their neighbours in Eel River Bar. Many of them carried signs spray-painted in red TAXES UNFAIR TO NATIVES. Another Oka crisis was feared.

Similar protests spread quickly. The Kingsclear Reserve set up a roadblock on the Trans-Canada Highway above Fredericton. A blockade was established at the St. Mary's Reserve in Fredericton and on Highway 11 near Burnt Church. Dozens of drummers and singers were heard well into the night, their chanting circling the orange glow of bonfires on Easter weekend.

In the meantime Augustine informed McKenna he would challenge the province's decision in court. The premier responded by announcing he would cooperate in putting the matter before the courts and, should the province lose, all provincial sales tax that had been paid by Natives who held on to their receipts would be reimbursed.

In Oromocto I watched the growing tension among the people of the community when they talked about the situation. A few hotheads suggested violent retaliation, and I became increasingly uneasy as plans were made to set up a roadblock beside the reserve. I feared I would be alienated more than ever by Chuck and his family merely because I was white, like McKenna.

At the university the protests were discussed openly in the cafeteria by students of all races. I was encouraged to hear there was a great deal of sympathy for the plight of Native Canadians among the non-Native students. In the end the Oromocto protest was handled diplomatically. It was a peaceful protest, but that didn't stop some of Chuck's relatives from making insulting remarks about white people in front of me.

"Bloody white land grabbers," a man in his mid-twenties—a cousin to the chief—shouted at a motorist who had expressed impatience over the blockade. "They take our land and now they want to charge us double."

What they never seemed to understand was that I felt as angry as they did when I heard tales about store owners taunting Natives with the new regulation. One store owner told my husband it was about time Indians were treated like everybody else.

"You cried for equal rights," the store owner said. "Well, you got it."

When Chuck came home and related the story to me, he acted as if I were the one who had insulted him.

In Kingsclear matters soon got out of hand. People in the community were angry and the police weren't backing down. A few of the protesters were drinking, and that only enflamed the situation. The RCMP moved in to break up the blockade. In an attempt to subdue the Natives, they fired tear gas into a crowd of men, women, and children, the same tear gas that was alleged to have knocked a chained dog unconscious in his own yard. Twenty-four people were arrested, including the Kingsclear chief, Steve Sacobie, on various mischief charges.

The Union of New Brunswick Indians was outraged. They played one card the provincial government couldn't ignore. The federal funds for Native children to attend provincial schools was to be sent directly to Native bands in the province so they, in turn, could pay the province for the spots the children required in public schools. At that time $4,550.50 was provided from the federal government for each of the estimated twelve hundred Native children enrolled in off-reserve schools. Augustine reasoned that the $1 million the province planned to raise through taxation of Natives was a paltry sum in comparison to the more than $5 million the province could lose if Native communities decided to find alternatives to sending their children to provincial schools.

The reserves would also counter the sales-tax imposition by setting up tax-free businesses on the reserve and by buying outside the province. Kmart Canada capitalized on this decision immediately by offering to supply tax-free goods for New Brunswick Natives through the Listuguj Reserve in Quebec.

After eight days of roadblocks and protests, the patience of Natives and non-Natives was wearing thin. McKenna and Mahar recanted, and Augustine announced that a compromise had been reached in favour of on-reserve status Natives. They would be exempt from the provincial sales tax if the purchases were made on the reserve or if items purchased off the reserve, such as vehicles or furniture, were delivered to the home reserve of the purchaser. Off-reserve status Natives were out of luck.

The government called the sudden change of heart a "clarification." Natives celebrated their victory by letting the media know they considered it a "white surrender." And I breathed a laboured sigh of relief when it was all over. Perhaps I could get back to pretending to fit in again.

WHAT A WHITE WOMAN WOULD SAY

I never dreamed the tensions that reared up between Native and non-Native factions would surface in my own home, with racial slurs coming from my own children. I often recalled the warning of Pastor Foster, the man who had married me and Stan. Mixed marriages *could* be difficult for the children. No doubt about it.

Heather was beginning to embrace the tenets of Native spirituality and was proud of her Mohawk heritage. The identity helped her feel more accepted by others on the reserve, even though some Maliseets quite openly let me know that a Mohawk didn't belong there any more than a white woman. Nevertheless, Heather was dating a Maliseet, and perhaps that balanced things.

My daughter, Sonya, was fed up with the mistreatment she'd witnessed from Natives against family members. She constantly urged me to quit the reserve and find a non-Native partner for a change.

One afternoon Heather stopped in to see Sasha, expecting to take her out for lunch. She was upset when she learned Sasha was visiting Jennifer and Billy for the day. I'd had a bad morning already, arguing with Chuck about his plans to take his daughter to Maine, so I had little patience when Heather started telling me how wonderful the traditional Native beliefs about peace and harmony were in comparison to the way white people attempted to get along.

I'd had just about enough. "Well, it *would* be wonderful if some of those people who talk about living in peace and harmony stopped calling non-Natives 'whitey'." I was fed up with eloquent speeches from Natives who, on the one hand, declared all human beings equal and, on the other, accused all white people of being greedy, hate-filled land stealers. "I'm sick and tired of having five hundred years of history dumped on my shoulders while I live here and get lied to and talked about by the same people who point fingers at me because I have white ancestors."

"What do you expect?" Heather countered. "Think about all the things the white men did to the Indians." Heather was pumped up by recent lectures from a group of community members who met to discuss the curtailment of their fishing and hunting rights. Chuck was one of the leaders, quick to share the information he'd learned in his Native studies course. Heather heard a great deal about the genocide Native peoples had suffered after European contact.

"Some people spend their lives complaining instead of doing something positive," I argued. "We all have pain in our past to overcome. And that's what survivors do—they get over it." I could feel the pent-up anger raging inside me. *How dare my own daughter stick up for the people who were abusing her mother and her, too. How naive could she be?* "Only losers bury their head in the past," I said bitterly. "You can't find peace and harmony holding on to grudges."

"That's exactly what a white women would say, isn't it?" Heather shot back. "How could you understand, anyway?" She stormed out without saying another word.

I was in shock and speechless. When the apartment door slammed shut, I sat at my kitchen table and felt myself drowning in sorrow and defeat.

BLESSINGS AND CURSES

Many Natives I met on the Oromocto Reserve were extremely superstitious, just as my own Gypsy ancestors had been. One of the elders in the community explained how the reserve had been cursed a long time ago by an angry member who was shunned by the rest of the community. When I asked Chuck's mother about the curse, she revealed it went back farther than anyone could remember. She thought it had something to do with infractions against ancient laws set down by the Creator.

Regardless of the source, people firmly believed in the curse. To them, nothing or no one could prosper while living there unless the curse was broken through traditional ceremonies or prayers. Even those who knew little about their heritage had heard, through stories passed down from generation to generation, about spirits who warned of danger or who tormented people for spiritual breaches.

I'd grown up believing in forerunners and spirit guides, who I later preferred to call angels. The surreal world of spirits and curses was a familiar one.

When we first met, Chuck had said that animals often acted as guides or protectors. Other times they were sent by those who had special powers to spy on people and report back to them.

"If you see a certain animal following you around, he's either there to protect you or watch you," Chuck had told me.

My secret fascination with crows and ravens was called to mind. They were always following me, and I wondered which job they were carrying out: protecting or spying? If a solitary crow swooped near me, I automatically said a prayer.

One crow sorrow
Two crows joy
Three crows money
Four crows a boy

I had read about how animals could shift shape. Chuck claimed this was a ploy used by the trickster. To my mind, the trickster was the Native equivalent to Satan, the evil fallen angel spoken of in Christian literature. Both could transform into beautiful creatures and both were bad news. Chuck's story of the man by the river had made the hairs on the back of my neck stand on end.

Over the years I met several people who were professed Catholics yet spent more time with tarot cards, Ouija boards, and books on how to curse people than in church. Others didn't need books, seeming to possess dark knowledge derived from other sources. One Maliseet woman told me once, quite openly, that she knew how to curse and to bless people, and practised on a regular basis. She revealed that she was a *white* witch.

It wasn't that I didn't believe these sorts of things existed. Certainly I'd witnessed and heard about supernatural occurrences all my life. But I wanted no part of the dark side anymore. I strove toward light and the protection it ensured. I believed there was no such thing as a "good witch"; I'd been around plenty who had made that assertion and nothing *good* had ever come of it.

Several of the women met regularly—even Naomi's mother—to share their interest in the dark arts. But none of these women appeared the better for it. Their lives were plagued by turmoil and crisis. Even the dead spiders one woman took to a bingo game as a good-luck charm never improved her winnings.

I'd heard stories of the practice of Satanism on other reserves, especially among young people. Perhaps the powerlessness many of them felt over situations that didn't seem to mend drove them to find alternate sources of power. I often wondered if anyone had told these children about the Jesus I'd encountered as a child.

I used to suspect Chuck had tried to send something wicked my way after I left him the last time. The crows that had once fascinated me now seemed dreadfully ominous. I noticed them everywhere, their glassy black eyes fixed on me. I even found a dead one on my doorstep. After talking about my fears to a Mi'gmaq friend, she suggested I make an offering of food to the crows for three days to appease their displeasure toward me. I did what she suggested.

After that I felt incredibly better. I didn't care if the change had actually come about through some supernatural force, or because the ritual had helped me face my fear. What mattered most was that I was able to greet all crows as friends again, even the one that often sat on my windowsill, staring through the glass, watching me.

THE NIGHT I HIT CHUCK

No matter how hard I tried to please Chuck, nothing was ever good enough. His jealousy and paranoia intensified. Every morning he'd question my plans for the day, even though he knew exactly where I was going. At suppertime he'd grill me about my hours away from him. If we'd both been on campus, he'd ask who I spoke with, whether I'd had coffee with anyone, and sometimes he'd declare he'd seen me speaking with a guy when I hadn't been near one at all.

Nights were often worse. Usually he'd go out for the evening, but when he stayed home it would only be until Sasha went to bed. If anyone saw him watching television with her, often cuddled on the couch, they'd have thought I was imagining all the verbal and psychological abuse he reserved for me.

One night in bed, after a particularly tender episode of lovemaking, Chuck held me closely with true feeling and stroked my skin. At first I believed he was having a change of heart.

"You know, I really do love you, Eve," he said as I snuggled against his warm, firm body.

"And I love you," I answered, closing my eyes to savour this welcome lull from the torment of the past few months.

"You know I love you so much," he whispered. "I'd have to kill you if you ever left me."

My heart felt heavy in my chest. The smile of contentment wilted from my lips. Not saying another word, even though I was scared, I pretended to go to sleep.

Chuck stayed away many nights until two or three in the morning. He spent most of this time in Kingsclear. When he returned home, he'd wake me up and begin accusing me of being with someone else earlier that evening. One night he pulled me roughly out of bed at 3:30 a.m.

"Get up," he said, dragging me. "What kind of wife are you, sleeping when her husband needs a little loving?"

The very thought of making love with him when I knew he'd just crawled out of another woman's bed made me sick to my stomach. But I wasn't about to protest, as I didn't want to wake Sasha. I did insist he use protection, though. His crazed insistence for a marathon of sex left me feeling like an old cleaning rag tossed into a cupboard. Constant ridicule about my lack of enthusiasm during these times soon exhausted any early spark of passion I might have felt. Chuck wanted a wild woman, and I was trying my best not to be one.

He grew increasingly possessive and would often follow me to the bathroom and stand over me while I did my business. Chuck had grown up in a home where physical violence was disguised as discipline. Still no one would talk about it. It was easier to pretend that threats with knives or a stick of wood across the back were normal motherly responses. Alcoholism was prevalent. No one ever spoke up. It was considered a shame to reveal any truth. For that a person would be branded "disloyal."

"I knew I should have never married a white woman," Chuck often said. "You're all bad blood. You stink. You're used goods. No one will ever want you."

After a while, my fragile self-image couldn't take much more. I thought about drinking a couple of beers to take the edge off my pain but knew I'd never stop with two. This pain was too immense for any amount of alcohol to deaden. *There's always suicide. No pain forever.* Old, familiar thoughts teased my mind, but they were no match for my love of Sasha. When I thought about her, I grew more determined to find a way to rise above this misery.

At the end of my marriage to Chuck I became more violent. For a long time I'd buried my anger. I tried hard to hide my pain from Sasha, but the rage that festered inside me finally came to a head.

Long after I quit drinking, I still carried the poison within me. It had started seeping out shortly after I married Chuck. I'd been so determined to be a proper wife, then discovered he had no intention of being faithful to me. At first I'd only yelled at him, called him names, but as my pain grew so did my fury.

The first night I hit him it was late and I was exhausted. I thought I was coming down with a cold and couldn't sleep. The clock said 1:30 a.m. and I knew I had to awaken by 7:00 to get ready for class and prepare Sasha for Headstart. When Chuck waltzed in a few minutes later and accused me of just getting home, my already-taut nerves were on the verge of exploding. Chuck stuck his face close to mine and I slapped his cheek as hard as I could. As soon as I realized what I'd done, I was frightened.

Chuck merely laughed it off. "Wait till I tell everyone about this," he said.

I knew I'd crossed the line. What I had done was strictly taboo on the reserve. No matter what your husband did, you didn't slap him across the face. You could hit him over the head with a stick or a frying pan, but the face was off-limits. Of course, it wasn't the same for men. Female faces could be shoved into dirty toilets or rammed against the wall. Chuck often told me horror stories of how some of the Native men treated their wives or daughters: women with teeth knocked out, tied up or beaten with sticks; sisters forced to have sex with their brothers while their fathers watched.

Chuck talked about these things matter-of-factly as if relating stories of normal family dynamics. What he told me was repulsive. "It's none of our business," he explained without the slightest hint of emotion.

As the days went by, the weariness I felt because of my lack of sleep, my rigorous schedule at university, and my determination to shield Sasha from the abuse I was experiencing was compounded by Chuck's constant questioning and intimidation. He was always demanding that I give up my white ways and my white friends. He wanted me confused and isolated.

Chuck was an intelligent and cunning tormentor. I suspected his army training had served him well. He'd learned to shut off his emotions at will and ignore pain—his own and that of others. Sometimes his words brought terror to my heart.

"That crawl space under our apartment would be a good place to hide a body," he'd joke.

One night, when Chuck showed up unrepentant after spending two days with his ex-wife, I grabbed shirts, coats, and boots— whatever I could carry—and threw them outside our reserve apart- ment onto the slushy ground.

"I've had enough!" I screamed. "You want to spend your time somewhere else, take your clothes with you."

Amazingly Sasha didn't wake up that night. Perhaps she'd

grown accustomed to the high level of night noises that were normal for our area of the reserve. Or maybe my prayers for her protection had beckoned an angel to place palms gently over her ears. Whatever it was, Sasha slept through the entire affair, even though the neighbours across the street woke up to witness my breakdown.

I made at least three trips back and forth on my crazed mission to destroy anything that belonged to Chuck, knowing full well by my insane behaviour that I was the one who was suffering. I had to keep moving or I'd rush into the kitchen and grab a knife, lunge for Chuck, and stick the blade right through his filthy heart.

While I raged, tossing clothes outside and screaming, Chuck said, "I've been through this before. You're just making me look good." He went to the phone and dialled a number. "Terry," he said into the receiver, "have a look out the window." Terry was our neighbour. Chuck just laughed the whole incident off, knowing I'd be the one to clean everything up later, anyway. And I did.

After that night, whenever he returned from spending time with another woman, I threw his clothes outside as he drilled me about what I'd been doing. Once, when he barred me outside in the winter without a coat, I tore up everything I could find inside his car: AA meeting lists, old newspapers, envelopes, even discarded paper coffee cups. Anticipating such behaviour, Chuck never left important papers, like his registration or insurance, in the car. Anything of value was locked in the trunk.

As I vented my fury, the neighbours, relatives of Chuck's, watched briefly but with little interest, familiar with this sort of behaviour. Everyone knew I was crazy. After my first outburst, Chuck had visited around the reserve to pass the word to those who might have missed the show: his wife had finally shown her true colours. One of Chuck's sisters, who often fought and drank as hard as any man, took delight in informing me of this.

My children seldom came around after I moved to the rez. Only

Heather showed up, often to see Sasha but also because she was dating my husband's nephew, who lived up the hill from us, not far from the Headstart building. I tried to spare Sasha, reserving my fits of temper for times when she'd fallen safely asleep. She never witnessed much of the violence, yet she saw me weeping with frustration practically every day. She'd offer me hugs and teddy bears. Her presence would compel me to concentrate on doing something to make her days happy—play puppets or cuddle on the couch to watch one of her favourite movies like *The Ewok Adventure*.

It was a monumental effort to complete course work at STU, but I held on desperately to my studies. STU was my safe haven; I wouldn't allow myself to let that go.

FIST

By the beginning of 1994, I had already left Chuck at least four times. What drew me back was my dedication to my marriage vows and my tenacious love for my husband. Each time I left, Chuck assured me he'd change. I'd reason with myself that I had to try, for Sasha's sake and my own sake. It was the responsible path to take. I was still Chuck's wife and I'd been serious when I said "I do." I didn't want another failed marriage.

With Chuck's history of cheating, I could never be sure when he was actually being faithful. Even on the rare occasions when he was away fishing or hunting, I was sure he was with another woman. There was no trust left as jealousy ate away at me.

I'd slapped Chuck across the face on three occasions, even though I hated myself for doing it. The last time I hit him I knew I had to leave forever. I despised violence and I was losing control. On this particular day I had taken extra care to prepare an appetizing meal. I was trying to smooth things between us, tempt Chuck into settling more devoutly into married life. I knew I was a good cook, so I figured I'd appeal to his taste buds. Maybe then he'd have something nice to say to me.

I went to the stove to check on the steak, smothered in mushrooms and fried onions, that had just finished cooking. There were potatoes, buttered fiddleheads, and Indian fry bread fresh out of the pan. To entice Chuck further, I was wearing one of his favourite outfits: black jeans and a black top with a crocheted red design on the three-quarter sleeves. And I had my hair tied back in a ponytail.

Sasha wasn't quite four years old, but I let her set the table. She took great pride in helping out, positioning the knives and forks in their exact positions, taking things from the fridge and placing them down just so. She was a quick learner, and I enjoyed teaching her.

Deep down I felt uneasy, knowing something wasn't right with what I was attempting. This was all quite pleasant on the outside, but on the inside there was desperation.

When Chuck arrived home, he was scowling nastily. "Don't open your mouth," he said. "Just listen to what I have to say."

I stood still, looking at him, the steak sizzling in the pan. His beady eyes were fixed on me. He hadn't even said hello to Sasha. She was watching him, waiting.

"I saw you talking to that honky at the mall," he accused in a slow, controlled voice. "Screwing around behind my back again, eh?" He jabbed his index finger in front of my face and held it there, glaring at me.

Sasha regarded us in confusion. I didn't want to alarm her, so I forced myself to speak softly. "I haven't been outside the house."

"Are you calling me a liar?" he shouted.

Before I could answer he peered at the stove. "What's that crap?" He strode over to the frying pan and poked the steak with a paring knife. "Tough as usual. You wouldn't know how to cook meat if your life depended on it." He snatched up the pot with the potatoes and was about to fling it. I reached out to grab the handle, and he jerked his hand away. A few potatoes thudded to the floor, and we both looked at them. Then I checked Sasha. She was scared.

"Clean up that mess!" Chuck demanded. I bent to pick up the potatoes. "I'm not eating this. Just give me some bread and then I'm out of here." He went over to the table and sat. I straightened with the hot potatoes in my hands as Chuck held out his arms to Sasha, who glanced over at me. I managed a small smile, and Sasha hesitantly made her way to Chuck. He picked her up and sat her on his lap. When he smiled, the frightened expression left her face completely.

"Your grandmother's crazy, did you know that?" He grinned at Sasha, then smirked tauntingly at me. "Good thing you got some Indian blood in you, kid."

"Shut up!" I screamed so loud and unexpectedly that Sasha jumped off Chuck's knee and stood stiffly beside the table. Seeing her eyes fill with fear further incited my rage. I couldn't contain the words. Not this time.

"Why don't you grow up?" I yelled, tossing the potatoes into the pot and mashing them. "My parents raised me with some values."

"White values. Nothing to be proud of."

"At least I've got some." I slapped the steak onto his plate, added potatoes, fry bread, and fiddleheads, then slammed the plate on the table. He looked at me and sneered, his dark brown eyes almost black.

"Too bad your mother didn't teach you how to cook."

Twenty-five years of hurt were doubled up in my fist as I thrust it back and swung it forward, connecting with his nose. I watched with dreadful awe as the responding flood of red dripped onto the fry bread on his plate. As soon as I realized it was blood, my heart melted with unspeakable regret. Sasha was standing with her mouth hanging open, as shocked as Chuck was. His eyes were wider than I'd ever seen them before. He vaulted to his feet and headed for the bathroom, blood running down his shirt and dripping onto the floor behind him. I was ashamed and immensely sorry, not for Chuck but for Sasha. My granddaughter was caught up in the violence now. The circle had reached her.

GIGNOO HOUSE

Two days later I was seated at a large mahogany table in Gignoo House, a Native shelter for battered women in Fredericton, wondering if Chuck missed me. At the time I was the only resident in the shelter, a large comfortable house with six bedrooms that offered a safe place in the basement away from the entrances. It bore no resemblance to any institution, unlike the transition house I'd stayed before my surgery, with its monitors and locked bedrooms. Even the curfews weren't rigid at Gignoo. They understood that most abused women didn't sleep on schedule.

I had taken Sasha to spend a few days with Debbie and Dwight Palmer in Geary, the night after I punched Chuck in the face. They were the couple who had helped my daughter, Jennifer, when Billy was born. They had also baby-sat for me before, and Sasha was comfortable with them. I wanted a secure place for her while I figured out how to find a new location for us to live.

Chuck had walked out without a word after I hit him. I had stayed in our apartment that night and slept with Sasha in her bed. I had bolted the door from the inside, even though I'd known Chuck wouldn't return. He'd called Ruth in front of me and told her he was on his way to Kingsclear to escape the "crazy white woman" he'd married. Now I was so troubled and flooded with anxiety that I could barely perform routine tasks. I knew I was on the brink of a complete mental breakdown. For the past couple of days I'd wept openly, turning ceaseless unanswerable questions over in my head. Why did I love this man? Why was I attracted to this darkness in men? What was the matter with me that I would allow these things to happen to me and my children?

Mary Jane, a Native counsellor at Gignoo, never seemed to notice I was white. Before wrapping me in her muscled chestnut arms and allowing me to cry on her shoulder, she didn't bother checking for a status card. She was a warm, self-assured woman about five years younger than I was. Tall and solid, she lived on the Mi'gmaq Big Cove Reserve, about 168 miles from Fredericton. Big Cove was the largest reserve in New Brunswick. It had received a great deal of publicity about the escalating suicides among its youth, but an increasing number of people in the community were dedicated to spreading the practice of traditional Native spirituality in order to facilitate healing. I knew this because my friend Irene had moved there and married an elder named Joe John Sanipass. Mary Jane was involved in traditional Native religion herself, often attending sweat-lodge ceremonies. She had immense faith in the Creator and the spirit helpers he provided and let me know she'd had her own battle with alcohol and a bad marriage. It was the spiritual beliefs of her people, introduced to her by elders such as Joe John, that directed her toward a more rewarding life.

Mary Jane enjoyed a good laugh and tried to find humour in even the most difficult situations. Her generous wit taught me to buffer the pain with humour and use it as a survival skill. Her nickname was Mousie, but I never learned why. Mary Jane was far from a mouse in my eyes. She reminded me more of an elk—regal and dignified, extremely proud of her heritage.

I bonded more with her when I learned she had been married to a white man. The marriage didn't last but eventually she found her soulmate, a beautiful traditional teacher from the Western Blood Tribe. Having experienced a mixed marriage, she knew firsthand about the split between the two worlds and how that affected children born from such unions. She had two teenage boys from the white marriage, and that augmented my affinity with her.

Nighttime at the shelter was when I felt like talking, when the shadows brought back the sneaking fear and loosened my tongue. It was then that I would sit in the kitchen and talk to Mary Jane, sipping cups of hot tea, tears plopping into my cup.

This was my second move into a shelter for battered women, and I felt great embarrassment. I had believed I was strong enough to handle the home situation, but now had to admit my life was completely out of my control. That—coupled with the fact that I was still struggling with my identity and had lost it by giving up everything—deepened my depression.

I was seven years clean and sober and regularly attending Alcoholics Anonymous meetings. I was a respected member of a recovering community who often counselled others about their addictions and life problems. I had all the answers for everyone. I even sponsored other alcoholics and believed strongly in God and the power of prayer. Yet I couldn't break my addiction to bad boys who I now knew grew up to be sick, abusive men.

I felt like a phony. My faith was shaken. I became short-tempered and forgetful, couldn't concentrate, couldn't write, and I was gaining weight—compulsively eating to fill the growing void inside me. I fantasized about drinking again, to find buoyant comfort in the bottle. I thought about starting to smoke—I'd given that up three years earlier—but didn't think I could afford it. I fidgeted for a habit. I needed a crutch.

It was fortunate for me that I had come to a Native shelter, even though I'd had qualms at first. In the non-Native shelter the realities of reserve life were alien to most of the workers. They could never comprehend that stepping in to stop a fight between a man and his wife might turn a whole community against you. I didn't fathom it, either, but knew it was a reality.

Because my earlier abuses had been mostly physical—split, swollen lips, bruises, and scrapes—I'd considered verbal insults and intimidation a holiday in comparison. Back then, you didn't even call that "abuse"; it was just "marriage." That was why I'd downplayed Chuck's attacks.

"The Creator never gave anyone the right to abuse," Mary Jane would say. "That's their own decision. They're in pain, so they take it out on you. To realize and dissolve the pain, that's the great deed. The only way to healing."

Mary Jane told me about a man in Shubenacadie, Nova Scotia. His name was David Gehue, a big gruff blind fellow who worked with wounded people and helped them to heal and find direction. She said he might be able to help me.

UNLIKELY HEALER

I took a quick trip to see David Gehue in Nova Scotia with Sally and Bella, two white women I'd met in AA. Sally and Bella were fascinated with the New Age movement and Native spirituality. My travelling companions were politely cordial to me, making sure to stop if I needed to use the bathroom or buy a soda, but it was obvious they weren't fond of me. There was no easy casual conversation between us. They talked mostly to each other, and I pretended I was alone in the car as I gazed out the window at the endless display of trees from my view in the back seat. I was on a personal quest and wanted to be healed. At one point I thought I heard Sally or Bella speak to me, so I looked in their direction.

"Maybe she's uncomfortable with lesbians," Sally joked to Bella.

I must have missed something.

"What?" I asked.

"All human beings are really bisexual," Sally said.

"Well, I'm not one of them," I countered. "I like men too much."

"Maybe you're a lesbian in denial."

Sexual orientation was the last thing on my mind, coming from a shelter for abused women. But I was sure it was a man I was fighting to forget, not a woman.

"You probably wouldn't be in the situation you're in if you'd been living with another woman."

I was about to ask if lesbians really were all doelike creatures who never hurt one another but, concerned I might get thrown out of the car, I kept my mouth shut.

Eventually we pulled up in front of David Gehue's weather-beaten house on the Millbrook Reserve in Shubenacadie, the same reserve where I'd attended my first sweat a couple of years earlier. As we climbed out of the car and glanced around to see if anyone was about, a loud roar came from the house. "Who put that fucking chair in front of the door? Don't they know there's a blind man in this house?"

A large man with uncombed hair and wild eyes appeared on the doorstep, leaning on a wooden walking stick. I was ready to turn tail and duck back into the car, but the elder's voice softened when he sensed the presence of guests. Sally and Bella were standing beside me, and I could tell by their surprised expressions that they were a bit uneasy, too.

"C'mon in," David said. "Where have you been? I was expecting you hours ago." The anger had vanished from his voice. We followed him into a small, cluttered kitchen with a cast-iron wood stove. A Native woman was busy at a counter, kneading bread dough. David said something to her in Mi'gmaq and walked away from us without a word.

The house was crowded. An overweight Native woman sat at a small table beside the door. She had long black hair pulled tightly into one thick braid and paid us no mind. A baby with fat brown cheeks played with a plastic animal on the floor beside the woman. The animal might have been an elephant once, but it now bore the marks of the teething toddler and an ear was missing. The baby started crying and the woman made no motion to pick it up. Directly in front of us, there was a living room off the kitchen. I could see at least three men sitting on a couch, chatting and drinking from mugs. A little girl, about five or six with long dark brown hair, stood by the doorway, finger in mouth, staring at me.

The woman who was making the bread turned around. "I'm David's wife. Pull up a chair," she said with the Mi'gmaq accent I'd come to recognize. "Don't be shy. David's gone talking to someone else. He'll be a while. Have some tea."

We waited in the kitchen, sipping bitter black tea. David had run out of milk. I wasn't surprised. People I hadn't even seen when I first entered the house made regular trips to the kitchen to refill their cups. I was happy to notice there were two other white women in the house, besides me, Sally, and Bella. Everyone was seeking advice or medicines. The front door kept opening and closing. The house was constantly full, and so was the teapot.

After a few minutes, Bella and Sally decided to go for a drive to pick up milk. I waited at the house because David had told Mousie on the phone that he'd see me as soon as I arrived. After my third cup of tea, David's wife left the kitchen to put in a load of laundry, then returned. "He'll see you now."

When I entered the room where David was, I glanced quickly around the modest blue-walled den. A statue of the Virgin Mary was perched on a corner shelf. David was sitting in a rocking chair near the far wall. He gestured for me to sit on the floor in front of him, and I nervously did as instructed.

"Your name's Eva?" he asked, staring straight at me.

"Yes," I replied, even though I'd told him my name was Eve. The only people who still called me Eva were my mom and dad.

"There's nothing to fear. You have protectors all around you, Eva. I see them, so relax."

I took a deep breath; my stomach was in knots.

"That's good. Now tell me about Eva, the little girl who cried all the time."

Tingles rushed through me. He emphasized my name each time he spoke, a sense of familiarity that eased the tautness from my body. Within minutes I was blurting out confessions from my childhood and my tempestuous marriages. I cried quietly, wiping tears away with tissues I fished out of my sweater pocket. It seemed as if my unburdening lasted hours. The whole time David never stirred.

When I stopped talking, he said, "Take it easy for a minute." He used his walking stick to pull himself from the rocker, then easily navigated toward the door. He didn't need to use the stick to find his way. I could hear him in the hallway outside talking in Mi'gmaq.

The same little girl I'd noticed when I first arrived entered and stood before me, intently studying my face. She wore a pink cotton dress at least a size too big with white flowers along the front. She wasn't wearing shoes.

"I am bringing little Eva to you," David said as he returned to the rocker.

The child bent toward me, seeming to float into my arms, fitting perfectly as I held her. She nuzzled her shiny head against my breast but never said a word.

David told me to close my eyes. "This is little Eva," he said. "This is you."

My lips began to tremble and, again, warm tears spilled down my cheeks.

"Hold her gently and tell her she's all right," David prodded, his voice low, soothing, and hypnotic. "Go ahead. Tell her you'll protect her."

"I will protect you," I whispered.

"Tell her how beautiful she is."

"You're so beautiful." I held her tighter, gently rocking her, pacifying her.

"Tell her you'll never, never leave her."

"I won't leave you. I won't." The tears flowed freely, and soon I was sobbing. I was transported to another time. A little girl hiding in

305

an apple tree, avoiding the fights at home. I held the child closer to me and started to sing.

"Lullaby and good night,
There'll be angels around thee,
There'll be angels overhead
In my baby's little bed."

I repeated the caressing verse as I continued rocking back and forth. The little girl was so warm in my arms, such a flawless fit. I was holding a child who was not only me but every child who had come from me, every hurt child who ever sought solace.

"Lullaby and good night,
There'll be angels around thee,
There'll be angels overhead
In my baby's little bed."

When I opened my eyes, David was sitting in a chair directly in front of me. I hadn't heard him move nearer. The little girl was gone. I had no idea when David's daughter left. I had never felt her go. David remained silent and I was tranquil though exhausted.

"Now," he said, "tomorrow, after you sleep, you go to the ocean." He gestured toward the door, but his unseeing eyes looked straight at me. "Throw away your pain and rage." There were a few more moments of silence during which he seemed to peer through me into another dimension. I was still picturing the child in the apple tree. Was that the hint of a smile on her lips?

He nodded. "You're gonna be okay, *dus.*"

I stood and David reached out. Stepping toward him, I let him hug my belly. We both laughed with relief and triumph. When I moved back, I remembered the gift I'd brought along. I reached into my pocket and pulled out a pouch of tobacco that Mary Jane had suggested I bring as a thank-you offering. I handed it to him, and he raised it to his nose and sniffed.

"Thank you," I said.

He nodded again and asked me to tell his wife to bring him tea.

That night we all slept at the elder's house. Bella, Sally, and I had sleeping bags, so we camped out on the floor in one of the bedrooms. Later that evening, when I was settling in, David called out that there was a phone call for me. It was Mousie from New Brunswick with some bad news. Chuck's nephew, Matthew had been in a car accident and was in a coma in the Moncton hospital. When I hung up, I asked Sally and Bella if we could stop and check on Matthew on our way home. Moncton was halfway between where we were and Fredericton. Sally told me that wouldn't be a problem, so I put the accident out of my mind. To complete my spiritual journey, I needed to take care of myself.

The next day Sally, Bella, and I headed to Joggins. It was a warm, sunny day, and I felt optimistic. This trip to Joggins was an important pilgrimage for me. Sally and Bella were friendlier toward me and didn't make further references to sexual orientation. Bella was a social worker and familiar with anger therapy. When I outlined what David had instructed me to do, she offered her assistance. It was the first time she showed any real compassion toward me. Sally remained polite but distant.

We were soon in Joggins, the same village my mother had visited as a child and the same place my second husband, Bob, and I had brought my children to for a holiday. *How ironic,* I thought. When we arrived at the ocean with its golden sandy beach, I was awed by its majesty. It was a windy day and the tide was rising. The waves roared as they pounded the sides of the fossil cliffs. *So powerful. So much bigger than we are. So constant.*

Bella coached me as I picked up rocks and tossed them half-heartedly into the ocean. I didn't think I was getting the point of the exercise. Sally had left for a walk down the beach to find some special treasures to bring home with her.

"Put a bad memory or resentment into each stone," Bella said, "and scream out your pain as you throw them into the ocean."

My eyes searched the beach. "I don't know if I can find rocks *big* enough."

"Size doesn't matter," Bella assured me. "It's your mental concentration that'll do the trick. Try to start with your earliest memories. Just let them come."

Along with the anger, I needed to rid myself of any residual pain or fear I felt when I remembered people who had hurt me. I picked up a rock and thought of my grandfather, then tossed the stone with as much conviction as I could summon. It plunked into the water fifty feet from shore.

I thought of the elementary school teacher who had told me I'd never amount to anything, then reached for another rock. Soon I was grabbing two or three at a time and hurling them, moving ever nearer to the ocean. The waves soaked my feet, and I wanted to climb right in, fully submerge myself. I picked up a bigger stone and thought of baby Aleshia's death. Screaming, I threw it as far as I could. Another rock, another memory. I cried out my frustration, tears mingling with the waves that grew stronger around my legs. I scrambled for a rock, one rock that would represent Chuck. Snatching it up, I stared at its contours. It was hard and impenetrable, and an overwhelming sadness washed over me. I tossed the stone away, but my heart wasn't fully in it. I was utterly spent.

I searched for Bella and Sally. They had gone back to the car, which was parked at the top of the hill overlooking the ocean. I scanned up and down the beach. Thankfully no one else was there, or I might have felt foolish. Any onlookers probably wouldn't have stuck around long, anyway. I was certain I looked like a madwoman. Happily the opposite was true: I was just beginning to gain control of myself.

For those fleeting moments on the beach I had thought Bella might be genuinely concerned about my well-being. I was feeling a little more at one with her and Sally as we headed out for Moncton. Back on the highway, Bella called over the seat, "You can mail me the money for my assistance if you're short on cash right now."

"What?"

"The money for consulting."

I was struck speechless.

"How much?" I finally asked, resentment toward her growing.

"I usually charge $80 an hour."

"Sure," I said quietly, then turned to watch the trees flash by, wishing I was back on the beach with one more stone in my hand.

When we arrived in Moncton, we drove directly to the hospital. Chuck's brother, Wayne, was smoking a cigarette outside as we pulled up. When I climbed out of the car, I hurried over to him and asked what had happened.

"It's Matthew," Wayne said. "He was in a car accident. He's in a coma and his friend's dead."

I'd expected maybe a few broken bones, but not this. Matthew was an active teenage boy who played hockey with conviction. He even baby-sat Sasha for me occasionally. He wasn't into drugs or booze like some of the others his age on the reserve.

"How's Sarah taking it?" I asked. Sarah was my sister-in-law. I knew her children were the most important part of her life.

"Not good," Wayne told me, flicking away his cigarette butt.

"Is Chuck here?"

"He's with Gary getting a coffee." Gary was Sarah's husband.

"Maybe you should stay and talk to him," Wayne suggested. "He's pretty shook up. This isn't any time to worry about your differences."

As I debated my options, Chuck and Gary walked up with cigarette packs in hand. They looked worn out.

"I'm glad you came," Chuck said, taking out a cigarette and placing it between his lips. "You want to see Matthew?"

I indicated the car in which Bella and Sally patiently remained. "I've got people waiting for me. I need to get back to Fredericton."

"I'll take you home later," Chuck responded with sincerity. "No tricks. I promise." Despite all the trouble between us, I couldn't abandon him or his family during this crisis.

"All right." I went back to the car and told Bella and Sally I was staying. They were both disappointed. As Sally handed me my bags, she shook her head and said, "I hope you know what you're doing." Before I could reply, they drove off.

The sterility of the hospital corridors nauseated me. I had been in too many hospitals over the years. I found Matthew's room and entered. He was hooked up to various pieces of medical equipment. Sarah was standing over him.

"Hi," I said, giving her a hug. "He'll come out of this," I assured her with more certainty than I felt.

Chuck stood there, watching his nephew, tears in his eyes. Again I saw the man I once admired.

That night I went back to Gignoo in Fredericton with new hope. Chuck dropped me off at a coffee shop with my bags and I phoned a taxi. I'd have been kicked out of Gignoo if I'd let him drive me there.

I was really missing Sasha, so I called her as soon as I put my bags in my room.

"Where you been, Mommie?" the sweet little voice on the other end of the line said. I suddenly felt lonelier than ever.

"I've been sick, baby, but I'm almost better," I told her. "I'm coming to see you tomorrow." My sense of compassion for Chuck and my longing to provide Sasha with a proper family led me back to the reserve for a few more weeks.

Early one morning, while we were still asleep, the phone rang beside the bed. I picked it up to hear Wayne's voice. "He's gone," he said.

"Oh, my God," I gasped. "How are Sarah and Gary?"

"Not very good."

I glanced at Chuck, who had awoken beside me. He was watching me, suspecting the worse. I said goodbye to Wayne and hung up.

"It's Matthew," I told Chuck.

Chuck broke down and sobbed. I put my arms around him and started crying, too.

A few minutes later I gazed up to see Sasha standing in the doorway.

"What's the matter?" she asked. "You have a bad dream?"

"No, baby," I said, wiping my eyes secretively. "Why are you up?"

"I had a bad dream." She drifted over and I lifted her onto the bed, cuddling her.

"Tell me about your dream."

"I saw Matthew. He was smiling, but everyone around him was screaming."

At the wake Sasha approached the casket and wiped Sarah's tears away with her fingers. "Don't cry," she said. Then she came to me and asked, "How come everyone's crying?"

"'Cause everybody's sad about Matthew, sweetie."

"But Matthew's not sad."

"I believe you're right."

I stuck by Chuck during the funeral and for the required period of mourning. Then a month after Matthew's death, while I was doing the dishes, Chuck called on the telephone. He sounded angry.

"What's the matter?" I asked.

"Someone told me something very interesting about you, and

I'm going to get to the bottom of it." The tone of his voice sent that familiar shock of fright through my nerves. I knew I shouldn't wait around for him. I called Gignoo House, but the person who answered told me it was full. I hung up and called Transition House, and they instructed me to come right away. I gathered my stuff, took Sasha with me, and drove off, fearing Chuck was close behind.

SASHA'S CRASH

Even after I moved off the Oromocto Reserve, I kept in touch with a couple of the families living there. I frequently called Chuck's sister, Sarah, and often visited Naomi's house so she and Sasha could play together.

Naomi lived with her mother, Anna, in a small cabin-style house on the Oromocto Reserve. All the while we had lived on the reserve, Naomi and Sasha had been inseparable. Before we left for good I'd promised Naomi she could visit Sasha, and I kept my promise.

On Thanksgiving weekend, October 1994, I was looking forward to the celebrations with my children. Dinner was at Sonya's home the following day, which meant I didn't have to cook the turkey. A meal that didn't involve me sweating in the kitchen was a welcome thought.

I dropped Sasha off to play with Naomi that Saturday around lunchtime and headed for the mall to shop. Anna was home with her fiancé, Rick, a young Mi'gmaq writer. He was from Big Cove where New Brunswick's largest Native population resided. Big Cove was approximately 180 miles north of the Oromocto Reserve. Naomi was so excited to see Sasha that she had her arms out for a hug before I could open the car door.

When I returned at suppertime to pick up Sasha, the girls pleaded with me to let Sasha spend the night. Anna, Rick, Naomi, and Anna's cousin, Sylvia, were leaving for Big Cove to spend Thanksgiving with

Rick's family. I felt uneasy and refused.

"Please, please can she go?" Naomi begged, her big brown eyes pleading.

"I'll be good," Sasha chimed in.

The two of them were jumping up and down and hugging me. It was difficult to harden my heart against Sasha's wishes. Anna assured me the girls wouldn't leave her sight. So I gave in.

I stayed to see them all off. Anna poured me a cup of tea, which I slowly drank while she finished preparing for the trip. I chatted with Sylvia, who was pregnant with her second baby, and teased her about not wasting any time. She smiled and told me she was glad because the responsibility was helping her get her life back on track after problems with alcohol and bad relationships.

Standing and moving outside, I watched as everyone piled into the minivan. Sasha and Naomi, best buddies, sat close together in the back seat. They smiled widely at me and everyone waved as I said, "Be careful," then "I love you," to my granddaughter. Rick, who wasn't much of a talker, gave me a warm, reassuring smile as he pulled out of the driveway.

Finding myself unexpectedly alone and still apprehensive, I decided to see Sonya and her family, although I'd planned to wait until tomorrow to visit.

Still, Saturday nights at Sonya's house were special times for me because, often, all my grandchildren were gathered there. Sonya baby-sat for Jennifer while she worked at a nightclub as a bartender on weekends. Usually she and I would gang up on her husband, Harry, for a game of Scrabble while Sasha played with cousins Brittany, Mitchell, and Billy. Once in a while Miles would join us. Both Sonya and Harry had a great sense of humour that kept me in stitches for hours. When Miles was present, it was like watching a group of stand-up comics.

"C'mon, Big Mama," Harry would start, "set up the game so I can show you women how a real man plays."

"Why thank you, Harry," Miles would say, imitating Elvis. "Thank you very much."

"I wasn't talking about you, you idiot," Harry kidded back.

"He must have invited someone," Sonya joined in. "A real man flown in to Geary just for the game. There you go, Mom. We'll marry you off to a real man yet. He just has to prove himself at Scrabble first."

"Can I cheat?" Miles asked.

"Ask your ex-wives," I said, keeping up the playful banter.

These sorts of evenings spent with Harry and Sonya were entertaining, as long as everyone limited their drinking. If Harry or Sonya had been arguing earlier in the day and either of them had drunk too much alcohol, things could turn nasty.

When I arrived, I was relieved to detect no signs of drinking. As usual Brittany, then six, and Mitchell, three, gave me enthusiastic hugs that dispelled some of the trepidation I'd felt about Sasha's departure. My grandson, Billy, also six at the time, was spending the night and gave his fair share of hugs.

Brittany was a petite blond with big brown eyes, just like her mother. She loved horses, stuffed trolls, and dolls. Mitchell was short and stocky with a face like one of those ceramic smileys often used to make lamps. He was a wind-up toy in constant motion, and asked question after question without taking a breath to allow an answer. Billy was dark and handsome, with a charming smile that never failed to tug at my heart. He was my favourite little hockey player. I adored them all.

"Where's Sasha?" Brittany asked. No doubt she was eager for company to set up her Barbie doll collection.

"She went away with Naomi."

"Is she coming back?" Mitchell piped in. His wide-eyed look of alarm suggested he'd taken my statement literally.

"No, she's just gone for the night," I assured him but again felt a twinge of uneasiness.

"Go play, you guys," Sonya interrupted. "C'mon, Mom, let's get some supper on."

"Yeah, put yourself to work, you lazy thing," Harry said.

"Someone has to feed you," I shot back. "How else could you have strength to lift that TV remote."

"Good one, Mom." Sonya smiled and gave me an elbow nudge.

After a light dinner of fries and fish sticks, Sonya and I piled the dishes into the dishwasher and sat in the kitchen over coffee to discuss plans for Christmas. The kids and their partners always picked names for a gift exchange and usually we gathered on Christmas Eve at Sonya's house. While we were debating who should cook the turkey that year, Sonya's friend Shelley stopped by and joined us.

Harry was in the bedroom watching football with a cold beer, while Sonya and I listened to Stevie Nicks as the mellow strains of "Leather and Lace" drifted in from the stereo in the living room. Billy and Mitchell had thundered down to the basement to play war with toy soldiers and tanks. Brittany was in her bedroom singing Barney songs to the cat. It was a wonder anyone even heard the phone when it rang.

"Get the phone!" Harry yelled from the bedroom. I jumped up to turn down the volume on the stereo as Sonya sprinted to the phone on the kitchen counter.

"Mom, it's for you," Sonya said, holding the receiver out to me with one hand cupped over it.

"It's Chuck," she whispered. "He says it's important."

I accepted the receiver with misgivings. He'd feigned important issues before so he could talk to me. "Hello," I said, my tone firm and even.

"There's been an accident, Eve." His voice was barely audible. "An accident with Sasha."

"What in hell are you talking about?" My scream brought my son-in-law hurrying into the kitchen.

"The van, it got into an accident," Chuck said. "The police just came to the reserve."

"Oh, my God, no!" I gasped, starting to sob crazily.

Sonya grabbed the receiver, my sobs becoming louder. "Make her stop," she said to Harry, turning away.

"What's going on, Chuck?"

Harry had his arm around me now. Trying to calm myself, I focused on Sonya's back as she stood there, saying nothing, obviously listening to what Chuck had to say. It seemed to take forever before she uttered another word.

"Where?" Sonya pressed. "What police?" She was so composed. I couldn't stop shaking.

Shelley took my hand and squeezed it in reassurance.

"You want some water?" she asked quietly.

I shook my head and tried to pray.

"You'd better come out here," Sonya said as she hung up. When she turned to face us, she was as white as a ghost. "Sasha's been in an accident. I don't know how bad." She paused. "The police were just talking to Chuck on the reserve. The accident was near Newcastle. Someone's dead."

I trembled harder and began to scream uncontrollably.

Sonya gripped my face, her eyes narrowing in near anger in an attempt to calm me. "Stop it, Mom. You have to stop it." She was losing her composure, close to tears herself.

A few minutes later there was a knock on the door.

"Come in!" everyone yelled at once. It was Chuck, and I could tell he'd been crying. I ran to him and let him hold me. One truth about Chuck was that he loved that little girl, too.

"Who told you all this?" Sonya asked.

"The Fredericton RCMP. They came to my mother's house with the reserve cop. They didn't know how to find your mother."

Sonya went to the phone again and dialled the Fredericton RCMP. After Sonya explained why she was calling, the dispatcher connected her to an officer. We waited while my daughter sat with the receiver against her ear.

"I need a cigarette," she whispered as she listened. After that she was on the phone for about five minutes without saying a word until: "I have to go." Then she disconnected and dialled again.

"What's going on?" Harry and I asked in unison.

Sonya held her hand up to silence us and spoke into the receiver. "My mother just got a call about a car accident her granddaughter was in. Can I speak to an officer?"

Sonya had to hang up again and wait while the dispatcher contacted an officer to respond. "I had to call Newcastle," she said. "Fredericton's not sure what's going on yet."

We waited in silence. The boys were still playing downstairs, and Brittany continued singing in the next room, oblivious to the developing chaos. Her sweet voice drifted into the kitchen: "I love you, you love me. We're a happy family..." The words were interrupted by the ringing of the telephone.

Piece by piece the story unfolded. The minivan had left the road and rolled several times on a turn near the Renous prison, just outside Newcastle. Some of the occupants had been taken to hospital. Two were dead. No one knew which two. We were advised to sit by the phone and wait until the police contacted us.

That was when I lost it completely. I screamed so loudly my grandchildren ran to see if I'd been hurt. Harry shook me to bring me back to myself. Chuck stood by the door, muted by his grief.

"Stop it!" Harry said. "You've got to pull yourself together, Eve."

I stared at him, saw his wet eyes. "I shouldn't have let her go. I knew better. Please, God, don't let her die." *Please, God, don't let her die...*

Shelley led Billy, Brittany, and Mitchell out of the room, assuring them that Nannie Eve was all right. "Someone should call Jennifer," she said over her shoulder as she whisked the children, into the bedroom to further address their concerned questions.

"What about Heather?" Chuck asked. "Shouldn't someone call her?"

"She's somewhere in Red Bank," I said. "I don't know where." Red Bank was the Mi'gmaq community adjacent to Newcastle.

"There's no sense trying to find her right now," Sonya cut in. "It could make things worse. She's probably out of it, anyway."

We all knew Heather had been on a cocaine binge for months.

Sonya tried four times to obtain more information from the RCMP, but there was no news. When Jennifer arrived a few minutes later, I said, "That's it. I'm going. I'm not staying here. Sasha needs me."

"I'll drive," Chuck said.

Sonya, Jennifer, and Shelley joined Chuck and me. Harry agreed to take care of the children and wait by the phone.

Everyone in the car was unusually quiet. It was dark outside and we had to be cautious, as moose often crossed Highway 8. The sound of lighters flicked as everyone in the car except me gradually depleted their stock of tobacco. *I'm on my way, Sasha.* I refused to believe she was among the dead.

I could hardly tell where we were most of the time, though I recognized the Woodsmen's Museum in Boisetown when we passed it. We were still a long way from Newcastle, at least another sixty miles. It was ages before I saw the road sign that signalled we were close to Newcastle—only eight miles now.

As soon as we pulled up in front of the hospital, I was out of the car. A nurse met us in the Emergency hallway.

"The accident," I blurted. "My little girl..." I tried to talk, but the words were tangled.

Again Sonya took charge of the situation. "Where are the children from the accident in Renous?"

"Are they here?" I asked. "Are they alive?"

"Yes, they're alive, dear," the nurse assured me. We all breathed a collective sigh of relief. "But they're not here," the nurse continued. "They've just been transferred to the Chatham hospital."

"Are they all right?" I'm not sure who asked that question. It might have been me.

"Well, one little girl is still unconscious. It's a bigger hospital and we wanted to be safe..."

We were out the door and back into the car before she finished talking. Chuck was familiar with the area, so he drove. Again we were moving through the night in grief-sticken silence.

When we arrived at the Chatham hospital, the head nurse and a doctor were waiting for us. They indicated that a nurse from the Newcastle hospital had called, then took us directly to the two girls who had been transported on the same stretcher and were now sharing a room.

As I raced up the corridor, nearing the door to the children's room, I heard Naomi crying.

Oh, dear God, Sasha.

I burst into the room and spotted Sasha in a hospital crib. Her eyes were closed and there was a bandage on her forehead. She wasn't moving. I reached for her small hand and wept through my dread and sorrow.

Jennifer focused her attention on Naomi and tried to hush her. Chuck went to talk to a nurse, seeking the complete details of Sasha's condition. The nurse suggested we wait for the doctor.

We took turns talking to Sasha, even though she never responded. The doctor finally arrived and said he felt Sasha would be fine, but he was concerned about the swelling in her abdomen and told us he'd keep an eye on her. Naomi appeared to have only a few cuts and bruises. We learned from the doctor looking after Naomi that her mom, Anna, was in the Dr. Everett Chalmers Hospital in Fredericton in critical condition. Rick and Sylvia had been killed instantly. The two girls were thrown from the car and had been found near the side of the road by an elderly couple who had come upon the accident. The couple had covered the girls with a blanket and stayed by their sides, trying to calm their fears until the ambulance arrived.

The windows were dark in the hospital room. I didn't know what time it was but had no intention of leaving. Chuck, Sonya, and Shelley had gone in search of coffee. Jennifer was sitting with Naomi while I stood over Sasha and held her hand, watching her beautiful face and praying for her to wake up. Minutes or hours later Sasha's eyes slowly opened. She gazed at me but didn't say a word, her vacant expression flashing a chill through me. I wanted to shake her back into the world but knew better than to touch her. I asked Sonya to find the doctor to give us an assessment of the situation.

Holding Sasha's hand, I sang the Barney song I'd heard Brittany sing earlier that night. She just watched me, the blank pools of her eyes intensifying the gravity of the situation, drawing me deeper into despair. Sasha's eyes weren't seeing me. I was terrified, and that desperation transformed into a need to find Heather. She should know about her daughter. Chuck agreed to take me to her. He was familiar with Red Bank, knew the person Heather had been staying with, and was able to locate the house readily.

When we arrived, we faced a run-down shack with the front door hanging open on one hinge.

"What if she's not here?" I asked Chuck as we stood outside. It was almost midnight, and I felt the threat of darkness in a neighbourhood like this. "I don't want to go in there. It's too dangerous."

A faint light shone in the window. I couldn't hear any music or talking. Maybe there were people doing drugs. This was clearly a crack house. I glanced up the street and noticed the shadow of a man walking into a house where a light was on a few doors away. I wasn't thrilled about looking around, but Chuck was determined.

"We'll go in together," he said. "I can't hear anyone moving around. They're probably sleeping. We'll be fine."

Chuck entered, then paused to knock softly on the inner door. There was no reply, so he rapped louder. When no one answered, he tried the knob. It was unlocked, so we stepped into the dimly lit kitchen directly in front of us.

Garbage littered the torn linoleum. I made out a figure sleeping on a mat on the floor. When I approached and leaned over, I saw it was Heather. She had always been such a clean girl. She couldn't abide dirt. She couldn't even tolerate the clutter sometimes around me while I worked on the computer at home. Through a doorless opening a young man was sleeping on a cot in the room off the kitchen. A lamp on a table in front of him emitted weak light. The discarded door was propped against a wall.

Chuck bent and tried to wake Heather, nudging her. "Heather," he whispered. She was in such bad shape that she had a hard time keeping her eyes open. She seemed to watch us, not recognizing who we were. Then her eyes shut, opened, then shut again. *Oh, God,* I thought, *Heather can't even see me. And Sasha doesn't recognize me, either.*

"Sasha's hurt," I yelled, but Heather gave no response. "She's in the hospital!" The guy in the other room wasn't moving, either. I wondered for a moment if he were dead.

"Sasha?" Heather called out, unknowing, as if the child were somewhere in the house. I tried to tell her again, but the information couldn't make it through her drug-sodden brain. I ran back to the car and grabbed a pen and a piece of paper out of my purse.

In large block print I wrote: SASHA IS IN THE HOSPITAL. CALL SONYA'S. Then I put the note beside Heather and kissed her forehead, stroking her hair as she remained oblivious to my presence.

"We've got to go, Eve," Chuck said, checking over his shoulder. "Before someone comes here for drugs."

On our way out I glanced back at my daughter on the floor, her long dark hair accenting the ghostly paleness of her face. In the car outside I studied the house. It was grim and quiet. A black hole in the world.

The next morning Naomi was released from the hospital. A family friend, Penny, picked her up, and we all gave her a hug. Naomi said she wanted to hug Sasha before she went. Penny lifted Naomi in her arms so she could see into Sasha's steel crib.

"Bye, Sasha," Naomi said, waving her fingers at my grand-daughter's unseeing eyes. Penny leaned near the crib so Naomi could kiss her playmate. "See you soon."

After Naomi's departure, Sasha's eyes seemed to recognize me. She reached out so that I might hold her, but she still couldn't talk.

Sasha's belly remained swollen and she wasn't very responsive. The doctor was worried about damage to Sasha's spleen and wanted her to see a surgeon, just to be on the safe side. He said she'd need to be transferred to Fredericton. Sasha's face was so white. Her eyes, now fully fixed on my face, were frightened.

As they loaded Sasha into the ambulance, tears rolled down her little round cheeks. She continued staring at me but didn't say a word.

I placed a teddy bear beside her on the stretcher. "Mommie loves you and she'll be right behind you in the car, baby."

The drive to Fredericton was a crystalline nightmare. Daylight. Brightness. The reality of the situation coupled with fatigue put everyone on edge. The ambulance raced with such speed that Chuck couldn't keep up. When we passed the spot on the highway where signs still lingered of the accident, the ride assumed a graver tone.

At the Fredericton hospital we had to wait while Sasha was examined and sent for X rays. Sonya, Jennifer, and Shelley went in search of Anna's room and Chuck stayed with me, holding my hand and telling me everything would be all right.

"I know God's been hearing your prayers," he said. "You're a good woman."

When Sasha was settled in a room in the children's ward for

observation, Chuck drove the others home to rest.

Sasha remained in the hospital for the next four days. Her body healed without surgery and her spirits showed a marked improvement.

After the first day in the Fredericton hospital, she spoke to me. "Don't go home," she pleaded. It was the first time I'd heard her voice since I'd let her take the trip with Naomi.

I got down on my knees beside her bed and put my head beside hers. "Don't you worry, baby. I'm right here."

"I don't want you to leave," she told me every time I rose to go to the bathroom or to find a coffee. "I want you to stay right here."

I spent the entire time with her. I was so wrapped up in Sasha's recovery that I wasn't sure if Heather ever made it to the hospital. Chuck dropped by again to bring me coffee, but as soon as he determined Sasha would survive, he never showed up again. Some of my new friends dropped me off a change of clothing.

The kids from Sasha's day-care sent cards and a stuffed lamb with a bandage on it. Sasha loved the lamb and slept with it every night at the hospital and when she came home.

While at the hospital I visited Anna and was broken-hearted by the state she was in. Much of her body was covered by bandages or splints, and her face was so bruised and swollen I hardly recognized her. She was in rough shape, physically and emotionally.

"It'll take months of physiotherapy before she'll be able to walk normally," Anna's mother told me. Not only had she lost her fiancé and cousin, she had also lost the unborn baby she'd been carrying. Her pelvic bones had been broken along with one of her legs.

Naomi had made a remarkable recovery, but her life was never the same again. Her mother, in emotional and physical pain, turned to drugs for relief. For months after Anna's release from hospital, Naomi was shifted from relative to relative while Anna recovered.

Expectedly the accident made me overprotective. I couldn't

imagine letting Sasha go to day-care while I was at university, let alone allowing her to visit any of her little friends again without me there by her side.

No one knew for certain how the accident had occurred. Anna believed they had swerved to avoid a deer, but everything had happened so fast. The police brought me a small bag of Sasha's belongings a week after my granddaughter was released from hospital. They'd been able to retrieve a few articles from the wreck. I thanked them for their kindness, studied the change of clothes, one small sneaker, and a *Curly Sue* video, then threw the items in the garbage. Sasha didn't need souvenirs from a death scene.

I considered how Sasha's accident had taken place while travelling from one reserve to another. Nothing good had ever happened for us on the Oromocto Reserve. It was time to sever connections completely.

When Heather returned from Red Bank to Joe and announced she would be marrying him in January 1995, I sank deeper into despair. *How far does this vicious circle reach?*

GRAMMIE BREWER

Over the years I had continued to visit Grammie Brewer, the Gypsy grandmother who had once predicted my future. She was living in Dixon Lodge, a nursing home in Nashwaaksis on the north side of Fredericton. When her husband, Perley, suffered a stroke in the 1980s, it seemed more practical for him to be cared for in a nursing home, so Grammie moved in, too. When he died on November 24, 1991, she stayed, though she was quite capable of taking care of herself.

If you crossed Grammie, she was a tough lady. On one of my visits I couldn't help but laugh as she told me about chasing away another patient when the woman mistakenly came into her room and started going through her dresser drawers. "You can't trust half these people," Grammie Brewer said with a nod of her tiny head, which was covered with white curls.

I usually went to see her once a month. On one of my weekend visits Chuck accompanied me. My grandmother seemed to like him but later, when we were alone, she said, "He's a troubled man and that means trouble. You be careful."

Although Grammie no longer told fortunes, she was still quick to issue warnings about visions that came to her. I didn't dare tell her I'd taken up telling fortunes again, just for two days as a fundraiser for the Mature Student Association at university. She'd have scolded me and declared that was why I was having problems with men.

On one visit I found my grandmother having tea with a man who also lived in the home. The two of them were in their nineties, yet were engaged in a spirited conversation. While I walked across the cafeteria, I could see my grandmother smiling as she listened to the man.

The next time I visited I teased Grammie. "Where's your boyfriend today?" I asked, sitting on the edge of her bed.

"What boyfriend?"

"The man you were having tea with."

"Oh, him."

"Yes, him. Is he your new boyfriend?"

"Of course not," she said, indignantly. "We're just friends."

I could have sworn my grandmother was blushing. After a few moments of quiet contemplation, she gave me a serious look. "I don't think I'll get married again. I think I'll just have a companion."

I never saw my grandmother when she wasn't moving or talking, so I wasn't prepared when my mother called to tell me Grammie was sick. I hadn't visited her for three weeks, but she had been fine then. I was in the middle of a summer course at Saint Thomas University and sometimes had difficulty arranging baby-sitters for Sasha.

Finally I managed to get away one Thursday evening. When I

saw Grammie, I knew she was seriously ill. She could hardly speak and wasn't eating. I sat with her for a while, and she studied my face, no doubt knowing the end was near. All I could do was hold her hand and tell her I was praying for her. Then I hugged her goodbye and said I loved her.

"I like you, too," Grammie whispered.

When I returned the following afternoon, my grandmother was in a coma. The nurse reported to me and other family members that in a few days Grammie would be gone. Seeing her in this state, I figured she had already left and my heart ached to hear her voice one more time. *Thank God we have those five-generation photos,* I thought.

My parents, who had faithfully visited every week, stayed that day until nine o'clock. For the next three days family members took turns sitting with Grammie. On the fourth evening I relieved my parents. They were completely spent, so I urged them to go home. "I'm prepared to stay the night," I said. I'd taken Sasha to Sonya's house in Geary.

I'd always prayed that God would give me the opportunity and strength to be with my grandmother at the end of her life, to help her with the transition. Her ninety-second birthday was four months away. *What a remarkable woman,* I reflected, studying her wrinkled face. *Life had never been easy for her.* Coming to Canada as a child to escape certain death in Europe. Life in a strange new land. The loss of her father through suicide. An abusive, alcoholic husband who dragged other women home with him. Raising seventeen children. Losing the husband and granddaughter, Nancy, she'd loved so dearly.

Death must be a relief.

I pulled the blankets up to her chin. Her tiny hands felt so cold, as if they belonged on a porcelain doll. I stroked her hair and kissed her soft, withered cheek, which was chilly, too. For a minute I wondered if she was still breathing. I placed my hand on her chest and detected a dull heartbeat.

Then I recalled the Valentine's Day cookies Grammie sent me through the mail every single year until I finally left home at fifteen. Heart-shaped brown sugar cookies frosted with pink icing, they'd arrived wrapped in waxed paper and always survived the three-day trip through the mail in one piece. *When did she have time to make them while caring for all her stepchildren and a grand-daughter on a farm?* I wondered.

I sang to Grammie for hours. I had brought along a hymn book, the one she used on Sundays, and since I was familiar with most of her favourites, I worked my way through, repeating those I knew by heart such as "Amazing Grace" and "Jesus Loves Me." Occasionally I took a break to go to the bathroom or drink coffee the nurses brought. Sometimes I spoke a few words.

"I love you, Grammie," I'd say. "You're going to see Perley and Nancy soon. You don't have to be afraid. They're waiting for you. They're with Jesus."

Once in a while my grandmother would gasp for air, and I'd be convinced it was her last breath. Panicky, I'd call the nurse, who would check Grammie's pulse.

"This may go on for a while," the nurse would tell me.

Sometime before midnight, as I sat beside Grammie's bed study-ing her face, I sensed a difference in the quiet room. It was nothing I could see, but everything appeared lighter, brighter somehow. I actually felt a presence, and a peaceful lull washed over me as I grasped my grandmother's cold hand and sang, "Shall We Gather at the River."

Grammie's head began to stir slightly and her mouth opened as she laboured to breathe. There was a choking sound in her throat, but her eyes remained shut. I stopped singing and started to talk, to calm her.

"Don't struggle, Grammie, don't struggle," I whispered. "It's okay. Go toward the light. Jesus is there." I continued holding her hand

and stroking her hair until she stopped resisting. Her eyes never opened. For a few seconds there appeared to be a spirit in the room. I actually felt a coolness in the stuffy room, convinced it was a Godly presence.

Three days later, on September 1, 1995, I gave the eulogy at Grammie's funeral, saluting her dedication, determination, and resilience as a woman. The following week I went back to university to complete the final year of my undergraduate degree.

FULL CIRCLE

I continued to travel to Woodstock for gatherings, sweats, and social visits. Elder Ervin and Nadine were always willing to counsel me whenever I was uncertain what the next step in my life should be. For a time their house seemed like a second home for Sasha and me.

My encounters with Native spirituality appeased the part of me that had felt empty and neglected, yet it was inside a sweat lodge that I first experienced a kind of homesickness to share my faith with others who practised the same Christian tenets I'd embraced as a child.

I was invited by Nadine to a special sweat-lodge ceremony that had been arranged for her. I drove to Woodstock, wondering if she might be sick. The sweat-lodge keeper was a woman named Anne, a robust, friendly Passamaquoddy with a penchant for hugging everyone. She was a close friend of Nadine's and had promptly agreed to make the two-and-a-half-hour trip from Old Town, Maine, to conduct a healing sweat for Nadine. Doctors had found a lump in Nadine's breast and suspected it might be cancer.

As usual the sweat was preceded by warm, hearty conversation and steaming cups of tea in Ervin and Nadine's spacious kitchen. The gravity of the ceremony seemed unapparent as the eleven other women, and the men who were there to support them as firekeepers, told funny stories of past gatherings and caught up on the gossip. Even Nadine appeared to be in high spirits.

"I heard Marilyn and Buck are back together," Nadine said. "How many times is that?"

"Probably one time too many," Anne answered, and everyone laughed.

"Almost as bad as Eve," Ervin threw in with a mischievous twist of his lips. "She looks in the welfare lines for men she can help."

"Thanks, Ervin," I said. "You're a pal."

I chuckled along with the others but found it hard to see the humour given Nadine's condition. *Now there's a real warrior,* I marvelled as I watched her wonderful smile.

It was mid-evening when we headed for the sweat lodge that had been constructed earlier that day in the backyard of Nadine's country home. It didn't take that long to erect. The frame that supported the walls of tarps and blankets was constructed from bent willow or ash branches.

The sweats in Woodstock never utilized tobacco ties like the ones we'd prepared in Shubenacadie. That was a Sioux custom adopted by some Mi'gmaq sweat-lodge keepers. The Maliseets followed a different format. They simply offered tobacco to the fire outside the lodge.

As we departed, four women remained in the kitchen to prepare the feast that would await our return. Ervin had left to attend a sick relative on the Tobique Reserve an hour away downriver.

Surprisingly the late-October air was warm. It carried the sweet, pungent smells of fall—newness through decay. Most of the women were wearing cotton nightgowns. Mine was sleeveless and made of red flannel, and I carried a large navy beach towel. By now I had lost my original fear of the sweat-lodge ceremony and had come to welcome not only the physical cleansing of the sacred act, but the sanctuary offered to my mind and spirit.

I had memorized the words to many of the chants sung during

the four rounds. I didn't understand the prayers in Mi'gmaq or Maliseet, but that no longer mattered. I prayed in English, sometimes not even out loud, and that never seemed to bother anyone. It was a time when all differences and prejudices, if any existed, were put aside for a common purpose.

That night, after each woman gave heed to her own spiritual purging and remembered the children, the men, and the elders in their meditations, all the focus was then placed on Nadine's protection and healing. I expected the sweat lodge to grow hotter; it always seemed to do so when we prayed for someone's healing. Otherwise I didn't anticipate much difference in the general routine. Then I heard the flap of the tent being secured by the men outside. My heart sped up as I waited in anticipation, welcoming the gentle darkness, imagining myself inside Mother Earth's womb as the sweat lodge was intended to represent.

I waited for Anne to begin the ceremony, to start a traditional chant, perhaps one I'd never heard before. A few moments passed and then Anne's beautiful voice rose above us all. She was singing delicate words I recognized and held dearly. It was an old, familiar hymn reaching out to me in the dimness:

"Amazing Grace, how sweet the sound
That saved a wretch like me
I once was lost but now I'm found
T'was blind but now I see."

I couldn't believe my ears! Surely there would be an uprising right here, I assumed, trying to picture the surprised looks on the faces of the other women. I expected anger, but instead the singing grew louder as the women, one by one, joined in. I listened to the wondrous, soul-lifting harmony, realizing that everyone was singing except me.

Sitting there in beatific awe as the steam drew large beads of sweat from my body, I wiped the droplets away from my eyes with my towel. My back was soaked already with the rivulets that had worked their way down from my neck. I took a deep breath and joined in.

With the final words of "Amazing Grace" still lingering in the sweat lodge, Anne began to sing another hymn that soon melded into a Mi'gmaq chant. When the chant was done, Anne talked about Jesus cleansing our hearts and minds.

"We all need to be cleansed so sickness and pain will leave us," she said. "That's why we pray while the toxins pour from our body in this sacred place. Our Creator hears our prayers when we send them together."

I recalled the night when, as a child, I'd run to the makeshift altar at the Billy Graham Crusade. In the protective darkness of the sweat lodge I urged my mind to carry away the resentment and pain I'd fostered toward those church people who had hastened to condemn me in the name of God. This open acceptance by people within the sweat lodge reacquainted me with the special God of my youth. As the prayer rounds commenced, I listened with respect to the petitions presented in varying languages to the Creator. When my turn came, I offered up my pleas to Jesus.

"Please heal my friend Nadine," I implored. "Dear Jesus, give her the strength she needs, and the courage."

My spiritual journey had come full circle. For the first time in years Jesus and I were back on a first-name basis. Up until that day I'd addressed all my prayers to the Creator or God.

When I emerged from the tiny dome-shaped lodge six hours later, my skin glowed from the heat and felt as soft as a newborn's. No one could believe we had been inside the lodge for so many hours.

"We thought you'd all left for a restaurant," one of the women joked as we entered the house where the feast awaited us.

"I even had time for a nap," another said.

It was as if motion and time had been disengaged in that holy place. Our common purpose and love for our sister had transcended any thoughts of the outer world. Even when the sweat was over, we'd stood near the flap, reluctant to leave. I, for one, had wanted to stay inside and savour the experience, but when Anne mentioned the fresh barbecued salmon that would soon find a welcome home in our bellies, a rumble in my stomach underscored the necessities of the physical world.

Back inside the house, with a plateful of lusginigan and fiddleheads, I silently thanked Jesus for giving me food and the great gift of these noble friends.

As strange as it might seem, it was the Native sweat-lodge ceremony that prompted me to embrace Christianity fully. I had listened with tears in my eyes as some of my Native friends told me about the horrors they'd experienced at the hands of Christian leaders in residential schools—heads shoved into buckets of water for daring to speak their Native languages, beatings with hairbrushes. I'd read the many accounts of European contact with the First Nations peoples of this continent and was appalled by the atrocities committed, in the name of God, against such a trusting race.

Fully accepting Christianity was a struggle. There was the guilt of betraying my Native friends, but also the memories of the heavy hand of a preacher prodding me to my knees in front of an entire congregation when I was only thirteen. He had insisted I repent for wearing jewellery to entice men. When I read how Native people were considered less than human, assigned Indian agents to dictate to them, and forbidden to vote or travel outside certain areas, I remembered the day I was told to keep silent in the church and turn my back on worldly friends and relatives or I would burn forever in Hell. My suffering had been microscopic in comparison with many Native people, but I'd suffered enough to feel an affinity with them.

How could I reconcile all that I believed and still be true to my own spirit? How could I tell my Native friends I understood their pain, empathized with them, and wanted no part of an order that tried to destroy an entire people's belief system, yet still worship the faith that was the source of so much of their pain? How could I, with a pure heart, follow Jesus?

MY OUTLOOK ON DEATH CHANGED

Elder Ervin was patient answering the many questions I put forth about life and death. Since Grammie Brewer's passing, I had speculated about death and wasn't sure what to believe anymore, so I decided to ask Ervin what he believed.

Ervin was a tall, slim woodsman with long, knotty arms. He was always good-humoured, laughing as if at some inside joke between him and the world. A handsome, clean-shaven man with a strong jaw and high cheek bones, he had a body that was fit despite several ailments. Ervin had already experienced two heart attacks and was developing diabetes, but he walked with great dignity whether he was wearing jeans and a plaid shirt or his special leather regalia.

I only saw him angry once. We were walking into the woods behind his home in Woodstock in late November to pick cedar for a sweat-lodge ceremony scheduled for sunrise the following morning. Sasha was in the house playing. Nadine, who by then had been diagnosed with breast cancer, was resting inside.

Ordinarily I wouldn't have ventured into the woods that late, but I wanted to ask Ervin how he felt about death. When I told him this, he invited me along, saying, "C'mon then, no use in sitting idle."

As we made our way into the trees, I had to walk fast to keep up with Ervin, who cut through the snowdrifts without problem.

When he tensed and paused, I stopped.

"Someone up ahead," he said, his breath misting in the still air. I held my own breath and listened, but I couldn't hear a sound. I remember thinking, *He's either got awfully good ears or he's losing it.* But the next turn in the path confirmed his suspicions. Straight ahead of us, in a small clearing, a burly white man was dragging a fat young spruce tree behind him. The sharp needles at the tips scratched an erratic path in the snow.

I watched the muscles in Ervin's neck clench and his eyes narrow into steely bullets. "How would you like me to try that on you?" he called out.

The intruder dropped the tree and stared at Ervin. He seemed scared, and my heart began to pound anticipating a violent altercation. The sun was close to setting and there was an orange-red light on the snow. The white man stood motionless, glanced at the tree he'd cut, then looked at the stump, sawdust, and chips of wood on the snow. "Didn't think anyone would miss an old tree," he muttered.

"Don't think anyone'd miss you if I planted you in its place, either," Ervin said, raising his hand and pointing. "That tree's got more right on this land than you, mister. Now get out of here before I decide to decorate you for Christmas!"

The trespasser didn't argue. He held his ground for a second, then decided to move on. "Stupid old Indian," he said under his breath as he tramped off.

Without warning Ervin let out a loud growl like that of an angry she-bear. I jumped almost as high as the retreating invader, who broke into a run, stumbled, and partly fell into the powdery snow.

Ervin watched the white man go with steady eyes, then burst out laughing. "Did you see that honky run!"

After a few seconds, trying to quiet my fast-pounding heart, I laughed, as well. A big belly laugh that broke the tension inside. *Honky* seemed appropriate for the occasion.

"Now let's get back to business," Ervin said, gesturing to a huge log. He was still snickering; no doubt a bad taste lingered in his mouth due to the stranger's presence. "Let's sit."

After brushing off the shimmering overcoat of snow, we parked our backsides on the log. Motionless in the dusk, Ervin resembled an ancient statue. He wore his silver hair in a single long braid under a Boston Red Sox cap. It glistened like Christmas tinsel. When he took out his pipe, filled and lit it, I knew he was ready for serious conversation.

I sat quietly, breathing in the apple aroma of pipe smoke, sensing that whatever he was about to say was exactly what I needed to hear. There was no need for questions.

Ervin smiled. "That man is out of balance, you know. That tree could teach him something. If he learns, he'll be okay." He puffed on his pipe and watched me intently. "It's true that what goes around, comes around. We get back what we give out. It doesn't even end with death. That's just another gateway." His eyes shifted to where the white man had been, as if he could still see him doing damage, taking what wasn't his. "I don't think he'll be back for a while."

I didn't want to say anything. I was afraid to interrupt. So I sat, shoulders hunched against the chill, looking at my new mentor as he stared into the distance. I wondered if he realized I was still there.

After a period of contemplation and a few more puffs on his pipe, Ervin glanced at my face. "I'll tell you this story," he said, casually pointing the stem of the pipe at me.

I nodded. "Great."

"Every person must travel the circle of life. We journey always toward becoming complete and healed. Sometimes that means we have parts of our circle that become weak or broken. This can be caused by bad happenings in our life, by abuse or by things like alcoholism." He let his last words sink in, not in a condemning manner but as a sign of recognition. His eyes knew. They probed deep and recognized the clot of black that was stuck in my spirit like a cancer, resting, then eating, then resting. "Always we are trying to find balance so our circle can be healed and strong." Again he paused and searched my eyes. Above us a few small birds swept past. I heard the movement of their wings. In the distance a crow cawed, then another in return. "Sometimes we need to join with others to make the circle stronger. Sometimes we have to get away from someone to do that." He nodded slightly. "This journey doesn't end. We just keep developing our spiritual nature. Here in this life we make choices to grow and change so we can become stronger spiritually. We finally realize we are all equal and connected or we make the growth slower by refusing these lessons, like our friend here tonight."

He drew on his pipe, then peered into the bowl. "But it doesn't matter, fast or slow, we all learn, and like the tree that dies in winter, we all eventually see spring."

The dusk air was calm as the pipe smoke wafted in the tranquil wilderness. I gazed at Ervin, astonished by his interior peace, the peace he had instilled in me. I wanted to embrace him. I felt something close to love for him, familial love.

I thought of earlier Sunday School teachings that had once frightened me with images of fiery damnation. Ervin's words seemed so much closer to *actual* Christian compassion. In Ervin's presence I felt for certain that God, the Creator, was very much around me. With his steady, patient words, Ervin had offered me a great gift: the realization that only I could make the necessary choices to restore the circle. And I knew my grandmothers weren't really dead. I'd see them again when I reached the same part of my journey.

DON'T FORGET THE MOON

Nadine continued to get sicker, but her Creator gave her the energy and courage she required to endure. Her optimism never faded right until the end. She passed away, surrounded by her family, on December 20, 1995.

I visited her three days before her death. My old friend Elizabeth from Kingsclear joined me. I asked Ervin if I could talk to Nadine alone. The downstairs parlour, where we'd held AA meetings for kids seeking counselling at the house and had gathered for drumming afterward, was converted into Nadine's bedroom.

When I entered the room and saw her lying on the bed, I was struck by her physical appearance. I had already seen her after she lost most of her hair to chemotherapy, but I wasn't prepared for the bloated body or the pain-glazed eyes that were all the more promi-nent now that even her eyebrows were gone. When she smiled at me as she laboured for breath, I broke down and cried.

"I'm so sorry, Nadine," I said. "I promised myself I wouldn't do this."

"It's okay, Eve," she whispered, weakly holding out her swollen arms for a hug. "It's normal to cry when you're losing someone you love."

Carefully I held her close for a few seconds, trying not to add to her pain. Her body felt feverish.

"How are you making out?" she asked before I had time to utter another word.

"I'm fine."

"I hope you're not back with Chuck. Tell me you won't go back to that."

"No, I learned my lesson. I promise."

"And how's Heather?"

"Not doing well."

"That's all right. She'll find her way," Nadine said with more assurance than I could muster. Her breath was ragged, but she continued to talk. "And Sasha? How's my little Sasha?"

"Doing well. She loves school."

"She's a special girl. You've taught her well."

I knew Elizabeth wished to see Nadine and I didn't want to tire her out. "Elizabeth's here," I said. There was a silence as Nadine thought for a moment.

"Eve, you make sure to keep in touch with Ervin when I'm gone."

I nodded. "Okay."

"Don't forget the moon," she said. Grandmother Moon, as Natives referred to it, was one of her favourite wonders of creation. "Remember me when you look at the full moon."

I kissed her goodbye. "I love you," I said studying her face intently before walking away with a heavy heart.

That was the last time I saw Nadine.

The following spring I entered the Saint Thomas University History Writing Competition. The topic was "Women Who Have Influenced My Life." I wrote about Nadine and won first prize.

HEATHER'S MARRIAGE

Heather's marriage to Joe put her in greater danger of abuse. When riled, Joe was even more vicious than his Uncle Chuck. Heather had already received a number of bruises and black eyes, no doubt the result of lost temper long before she and Joe were married.

After one of the beatings, a vicious attack that left her with the worst black eye I'd ever seen and legs bruised black and blue from the imprint of a hockey stick, Heather turned to painkillers for help. Only this time she didn't simply swallow the pills; she crushed them with a spoon and snorted the powder. She was with another girl on the reserve when she first snorted Demerol and Leritine.

"I vomited for hours," she told me more than a year later. Deep, retching belly pulls had followed her ten-minute escape from agonizing memories of being beaten by the hockey stick. After snorting the drugs, her head ached for days as if fists were pounding in her skull. But the euphoria was her bliss against hopelessness, and given her pattern of substance abuse, she was easily hooked on a whole new level.

Sometimes Joe and Heather got along. They'd go fishing or take in a movie, like any normal couple. Occasionally Sasha would accompany them, but I never let my granddaughter visit until I checked out the emotional climate first. If everything seemed peaceful between Heather and Joe, it usually stayed that way while Sasha was around. Joe appeared to enjoy her visits.

Whenever Heather disappeared from the reserve to drink with friends without letting Joe know, he became extremely angry. If Heather returned drunk or high, the couple would fight. Heather never backed down when she was intoxicated. Still, her slight frame was no match for Joe. He weighed well over two hundred pounds.

I stayed away from Heather and Joe as much as possible because I couldn't stand the violence—what it did to me, what it brought back.

PART FIVE

1996-2000

WINTERGREEN

PALM AGAINST MY WINDOW

I had tried to remain in touch with old friends while I was married to Chuck, but it was next to impossible, especially if those friends happened to be males like Miles. Chuck was just too possessive. Miles and I had talked off and on over the years. When he was married to Marg, he seemed content, but Chuck became jealous at the mere mention of Miles, so I stopped trying to maintain the friendship.

Later I heard through the AA grapevine that Miles and Marg had broken up and he was having a hard time. He called me at my apartment and asked if we could get together for coffee.

Drawn together by pain once more, we began to spend almost every day in each other's company. We had both changed so that we valued our own special kinship too much to ruin it by stepping over boundaries that would hurt us. But that didn't prevent people from talking. I suppose it was difficult to believe that a "womanizer" and a woman with three broken marriages could spend so much time together without becoming intimate. To be perfectly honest, I was surprised, too, but even more so when I realized we were closer than I'd ever been with any man with whom I'd shared a bed.

After my stay at Transition House, Sasha and I moved into Liberty Lane, a safehouse for abused women and children. It was a complex with seven apartments secure from any threat of abusers. In fact, men were prohibited without written permission. That included nice guys like Miles.

If I were sick, Miles would call to tell me he'd be dropping off ginger ale and I would meet him at the front door, which was locked at all times. I often cooked him meals at his house a few miles away. For the first time in years I had met a man I knew was truly my friend and who appreciated me for exactly who I was. I knew if I was in trouble or in pain he'd be there, maybe not forever but at least for as long as he was able.

Miles and I went on leisurely drives to Saint John or McAdam just to talk. Sometimes we'd take Sasha to the park. We rented movies (we both enjoyed westerns), attended a few dances at AA functions, and even visited my children together. They all loved Miles, especially Sonya, who jokingly called him "Dad" and tried several times, with Miles's approval, to nudge our friendship toward romance. He was a regular at birthday, Thanksgiving, and Christmas dinners and often spent time alone with one of the children. He went out of his way to help Heather whenever she reached out to him, visiting her in detox, driving her to a rehab, and never criticizing her when she slipped again. He even took Sasha to watch the fireworks one Canada Day when I was too sick to handle the excursion.

Naturally our time together didn't go unnoticed by Chuck, who often followed in his car to harass us.

One day Miles drove me to Oromocto to pick up a part for my car. No sooner had we pulled into the garage beside the Oromocto Shopping Centre when Chuck raced in front of us to block our way in the parking lot.

"Oh, my word!" I cried out when I realized who was rushing out of the offending car.

"Relax," Miles said. "He can't hurt you in plain daylight with all these people around."

"What are you doing with my wife?" Chuck roared as Miles rolled down his window.

"I'm giving her a drive," Miles answered calmly.

"I bet you're giving her a drive. More likely a ride," he yelled loud enough to get the attention of a burly mechanic inside the garage. "You better watch your back."

He stuck his finger in Miles's face, then backed away from the car to glare at me as I started to cry.

"Is anything the matter?" The big guy from the garage had walked up to the car and was studying Chuck.

"Nothing I can't take care of," Chuck said, climbing back into his car.

"Are you all right?" the man asked, looking at my teary face.

"Yeah, I'm okay," I said. "We were just leaving."

I was so shaken that I wouldn't even stay long enough to pick up the car part. I insisted Miles head back to town.

Another time Chuck stopped behind me at a busy intersection in Fredericton, leaped out of his car, and ran up to my window while the light was red.

"I'll get Miles for stealing my woman!" he screamed, slapping his palm against my window.

I yelled back through the closed window, "Miles is my friend—nothing more!"

Chuck just laughed.

When the light turned green, I pulled away quickly, leaving him to shake his fist while the cars behind honked.

It was difficult to keep up appearances at the university, so I stopped trying. I talked to the assistant registrar, Anne Forrestall, and told her the whole story. She suggested I secure a peace bond. I also let my professors know I was under extra stress due to personal matters. A couple I'd met while attending university, Jim and Joanne Wilson, offered to baby-sit if I needed a break and they invited us over for dinner every week, which was a welcome reprieve.

I had resolved to graduate at spring convocation next year, so I knew I'd have to find a way to concentrate and keep supportive people around me if I was going to make it.

One evening I left early from a lecture on aboriginal childcare practices by Professor Laurel Lewey, telling her I didn't feel well. I walked out to my car in the parking lot, too exhausted to care about any danger from Chuck. I hadn't seen him for a few days. He was only taking one class in the afternoon now at STU, and I made certain I was somewhere else then. I was impatient to get home and tuck Sasha into bed so I could have a hot bubble bath.

Taking the car keys for my Ford Tempo out of my shirt pocket, I started to open the door when I realized it was already unlocked. *I must have forgotten to lock the car doors,* I thought, *in my haste to get to class*.

Uncomfortably I lowered my body behind the steering wheel. I'd gained fifty pounds since my surgery and found it difficult to breathe. I made a mental note, as I had so many times in the past year: *I've got to get that weight off. I've got to start walking more. Tomorrow*.

As I slid the key into the ignition, I heard a noise in the back seat. Frozen with fear, I was certain my heart would explode, every beat loud in my eardrums.

"You're early tonight," a familiar voice said. When I whipped around, I saw Chuck grinning in the half-light from the streetlamps. "Did I scare you?" he asked.

"Scare me!" I gasped. "You idiot!" I was so angry I could have killed him. All fear fled as I struggled out of the car and ordered him to do the same. Surprised no doubt by the confidence in my voice, he obliged. "I have to go home. Sasha's sick," I lied.

"What's the matter?"

"Nothing. Look, if you really want to talk, I'll meet you tomorrow at Odell Park. Okay?"

Chuck nodded. "Sure. Around three o'clock?"

"Okay."

He let me go without a problem. I inched toward the driver's door, climbed in, started the car, and roared away with a bad case of the shakes.

By the time I arrived home, I was a nervous wreck. My friend Jill carried a sleeping Sasha upstairs to my apartment, then suggested I call the police. Instead I phoned Miles. He told me Chuck was obsessed and might be capable of anything.

"Call the police," he insisted.

The next morning I went to see Anne Forrestall and told her what had happened. Since Chuck and I had been on university property at the time, she was able to write Chuck a letter, warning him to refrain from harassing me or face possible suspension from STU. And she made certain he received it in his class that afternoon.

I never knew if he showed up at Odell Park the next day or not. In fact, I stayed away from the park for a whole year, just to be safe.

MY STOLEN COAT

It was Sunday and Heather was trying to kick drugs again. She and Joe had reunited after a brief separation and were living in the same apartment I'd occupied before I left the Oromocto Reserve. Many of my belongings were still there.

Both of them wanted to spend some time with Sasha. I felt more confident Sasha would be in safe hands, so I allowed an overnight visit with her mother. When the telephone rang, I was planning to catch up on laundry.

"How does a delicious spaghetti dinner with a gorgeous man sound?" It was Miles on the other end.

"Sounds good, but who's cooking?"

"Me."

"Then who's the gorgeous man?"

"Me, of course," Miles replied suggestively.

"Well, I've got tons of laundry to do."

"Bring it with you. I won't charge much."

"What time?"

"Around six. Dinner will be served then, madame."

"Okay, see you then."

I hung up and chuckled. *What would I do without Miles?* I wondered as I set two baskets in the middle of the kitchen floor to sort the dirty laundry.

When I arrived at Miles's house in Silverwood, three miles from where I lived, dinner was on the table.

I ate two platefuls of the spicy pasta while sipping on a cup of tea.

"You'll never fit into your bikini eating like that," Miles said.

"Maybe you should try a couple more plates before we lose you in the shower drain," I teased back.

One of Miles's boarders, Bill, was having dinner with us. The other boarder, Bradley, was away for the weekend. Bill merely shook his head and smiled as we traded insults. He'd heard it before and knew we meant no harm. "Some people's children," was all he said as we headed for the living room where Miles and Bill kept their guitars.

I had already washed two loads of clothes and was still waiting for the first one to dry before I put the third into the washer. Miles's dryer had certainly seen better times. It took hours to dry one load, but I was glad for the opportunity for benign adult company and a washer and dryer that didn't demand more quarters than I could usually scrape together.

We sang country songs. Miles liked Conway Twitty and knew most of his numbers. "Hello Darling" and "Fifteen Years Ago" were two of my favourites. I sang along during the choruses. When Miles paused to make tea and coffee, Bill filled in. He preferred folk and gospel. I knew a lot of songs in those categories, too, and hummed or sang along on "Four Strong Winds" and "Why Me Lord?"

After Miles brought in tea for me and coffee for himself, we talked for hours about the government, the Bible, pets, and food.

It was a terribly cold night and, as the evening wore on, I became a little worried that my car might not start. The battery was old and sometimes left me stranded. Miles had no outside receptacle, so I couldn't plug in the block heater.

"I should probably get going," I told Miles as I swallowed the last mouthful of tea. "I can pick up that load in the dryer tomorrow morning before I go to class."

"Why don't you stay?" Miles asked. "You can sleep in my room." He faked a lecherous grin and batted his eyelashes at me.

Bill and I both laughed.

"Yeah, right," I said.

"No, seriously, you can have my bed. Bradley's not coming home. I'll sleep in his room."

Bill nodded and rose from the couch. "That'll work. I'm off to bed."

It was almost midnight and I didn't relish the thought of climbing into a freezing car and driving home to an empty apartment. Still, I was nervous.

"What if Chuck comes here and tries to cause trouble?" I asked.

"He'll never come here." Miles was in the kitchen, making certain he'd turned off the stove. "He doesn't even know where I live."

Reassured, I gave Miles a hug and trod down the narrow hallway, passing Bradley's room and then Bill's before coming to the master bedroom at the rear of the mini-home.

The clock's glowing red numbers on the stand beside the bed said 11:50. I buried myself under the covers and felt the warmth of the waterbed chase away the chill as I sank in. Immediately I fell asleep, not even finishing the prayer I'd started.

Two hours later—1:55 on the clock—I was awakened by a large thump that shook the trailer. At first I thought I had imagined the sound, that the noise had crossed over from a dream. Sitting up, I heard angry voices outside but couldn't understand the words. I knew it had to be Chuck. Falling back on the bed, I pulled the covers over my head and peered into the blackness. *He's going to kill me.*

He's finally going to do it. I wanted to run, to hide in the closet, but I couldn't move. The air was stale under the covers. I thought I might suffocate, slip into unconsciousness, and be found by Chuck. *Please, dear God, help me,* I prayed over and over again.

Then I heard a door slam and after that complete quiet. Eventually I detected water running in the bathroom next to the room I was in. Slowly I inched the covers from my head and felt the cool air on my face. I paused, listened, then carefully slipped my legs over the bed. Standing, I held my breath. No sound, except the running of water in the sink. I opened the door and saw a light in the bathroom. "Miles?"

No reply.

I took another step.

"Miles?"

A muffled reply came. I reached the bathroom doorway and cautiously peeked in. Miles was holding a cloth to his nose. There was blood all over his face.

"What happened?" I asked.

"Get back in your bedroom until I tell you to come out."

My eyes darted toward the front door, then I hurried back to the bedroom, where I shut the door, locked it from the inside, and waited, leaning against the door just in case. Then I decided I'd probably get knocked down if Chuck barged in, so I sat on the edge of the bed and tried not to cry as I rocked back and forth, hugging the pillow, and hoping Miles would be all right.

Help me, Lord, I prayed. *Help me stay calm and protect Miles.*

When Miles finally came to get me, Bill was right behind him.

"Chuck saw your car in the driveway," Miles said, obviously shaken. "He must have asked someone where I lived and checked here."

"He knocked on the door first," Bill interjected. "I heard him when I got up for a drink of water. He asked to use the phone. I didn't know who he was. So I told him we didn't have a phone and to go away—"

"That's what I have to do now," Miles cut in. "I've got to phone the police." He grabbed a coat to cover the jogging outfit he was wearing, pulled on some boots, and headed out the door to the nearby pay phone.

"I told the guy to leave," Bill continued. "I assumed he left."

The loud noise I'd heard was Chuck breaking down the door. No doubt he assumed Miles and I were sleeping together. Once inside, he charged his way into the first bedroom.

Just then Miles returned. "The police are on their way." He explained how, still dazed from sleep, he had attempted to stand and push Chuck out of the room. But Chuck had grabbed a dumbbell lying on the floor and swung it, striking him in the face. Dropping the dumbbell, Chuck had lunged for Miles, hands gripped around his throat, choking him.

"I thought I was a goner," Miles told us. "All I could do was pray. I was pinned against the door and couldn't move." Suddenly Chuck had let go of Miles's throat and raced for the door, grabbing my winter coat from a hanger on his way out.

Five minutes later two police officers arrived. The female was petite and sympathetic. She did the majority of the talking, and Miles answered most of the questions. Bill and I filled in details when asked.

The policewoman radioed the information to the RCMP dispatcher. In a few minutes another RCMP officer radioed back to say he had stopped a man on the Trans-Canada Highway near Nackawic, forty miles away, who fitted Chuck's description. The man said he couldn't speak English. He was talking in another language.

"Maliseet," I said. "He's talking Maliseet, but he can speak English perfectly well."

The female officer radioed the information. Confronted with this news, Chuck dropped his act immediately.

Miles drove himself to the hospital around 4:00 a.m. Chuck was in custody, so I went back to bed and eventually fell asleep.

The police transported Chuck to the same jail where Sonya was working as a corrections officer. My coat wasn't returned for a couple of days because it was held as evidence. Why Chuck wanted it was a mystery. Maybe he felt it was a part of me, a symbol he could cling to.

Miles had been lucky. Nothing was broken, but he had a cut on his cheek and bruises on his neck and around each eye. He eventually healed but took a lot of kidding from his friends, often telling them he was trying a new kind of weight lifting with his face.

When the case went to trial, Miles didn't show up, but I did. I couldn't believe my eyes when I saw an elder from the Oromocto Reserve enter the courtroom in full Native regalia, headdress and all. He certainly had everyone's attention. Although the elder had always been friendly whenever we'd met before, this time he didn't acknowledge my presence.

Luckily Judge Greydon Nicholas, who also happened to be Maliseet, was quick to glean the truth. He wasn't distracted by the elder or the feathers on his head when the man stood to plead Chuck's case.

"I have been teaching this man the traditional ways of the Maliseet people," the elder informed the judge. "He is trying to follow the Red Path. He was upset by the loss of his wife. It knocked him off balance, but he knows what he must do now to get back on the path."

The judge listened patiently, then recessed briefly to review the police reports and consider testimony. When he delivered his verdict fifteen minutes later, he pointed out quite adamantly that it wasn't the "way of Maliseet people" to break into the homes of others and become violent, nor was it the "way of Native people" to terrorize women. Chuck would have to spend seven more days in jail, write a letter of apology to Miles, attend sweat-lodge ceremonies on a regular basis, and perform community service. Outside the court-room the elder removed his headdress, looked at me, smiled, and shrugged before getting into his car to drive away.

Although Miles admitted he'd never trust Chuck, he amazed me with the sympathy he showed. Despite the fact that Chuck could have killed him, Miles would often say, "I know where he's coming from, what it's like to be obsessed, and it's no fun to live like that. I hope he gets some help."

A few weeks after the incident with Chuck, Miles attempted a reconciliation with his wife, but it didn't work out. Our times together became more infrequent. I started dating a Mi'gmaq man from Cape Breton Island who regularly visited Fredericton, thinking a long-distance relationship might work better for me. I wasn't ready for a commitment and still had my honours thesis to finish so I could graduate in a couple of months.

After dating a new woman for a few weeks, Miles moved with her to Chipman, about forty-five minutes from Fredericton, and we stopped talking to each other altogether. The loss left a gaping emptiness. When I spoke with some of Miles's friends, I learned this was just part of his usual pattern. "Miles is in love again," they'd say with amusement. "Don't worry. He'll come to his senses in a year or so and you'll be one of the first people he'll call."

I threw myself into my studies and made plans to move again. This time I would be leaving the protection and support of a build-ing filled with fellow survivors. I was nervous and excited at the same time when I learned there was an apartment available only a block from the university. I would qualify for subsidized housing because I was living solely on student loans and the occasional pay from writing contracts.

In the summer Sasha and I moved into our new apartment. She would soon begin kindergarten at Montgomery Street School a few blocks away. We would both have a new start.

ACADEMIA—A NEW SLANT ON PREJUDICE

I thought Professor Paula Eagle Stone, director of Native studies at STU, would be thrilled with my decision to explore how Native women writers make sense of their worlds through narrative. Historically women were the keepers of the stories in oral societies.

I could never quite gauge Eagle Stone's moods. At times she appeared outgoing and friendly, but then suspicious and angry. She was a brilliant scholar, even though she never had a doctorate, and I admired the thoroughness of her research when I read articles she had published.

Once, during a meeting in her office, she asked me why I was writing about Native people. I tried to explain my vested interest but could see she was unimpressed. She mumbled something under her breath about "misappropriation."

"It's time Native peoples did their own writing," she asserted. "We've had enough of non-Natives writing our history."

I was insulted but said nothing. I continued to remain quiet even when she insisted on reviewing an inconsequential article I'd written for the campus paper about a social event hosted by the Department of Native Studies. She wanted to check it prior to submission.

During my third year, I took an independent study course from this same professor, and although I worked diligently to prove myself, I couldn't please her. The tension between us seemed personal.

Thankfully the Native studies courses I signed up for at UNB offered much more amicable experiences. They were taught by Dave and Imelda Perley and Dr. Robert Leavitt.

Dave Perley was a consultant with the Department of Education Branch, Aboriginal Services, who was concerned mainly with curriculum design. In 1995 he asked if I was interested in working on a book to be used in middle schools throughout the province. Of course, I jumped at the opportunity. However, I wasn't prepared for the role he had in mind. He wondered if I would like to be the *editor*. That meant I'd travel to reserves in New Brunswick and even Maine to interview Natives. The book would be called *Welcome to Our Talking Circle: Voices of the Wabanakis*. That same year Dr. Leavitt, the director of education at the Micmac/Maliseet Institute at UNB, asked if I would edit the newsletter for the institute. I readily agreed.

In my final year at STU I informed Eagle Stone that I wished to complete an interdisciplinary honours thesis. She was concerned about my decision to mix Native studies with other disciplines, particularly English and psychology.

"I've never heard of this combination," she told me when I brought the idea to her one afternoon in her office. "Who are you proposing for your honours committee?"

"I was hoping you'd chair it," I replied hesitantly. She stared at me with cold black eyes that reminded me of those of a hawk I'd encountered at a zoo once. "Dr. Donovan and Dr. Thornton have already agreed to be part of the committee."

"I'll have to talk to them. Get your written proposal into me as soon as possible."

Wanting as little contact as possible with Eagle Stone, I left it to my other professors to smooth things out with her. But as soon as I submitted my proposal to investigate how Native women writers and storytellers employed stories to make sense of the world, Eagle Stone contacted me.

"I don't like the sound of your thesis," she said. "And I have some concerns about your title, 'The Myth of Silence Among Native Women Writers.'"

I went back to Donovan and Thornton and begged them to intervene on my behalf. Still, even after the initial proposal was approved and my committee officially set up, Eagle Stone found

355

fault with or rejected the majority of submissions during the entire writing process, although they met the standards of two other academically senior professors on my honours committee.

Regardless, I kept at it, writing and rewriting chapters, scouring history books and *Form and Format* to meet the high standards established by my chairperson. Eventually I made it through. When I marched up to the podium at Aitken Centre on May 8, 1996, to receive my diploma, I was prouder than I'd ever been in my life. Onstage, wearing my black gown with STU's traditional green-and-gold coloured sash, I took my seat with the rest of the graduates. There was a loud call of "Hey, mother!" Searching in the direction of the voice, I saw my son, Jody. All of my children were standing and waving at me.

Beryl was there, too, and my Aunt Lena and cousin Heather. Even my latest AA sponsor, Marg W., and her husband were present. I didn't see my brother, Carman, but I learned later he had come. I knew Mom and Dad wouldn't be able to attend. Dad was feeling sick after receiving treatments for prostate cancer, and Mom seldom left his side. I'd promised them I'd visit with my gown and diploma after the ceremony.

Patiently I waited while the names were called and the students stood to accept their diplomas. There was a knot in my stomach the size of a boulder. I hoped I wouldn't trip in my long robe. Finally my name was announced and excitement coursed through me as I bolted from my seat. My kids cheered and whistled from the bleachers as I strode across the stage to accept my Bachelor of Arts from the president of the university.

I'd really made it! I didn't care any more about Professor Eagle Stone. Her attitude had only spurred me to work harder. I had graduated with first-class interdisciplinary honours and my thesis received an A. I was also awarded the prestigious David Velensky Graduation Prize for Creative Writing and the STU Campus Ministry Certificate of Appreciation for my participation in advocacy groups that protested poverty and abuse.

As I returned to my seat, I caught Dr. Donovan's smile. He was seated onstage near the steps. Walking by him, then quickly down the steps, I almost stumbled but recovered before anyone really noticed. And, as my friends Jim and Joanne stepped up to the podium to receive their diplomas together, I let out a cheer.

A woman from the Alumni Association interviewed me for the alumni magazine. I was delighted to be on the other end of the pen as I detailed my plans to attend graduate school as soon as possible. After the interview, I headed to the reception for graduates to meet with my children. My head and heart were in the clouds as I thought about the celebrations to come and hurried across the manicured lawn of the campus toward Edmund Casey Hall where the reception was under way. In my glee I was invincible, indestructible, higher than a kite. But as I approached the hall my brow furrowed when I spotted a man on the steps. It was Chuck, and he was holding a camera.

"Do you think I could get a picture?" he asked.

I stopped in surprise.

"Congratulations," he said before I could speak. As I stood in sudden indecision, he snapped a photograph. I shook my head in disbelief and marched past him into the hall, mumbling a quick thank-you.

Inside, I vowed not to let my spirits sink. Enthusiastically I greeted my family and posed for photographs with my children and friends. Then I made my way to my favourite professors, Trish Thornton, Stewart Donovan, and Frank Cronin, and gave them each a big hug, thanking them for helping me to make it despite all the obstacles I'd had to face.

"You're the one who did all the work," Cronin told me. "You should be proud."

I promised my professors I'd keep in touch. Feeling magnanimous, I scanned the reception for Eagle Stone but couldn't see her anywhere. In fact, our paths never crossed again.

When I left the university, I picked Sasha up from day-care and, still clad in my graduation gown, headed off to visit my parents for more photographs.

REUNITED WITH FRIENDS

I applied for graduate school at the University of New Brunswick as soon as I received my final marks from STU and was accepted into the creative-writing program for autumn 1996. My graduate studies at UNB were nothing in comparison to my days at STU. I made few connections, but I did enjoy my seminars.

As I was finishing my first year at UNB, I met Brandee, a young woman who was new to AA. Only twenty years old, she was studying for an undergraduate degree in French. At an AA meeting Brandee talked about the sadness she carried with her since her mother, an alcoholic, had died two years earlier. Her father was also an alcoholic and had been diagnosed with cancer. Brandee's fifteen-year-old sister still lived at home with her dad on Campobello Island, more than 150 miles away. Sober only for a few months, Brandee was struggling to stay clear of the party crowd at university.

As I listened to her story, my maternal instinct was aroused. Here was a girl who needed a friend, I thought. After the meeting, I offered my telephone number and told her I lived close to the university. She called me the following evening. When she asked me to be her sponsor, I agreed immediately. My circle grew a little brighter as my new friend began to visit on a regular basis.

Brandee had a soft spot for children and aspired to be a teacher. She often read to Sasha or played puppets with her, and sometimes the three of us would go to a restaurant for supper. Once in a while Brandee would spend the night and we'd watch a movie and eat popcorn, but usually she just stopped by my apartment for coffee and a long chat. She called me her second mom, which warmed my heart.

It was around this time that Miles began calling me again. He was suffering the fallout from yet another breakup, while I was finally feeling pretty comfortable about being single. My studies, Sasha, AA, and my friendship with Brandee kept me busy. There wasn't much time to feel lonely.

Nevertheless, I invited Miles over to my apartment on Graham Avenue. He showed up with coffee for me and hot chocolate for Sasha. My granddaughter and I both gave him hugs, happy to see him again.

"It's been a while. I thought maybe you'd died," I joked, expecting sarcasm in return.

"Too long," he said with a serious look on his thin face, his high cheekbones more pronounced than ever.

"You lost weight."

"I almost lost more than that."

After Sasha drank her hot chocolate, I tucked her in to bed. Then Miles and I spent hours discussing relationships. His latest had taken its toll and he had been prescribed tranquillizers. The conversation drifted to how relationships had controlled so much of our lives.

"You need to feel content by yourself, Miles," I assured him. "You have to get a good relationship with yourself before you jump into something again."

As Miles was leaving, I made him promise to keep in touch.

"Don't worry," he said. "You'll be hearing a lot from me."

Miles and I had a number of mutual friends. I knew most of his family and he mine, so it was an easy friendship to resume. It was one of those rare relationships where we could be apart for long periods and still feel relaxed with each other, as if there had never been any distance between us.

BLAKE

Brandee and I attended a Christmas party on the STU campus with some of my friends from undergraduate days. We'd both been cooped up too long, hitting the books, and needed a night on the town.

Jim and Joanne Wilson were at the party, along with a few other people I'd met at STU. I was introduced to a guy named Ed and his full-figured companion, Mary, but they weren't really my type. The couples in the auditorium appeared to be having lots of fun. There didn't seem to be any single guys; the best-looking man in the room turned out to be Bill Brennan, the resident priest!

Brandee had a few dances, but I kept mostly to myself, unable to shake the feeling of solitude. Three of my fellow alumni led the music karaoke-style with their rendition of "Born to Be Wild." A few of us sang along and we all had a good laugh. Coming from where I had been in my life, I found it difficult to imagine the well-dressed trio as anything remotely close to "wild."

Later, while watching couples cuddle up for waltzes and smile into each other's eyes, I experienced such an acute sense of loneliness that I knew I had to leave. I went outside, thinking the fresh air might erase the dreary sense of nostalgia. Staring up at the almost-full moon as I stood in the parking lot, I heard the refrain to one of the songs I'd often listened to with Chuck—Colin Raye's "Little Rock." The familiar chorus drifted through the air: "Without you, baby, I'm not me." My heart tumbled into a vast abyss, then I felt a gentle touch on my arm and turned to see Brandee.

"You all right, Eve?" She watched me, concerned.

"I'm just so lonely," I barely managed to say before bursting into tears.

"I know," Brandee said, tears rimming her eyes and spilling down her cheeks.

The two of us stood in silence, quietly crying. Again, I looked at the moon and saw a blur as I blinked. I thought of my friend, Nadine. Her death had left Ervin alone. Brandee grasped my hand, and I knew her tears were for her dad, who was dying back home on Campobello Island. She was losing someone dear to her, and I was missing everyone I had ever known.

In 1997 I began to visit the churches around Fredericton. I felt like a newcomer trying to sneak into the back seat of an AA meeting, hoping no one would pay attention so I could make a hasty retreat if I felt too uncomfortable.

I often talked to AA friends, like my old chum Theresa, about God's importance in my life, but I knew something vital was missing. I believed this "Higher Power," as God was referred to in AA, was more than a necessary stepping stone toward recovery. I lacked a religious community with whom I could discuss the Bible or my feelings about the importance of Jesus in my life. That was strictly taboo in AA. I felt like a spiritual exile.

"I'm so alone most of the time," I told Theresa on the phone one night.

"I know what you mean."

"No, you don't. You still have a husband. At least you can get some physical satisfaction."

"You can be alone even in a marriage," she pointed out. "God's the only one who can really fix that."

After more than eighteen months without dating, except for an occasional dinner or dance with Miles, I began to have a few urges. When I was married to Chuck, I was used to sex as a stress reliever if nothing else. Now I felt as if I was missing something fundamental again. Maybe I should try exercise, I reasoned. Sex never failed to get me into trouble.

In February 1997 Brandee and Anne R. suggested we attend an AA Round-Up in Fredericton. I was in my second year of graduate work at UNB, and my relationship with Chuck was almost two years behind me. When I wasn't toiling on a paper or writing, I spent most of my time with Sasha, who was now seven and often pretended she was doing school work, too, while I did my assignments. I rarely left my apartment, except to visit the park or the mall with Sasha. My apartment was a safe place. Figuring the time was right to bust loose, I called Sonya to see if she could baby-sit Sasha while I was at the round-up.

Close to six hundred people—members of the twelve-step recovery groups AA, Al-Anon, and Adult Children of Alcoholics—piled into the Fredericton Inn for the convention. On Friday night, after the opening meeting, I ran into friends from the Miramichi who I hadn't seen since the last convention a year earlier. Harold, Bill, Peter J., Gerald, and Terry went out of their way to make sure I enjoyed the weekend. They ordered pizza and coffee and invited us to share. Whenever one of them saw me standing alone or looking despondent, they would come over and strike up a conversation.

The first night of the convention Brandee and I rented a room next to the guys. We ate pizza in Bill's room while he strummed his guitar and sang old Hank Williams tunes. A couple of other guitar players soon joined us. I sang along on every old country song I could remember before the guitar players took a break. We strolled to the hospitality room where everyone was drinking coffee. Then the stories started—fish too big to be believable, two moose killed with the same bullet. One story would hardly be finished before someone jumped in with a taller tale.

"You should have seen Peter," Harold piped up. "The time he chased his cow down the road with his pants around his ankles." He continued giving the details of his friend's unfortunate attempt to round up his livestock before he'd had time to finish his business in the outhouse.

Brandee and I laughed so hard we cried. We stayed up half the night. If anyone outside AA had heard us, they would have thought we were having a drunken party.

The next morning I was tired from the long night but raring to begin another day. The second night I danced for hours in the ballroom at the hotel—fast, foot-stomping tunes that sent my cares flying, and slow, romantic waltzes with Terry that reminded me I still had some passion left. Back in my own bed that night, I realized for the first time in many months that I missed the physical contact a male partner could provide.

After the round-up, I found it harder to quash the urges sparked by the dance-floor flirtations. It had been so long since I'd spent a night with a man, so long since I'd felt the climax of spent passion. I told myself no one would bother with me because I'd gained weight. Cold showers didn't seem to have the effect I'd heard about. Many nights I tossed and turned for hours before sleep sublimated my desires.

At the insistence of my AA friend, Sharon, I agreed to go out and celebrate St. Patrick's Day. With high hopes I attended a dance for singles—widowed, separated, and divorced—on March 17. Perhaps my hopes were unrealistic because I wasn't impressed by the gathering. People were friendly enough, but it reminded me of all the other bars I'd visited in the past, searching for men. The pickup game was depressing. After a few ginger ales, I noticed a man across the room looking at me. When he caught my eye, he came over, seeming more familiar as he neared.

"You used to go to AA, didn't you?" he asked, talking loud to be heard above the music.

"I still do."

"I used to go," he explained. "Back in 1990."

"That's where I've seen you," I said as the chords of "Boot Scootin'

Boogie," one of my favourite country dance tunes, started up.

"I'm Blake," he said, watching me consider the couples who were heading to the dance floor.

"Eve." We shook hands.

"You want to dance?"

"Sure."

Out on the floor I observed Blake dancing across from me. Trim and clean-shaven, he was attractive in a green plaid shirt and jeans. He was smiling at me, but his green eyes possessed a sad quality. When the music stopped, he escorted me back to my table.

"Thanks for the dance," he said, indicating his friends. "I'll stop by later."

But he never did.

Sharon and I left before the event was over. I'd become a homebody, and I'd had enough for one night. Besides, Sharon had to work the following day.

Thoughts of male companionship were briskly shelved as I dived into research for the final paper in my "Property and Gender in the Nineteenth Century" seminar. I relished going through books at the Harriet Irving Library on campus. While I was studying, I never felt alone. I could lose myself in the welcome complications of a textbook.

In spring 1997 I completed my final graduate studies paper. Since I hadn't been out of the house for days, I celebrated by going utterly wild with a visit to the local coffee shop. I asked a neighbour to watch Sasha and headed off, hoping I might see someone I knew.

When I walked in, lo and behold, there sat my old friend Miles, who I hadn't seen for weeks. He'd been tangled up in another romantic pursuit and usually disappeared when that happened. I waved at him as I made my way to the counter and ordered a large cup of coffee with double milk, which I took over to Miles's table.

"Who let you out?" I asked, sitting with a contented sigh. "I thought you were buried in Minto or something."

"Or something," he said. Miles was always tight-lipped about his relationships until he wanted to talk, but his quiet smile informed me he was okay.

"How's school?" he asked. "You a brain surgeon yet?"

"Why, you in need of one?"

Before he answered we were joined by someone else. It was Blake, the man I'd met at the singles' dance. He and Miles knew each other from AA, and Miles had given him guitar lessons.

Since Blake was there, I decided to stay for another coffee. I felt a familiar excitement as I peered into Blake's beautiful green eyes. He gave me an impish grin that lent him a boyish charm.

"Fancy meeting you here," he said. "How've you been?"

"Pretty busy at university. This is the first time I've been out in days."

We talked about music, AA, and cars. When the conversation turned to relationships and Blake mentioned arguing with his ex the day before in the parking lot, I decided to leave. I figured the two men would have a better time talking about ex-partners without me.

When I arrived home, I put Sasha to bed. A little later the phone rang. It was Miles.

"Well, you sure made an impression on Blake."

"What are you talking about?"

"All he talked about was you after you left. He asked if you were as nice as you seemed."

"What'd you tell him?"

"No, of course."

"Get serious, Miles."

"I told him the truth. You're the best friend I ever had."

"What did he say?"

"He said maybe he'd ask for your phone number next time he sees you at a meeting."

I was grinning and it felt liberating and reassuring. "Thanks, Miles."

"Hey, what are friends for?"

Three weeks later Blake and I ran into each other at an AA function in Sussex. I'd asked my old AA buddy, Mark A., to drive with me when he told me his partner, Joy, couldn't make it. As soon as we parked the car and started into the church hall where the event was held, Blake pulled into the lot in a well-polished dark blue Pontiac Parisienne. My heart skipped a beat, and I hurried inside before he saw the interest on my face. I wasn't adept at hiding such things and felt I wasn't ready for another relationship just yet.

To my surprise, Chuck was sitting with one of his friends at a table across the room. I hadn't seen him in months, not since before he went to jail. I hoped he wouldn't do anything to spoil my night out. He smiled, nodded, and kept watching me as I entered.

When the lights dimmed for the dance, I relaxed and got up with Mark for the first couple of fast tunes. After that Blake strolled over and asked me to waltz. I could see Chuck every now and then as the crowd shifted.

"You look nice," Blake said.

"Thanks."

Leaning my head on his shoulder, I smelled his aftershave and felt his body heat tempt my senses. Waltzing, I was more nervous of what Chuck might do. Blake was a fine dancer. His arms around me, guiding my subtle moves, seemed natural, as if they belonged there. We spent most of the night dancing with each other, and when "Boot Scootin' Boogie" began, we both smiled and jumped back on the floor. *He remembered,* I thought. Soon, to my relief, Chuck departed by himself.

I hated to leave, especially since I was travelling in my car with Mark, and Blake was driving his friend Chris home in his car. I suspected Chuck must be waiting for me outside, but I had so many friends around that I wasn't really worried.

"Are you stopping for coffee?" I asked Blake on our way out of the hall, holding on to the railing as I descended the steep steps to the parking lot. Blake hadn't asked for my phone number yet and I was hoping he would.

"Probably," he said, lingering near me. "Are you guys stopping?"

"Yes. At Tim Hortons."

"Good. I'll see you there."

When Mark and I arrived at the coffee shop, Blake and Chris were already there, but everyone was tired and had lost the spirit of adventure, so we decided to head home. In the lot Blake asked for my phone number and I quickly scribbled it on his cigarette package before we climbed into our cars.

It was 2:00 a.m. when I made it home. I kicked off my shoes, undressed, and went straight to bed. Sasha was spending the night at Sonya's house, but I wished she were there to hug and watch over. Lying in bed, I stared at the ceiling, fantasizing about Blake. His compliments and gentle caresses as we waltzed had endeared him to me.

A few days later Blake called and asked if I'd like to attend an AA meeting with him the following Saturday. And he wondered if I'd go to dinner afterward. When I called and told Brandee, she was as excited as I was. "I knew he'd call!" she said.

Two weeks after our initial dinner, Blake showed up with ten long-stemmed roses to commemorate my ten-year anniversary in AA.

We both took pleasure in long drives in the country and we loved eating in restaurants. Every Saturday morning Blake would treat me to steak and eggs at the Hill Top Pub, the best in the city. Sometimes we'd take Sasha with us for pizza.

Blake had charm and a wonderful sense of humour. He would regale me with tales about truck driving and the wounds of old drinking escapades. Yet despite his manly bravado he was never rough or demanding and was quite gentle when he brushed my cheek with his lips.

Charlotte, Blake's mom, was a soft-spoken woman who had

grown up in the country "over north" in Doaktown. Blake told me he'd joked with her, saying he was going to marry me long before we ever started going out as a couple. Blake's mom and stepfather, along with Blake's cousin, Kate, lived in a mobile home in Hanwell, one of Fredericton's suburbs.

In August 1997 I struck up a deal with one of my brother Nelson's old friends to purchase a mobile home. Freeman Blanchard owned several properties and apartment buildings. He'd bought the mobile home to help the owner out of a jam. Freeman, through his accountant, worked out a plan for me to purchase the trailer over a six-year period.

Sasha fell in love with her new room and the captain's bed that went with it. She started setting up her stuffed animals before any of my boxes were unpacked. We were both tired of living on the third floor of an apartment building without even a small yard for her to play safely. My lot, with a few trees in back and a spacious lawn beside us, offered a terrific place to romp. There were kids next door. And there was a church, Life Tabernacle, right across from the trailer park.

Blake lent a hand with the move. In fact, he was the only adult who showed up to help. Mousie let us borrow her truck, and Blake and I sweated out the whole operation by ourselves. I suspected he was pleased I was moving so close to where he was living with his mother and stepfather. It was Blake's mother and Miles who encouraged me to visit Life Tabernacle, which they both attended. The church would later become a cherished sanctuary for me.

LEGAL GENOCIDE—ADDICTS ON THE REZ

Since 1979 New Brunswick Natives have received prescription drugs *free of charge* and, subsequently, the use of pharmaceuticals has steadily risen. In Red Bank on the Miramichi River, two hours from Oromocto, the average cost of drugs per person jumped from

$302 in 1990–91 to $518 in 1994–95. These figures were obtained through an investigation spearheaded by Noah Augustine, a Mi'gmaq lawyer who lived in Red Bank. Most of these prescriptions were for narcotics such as Leritine, codeine, or Demerol. The increase in drug spending was the norm for all New Brunswick First Nations communities.

The National Native Alcohol and Drug Abuse Program (NNADAP) was set up in 1982 to establish and operate programs aimed at reducing the level of alcohol and drug abuse among people living on reserves in Canada. However, by 1998, the monitoring of prescription-drug abuse still hadn't been identified as a priority. Administration of NNADAP funding was, for the most part, left to the discretion of community leaders. Accountability in this area was practically nonexistent.

In 1997 the federal government handed ninety-six percent of the $53 million allotted for NNADAP directly to First Nations communities. A year later there were fifty-three Native-run treatment centres offering only seven hundred in-patient beds to serve every Native community in the country.

By 1999–2000 the total cost for drugs, medical supplies, and equipment for all New Brunswick band members totalled $3,489,258. Red Bank received $205,439 for its 488 registered band members (363 living on the reserve). Oromocto received $194,246 for its 437 registered members (204 living on the reserve). A large percentage of these funds paid for prescription drugs, including those rampantly abused and growing in popularity, like Dilaudid.

In March 1998 a notice from the newly established Wel-A-Mook-Took Health Centre went out to the members of the Oromocto First Nation. For many people its arrival was a little too late. The notice read: "It is common knowledge that there is an ever-increasing drug problem in our community. I am not talking about smoking marijuana. I am talking about the practice of dissolving narcotics and shooting them into the veins with the use of a needle…. It has been mentioned numerous times that young children have been finding and bringing home used syringes that have been discarded on the street." It was signed by the Oromocto Band.

What the notice failed to mention was that many of these syringes were found by children in their own homes, and that several of the children were in danger because they were beginning to experiment with the drugs used by their mothers, fathers, aunts, uncles, and cousins, supplied *free of charge* by the federal government.

When I lived on the Oromocto Reserve in 1993–94, the pill trade was openly discussed in most of the homes I visited. It was common knowledge, and everyone seemed to know which doctors more readily wrote prescriptions for narcotics without asking too many questions. At that time the drug of choice was Tylenol 3 with codeine, often washed down with alcohol. Tylenol 3 sold on the street for $2 a pop.

Another pain medication, Percocet, rapidly became the popular drug. Percocet could be obtained from a number of households on the reserve for $3 to $5 a pill. There were few homes that didn't have regular access to pain medications for real or faked ailments, and although none of the people who sold pills could have been considered big-time pushers, there was seldom any difficulty finding a painkiller for just a few dollars.

Fiorinol sold for $3 or $4 a pill, and once in a while Demerol might be available at $5 to $10 a hit. Then came Leritine, the latest painkiller, at $10 each. It packed a more powerful punch, so the price tag was higher.

I had personal knowledge of at least twenty-four people in the community who "used" on a regular basis. I suspected the number was much higher. Since that was more than ten percent of the adult population, the statistics were alarming. And it got worse.

As the habit of each addict grew, so did the dissatisfaction with the effects of the drugs. All of these potent little pills, regardless of their strength, took about an hour to kick in. For a growing number of people in various stages of addiction, the time factor became troublesome. Addicts required faster relief from their pain and desperation. Snorting, instead of swallowing, provided that sped-up rush.

By the end of 1995, many of the prescription-drug users on the rez were snorting a combination of Demerol and Leritine. The tiny pills could be easily crushed with a spoon and lined up in rows like cocaine.

In 1996 Dilaudid was introduced to the reserve by an outside pusher—the white boyfriend of one of the girls who had been regularly snorting painkillers. At that time a four-milligram pill of this synthetic heroin—also called hydromorphone—sold for $10. Twenty dollars bought an eight-milligram pill. The drug was usually snorted.

Prior to Dilaudid, all of the other prescription narcotics couldn't be broken down and used in a needle. Like cocaine, Dilaudid could be taken intravenously for an almost-instant high. This higher but less easily-sustainable euphoria plunged its addicts to an all-time low. Mothers who once spent most of their time with their children thought little of leaving them in the care of strangers for days on end. Teenagers once eager to play baseball or road hockey nodded off in crowded rooms known as pump houses so they could score another fix.

Dilaudid became the super-addiction that urged users to make greater sacrifices. People were hooked not only by the numbing effects of the drug, but by the sting of the needle and its assurance of instant relief.

Compared to the $100 cost of a gram of cocaine, a free prescription of Dilaudid was a sweet treat.

Heather sank deeper into Hell while I stood by, powerless to block her descent. When she drank too much, she could usually make herself look attractive after a day or so. With the drugs it took days, even weeks, before she appeared normal and could carry out day-to-day activities.

Heather's body deteriorated rapidly. Her doctor was prescribing two hundred eight-milligram pills every week. Liver impairment was inevitable. I told her I was going to confront her doctor or call the police, but she begged me to stay out of her business.

"You'll just make it harder for me with Joe," she said.

So I did nothing.

A few days later she told me she'd tested positive for hepatitis C.

"Oh, God, Heather, that's serious."

"I know," she said. "I'm having more tests to see how much damage has been done to my liver."

I hurried to the library at UNB and read everything I could about hepatitis C and was somewhat relieved to discover it wasn't easily transmitted from one person to another. "Through blood," the medical encyclopedia informed me.

The following week Heather called me with the results of her test. "My liver's not in good shape, Mom," she revealed, her voice quavering. "The doctor says I have to stop drinking and drugging or I'll die."

In an attempt to straighten out, Heather spent a night with us. She'd already been off drugs for days. I gave her Sasha's bed and put my granddaughter in with me. For the first twenty-four hours Heather rushed often to go to the bathroom to vomit and I'd hear Sasha asking if she was all right.

She was thin and had the shakes. Hugging herself, her skin a yellowish-beige, she desperately fought to quiet her body. Sasha and I took turns bathing her forehead while she lay on Sasha's bed. Then the diarrhea started. It lasted two days, and she had difficulty even keeping ginger ale down. Within a couple of days I noticed her skin was dry and her lips chapped. Heather was so weak she couldn't walk to the bathroom without help. She was dangerously dehydrated.

"I'm taking you to the hospital," I said, then helped her get into the car and delivered her to Oromocto Public Hospital.

Deep bouts of depression, violent bursts of anger, and a complete loss of energy and motivation became the hallmarks of her struggle with drugs. Withdrawal was so severe that Heather seldom stayed clean for long, choosing to use alcohol to buffer the panicky time between needles.

I'd watched her trying to come off drugs at a detox when I visited, and I remembered the torment others had gone through when I worked there. But I'd never seen a person look as ill as Heather did now. She was covered with sweat and trembled violently, while her skin had a greenish-yellow cast.

A week later she was finally able to keep food down, and her condition seemed to improve. Some of her colour was returning. When I visited her, the attendant met me at the door. I could tell by her expression that something had happened.

"What's wrong?" I asked.

"Heather's gone."

"Gone? Gone where?"

"She left AMA," the woman told me, which meant "against medical advice."

I turned away crestfallen and plunked down on the steps of the detox centre. The attendant joined me and put her arm around my shoulders. "Don't give up. One day she'll make it."

Listening on the telephone to Heather's anguished cries never failed to twist my stomach into knots and flood me with the darkness of her suffering. Once, she woke me from a deep sleep at three o'clock in the morning.

"Mom, please help me" came her terrified voice. "Please pray."

"What's wrong, Heather?" I asked, suddenly alert.

"It's so black. I can't see. I can't—"

"Where are you?" I sat up, squinting at the clock beside my bed.

"What's going on?"

"I want to die, Mom. Please pray for me."

Then the line went dead. I had no idea where she was. When I tried tracing the call using star 69 on my phone, the number was unlisted. There was nothing to do but slide my legs over the edge of the mattress, drop to my knees, bow my head, and pray. I'd been through this before. Crying seldom eased my pain, and when I managed to confine the tears, the ache in the centre of my chest only doubled.

I switched on the light, walked to the dresser, and picked up the poem I'd propped behind an angel candle holder. It was in Heather's slanted left-handed handwriting. She had written it a few weeks earlier. And I wept again as I read it.

So dark
So sad
So scary
Shattered dreams
Scattered thoughts
Silent screams
No one can hear me...I am dead

Heather's addiction prevented her from being the mother she wanted to be. The drugs wouldn't allow her to be the vital part of our family she'd once been. Most of the time I wasn't even sure where she was living. She'd call me from the Oromocto Reserve, from a friend's house in Fredericton, or even from a bar. Occasionally the calls were made by hospital employees or the police.

I wanted Heather to spend more time with me, but as her habit grew worse and more expensive, cordial visits to my home were undermined by the tension I experienced guarding my belongings. Once, I'd turned my back for five minutes only to have her load most of my videos into a bag so she could sell them at a pawnshop.

This was a distraction but never diminished my relief at seeing her on my doorstep and knowing she was still alive. She showed up a few hours after that middle-of-the-night frantic call. It was February 1999, and she looked sicker, paler than usual, emaciated, with dark circles under her eyes. She was trembling and carrying a small black gym bag.

"I'm so sick, Mom," she said as I let her in and put my arms around her.

"I've been so worried."

"I'm sorry about the call. I thought I was dying."

Sasha was just waking for school. It was about 7:00 a.m. and I'd been up for only ten minutes. I'd barely slept the rest of the night after the call and was still in my nightgown.

"Can I stay here today, Mom?" Heather asked, her eyes nervous and needy. "I have nowhere to go."

"Sure."

"I have to call detox or the hospital."

I knew I couldn't take a chance and leave her by herself. She might have a seizure. Her shaking seemed to worsen by the moment, so I decided to remain home with her. It was my first year working with the local school district as a behavioural intervention mentor for children with problems. I knew I could safely take a sick day.

"Mommy!"

We turned to see Sasha running to give her mother a hug. Heather bent and kissed Sasha, smiling and trying to act as if nothing was the matter, but her teeth were chattering. "Get ready for school, sweetie."

Sasha hurried into the bedroom to change into her school clothes—a white sweatshirt and a pair of navy sweatpants. There was a picture of kittens playing on the sweatshirt. Sasha adored kittens.

Heather put her bag down and removed her jacket. Despite the pain I knew she was feeling, she went into the kitchen, took a box of cereal out of the cupboard, and poured a bowl for Sasha. When Sasha ran into the kitchen, fully dressed, Heather smiled nervously again.

"You look beautiful!" she said. "Now come have some breakfast." Heather shakily set the bowl on the table. "Get the milk out of the fridge and I'll sit with you while you eat."

After Sasha left for school, I called my workplace and told the secretary I wouldn't be in. Then I made Heather and me tea and joined her in the living room. She was lying on the black chesterfield, covered with a pink quilt, her bare arms hugging Sasha's pink piggy pillow. I put her tea on the coffee table and seated myself in a chair across from her.

"Junkies aren't happy people, Mom, not even when they're high," she confided, clutching the pillow and studying the ceiling. "I don't even know what happy is anymore."

It pained me to look at her swollen and bruised arms marked with an excess of purplish-black needle holes. The incongruity of those arms against Sasha's pillow was savage. I glanced at a framed photo of Heather taken five years earlier. That girl looked so happy, so beautiful. Who was this stranger? The sparkling doe eyes that stared at me from the photo hardly resembled the dull opaque black ones gazing at me from the couch. There was no light in her. She had been a natural beauty, who now seemed to have lost something essential. Her long, thick black hair, so much like mine at that age, covered part of her face.

"Even when we're high we talk about how gross it is, how we're going to quit." She blankly regarded her tea. It was untouched. "Everyone wants to quit, but we can't. We hate how we look, how our arms get so scarred." She glanced at her arms and quickly hid them under the pink quilt. "I hate what I have to do to get a fix." She paused, then said, "But I can't quit, Mom. I just can't." Hopelessness forced her to the brink of tears.

"You haven't touched your tea, Heather," I said, standing, uncertain what to do. "Let me get you some ginger ale."

"No," she insisted, wiping her eyes.

I found it difficult to think straight. I wanted to leave, to pretend it was all nothing to me, but I couldn't deny its reality. I sat back down in my chair, my eyes fixed on Heather's ravaged body. She was trying to tell me something, trying to confess.

"Tell me about it, Heather," I whispered. "Let it out." I brushed a stray tear from my cheek.

"Junkies know they can die at any time," she said, numbly staring at me, her voice a dead monotone. "We know these things. If we screw with the wrong person, we might even get an intentional overdose. We'd just be another dead junkie."

It was the truth, but I didn't want to hear it. I sat there, feeling as if I were made of lead and sinking.

"It happens, Mom. Lots of times someone has a seizure. I know every time could be my last and it takes more and more drugs. There's all this work involved in a five-minute high." Heather continued to stare at me while she talked. Her shaking had subsided. Listening, I imagined what it might be like to be a priest. I pretended that was my role, so I could summon the strength to remain in the room. I couldn't allow myself to associate all these sordid details with my daughter. I had to feel detached. Without that my heart would collapse.

"The needle often misses the vein," she said. "That's what makes it swell and get infected."

I'd witnessed Heather's swollen arms and the deadly abscesses that attested to the abuse. She'd been hospitalized once for blood poisoning. They'd had a hard time putting in her intravenous line so she could receive antibiotics. The nurse had explained that the skin on Heather's arms was so callused it was almost impossible to find a spot a needle could penetrate.

Heather told me the veins in the arms become useless after a while. Hands, feet, neck—an especially dangerous spot—penis, or vagina became the only places left to use. She explained how junkies lived on Gravol and other anti-nausea pills. Vomiting often accompanied a "good" high, and always marked the withdrawal.

I had to have a break. "Would you like something to eat, Heather?" The information she was sharing with me, in her attempt to purge herself, was almost more than I could bear. "How about a piece of cheese?" I figured she'd never refuse her favourite food.

"I can't eat, Mom. I think I'll have to go to the hospital, but I needed to talk to you first. I want you to write some of this down. I need you to know, to be able to tell my story if something happens to me."

"Nothing's going to happen, Heather." I stood and walked over to the couch, then knelt to kiss her cheek. "Too many people are praying for you. You're going to make it." I stroked her hair. "Every day I pray and ask God to place angels around you. You won't die in this state. A mother's prayer is powerful to God." With the backs of my fingers I caressed her cheek the way Grammie Mills once did mine.

Retrieving a pad of paper and a pen from the cabinet in the corner of the living room, I returned to my chair and shifted to my familiar role of journalist as Heather began again. That way it was easier to pretend this horror wasn't really part of my daughter's life. She became someone else—a story. I could move outside the family and be the observer, protect myself. But I knew something truer deep inside. I suspected Heather might not live much longer and I wanted to preserve her words.

"No one wants to be a junkie," Heather said plainly. "We never planned to grow up to be junkies."

My mind wandered backward in time. Even with pen in hand it was impossible to pretend. I pictured a beaming ten-year-old Heather standing in front of a room full of people at King's Arrow Arena in Oromocto, accepting a trophy for placing first in the under-sixteen category of a singing competition. "I'm going to be a singer when I grow up," she'd told me later, floating from her victory. "I'll be famous."

I refocused on the couch. Heather's throat was so burnt out by the drugs, she'd stopped singing a long time ago. I doubted this fragile creature on my couch had a song left in her.

"There's no pleasure. It's just too powerful. The need is too great and you ignore the risks. I'm in pain every day, and every day I want to die. After a while, you give up. Some things are worse than death, Mom."

I gazed sadly at Heather's wasted face, her imploring, tormented eyes, and kept going back to former days, seeing the bright-eyed girl who had yelled at the mean kids who had hurled insults at a friend in a wheelchair. The girl who had volunteered to buddy the mentally challenged kids who were often ignored or picked on by others. The girl who to this day never forgot Sasha's birthdays, or the birthdays of her siblings, nieces, nephews, and mother.

"You're my guardian angel here on earth, Mom. I know you pray for me all the time. I feel it. But, Mom, I want you to stop. I want you to let me go."

I couldn't hold back any longer. I sobbed openly as I rose to my feet and rushed over to the couch to embrace her. "You can't give up, Heather. I won't let you."

HEALTHY WAYS TO COPE

I'd worked with street kids, disenfranchised youth who had left home to escape pain and abuse or, in some instances, simply boredom. I'd worked with women in transition fleeing abusive and violent homes to begin new lives while living in Liberty Lane, the same place where I'd attained my freedom from Chuck. Since the start of my sobriety in 1987, I had always made a point of helping others struggling to find a new way to live one day at a time. I'd spent time at Elder Ervin's home for throwaway kids, trying to aid Native children who had been abandoned by their families when their parents turned to drugs or simply gave up on them. And in all of those situations I had felt the reassuring peace of giving something back. I wasn't taking up space on the planet. I was making a difference for the well-being of others.

I knew I was here for more than my own salvation and pleasure. I was a caretaker and nurturer by nature, and compassion wasn't something I needed to force, so I decided I should work in a supportive profession. I knew I'd always be a writer, no matter what other career I pursued. I had to write. It was in my blood. But so was the urge to help.

When I read the advertisement in *The Daily Gleaner* for an intervention resource worker for School District 18, I knew I'd found my calling. It was a pilot project aimed at creating a more positive learning environment for children in elementary schools. The successful candidate would be involved in implementing and devising programs and strategies to address problems in children such as inappropriate behaviours, lack of self-control in conflict situations, and inadequate social skills.

I possessed the right combination of specific training, psychology courses, and experience to meet the requirements, so I sent in my application. When I was called for an interview two weeks later, I was elated. Another call the following week convinced me this had to be the work of God when one of my new supervisors, Nic Plimmer, told me I'd been hired. In September 1998 I began work as one of three intervention resource workers chosen out of close to three hundred applicants.

That fall I visited schools to discover new ways to help kids deal with their anger and sadness. As I learned about their backgrounds, it became apparent that numerous children required assistance dealing with divorces that had disrupted their family structure and basic sense of security. Others had trouble channelling their anger in safe ways. Knowing that "hands off and feet off" was an important school rule did nothing for a child who had been called names like "sissy" and "loser" by a peer. These kids needed to learn and practise what to do with the feelings such encounters stirred up.

I decided to establish a "divorce" group to deal with grief and loss, and a skills-acquisition unit to demonstrate healthy ways to cope with emotions like anger. I had my work cut out for me.

The first morning I arrived at one of my north-side schools a little boy named Daniel walked up to me. "Who are you?" he asked.

"My name is Ms. Nash."

"Are you a teacher?"

"No," I told him as I moved toward the room the school had granted me temporary use of, "I work with kids who are having trouble."

"Well, I'm not getting into trouble then."

"Oh, I don't punish children in trouble," I said, squatting to reassure him. "I try to help them."

"Well, I don't need no help, either," he said firmly. "No needle's going to help me." His eyes were on the room I was about to enter. Suddenly I understood what he was trying to articulate. The word NURSE was on a plaque on the door.

Maybe I'd better see if I can find a different place to work, I said to myself.

I finished my master's thesis in time to graduate at spring convocation in May 1999. It was a rainy day, and although I was proud of my accomplishments, I had considered not participating. It just didn't seem as important as my graduation from Saint Thomas. There I'd made a number of friends, including several of the professors. UNB, though, was a different experience. Except for a couple of professors (Bill Gaston, Sunna Dhakir, and Mary Rimmer) who showed interest in my work and actually stopped occasionally to talk to me and fellow students Andrew Titus and Colin Smith who were never too busy to share their expertise in literary criticism, I slipped quietly through like a ghost.

I did manage to win twice in the Showcase Writing Competition at UNB, second place in the short-story category in 1997, and first place in the short-story category in 1998, but most of the time I wasn't part of extracurricular activities on campus.

For two semesters I worked as a tutorial instructor to under-graduate students. I was required to conduct seminars on grammar, writing techniques, and an introduction to the novel. During these exercises, it became apparent to me that I cherished teaching; I also tutored Native students and I continued to edit the *Micmac/Maliseet Newsletter* for UNB.

If I'd never met Kenneth Harvey while he was at UNB as writer-in-residence, or received my M.A. at the rainy convocation in 1999, I might have thought I dreamed the whole thing. However, the eyes of Shakespeare that watched me from the painting on the wall at Carleton Hall as I climbed the stairs to my seminars three times a week haunted me long afterward.

The following September, when the structure of the job with School District 18 was modified to accommodate middle- and high-school levels, I was rehired. This time I was to spend more hours one-on-one with referred cases from three assigned schools. In my third year I was allotted six schools.

PETTY TYRANTS IN MY LIFE

At first I found Blake's possessiveness complimentary. I wanted to be necessary to a man. I enjoyed the feel of it. But soon he began to resent my visits to Native communities where I gathered infor-mation for features I was writing for Dave Perley at the Department of Education or for the Jedi Aboriginal business series sponsored by the Atlantic Capital Opportunities Agency. Blake would often comment, "You must be still interested in Indian men. That's what you want, don't you?"

After a couple of months, I cut short my visits to old friends. Eventually I stopped seeing them altogether. The reality of my "between worlds" status resurfaced to confound me.

Six weeks into our relationship, on our way to an AA gathering in St. Stephen in Blake's car, he embarrassed me in front of one of his friends. We'd just had lunch in a restaurant, and when I didn't offer to pay for my meal, Blake picked up the bill and marched to the counter, mumbling hotly under his breath.

"What's wrong with him?" I said to his friend.

"Must be PMS—Poor Me Syndrome," the friend joked back.

When we got in the car, Blake was radiating anger.

"What's the matter?" I asked, assuming it must be about the bill. "Didn't you like your lunch?"

"I don't like women who try to take advantage of me."

"What are you talking about?" My face got hotter, and I knew I was blushing.

"You assumed I was paying for your lunch. I don't like women thinking I'm around just to pay the bills."

I felt the heat colouring my cheeks and drew a deep breath. "I can give you the money."

"Forget it," he replied, further darkening the spirit of the outing. I wished I'd stayed at home. Blake was having what AA people often refer to as a "dry drunk," and I didn't want to be the brunt of his bad temper.

Blake apologized the next day, confessing that his surliness was connected to the cravings he still had for alcohol. "It's hard to change that mood," he said, "when it comes over me."

I suggested this might be a good time for him to get away by himself.

At this point I had given up contact with most of my Native friends, including Irene and Elizabeth. I was tired of arguing with

Blake about my true motives whenever I mentioned visiting a reserve. One day I told Blake's mother, Charlotte, about his mistrust of Native people.

"That's funny," she said. "His great-grandmother, my grandmother, was a Native. A Mi'gmaq, I think. He shouldn't have anything against Natives."

I brought this interesting piece of information up the next time Blake and I got together.

"My mother's crazy," he said dismissively, and I left it at that.

But it wasn't just my Native friends Blake resented. It was anyone or anything that diverted my attention from him. He particularly disliked my second job as a freelance journalist. He couldn't see why my work for the school district wasn't enough, even though I'd confided in him the large financial load I was carrying.

Blake had supported my desire to finish my master's thesis. He even fixed my car or repaired things that broke in my mobile home. Occasionally he'd take Sasha for a drive so I could work on the computer, and we went on short overnight trips to Sussex, Miramichi, or Saint John. These jaunts were often related to AA events, but sometimes we took in the sights and stopped for dinner along the way.

When I purchased my mobile home, he helped spruce it up. He knew a bit about almost any kind of house or car repair, and he certainly wasn't lazy. Yet it was hard to adjust to his moods and extreme jealousy. I talked to Theresa, Chrissy, or Brandee about my feelings. I'd made another friend, Joan, through my daughter, Heather, so I counted on their telephone conversations to help me stay patient with Blake.

Unfortunately Brandee decided to move back home to Campobello to work after she graduated from UNB. We spoke frequently on the phone, but I missed her companionship. I rarely communicated with Miles anymore and Mousie seldom called.

I didn't stop to think about where Blake was in his AA recovery. I had several years on him. He was still teetering, and I was an easy target when he needed to vent the uncomfortable feelings he was experiencing.

Prior to my relationship with Blake I had been alone for almost two years and wasn't used to being told what I could or couldn't do. I'd fought hard to win the right to control my own life and wasn't about to give in easily. Blake couldn't understand that his "caring" for me bordered on control. He reacted in the only manner he knew: he became angry and sullen, like many of the kids I worked with at school. After I started attending church more than the occasional Sunday-night trip to Smythe Street Cathedral, he became upset the way he did when I spent too much time with friends.

When Charlotte first mentioned Life Tabernacle, I told her I'd heard good things about the church already from Miles. I said I'd visited other churches in Fredericton, mainly Smythe Street, off and on for the past couple of years but always felt like an outsider.

"It would be nice to visit a smaller church where you could get to know people," I admitted. "But I wouldn't want anyone trying to haul me up to the altar to pray for me."

"They're not like that at our church," she assured me.

I longed for a comfortable place of worship where I might relax in peace and pray, so I could try to finish recovering from the childhood hurts I knew had played such a detrimental role in shaping me. The AA recovery program had helped a lot, but I knew there were wounds inside me only God could heal and that I'd need the prayers of God-fearing people to let go of some of the deeper hurts.

When Miles and Charlotte prompted me to visit Life Tabernacle the following week, I agreed to try it. I asked Blake to come along, but he wasn't interested.

Life Tabernacle was a small white church that comfortably seated about 250 people. I had decided to leave Sasha with a baby-sitter because I didn't think she'd enjoy listening to a preacher. She was only eight. At Smythe Street she had attended activities with the other children in a room upstairs while the preaching was under way. Charlotte had told me Life Tabernacle didn't offer programs like that.

Four or five people were talking in the foyer when I walked in with Charlotte, her husband, Jack, and Charlotte's niece, Kate. The people at the door extended their hands to shake mine. One of them, a short, stocky woman in her sixties, was introduced as Ferne. Charlotte said Ferne was the Sunday School superintendent and also operated Busy Wee Lambs, a day-care in the church basement. I made a mental note to call her the next day to find out more about the day-care's after-school program. I would have to settle Sasha somewhere when I returned to work in the fall. It was summer and I was only doing contract work, so I usually asked Charlotte or Marlie Judd, a young girl in the trailer park, to baby-sit when necessary.

Service was about to commence, and I heard someone playing the organ near the front of the church. I followed Charlotte to a pew halfway up the aisle and sat. There weren't more than thirty people in attendance.

I shut my eyes and absorbed the music. At Smythe Street Cathedral the songs had been more contemporary. I'd recognized none of them from my earlier years in Pentecostal churches. At Life Tabernacle I knew almost every song and chorus they sang. The words and melodies rose easily from memory as Mary Messer, the pastor's wife, led from her seat at the organ. Miles was behind the podium stroking his rhythm guitar, while the pastor gently played bass. Mary had a clear soprano voice I could have listened to for hours. And I was soon singing along to "Power in the Blood."

Contrary to my expectations, Terry Messer, the pastor, preached about God's love, for everyone no matter where they'd been or where they were in their life journey.

"God does not want to put condemnation on you," he said. "God *does not* want to put condemnation on you."

Were those tears in his eyes? I wondered.

"God does not want to bring you down."

I squinted for a better look. Yes, his eyes shone with tears.

"God wants to lift you up. He loves you." On the word *love* the tears broke loose and spilled down his cheeks.

The guilt and sorrow that even my recovery program couldn't extricate began to recede. Through Pastor Terry's passionate faith it was as if the presence of Christ had been summoned around me. I had sensed this phenomenon before, the lingering of the Holy Spirit, but I'd never felt it fully enter me. It was a moment of penetrating clarity, an epiphany. I had heard this moment described by others as a point in time when you know that you know that you know. I knew I had found my church home.

I had to take a new look at how I evaluated others in my life, people like Blake who spent so much of their energy harassing me. Blake's pain was of his own making. He knew where to find help. I'd shared with him the relief I'd experienced attending services at Life Tabernacle and asked him to accompany me, but he refused. I also suggested he talk to a sponsor in AA so he might get rid of his anger, but all he would say was: "What anger?"

Through feeling compassion for him, through assuming his pain equalled mine, I saw how he had been a catalyst for my own healing and growth. The distress from our relationship had drawn me closer to God and farther from the desire to "fix" unhealthy men. And soon I couldn't handle any more criticism and control in my life.

When Blake threw tantrums and refused to escort me to gospel concerts because Miles and Brent Hickey, another Christian friend, would be there, I dejectedly told myself it was all too much. Whatever Blake and I once had was dying and there was no hope. With new clarity I saw that our relationship was built on something other than love. It hung together by desire and obsession and was hurting my renewed relationship with God, the most important friend in my life.

Sasha was fond of Blake but not of our arguments. Though not physically violent, they were heated. My old insecurities returned precisely at a time when I was giving women's self-esteem workshops for local service groups and family-oriented organizations such as the Family Resource Centre.

No drug or man would satisfy the deep-rooted loneliness I'd carried for so long. If I was ever to be in a healthy relationship, I needed to be free from the craving for fulfillment, the bleak hole in my unnatural self that had been the driving force behind most of my actions.

Blake and I had talked about marriage, but in my heart I knew it would be a mistake. We weren't right for each other, and I wouldn't marry him simply because I had to be somebody's wife.

One breezy summer day Sasha and I were driving in the black Tempo I'd bought from a friend in AA. We were on our way to the Farmers' Market downtown to search for fresh pork chops and spinach—Sasha's favourite vegetable—for dinner. Sasha was hoping to have her face painted by one of the young people who circulated at the market. It was a sunny day and we were both in an upbeat mood, singing our special song, "You Are My Sunshine."

Three days earlier Blake and I fought over my decision to take on another writing contract. Dixie vanRaaltee had called to tell me she needed an editor for a national research report. That meant I'd have to work evenings for a while and wouldn't have as much time to spend with Blake. When he heard the news, he threw a fit. I'd told him I'd had enough, suggesting we spend time apart, and he'd stormed out of my mobile home, slamming the door behind him.

"When I grow up, I want to be just like you, Mommie," Sasha had said with a big, dimpled smile.

Pride had swelled in my chest. After all these years, I was finally doing okay. Sasha wanted to be like me.

"Except in relationships," she'd added with unusual wisdom for an eight-year-old. "Don't get me wrong, Mom, but you're way happier without a man. And we can visit our friends."

There it was in a nutshell—out of the mouths of babes! Whenever I was with a man, I ended up feeling miserable. In fact, I *never* felt good with the man choices I made. Sasha was right: we rarely saw our friends when I was involved in a draining relationship.

I was so grateful to her. I squeezed her hand and smiled. "Thank you so much, Sasha."

She smiled back. "You're welcome."

It took a few more months to make the final break with Blake. Bouts of loneliness and desire would draw us back together for brief periods. Once the illusion of romance wore off, the hopelessness of the situation sank in. We fought again and again over the same issues. Blake demanded more of my time. He couldn't understand or believe that men like Miles were no threat to his claim on me. I wanted to help people through AA and church and saw little point in spending time at dances where the music reminded me of my drinking days. Furthermore, I was losing interest in sitting for hours in a coffee shop when I had such a busy schedule. Blake insisted church be a token part of his life, while I was keen to devote more of my time to it. We were two people with totally opposite aspirations.

As we grew ever distant, Blake became angrier and more confused. His domination surfaced frequently. There were days when I was afraid to answer the telephone. Eventually I just let the machine take all calls, and even Sasha learned to ignore Blake's harassing messages. We'd both raised our eyebrows when he said he wouldn't phone anymore, then call right back. It became a joke guessing how long he would keep at it.

Like a spiteful child, he left unpleasant rants, calling me a bitch, lesbian, fat pig or hypocrite. After a while I really didn't take the insults personally. Through my work with angry children I knew Blake was name-calling to spark a reaction. If I retaliated, he'd focus his wrath and pain on me. If I didn't respond, he'd eventually stop and be forced to deal with his feelings some other way. Since he was still attending AA, I hoped he'd get help from a sponsor or see a counsellor. I just needed to be patient, and that was a tall order since I was trying to deal with my own resentments toward him for treating me so shoddily. It didn't matter that I could reason intellectually why he behaved the way he did; I was still hurting emotionally.

The telephone calls went on for three or four months. One day I came home to find eighteen messages from Blake pleading with me to give him an opportunity to explain his feelings, to make amends, to listen to his reasons for his behaviour. When I didn't respond, the messages decreased. Soon they stopped.

I continued to pray for Blake's recovery and some days I missed him, but I had to admit that things were more peaceful without him. I wondered how I could have fallen for such an unhealthy man after all my years of life-changing recovery work. Why again did I have to hug my old black teddy bear and cry myself to sleep? Thereafter I resolved firmly to forget about finding a partner. It was preferable to be alone.

My friend Glenn Murray, who worked for the Department of Education School District, introduced me to the "petty tyrant" theory. Glenn was well read and had a commendable grasp of language. When I first met him, he had just made some lifestyle changes that included giving up drinking, and we talked about how it was possible to turn the hurts inflicted by others into workable assets.

I spoke to him about the pain I'd suffered with Stan, about how I had to learn to be stronger, more cunning in order to survive. So many years later I accepted the idea that Stan hadn't planned things to go the way they had. He was sick in his spirit and mind. I had to overcome that and grow from it.

I hadn't set out to subject my children to the turmoil they'd experienced as teenagers because of my drinking, and I never thought I'd be able to tell anyone about the mistakes I'd made as a parent. There was far too much shame attached. I suspected I'd just carry the guilt around with me. When I worked with parents (both in my capacity as a behavioural intervention mentor and as a volunteer for twelve-step recovery groups) who spoke openly about guilt from violations they'd committed against their children or family responsibilities they'd neglected, I was able to share not only my experience, but my zeal and hope that conditions could get better. That granted me greater empathy for people that others dismissed as uncaring or cruel. I knew neglect and abuse weren't always intentional but rooted in instability and a legacy of pain.

Our instinctive response to pain is the desire to retaliate. That was why Blake reacted to my rejection with insults that were completely ridiculous. If I'd kept taking his behaviour to heart, I would have had to reply in kind. Only altruism soothed that gut-wrenching need for retaliation.

That was how Glenn explained the "petty tyrant" philosophy. We were sitting in a coffee shop in King's Place, downtown Fredericton, one afternoon as people went about their daily duties, oblivious to the mindful conversation we were engaged in.

"In the works of Carlos Castaneda," Glenn explained, "Don Juan, the old Yaqui sorcerer, tells Carlos: 'You are like you are because you tell yourself you are that way. We are all victims of self-hypnosis, in this sense, and our problems are as big as we imagine them to be—and our ability to adapt ourselves to challenge is as helpful as we allow it to be.'"

Glenn tweaked his manicured moustache as he talked. His eyes were dead serious, but he smiled as he continued. "Don Juan is trying to encourage Carlos to change and to grow—to become a warrior. A warrior in Don Juan's terms is one who is constantly at war with himself, continually battling against the worst in himself, always pushing forward the frontier of what is best in himself. A warrior struggles each day, no matter what is happening in the world around him, to rescue the possibility of choice—choice about how to live and how to be in every moment and every situation. The goal of the struggle is freedom from the habit of past choices, freedom from the overwhelming weight of what one believes to be true. It is a way of life that demands one place all one's attention on what is actually occurring right now, and then act strategically to do what is correct, what doesn't waste time and energy, even if one has always done something else in the past."

"That's a hard task to accomplish," I said.

"Yes," he acknowledged. "One of the most helpful things that can come along in one's life to assist in learning this strategy is what Don Juan calls a 'petty tyrant'—someone who plays a significant ongoing role in your life and who drives you nuts on a regular basis."

"I know lots of them," I admitted with an understanding nod.

"Don't we all." Glenn smiled and paused to gulp some coffee. "Ideally a petty tyrant has some real power over you. It may be a boss, a parent, a demanding spouse. This means you're forced to find ways of dealing with this person, and in doing so, you learn to act like a warrior. Each time the petty tyrant roars to life, each time he or she 'pushes your buttons,' each time you feel like throwing your hands up and collapsing in a heap, there's a moment in which you can choose to act impeccably despite what appears to be happening. There's a moment to reach within and remember who you really are, to ask if you were put on this planet to be irritated by this person, to question if this person was really here to help you find a way to change and grow."

"That's a tall order," I said. "But it sort of makes sense."

"It's our own self-centredness that makes us think we're victims."

"Oh, I don't agree with that." I shook my head and sipped my coffee. "There are innocent victims, too."

"Of course, but most of us are really volunteers after a while. We stay or return to situations by our own choosing."

"Until we learn the lesson, right?"

"Exactly."

"Go on," I urged him.

"As someone once said, whatever doesn't kill you always makes you stronger. How can you shift gears and change strategies in dealing with your petty tyrant? That's how you'll prove to yourself that your real value lies in your ability to stay focused on what's important and to use your resources wisely. Remember, resentment is a powerful emotion to waste on someone you don't even like. Each time you succeed in choosing to act with calm self-assurance instead of losing your temper or your train of thought, you add to your own reservoir of strength and self-conviction. What a terrific gift, and it's a gift we can only receive from jerks and know-it-alls who don't even understand how they're helping us!"

"Sounds very idealistic, Glenn, but there are times I'd love to wring Blake's neck."

Glenn nodded. "Yes, of course, you'll feel that. It's changing that feeling that does it."

"So if I follow your line of thought, then I should stay with the petty tyrant who's dragging me down just so I can learn that lesson?"

"No, not at all. Some lessons are safer learned at a distance. And besides, you can be sure life will provide you with an ample supply of petty tyrants for all the lessons you've yet to learn."

"That's right." I peeked at my watch, having lost track of the time.

"I've got to get home." I drained my cup and stood, hooking my purse strap over my shoulder. "Thanks for the coffee and the words of wisdom."

"Now if I could only apply all of this to my own life," he said, chuckling as he rose and sent me on my way with an enthusiastic bear hug.

SIX GENERATIONS

At least once a week Chrissy, my friend from our days in Transition House, called to chat. The telephone usually rang around 6:00 a.m. because she realized I was a "morning person who was hard to catch after 8:00 a.m.," as she put it. It was an ideal way to kick off the day. She was always so optimistic and never failed to offer a humorous observation that made me laugh.

One of Chrissy's main worries was whether or not she would ever meet a "nice" man who would love her unconditionally. She was exceptionally lonely. She had few friends in Fredericton and I was so busy I couldn't spend much time with her, though I made an effort to visit her apartment on Aberdeen Street at least once a month and always for holidays.

Her two grown children were preoccupied with their own lives, even though her son, Raymond, and his girlfriend, Florrie, made certain Chrissy never wanted for anything. They lived in Fredericton. Her daughter, Bonnie, lived in Woodstock.

When Chrissy called me one day to let me know she'd met a very special man, I offered up a prayer of thanks on her behalf. *If anyone deserves a good mate, she does, God*. During my relationship with Blake, Chrissy had constantly encouraged me not to settle for a man who was incapable of treating me the way I deserved.

Her new boyfriend, Len, turned out to be a gift from heaven. At fifty-two Chrissy sounded like a giddy schoolgirl when she talked about the little gifts Len would drop off or how he'd take her for a drive to Woodstock to visit her daughter. When I met Len, I saw why she was so fond of him. He was a perfect gentleman, friendly and charming, holding the chair out for Sasha to sit in Chrissy's living room.

"Can I get you anything?" he asked, even though it was Chrissy's apartment. She told me he was always popping in to help out. She was unsteady on her feet since she'd had a stroke years earlier.

They'd dated for several months, then on New Year's Day 2000 the phone rang.

When I picked up the receiver, I heard Chrissy all out of breath. "What's wrong?" I asked, expecting the worst.

"Nothing's wrong. Everything's right," she sang into the phone. "Len proposed last night!"

"He did?"

"Yes, he took me out to the Diplomat for Chinese food and gave me a diamond. You should see it. It's big!"

"Oh, Chrissy, I'm so happy for you."

"And when we got home, he dropped to one knee and asked me to marry him."

"That's so exciting!"

"We're going to be married in the summer, and guess what?"

"What?"

"You have to sing at our wedding and we want Sasha to be there. And Miles, maybe he'd play guitar. What d'you think?"

"I'd love to sing."

They intended to be married in July in the small stone Anglican church on Westmorland Street. When I told Sasha, she asked, "Is Chrissy wearing a wedding dress?"

"Of course," I told her.

"Cool," Sasha said with a smile that made her dimples pop out.

Chrissy called me often in 2000. With full responsibility for Sasha, bank loans, car and trailer payments, lot rent, power, telephone, and cable bills, and monstrous student loans, I was in tough shape financially, so I took on more and more writing contracts in addition to my regular job. That meant I had little time for anything except work and Sasha. When Jody moved in with me in July, he gave me a break by spending time with Sasha. I didn't ask him for rent money. He had a minimum-wage job and bought his own groceries.

I was fairly certain Chrissy missed our visits as much as I did. I always promised to stop in as soon as I finished a project, but there would be yet another deadline looming.

Chrissy was often hospitalized for various ailments. She had bowel disease, had experienced at least two strokes that I knew of, and was a heavy cigarette smoker. I worried she might suffer another stroke any moment. When she called me from the hospital at the end of July, I was relieved to hear she was only in for a kidney infection. A couple of days later I went to see her.

"What some people will do to get a little attention," I kidded as I bent over to give her a hug and a small stuffed teddy bear from Sasha.

Chrissy smiled back. "Well, it's the only way to get a visit out of you."

We chatted for a while until Len returned from an early dinner. After a few minutes, I left them with a promise I'd return in a couple of days. Another big project for Dixie vanRaalte, a final report on the quality of services provided in childcare facilities in Native communities, was hovering over me. The eternal deadline.

Three days later, when I was almost finished my assignment, I received a telephone call from Chrissy. She said she'd leaned over to reach for the phone beside her bed and felt a sharp pain in her chest. When the pain didn't go away, they'd sent her for an X ray and discovered she'd broken some ribs. After that they did a CAT scan.

"They're pretty sure it's cancer," she said quietly.

My knees weakened, and I stumbled back to the nearest chair to sit.

Chrissy informed me they were doing further tests right away and asked if I would pray for her and visit soon. "I need to see you, Eve. I'm scared."

"I'll be there, Chrissy." That afternoon I went to the hospital. I couldn't believe the change that had come over her in such a short time. She was so heavily medicated she couldn't talk or sit up straight.

"Chrissy," I said softly as I entered the room. She tried to open her eyes, but they seemed to roll back in her head. I hugged her and attempted to prop her up, but she kept slipping down in the large hospital bed. She couldn't have weighed more than a hundred pounds.

Len was there and I could plainly witness the helpless sorrow in his eyes.

"What's going on, Len?" I asked.

He was standing by the foot of the bed, watching Chrissy. "She was in so much pain the doctor ordered more medication. He thinks the cancer's spread to other parts of her body."

"So it's cancer for sure?"

He looked at me for a moment without comment, then said, "Yes."

I gasped for breath, my hands rising to my mouth.

He reached for my shoulder. "She thinks the world of you and Sasha, you know."

"Excuse me," I said, darting from the room.

Less than a week later, Len and the family were informed the cancer had taken over Chrissy's body and treatment would be senseless.

"Mom only has a few weeks to live at most," Raymond told me when I went to visit again.

"Are you sure?" I asked.

"The doctor said there was no mistake,"

When Raymond asked me if I would sing at Chrissy's funeral, I fought back the anguish and said yes. I was supposed to sing at her *wedding*, not at her *funeral*.

I spent as much time at the hospital with Chrissy as I could during August. Len was constantly there wiping her forehead with cool cloths, feeding her, running around town to find grape Popsicles because they were her favourites. The dosage of pain medication was eventually lowered, at her insistence during a lucid moment, to a level that allowed her to maintain a conversation. During that period, I apologized for neglecting her over the past year.

"I understand, Eve," she said. "I knew you were busy. You're here now. That's all that matters."

We talked about Len, her children, her relationship with God, but only twice did we mention her imminent death. She had decided to be cremated.

"I dreamed they took me to that crematorium downstairs," she explained to me and her daughter, Bonnie, who was also at Chrissy's bedside. "But when they put me in I started to wake up." She regarded us as if she was telling a joke, as if we didn't get the punchline.

"That could never happen," I assured her. "They make certain before they do anything like that."

Once, when we were alone, Chrissy gazed at me and said, "I'm dying, Eve. I can't beat this one." She paused. "What'll happen to Len?"

"I'll keep an eye on him," I told her. "I will."

Every time I visited I sang to Chrissy, even when she appeared too medicated to notice. She still had her clear moments and loved to hear the hymns I chose for her. Near the end, when she could barely talk, I noticed her trying to sing along with "Jesus Loves Me."

I spent a night alone with her in the palliative-care unit of the hospital. Although she was being administered frequent large doses of medication, her pain was incredible. I held her hand and prayed most of the night, pausing occasionally to sing a familiar hymn or talk to the nurse who checked on Chrissy.

Sometime before morning the reality of the situation hit me. *Chrissy is dying.* The warm tears trickled over my cheeks as I watched my wasted friend on her deathbed. I imagined her wedding to Len. Where was the joy she deserved, the joy she had longed for all her life? She had come so close to attaining it. The more I contemplated how she had been robbed of her happiness, the faster the tears spilled until I was crying so hard the nurse came in to see if there had been a change in Chrissy's condition.

Less than two days later, August 27, 2000, she passed on.

I took Sasha with me to the funeral home in Minto so she could say a proper goodbye during the wake. She had brought along her Garfield angel to place in the casket.

"She looks so pretty," my granddaughter said as she tucked the stuffed animal beside Chrissy's head. "Is that her wedding dress?"

"Yes, baby, it is. It's beautiful, isn't it?"

Without further word, Sasha leaned in and kissed Chrissy goodbye.

I didn't hang around the casket for long. I couldn't bear the funeral home, the smell, the sense that what was being mourned in the casket wasn't actually the person at all. It was a morbid rite.

The next day I dropped Sasha at the baby-sitter's and prepared for the drive to Minto for Chrissy's service at the funeral home.

I didn't weep much during the ceremony. I felt empty, as if the pool had run dry. Standing in front of the mourners to sing "Amazing Grace" and "The Anchor Holds," I watched Chrissy's granddaughter crying in her seat at the front, her chest bucking so violently that she became sick to her stomach. After the service, I left as quickly as decorum would allow and headed for my car where I said a prayer asking God to help me give my friends and family a greater priority in my life.

I often paused to ask myself: If I knew I only had one week left on earth, what would be the three most important things I'd want to accomplish? Always my answer involved letting people know I cared deeply for them. The solution might be something as simple as a five-minute phone call to a friend or a leisurely walk in the park with my granddaughter.

Or it might take the form of visiting friends and relatives I hadn't seen in years.

In fall 2000 Sasha and I set off on an adventure to Nova Scotia. I'd never really had time to relax in the summer. I had attended the University of Moncton for a weeklong course on quantum teaching and the rest of the time I wasn't far from the hospital. Now we were headed for Porter's Lake, just outside Halifax, to visit Donna, my friend from adolescent days. Donna was stationed there as a sergeant in the Canadian Armed Forces. It was important for me to connect with someone from my past so I could get my life in perspective again. I was emotionally drained and needed the downtime, to feel carefree for a while, to not think, to enjoy life without obligations nattering in the back of my brain.

I had loved my previous trips to Nova Scotia, especially to areas near the ocean. The coastal towns, like Joggins, bordered a spectacular part of the Atlantic, and I was awed watching the waves crash against the high cliffs. Porter's Lake was fifteen minutes outside Dartmouth, Halifax's twin city, separated by only a tall bridge over the harbour that welcomed ships from around the world.

Even the five-hour car ride relaxed me. I didn't care if bill collectors were looking for me or if Blake had left a hundred messages on my answering machine. No one would be able to find me on this trip.

We actually drove by Donna's house twice before we realized we were at the right place. I had instructions written down and Sasha was acting as my copilot, searching for road signs, but it was turning dark and I soon became disoriented. Finally I stopped at a store to ask directions and discovered I was on the correct road and only a half mile from Donna's house.

When we pulled into the driveway of her large split-level home, she was waiting by the door, laughing. "I figured you'd get lost."

"You figured right," I told her, giving her a hug. Like me, Donna had put on a few pounds, but I decided we both carried it well. Her hair was blond instead of the auburn I was used to, and it suited her flushed complexion.

Sasha was right behind me, smiling. "If I hadn't told her to ask someone, I think we'd still be driving back and forth," she told Donna as she reached out for a hug, too.

Donna's partner, Bruce, a tall, stocky man, was standing behind her inside the door. He grinned and said hello.

It was around 11:00 p.m., and we'd had nothing to eat except peanuts since three o'clock, so Donna suggested we venture into Dartmouth for Chinese food. It was almost 2:00 a.m. when we returned and were settled for the night.

The next day I phoned Norm Gardner, my biker friend from the old days who had kept in touch over the years. He was living in Hubley, a small community on the outskirts of Halifax, and I was anxious to see him.

Sasha and I met Norm at a coffee shop in Dartmouth. He still weighed about 250 pounds, but his hug was as friendly and gentle as ever. Norm was dressed in the same sort of black Harley Davidson T-shirt, ball cap, and jeans he'd been wearing the last time we'd gotten together. Sasha didn't remember him at all. She'd only met him once when she was a toddler.

"Hey," he said to her, "I sure like those dimples."

That was all she needed to warm to him.

Whenever Donna was too busy to escort us, Norm became our tour guide. The first day we visited the Museum of Natural History in downtown Halifax, as Sasha wanted to check out the insect display she'd seen advertised on TV. Norm and I chatted as we tried to keep up with her enthusiastic investigation of all the displays.

"You know I'm glad to see you're still sober," Norm told me when we stopped to study a case of spiders. "I've been slowing down myself. I don't do the hard stuff no more. Just a few beers here and there."

"Good thing," I told him. "I guess my prayers for you have been paying off."

On our way to Citadel Hill I chuckled as Norm pointed out the Hells Angels clubhouse as one of the important sights. *You've come a long way, baby*, I thought.

The second day Norm took us to visit Peggy's Cove. I'd been there in 1988 before the Atlantic Ocean claimed hundreds of bodies after the Swissair disaster. I gazed at the beauty of the cove with different eyes this time. I could feel the moroseness in that place, the sense of loss.

Sasha, of course, saw only the challenge of small mountains of rocks to climb, and quickly darted barefoot toward the top of the higher ones that stood closest to the open water. Fearful of rogue waves, I hurried after her.

Norm remained behind, smiling at Sasha's adventurous spirit. "I don't do hills," he said as I struggled to keep up with my inquisitive ten-year-old.

On our way back to Fredericton, Sasha and I stopped briefly to visit my maternal grandmother's sister, Sophie, in Wellington Station. We had never met, but she was delighted to have us turn up on her doorstep. Right away she reminded me of Grammie Brewer. She had the same smile and way of hurrying around her small, scrupulously clean home, insisting I have a cup of tea.

I met another of the sisters of my beloved European grandmother Eva in Joggins. Annie, who was married to one of my grandmother's brothers, accompanied me to see Rosie, my great-aunt.

Rosie related stories about her mother, who had been born

Franchiska Berets in a Romanian village before marrying my great-grandfather, Franz Skoupi.

"She was a wonderful cook," Rosie told me in her sandpapery voice. "Best cook I ever met."

I thought about my own mother when she said that: *So culinary artistry is passed through the genes*.

Everyone adored Sasha, plying her with homemade chocolate-chip cookies and asking her questions about school and her personal interests. She soaked up the attention and listened attentively while Rosie detailed family history.

Aunt Rosie, who had been born in Canada after the Skoupi family immigrated to Nova Scotia, said her daughter had been able to make contact with a relative still living in Germany. I was captivated by the information that provided pieces of the puzzle from a past I'd often speculated about. Sitting between me and Sasha with the old photo album on her lap, Rosie showed us snapshots of her family.

She tapped her fingernail against a sepia photo. "That's your great-grandmother Franchiska. Your mother's grandmother."

"I can see the resemblance," I said. "Can you see it, Sasha?"

"Yeah. She looks like your mom."

I found it incredible that I was sitting in Joggins, the same village where my grandmother and her mother once lived, and where my mother had lived as a child. The same place I'd visited with my husband, Bob, and where I'd thrown rocks into the ocean to wash away my anger only a few years earlier.

Now we were sharing our history with Sasha. Six generations had been touched by this humble site beside the ocean.

"Do you like the photographs, Sasha?" Rosie asked.

"They're great," Sasha replied, staring up at her great-aunt's lightly wrinkled face.

When I walked with Sasha down the road from Rosie's house to see the cliffs that overlooked the beach, she was as enthralled as I had been the first time I'd watched the waves smooth the landscape. I'd mentioned we could search for fossils on the beach, which had really excited her.

Six generations of women from my family have walked these shores, I reflected as I reached for Sasha's hand. We strolled up the beach, enjoying the tranquillity, but then Sasha broke free to run ahead. Watching my granddaughter hunt for fossils on the beach, I knew it was now our special place, a place we'd often return to.

LOOKING AT FAMILY WITH NEW EYES

That same year, 2000, my mother and father marked their fiftieth wedding anniversary by renewing their vows. The entire family would be gathering, and I knew the celebration would be particularly special if I could convince Heather to attend. Sasha was living with me on a permanent basis, and so the function would allow Heather and her daughter some time together. But more than that, it would give my daughter a short reprieve from her hellish existence.

I didn't tell Heather about the anniversary until the morning of the event. Because she had no fixed address, I had no way of reaching her. I learned through her sporadic telephone calls, sometimes from the hospital, that she was still alive. I prayed for her constantly. Sometimes I'd wake in the middle of the night hearing my name whispered. It was Heather's voice and I'd immediately ask God to send angels to protect her. I knew He had answered those prayers, otherwise she wouldn't have evaded the death that lingered, waiting to snatch her away.

There was another reason why I hadn't mentioned the anniversary to Heather. I knew she could only last three or four hours without using some sort of drug, usually by needle, just so she could function. Otherwise her body would start to cramp up and she might even slip into an uncontrollable rage.

As luck would have it, Heather called me the morning of the celebration. When I asked her to come to the anniversary, there was a long pause, then she said in a teary voice, "I don't have anything to wear, Mom."

"Some of your clothes are here," I reminded her. "If there's nothing there, I have a dress that'll fit you and some panty hose."

Heather had always been a fashion-conscious girl, with nice clothes, jewellery, and footwear that matched her outfits. Now her clothes were left behind in so many different houses she no longer had any idea what she owned. Most of the time she carried a small sports bag with a change of clothing and drug paraphernalia: syringes, spoons, matches, and filters removed from discarded cigarettes. The bag also contained makeup and perfume.

My daughter always smelled nice; she loved perfume. I usually gave her a bottle for her birthday—*White Shoulders*, *Ananya*, and *Amari* were her favourites. Somehow I was always able to track her down around her birthday. Usually she'd call if she remembered the day. I tried to make these occasions memorable by taking her out for a quality meal if she could stomach food, or shopping for a new outfit. I believed she counted on these short reprieves. At least when we were together Heather was treated with respect and dignity, considerations that were missing from the underground existence she generally lived.

"Do you think you can make it?" I asked. "Without having to take off to use a needle?"

"I'll be all right for a while, Mom, honest."

Heather had always possessed beautiful creamy skin, large expressive eyes, and long, thick, shiny blue-black hair. The tallest of my girls at five feet five inches, she looked good at 125 pounds. As an addict, she had dropped to ninety-eight pounds. She wore sweatshirts to hide her scarred and often infected arms. Heather always walked slightly bent forward, most of the time in pain from abused organs—her liver, bladder, kidneys, and ovaries were chronically damaged. She told me her back ached nonstop.

"I'll get you in two hours, okay? Sasha and I can't wait to see you."

"I'm anxious to see you guys, too," she answered. "I need this. I'll be ready."

Heather's hair was falling out from poor nutrition and there were patches she had torn out when she'd suffered through withdrawal. The shine was nonexistent, and her face was frequently covered with sores and scratches; sometimes she had black eyes or a broken nose.

"My face doesn't look real good," she said softly. "My eye's still kind of purple, but maybe I could cover it with makeup."

"You should be a makeup artist, Heather," I said feebly to lighten the situation. "I've seen you work wonders before. Two hours, okay?"

"Sure."

"Bye now." I hung up, my heart heavy, yet I sublimated the melancholy by busying myself with preparations for the day.

"This is going to be a good day," Sasha said delightedly when I told her we'd be picking up her mother. "I just know it!" She smiled as she laid out her sleeveless lavender dress and headed for a bath.

I prayed nothing would change in the next two hours.

Even a minute was a long spell in the life of a junkie. In two hours Heather's entire world, her emotional centre, could begin to boil, but she had assured me she had enough pills—Dilaudid, I supposed—to get her through the event and keep her clearheaded.

Concentrating on the positive, I was grateful for the opportunity to show my daughter how important she still was in my life, how special I believed her to be. I knew love was lacking in her days of torment and degradation. She needed proof she was a valued human being, even though she no longer believed that herself.

At this point I considered any chance to hold my firstborn, even for a few seconds, in my arms to be a gift from God.

Sasha kept asking when we were going, and I repeatedly told her the time. I put on a long sleeveless wine-coloured dress I'd picked up for the occasion. It had a short-sleeved matching jacket.

Better cover those upper arms, I warned myself. *That should be enough. Sasha was young enough to be forgiven the exposure of bare arms, but I'd never get away with it.* I found a dress Heather had forgotten at my place. It was black with tiny blue and yellow flowers. I also collected some panty hose and a pair of black pumps—we wore the same size—in case she required shoes, then placed everything in a plastic grocery bag.

After taking a long look at ourselves in the mirror, we went outside and headed for the car.

When I picked up Heather in Maugerville, beside Portobello Drive, a quiet area as far as I knew, she appeared happier than usual. I watched in the rearview as Sasha gave Heather a big hug.

"I missed you so much," Heather told Sasha.

"I missed you, too," Sasha pledged. "I pray for you every night."

Heather was wearing a T-shirt and sweatpants. One of her arms was bandaged to cover the track marks where she'd shot up. The drugs she injected made her appear normal, even though I knew she'd probably taken enough to provide a high for two or three people. Heather no longer used drugs to get high but to keep the constant physical and emotional pain at bay. To the unwitting eye, she would seem completely straight.

"You don't look too bad, Heather," I told her. I couldn't see traces of the bruises she'd told me about. "I'm really glad you're coming."

"I wouldn't want to miss this. Grannie and Grampie will be glad to see me, I think."

Sasha cuddled into her mother's side. "I'm glad to see you."

"And I'm happy to see you, my little angel. You look beautiful in that purple dress."

Sasha's smile stretched to the bursting point.

Along the way to the church in Waasis, I stopped at a service station in Oromocto and handed Heather the plastic grocery bag. "Here's your stuff to change into."

"You coming?" Heather asked Sasha as she accepted the bag.

Sasha jumped at the opportunity, and they went off together. I watched them stroll toward the service-station doorway. Sasha's slim frame wasn't much smaller than her mother's. From behind they could have been sisters, with the same petite figure and dark hair.

I breathed a sigh of relief at the thought of Heather asking Sasha to accompany her. I knew Heather wouldn't use any needles in Sasha's presence.

The church Mom and Dad attended in Waasis was packed with friends and relatives. My father had been quite sick after surviving a battle with both prostate cancer and depression, and his recovery made the celebration all that more poignant. It was great to see him in such high spirits. My mother, now seventy, was grey-haired and even tinier than I recalled. She was absolutely radiant, her excitement erasing years from her face, the wrinkles smoothed out by a perpetual grin.

When she joined my dad at the altar and I checked over my shoulder, I could see from my vantage point in the front pew that everyone was happy to be part of the event. Friends and relatives were dressed in their Sunday best, observing intently as the minister beckoned my parents to repeat their vows.

I glanced at Heather, who was just as pleased with the proceedings as anyone else. There was sweetness in her face, as if she were witnessing a fairy tale come true. She was seated between Sasha and her brother, Jody, who had arrived late from his stay in Lake Eutopia, 110 miles away. Jennifer and her boyfriend, Brad, were sitting with my twelve-year-old granddaughter, Brittany. Sonya had to work, and I figured she'd decided it would be better to keep her son, Mitchell, home. He was a hyper nine-year-old. Jennifer's son, Billy—also twelve—was paying strict attention.

I was close enough to catch the look in my mother's eyes when she gazed at my father. *Now that's love*, I thought, feeling a surge of emotion but forcing myself to remain dry-eyed.

Dad reached out to grasp my mother's hand even before the ceremony called for it. He held her hand in both of his and regarded her with unmistakable devotion.

Their love had overcome so much. Life hadn't always been easy or kind to them. Both had fought their own demons along the way, but time had mellowed them, particularly Dad. He'd lost most of the sharpness, and his adoration of my mother shone through. Recently, when I visited briefly, I'd heard Dad tell my mom how pretty she was.

As my parents exchanged vows, I was moved by the tenderness of the event yet saddened by the idea that I would never share such a significant occasion with a partner. Even if I did find someone I wanted to marry, we'd have no time to foster such an enduring legacy. Watching my parents kiss, I thought, *Only through love.* I wondered what might have happened if I'd stayed with Bob and worked things out. Now I'd never know.

After Mom and Dad finished their vows, I joined two of my sisters-in-law, Shianne and Marylynn, and Shianne's brother, Darren, on the platform beside the piano. Mom and Dad sat on chairs on the same platform to hear us join together to sing a song I'd written in honour of the anniversary.

> "She's the queen of her kitchen
> He's a king with his pen
> They've both made a difference to family and friends.
> Today we salute you, share your happiness
> May your life be rewarded and forever blessed."

As I sang the second verse, I spotted my mother wiping her eyes. Dad was smiling with gratitude. He'd always worried about not being a good father. If I gave him a card on Father's Day, he'd say, "I don't really deserve this" or "I made a lot of mistakes as a father."

I'd never felt more honoured to be their daughter as I let my voice ring out, singing their praises.

At the reception I chatted with my brothers Robin, Carman, and Steven. My eldest brother, Nelson, who was across the room with his new Native girlfriend, had arrived from Fort McMurray, Alberta, the night before in time to practise walking Mom down the aisle. We only saw each other at special family gatherings like this.

They're good men, I concluded, feeling sisterly pride. Yet I was also disheartened when I thought about the small part I had actually played in their lives. I had never been invited to a meal in any of their homes. Perhaps they considered my spiritual beliefs inferior to theirs. They knew I professed to be a Christian but often wore jeans and jewellery and kept my hair shoulder-length instead of letting it grow out. These were all taboos in their church. They also gave creedence to writings from a prophet named William Branham, and I was only slightly familiar with his teachings. Whenever I'd attended their church, I'd felt an almost palpable sense of condemnation dividing me from God. I'd never sensed any of the love I knew Christ wanted us to practise toward one another. My choice not to investigate their doctrine erected a wall between us. Still, I loved them and wished they'd value me as their big sister and the woman of principle I knew I'd become.

My brother, Allison, had remained at home, living with Mom and Dad in the basement of their mini-home. He wasn't much for social gatherings, and I respected that. Long before I'd quit drinking, we'd listened to music, discussed movies, and sometimes went for long drives to view the ocean we both revered. He'd been the best man when I married Bob. In the past few years we'd only spoken occasionally when I sought him out in his well-organized room in the basement during a visit to my parents' home.

Jody was delighted to attend Mom and Dad's anniversary and even happier to reunite with friends from the church he'd attended before moving in with a minister and his family in Lake Eutopia a year ago. He'd worked in a fish factory and then gone deep-sea fishing before taking a job pumping gas at a local station. Jody had also joined the Pennfield volunteer firefighters. He cut a dashing figure in his uniform. My little boy had grown into a man who weighed over two hundred pounds and stood close to six feet tall. I recalled how he'd devoted hours to sketching with a black pen or pencil. There was remarkable talent in his art, more than what might have been fabricated by an encouraging parent. Yet he never seemed to take time for his art anymore.

My son closely resembled his Mohawk father, Stan, but had a more serene nature. Although seemingly content with his position, he was keeping his eyes open for another job. I suggested he try Fredericton in order to be closer to me. Sasha was especially fond of her uncle, so she, too, urged him to move in with us for a while. Shortly afterward, he did find security work with his childhood friend Ron. It was a treasure to have him reunited with us on a steady basis.

My youngest daughter, Jennifer, was usually working at one of her two jobs and too busy to participate in most family functions. So it was wonderful to see her at the reception. She and her boyfriend, Brad, and son, Billy, were warmly greeted by all family members. At twelve Billy was already what most young girls called a "hottie"—dark good looks with a quick sense of humour, although I imagined some of his teachers didn't appreciate the jokes. Kids like Billy, who had been diagnosed with attention-deficit disorder, were usually medicated to keep them quiet. Thank God Billy still had some spirit left, even though he did depend on Dexidrine to maintain a steady keel.

As the sort of young woman everyone admired, Jennifer had always had a strong compassion and tolerance for people who were experiencing difficulties. Growing up in our dysfunctional family had no doubt added empathy to her character. She'd never considered drinking or using drugs even as a teenager.

Jennifer was a pretty woman with full lips, long auburn hair, brown eyes, and a dark complexion that attested to her Native heritage. I'd always hoped she'd find a good man. Now it appeared as if she had. I'd had no idea she was dating Brad until they'd been seeing each other for six months. I still remembered the phone conversation I'd had with Jennifer about the relationship.

"How come you never told me about Brad when you guys first met?" I'd asked.

"I don't know," Jennifer replied thoughtfully. "I guess we wanted to keep it to ourselves, to see how things went before saying anything."

"You didn't think I'd be upset because Brad's black?"

"Who *you*, Mom?" She laughed so hard it turned to static through the earpiece.

I couldn't help but burst out laughing, too.

My brothers, my mother, even my sisters-in-law, Marylynn, Shianne, and Shannon, and my nieces and nephews, were all glad to talk to Heather. They gave her warm hugs and passed friendly remarks: "It's so nice to see you! You're in our prayers. You're looking good." Heather's wilted spirit absorbed the attention and she'd smile, gaining a sort of self-preserving energy. My father, who Heather idolized, held her several times during the afternoon, patting her head while she clung to him. *The only man who never hurt me*, she'd often say when she talked about him. On this day my father kissed her on the cheek as he hugged her, studying her face. Heather watched him adoringly. It was enough to break a thousand hearts.

Nelson took Heather aside and spoke to her for a while. He'd had his own battle with drugs as a teenager, had stayed clean for fifteen years, then gotten back into cocaine. Three years earlier he'd been in the same shape Heather was in now. He'd lost everything he had, including his wife, but had built his way back up, entered rehab, and become straight. Nelson was committed to letting Heather know there was still hope for her. His daughter, fifteen-year-old Victoria, had accompanied him and his new girlfriend, Margie, a

Cree from northern Alberta. Victoria took to Heather and Sasha, and the three mingled easily among the crowd. Even my elderly aunts Lena, Lois, and Edna greeted Heather warmly. For a short while my daughter seemed to forget she was an addict. Instead she was a part of a huge family, watchful of their own, regardless of troubles and transgressions. The caring energy throbbed in the church hall, uniting everyone with the purity of loving and honest familial intention; we were suspended that day in a blessed state of grace. If only we could have remained there forever.

When Heather approached me and said, "I need to go soon, Mom," I didn't ask questions. It was enough for me to have witnessed the contentment in her face for a few hours. Watching her laugh and tease Jennifer as the children flocked around her was worth more than any sum of money I could have been offered that day.

My dad was reluctant to let go of Heather when he hugged her goodbye. I knew intuitively he was wondering if he'd ever see his first grandchild again.

On the way back to Maugerville, Heather and Sasha cuddled in the back seat.

"The cramps are getting stronger," she said. I glanced back and saw her hand on her belly, the other arm around Sasha. My grand-daughter had seen Heather like this before. She clung to her mother as much as Heather's condition would allow.

The spot where I was to drop Heather off was up ahead, so I pulled over and turned in my seat. "You looked beautiful today, Heather. Everyone was so glad to see you."

"I had a good time," she answered, wincing as she clutched the door handle. "Thanks for picking me up, Mom. I've got to go to the bathroom. The diarrhea will be starting soon."

I checked Sasha's face. She was smiling, but her eyes were worried. Heather kissed her, then got out of the car. Sasha shifted from the back seat, climbing over the console that divided the two seats in front. I waved goodbye through my window as Heather hurried off, turning quickly once to wave and blow Sasha a kiss.

"We love you!" Sasha and I called in unison through my open window. I couldn't help but wonder: *The next time I see her will it be in a casket?*

When we pulled away, Sasha and I were silent for a long time. My granddaughter looked heartbroken.

I reached out to hold her hand. "Are you okay, Sash?"

"Just tired."

It was only five o'clock. I knew Sasha's fatigue was stress-related. I'd seen her retreat into sleep many times when she was faced with similar unpleasant situations.

"Did you have a good time?" I asked.

"I certainly did!" she answered in her grown-up voice.

I started to sing the Meow Mix song from the advertisement on television, scrunching my face to mimic a cat sniffing for food.

Sasha laughed. "You're crazy, Mommie."

"I know it!" I said, wiggling my nose and trying to cross my eyes. That got a giggle out of her, and her eyes weren't nearly so sad anymore, but I knew her thoughts were elsewhere.

Sonya hadn't been able to attend Mom and Dad's celebration, as she was scheduled to work. I brought her a copy of the video a few days later and we discussed the anniversary. She, as did I, often felt alienated from the rest of the family because she didn't share their religious beliefs, but that in no way diminished the love either of us felt for them.

Watching the video, Sonya smiled warmly when her grandparents renewed their vows. But at the sight of the family gathered in the hall for the reception, my brothers laughing and talking to me and her siblings, her face became suddenly despondent. I knew she missed being close to her extended family. But the truth was that Sonya hadn't had much positive interaction with my brothers.

After Sonya and her husband, Harry, separated in 1998, it was a time of emotional upheaval. Having custody of her children only part-time really distressed her. She was working as a corrections officer at a minimum-security prison farm in Kingsclear, about six miles north of Fredericton. That was where she met Dan, her supervisor, who would later become her new partner.

She and Dan settled in Lincoln in an attractive bungalow and shared custody of Brittany and Mitchell with Harry, who still lived in the house Sonya and he had bought in Geary. Harry was living with another woman and they had a baby girl together. I despised what divorce did to the rest of the family. And I truly missed Harry sometimes.

But Dan was a lifesaver for Sonya. He was a strong, steadfast man whose authoritative nature helped Sonya to feel secure in the midst of the turmoil that followed her separation. Harry's mother, another of those staunch Christians I prayed never to turn into, tried to paint Sonya as an unfit mother, even accusing her, through the divorce lawyer, of being a witch because she'd once read tea leaves.

When the acrimony lessened, it was obvious to all that Sonya was a devoted mother. Seeing her with her children delighted me. Brittany looked just like her mom—stunningly attractive with big brown eyes and natural blond hair—while Mitchell was still the engaging child with a refreshing way of looking at the world.

I remember the laugh we all had when Dan told us about his experience with Mitchell at a Catholic Mass. Mitchell's only exposure to church at that point had been in a Protestant Sunday School, all very informal. Dan was a Catholic who attended Mass regularly.

One day, when Mitchell was eight, he asked if he could join Dan at Mass. Since Mitchell was a hyper boy, Dan at first hesitated and asked Sonya if she thought it was a good idea. After giving Mitchell a stern lecture about the necessity of remaining quiet and staying in his seat in church, Sonya agreed he could go with Dan.

According to Dan, once Mitchell entered the church, he appeared flabbergasted with his surroundings but never said a word. When it came time for the Eucharist, Dan indicated that Mitchell should come up with him but that he shouldn't accept anything from the priest because it was for the people who belonged to that church. Mitchell agreed with a quiet nod. He took it all in but never opened his mouth, seemingly mesmerized by the ritual.

On the way home Mitchell remained unusually quiet. Sonya, detecting her son's strange silence when he arrived, asked him how he liked the Mass. Suddenly, as if a switch had been flicked, Mitchell became quite animated.

"I've been thinking, Mom," he said. "I think I want to belong to that church."

"Why's that?" Sonya asked, surprised.

"Well, Mom," Mitchell replied. "You should have seen it. They served snacks halfway through."

Holidays finally became gratifying family times, no longer disrupted and blackened by alcoholism, nor the alcoholic's insecure need to destroy significant occasions as a means of demonstrating power. Rather than fear holidays, I drew comfort from the traditions and rituals we'd adhered to over the years. They became a time for cleansing.

Thanksgiving and Christmas dinners were usually celebrated at my home. No matter how small my living quarters might be, I always found a space for one or two more guests who might otherwise be alone, in addition to all my children, their mates, and their children.

Christmas Eve was spent at Sonya's where we opened one gift as we enjoyed Dan's seafood chowder or nibbled on Sonya's lemon squares. Christmas mornings at my house meant that everyone had to eat tangerines and a piece of cheese before they were allowed to open Christmas gifts.

We alternated the dinner site for Easter, and New Year's Day was negotiable. The kids were always welcome to visit. I usually cooked a large meal and invited friends over. On New Year's Eve Sasha and I never failed to attend a special service at Life Tabernacle. I no longer harboured any desire to greet a new year with a loud crowd of partygoers, with or without alcohol. Nor did I have the urge anymore to kiss strangers at the stroke of midnight.

SASHA'S NEW BROTHER AND NEW NAME

As I prepared for Christmas 2000 and I reflected on the years, I marvelled at the changes in my life brought about by the healing power of forgiveness. I sat in awe of my life while I wrapped a present from Sasha for my first husband, Stan. How did I make it this far? There was a time I'd have been so full of resentment and hate that I would have no part in any deed that would bring Stan the slightest shred of pleasure. However, with forgiveness, I knew I was responsible for how I treated others and now chose to treat them with compassion.

Stan had also tried to make amends. He wrote me once and described how sorry he was for the sins of the past. "I can't change what happened. But I'm a different man now and I want to let my children know I do love them," he'd written. He attended church regularly, sent the children presents on their birthdays and Christmas, and encouraged them to call him. There wasn't much else he could do. The scars were still there, but at least the gaping wounds had grown over.

Stan was no longer an entity I feared. He'd already reaped much of the pain he'd sown. Did that mean I'd welcome him back with open arms? Never. That wasn't the person I had become. Pardoning his ill treatment of me and our children allowed me to view him as the damaged man he was, rather than reducing him to a monster.

Everyone has the potential to commit dark acts if they nurture that side of themselves, if they allow the bestial urges to snarl to the surface. If we don't stay in the light, we grow sick and some grow sicker than others. Stan, Chuck, and all the men who had wounded me deserved my prayers, not my condemnation. *But for the grace of God, there go I...*

I've had to face the fact that even when friends I cherished slipped from my life, it was all part of a divine plan that allowed a place for new teachers. The loss of a person might have actually been for my own protection, to bring me closer to a higher good. I learned to follow a simple Native concept, which can also be found in the Bible: live consciously every day in harmony with all men and women.

The moments that really matter to me today are the ones spent in quiet communion with my God and those with family or close friends.

Not long ago Sasha informed me she wanted to have a family night when we could play Clue, Yahtzee, or maybe chess. My schedule was becoming too crowded, and I wondered if I was giving her the attention she deserved. So we designated a game night from that moment on.

On one of our walks through Odell Park, Sasha surprised me with a strange request. "I'd really like to have a brother," she told me as we strolled the path to where the deer lived behind a tall wire enclosure. We'd brought apples with us to feed them. To our delight, one of the smaller ones tottered toward us and began nibbling the apple Sasha offered through the links.

"I'm a little too old to have another baby," I explained. "And I don't think I can buy one in a store." I tried to turn the request into a bit of a joke, but I felt concerned that Sasha would express the need for family. She'd only seen her biological father once for a few hours since she was six months old, although he had been in touch by telephone. She knew she had a half sister named Evangeline living somewhere in Ontario. With all the other disconnections in her life, I guess she was interested in evening the score by adding a sibling she could actually grow to know and be with.

I sat on a large boulder near the deer enclosure and said, "Well, I don't think I can just go out and get you a brother, Sasha."

"Why not?" she asked. "There's lots of kids with no parents. You could get one." It was chilly for autumn, so she was wearing a blue sweatshirt with pink flowers on it and a blue beret. The hat made her look awfully serious.

"I can barely afford to take care of us right now, dear."

Sasha stared at me with disappointed brown eyes.

"And we only have two bedrooms," I added, hoping that might be the end of it. Sasha wouldn't want to share her bedroom.

"He could sleep in my bed. I'll sleep with you."

The simplicity of her reasoning made me smile. I stood and reached for her hand, directing her toward the horse stables. We both loved horses and had saved apples just for them. The path was wet and muddy in spots because it had rained earlier in the day. As we passed the duck pond, a goose honked loudly.

Intending to shift Sasha's train of thought, I pointed at the horses. "Look at that new Appaloosa. Isn't she beautiful?"

I glanced down at her and saw she was still thinking, trying to figure out how to get a brother. *God give me an answer for her*, I prayed.

I began to think about distant parents. Biological parents as opposed to adoptive parents. Then it dawned on me. I could adopt a foster child through one of those organizations we had watched on television. I'd even written down one of the toll-free numbers on a scrap of paper. I stopped walking and squatted to gaze directly into Sasha's eyes.

"I have an idea. Do you remember those children we saw on TV the other night? The ones who were looking for someone to help them?"

Sasha seemed confused. "That little black boy with no shoes?"

"Well, maybe not that boy exactly, but we could pick a boy and he could be black, if that's what you'd like."

Her confusion faded and a smile broke through, blossoming into a big grin. "Yes, I want a black brother!" she announced, jumping up and down so unexpectedly her beret flew to the ground and let her long brown hair tumble free.

"Okay, when we get home we'll call."

On the way back in the car Sasha sang her favourite Sunday School chorus, the one I'd taught her so long ago.

"Jesus loves the little children
All the children of the world
Red and yellow, black and white
They are precious in his sight
Jesus loves the little children of the world…"

Sasha checked the mailbox every day for a reply from World Vision. I'd told her the organization would mail us a photo and information about our foster child. Within a couple of weeks the envelope arrived.

Jerry Matsimbi from Zimbabwe is a year younger than Sasha. We keep his photo on our fridge and Sasha has her own, too. She calls him her foster brother and carries his picture in her purse. Every now and then she takes it out to study the perfect wonder that is her new brother.

In February 2001 a Mohawk minister from Tyendinaga, the same place where Sasha's grandfather, Stan, lived, visited Life Tabernacle. He was part of a TV ministry team called Spirit Alive, dedicated to helping Native people to discover peace and salvation through Christ. Ross Maracle and his team had just returned from a humanitarian mission in Labrador, attempting to aid the young gasoline-sniffing Inuit. I was scheduled to travel to northern Quebec the following week to work for the Naskapi people in Kawawachikamach, and I was anxious to talk to Reverend Maracle after the service. I felt a special comfort in this new connection with the community in which I'd once lived in fear.

Sasha and I made our way to the back of the church. There was a crowd gathered around Reverend Maracle, so we waited, leafing through a few pamphlets he had brought along.

The crowd finally thinned, and Sasha and I edged toward the reverend. He was more diminutive than he appeared at the pulpit, slender with glasses and short, straight black hair. His skin was lined and he had a wispy moustache. He was wearing a leather vest over his black shirt and dark trousers. I noticed a thick silver ring with a huge turquoise stone on one of his fingers.

I approached him and held out my hand. "I'm Eve Nash, the lady who did your press releases."

"Oh, your pastor told me all about you." He had a firm handshake, which he used with enthusiasm. "Thank you."

"I was glad to help."

He glanced down at Sasha. "And who's this young lady?"

"This is Sasha, and she's been wanting to meet you."

He bent slightly forward and thrust out his hand, which Sasha gently shook.

"I'm a Mohawk just like you," she blurted out nervously.

Reverend Maracle raised his eyebrows and grinned.

"Sasha's grandfather comes from your territory," I explained.

"That's interesting," he said to me. Then he looked at Sasha

421

again. "Do you have an Indian name?"

"No," she quietly responded.

"Would you like one?"

She nodded shyly and smiled, peeking back up at me as if seeking permission.

"That would be nice, wouldn't it?" I prompted.

"First I have to pray," he said, "and ask God to give me one." He laid his hand on Sasha's head and shut his eyes.

I watched Reverend Maracle and then studied my little girl, feeling this was inherently important for her.

A moment later Reverend Maracle opened his eyes and stared at Sasha. "Your name will be Wa tah hay nah. It means She Who Maketh the Path." Crouching, he hugged her, then straightened. "That means you are a warrior," he said carefully. "But you will use peace as your weapon. You are a bridge between the two cultures."

Sasha was bursting with pride, confident with her newfound purpose.

She Who Maketh the Path.

ACKNOWLEDGEMENTS

The retelling of history, personal or otherwise, is never a monologue. Often there are differing, even contradictory, versions of the same event. Sociologist Ruth Smith once said that the farther we live from the centre, the closer we are to the truth. *Little White Squaw* is a story about life lived in that precarious place, although not entirely far from the centre. It is my truth.

I want to thank my co-author and mentor, Kenneth J. Harvey, for urging me to keep writing this story. My appreciation to him goes beyond gratitude for sharing his expertise in the craft of writing. Without his support my courage to embrace the past would have failed me.

Thanks to the people at Beach Holme for their commitment to quality literature: Michael Carroll, an outstanding editor whose attention to detail astounds me; and Trisha Telep for fielding all my silly questions and changing schedules and still pulling off the impossible. She is a wonder woman!

Thanks to those, like Rita Young, who encouraged me to pick up the pen again. I will be forever grateful.

Thanks to my daughters, Heather, Sonya, and Jennifer, for the love and respect they've shown me, and for understanding my need to tell this story. I cherish all of you.

Thanks to my son, Jody, who was as enthusiastic as I was when I heard this book was to be published. I am grateful for his words of faith through the darkest days, and for his impressive artwork, which appears in this book.

Thanks to my beautiful grandchildren, Brittany, Billy, Sasha, and Mitchell. They are the motivation behind the writing of this book. I count on them to carry the message long after I am gone that all human beings deserve to be loved and treated with dignity. I love you deeply, my darlings.

Thanks to my birth family, especially Mom and Dad; my brothers, Nelson, Allison, Carman, Robin, and Steven; Aunts Edna, Lena, and Lois; and cousins Judy and Heather. I am grateful they were a part of my life. They've taught me many vital lessons.

Thanks to my faithful longtime friends, Beryl and Tom Johnstone, Donna Carpenter and Theresa Cox, who have made such a positive difference in my life. God bless them.

Thanks to special friends Pam Hatheway, Verda Warren, Grace and Weyman Brown, Ferne Bell, Dixie vanRaalte, and Lori Thomas, who listen without judgement and give good counsel. I am honoured to know them.

Thanks to my church family at Life Tabernacle in Fredericton, New Brunswick, especially Terry and Mary Messer, who are a very special part of my life. Thanks go out to them for supporting me and "lifting up the hands which hung down" during the writing of this book.

Thanks to my many valuable teachers in Alcoholics Anonymous, especially Ted, Faye, Ruth, Joyce, Lois, Marg, Heather and Dave, Marilyn, Harold, Brandee, Jeff, Anne, and Gail. I am grateful to them for carrying the message well.

Thanks to my many valuable teachers throughout the years, especially Carol Murray, Jim Davidson, Professors Stewart Donovan,

Frank Cronin, Patricia Thornton, and Bill Gaston.

Thanks to the New Brunswick Arts Board for its support.

Thanks to the caring people who helped me at crucial turning points in my life: Reverend Robert Foster, Frank and Deana Thomas, Gail and Robert Gardner, Reverend Ted Spencer, Kaye Foreman, Sharon Waters, Gloria Gallant, Gaynelle Cloney, Cedric Stewart, Irene Sanipass, Elizabeth Sacobie, Ervin Polchies, Anne Forrestall, Jim and Joanne Wilson, Mousie Milliea, Miles Blair, Tracey Mitchell, Glen Kennedy, and many, many more. They are blessed.

Thanks to Glenn Murray for sharing the "petty tyrant" theory, and to all the petty tyrants whose names have been changed in this book. Thanks for helping me strive for impeccability.

And, finally and most important, I want to thank my Lord and Saviour Jesus Christ who set me free and transformed my life through His Truth. To Him be the Glory.

Eve Mills Nash
Fredericton, New Brunswick

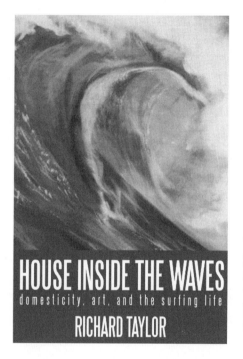